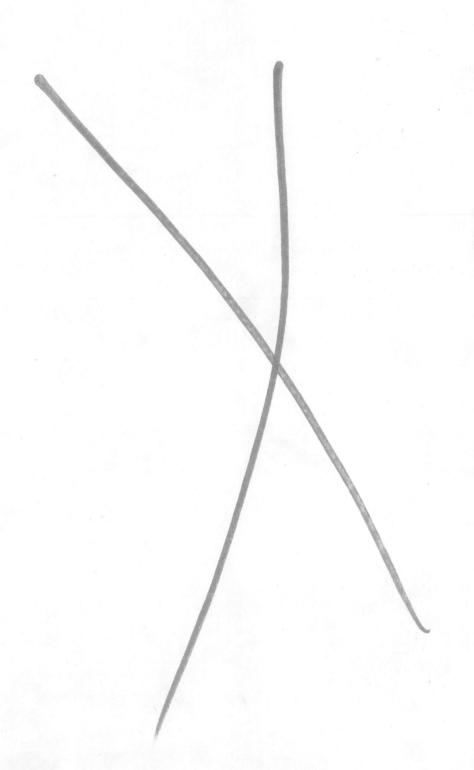

The Experts' Guide
to Managing and Marketing
a Successful
Financial Planning Practice

Andrew M. Rich, CFP

with

Jill Arowesty

PRENTICE HALL, *Englewood Cliffs, New Jersey* 07632

Library of Congress Cataloging-in-Publication Data

The Experts' guide to managing and marketing
   a successful financial planning practice.

   Includes index.
   1. Finance, Personal. 2. Financial planners
—Marketing. I. Rich, Andrew M. II. Arowesty,
Jill.
HG179.E96 1988   332.024′068′8   87–36024
ISBN 0-13-295155-X

Editorial/production supervision
  and interior design: *Carol L. Atkins*
Cover design: *Lundgren Graphics Ltd.*
Manufacturing buyer: *Marianne Gloriande*

The publisher offers discounts on this book when ordered
in bulk quantities. For more information, write:

   Special Sales/College Marketing
   Prentice Hall
   College Technical and Reference Division
   Englewood Cliffs, NJ 07632

Printed in the United States of America

10 9 8 7 6 5 4 3 2 1

ISBN 0-13-295155-X

Prentice-Hall International (UK) Limited, *London*
Prentice-Hall of Australia Pty. Limited, *Sydney*
Prentice-Hall Canada Inc., *Toronto*
Prentice-Hall Hispanoamericana, S.A., *Mexico*
Prentice-Hall of India Private Limited, *New Delhi*
Prentice-Hall of Japan, Inc., *Tokyo*
Simon & Schuster Asia Pte. Ltd., *Singapore*
Editora Prentice-Hall do Brasil, Ltda., *Rio de Janeiro*

To Bev, David, and Nancy

My real net worth!

Contents

Chapter III   Planning For Planners   **111**

Preface

The first thoughts of this book began to germinate while I was running back and forth between the McCormick Convention Center and my room at the McCormick Hotel at the 1986 IAFP National Convention in Chicago. I must confess that the reason for my frequent trips was the New York Met-Houston Astro playoff games and not financial planning. In any event, the spirit of the Met victory brought out enough creative energy to initiate this book.

I had great hopes of writing the ultimate book about successfully operating and managing a financial planning practice. Unfortunately, there are practical limitations. In my preliminary discussions with Jeff Krames, my editor at Prentice Hall, I had anticipated working with about forty practitioners on various practice management topics. On the basis of my idea, Prentice Hall quickly gave me the green light to proceed. And once started, I could not stop. Within two months I contacted about ninety-five practitioners and had commitments for eighty-five articles. The only thing that stopped me from gathering more material was the 200,000-word limitation including supplements and directories. Otherwise, I can not honestly say what the results would have been.

It is unfortunate that along the way I missed many deserving practitioners whose articles and ideas should be included in this manuscript. The constraints of time and of running a very busy tax-oriented financial planning practice—as well as the human aspect of not knowing every practitioner in the industry—kept me from approaching many deserving professionals. I am also sure that there are some very successful practitioners from whom the profession has yet to hear. Furthermore, without doubt, the selection of contributing authors was subjective and based to a great extent on my familiarity with the contributors and the recommendations of others whose opinion I respect.

The Experts' Guide to Managing and Marketing a Successful Financial Planning Practice is an attempt to provide objectivity to the topic of financial planning practice management. My first book, *How to Survive and Succeed in a Small Financial Planning Practice,* is highly subjective, since it revolves around my philosophy and my style of running a practice. Although it works for me, there is certainly a multitude of other ways to run a practice. Objectivity is, of course, necessary and there are many other ways and other styles that readers should be aware of—even at the expense of my ego!

The beauty of this book is that I do not agree with many of the contributors, yet I feel that their ideas should be heard and their styles brought to life. This business of financial planning is a very personal type of business, which planners should center around their own unique styles and the realities of their individual client marketplaces. The basic product is, without question, the financial planner—the individual. One must retain that individuality to be successful. What I have produced is a melting pot of ideas to help planners build and operate a practice that reflects their beliefs and concepts. This book is filled with treasures of helpful ideas and methods. My purpose is to offer useful ideas to make a financial planning practice more efficient and profitable. I caution the reader not to read or view these articles as doctrine, but as food for thought that could work in your financial planning environment.

In essence, what is clear is that there will be articles in the book that you should find quite helpful and stimulating and others that you just will not relate to. Some articles may even offend you, but that is the price we pay for freedom of speech and objectivity. To be objective is to allow others the freedom to give advice and present ideas in the way that they believe it should be told. Accordingly, the editing of this book was limited primarily to grammar and not to content. Otherwise, you would just be reading a book about what Andrew Rich, CFP, believes. The creation of this book has not only been stimulating and challenging in my role as editor but quite helpful to me in presenting new ideas necessary in my own practice. Successful practitioners are not only open-minded but quick to implement the good ideas of their peers into their own practices. This compilation has been a great experience for me, and my hope is that the reader will find good ideas that will ultimately prove quite beneficial. Be objective!

There have been frustrations and setbacks, to say the least. Quite a few necessary and worthwhile articles which some practitioners had committed to write never arrived. And then it was too late to get others to fill the voids. In a world without deadlines, there would be no problems, but this book needed to go to press with or without these articles. You may notice that in the organization section, there is not an article about the International Association for Financial Planning (IAFP). Unfortunately, I regret that my invitations did not elicit their participation.

Because of space considerations, each contributor was limited to one article, although some volunteered to do others. Only one contributor, myself, appears throughout this book, somewhat like Alfred E. Neuman in *Mad Magazine*. Enthusiastically, I invoked the doctrine of ''editor's privilege''; I hope that fact will not offend you. It is just that I felt that these articles were absolutely necessary and I could write them as well as anyone else. So much for objectivity!

This book has been an eye-opener as well as a wonderful and personal experience. It has proved to me that the financial planning profession is filled with talented and dedicated individuals who give a lot more to the profession than just time. It has shown me, without doubt, that there are a great many professionals who truly care about helping other people. In the process of creating this work, I have made new friends and have renewed friendships with others. It has been fun. It has been an experience. And it would have been impossible without Jill Arowesty.

Without Jill's organization, without her persistent hounding of this editor and the numerous contributors to meet deadlines, I would still be working on the manuscript. If it were up to me, the cover of this book would read, ''Edited by Andrew M. Rich, CFP, and impossible without Jill Arowesty, future CFP.'' One of the rewards of this book was detouring someone headed to a life of college teaching and rerouting it to the creative world of financial planning. Jill is a future asset to this profession, and it will give me great pleasure to watch her progress through the years.

Last, but not least, I wish to thank all the contributing authors for their time, dedication, ideas, and effort. None received any compensation, and all deserve more than just a simple thanks. I am just the technician who put it all together; they are the lifeblood of this book.

Andrew M. Rich, CFP

Chapter I

Financial Planning: From Beginning to End

Stephen P. Herman, M.D.
Colin B. Coombs, CLU, CFP
Felice Price, CFP
Joseph H. Clinard, Jr., CFP
Dale S. Johnson, Ph.D., CFP
Richard B. Freeman, M.B.A.
Loren Dunton
Ronald P. Hogarth, CLU, CFP

"People come to the financial planner with a variety of motivations. About the only thing that they may have in common is a desire to get in charge of their financial situation."

—STEPHEN P. HERMAN, M.D.

The Psychology of Financial Planning

Stephen P. Herman, M.D., is a practicing psychiatrist in Manhattan, New York. He is a graduate of Brandeis University, where he received his B.A. in 1968, and Milton S. Hershey Medical Center at Pennsylvania State University, where he received his M.D. in 1973. Dr. Herman is currently an Assistant Professor of Psychiatry at Cornell Medical College and is a consultant to both the Supreme Court and the Family Court in both New York and Bronx Counties of New York State. He is board-certified in pediatrics, psychiatry, and child psychiatry.

Dr. Herman is a member of the American Academy of Pediatrics, the American Psychiatric Association, the American Academy of Child Psychiatry, the American Academy of Psychiatry and the Law, and the New York Council on Child Psychiatry. He is the author of numerous professional articles and has made presentations throughout the United States.

"Money goes—it just goes places. Sometime today I just have to get hold of a Bromo."

Blanche Dubois in *A Streetcar Named Desire*, by Tennessee Williams

INTRODUCTION

People talk about money the way Mark Twain said they do about the weather. However, while something **can** be done about one's financial situation, relatively few individuals work at getting this kind of control. The reasons have as much to do with a person's psyche and interpersonal relationships as they do with the economy.

Psychiatrists have long been interested in the significance of money in people's lives as an expression of how individuals view themselves in the world and as one aspect of the manifestations of mental illness. Most people are aware of these opposites: the miserly hoarder who must account for every nickel spent, who never takes risks, and who denies himself pleasure at every turn; and the freewheeling, freespending character who may be a bit manic and who demonstrates the complete absence of self-control. But the psychology of money goes much deeper. It involves patterns set at an early age in a child's development. It reflects increasing self-esteem (or feelings of inadequacy), goals and ambitions (or lack of direction), and one's sense of mastery (or powerlessness).

A financial planner needs to know something about the psychology of money in order to better understand the particular needs of the client. That means recognizing that a person's approach to money is complicated and is based upon a lifetime's worth of conscious and unconscious attitudes. This doesn't mean that the financial planner has to become a psychotherapist. It **does** mean, though, that you need to be sensitive and aware of how emotionally charged this subject can be.

CHILDHOOD ROOTS

A child first learns about money from observing parents. Do they fight about it a great deal? Do they never talk about it? Is there one parent who uses money to control the rest of the family? Is there another who spends compulsively? Does a child see that one or both parents are constantly figuring "angles" to make more and more money?

A child can learn about money by getting an allowance. Some parents give money to a child with no strings attached; others put all kinds of conditions on these payments and make it hard for the child to come to an equilibrium about his or her own money.

Some parents use money as a way of maintaining control over their children. They may lavish all kinds of gifts upon their offspring and appear to be quite generous. However, psychotherapists know that such children later may develop serious problems when they try to assert their independence. These parents may then become angry, and the children may feel abandoned and alone. Other children may have been more fortunate. They may have learned that it's nice to have money for the pleasant things in life but that there are important values that go along with having money. Their parents may have helped them to put financial matters in a proper perspective.

ADULTS AND MONEY

For many adults, acquiring money and the apparent prestige that goes along with it are often linked to their feelings of self-worth. A person with an inner core of low self-esteem will be compelled to acquire more and more wealth in spite of being very well off. For someone like this, a major business success and the ensuing financial gain only provide temporary satisfaction. Because the underlying issue may be a poor self-image, the compulsion to make more and more returns. Such people may never be happy and able to use their wealth with any equanimity.

Other adults may have had several opportunities to acquire substantial wealth but have let those chances go by. A 36-year-old lawyer, for example, with the potential for being a high earner limited his practice to representing only the indigent. He justified this in terms of altruism, concern with society, and a seeming lack of concern for "materialism." Psychotherapy revealed, however, that he had always suffered from a poor self-image and a chronic depression. He had never learned how to enjoy himself and had never felt that he was worth very much. He was afraid that if he were to become monetarily successful, others would see through him and realize that he was a fake. In the course of his treatment, he began to enjoy himself and life more and was able to accept financial rewards even as he maintained a section of his law practice as public interest law.

Some people use money as a means of winning friends and of feeling accepted by others. They may or may not be aware of the roots of this behavior. A 10-year-old boy brought his aunt's silver dollar collection to school and began giving away the coins to other children. He later explained to his teacher that he had hoped at last to have some friends at school. He realized that this would get him into trouble with his aunt. However, the overriding need was to have friends to play with and not to feel lonely. A 25-year-old single woman had a large trust fund and a steady monthly income. She was constantly "lending" money to people who rarely paid her back. She was always the one to pick up the check in restaurants, and she had frequent, lavish parties. She justified this to herself in terms of helping out those less fortunate and in enjoying the pleasures of a vibrant social life. However, in psychotherapy she became aware that much of this behavior represented a compulsion to be accepted and adored by others. The compulsion grew out of deeply rooted feelings of poor self-esteem and loneliness and was an attempt to satisfy a need which was insatiable. As her therapy proceeded and her feelings of self-worth improved, she was able to conduct her financial affairs with more balance.

THE FINANCIAL PLANNER AND THE CLIENT

People come to the financial planner with a variety of motivations. About the only thing that they may have in common is a desire to get in charge of their financial situation. In general, this represents a healthy statement of wishing for more control in one's economic life. You as the expert must recognize that because of your authority in this position, the client will come to relate to you at least in part as he or she has with other authority figures before. This is the phenomenon of transference, which Sigmund Freud discovered. That is, you may be perceived as a parental figure who can do no wrong (or no right!), an older brother or sister, someone to be trusted, or someone to relate to with suspicion. You should be sensitive to this process, which will undoubtedly emerge as the relationship progresses.

As part of your evaluation of the needs of your particular client, you might well inquire about how money matters were handled as he or she was growing up. You will gradually get a sense of the financial world as perceived by this person. Be tuned in to levels of anxiety, distress, or comfort when various money matters are discussed. Bear in mind what psychiatrists are saying these days: In the "early days," no one could discuss sex with great ease. Now that's no longer the case, because all the anxiety, frustration, fear, and insecurity are about money!

As you work with your clients, be aware that certain developmental changes may occur. They can gradually feel more self-confident and in control with your help. As they take part in their economic lives more actively and begin to see results, they will, we hope, feel that much better about themselves. For one patient in psychotherapy, going to a financial planner represented his psychological growth as a mature adult, desirous of financial independence and ready to assume greater control and independence in life. Through his experience with the planner, he began to learn about various financial options and was not as insecure about making decisions. Using the insights he had gained with the advisor, he was able to carry these over into his professional and personal life. Without too dramatic a change in his finances, he was nevertheless psychologically ready at last to purchase a home and to make the necessary adjustments in his professional life to lead to much success.

Such improvements and the resultant pleasure and confidence they bring become part of a cycle which can add much to a person's psychological independence, self-esteem, and general well-being. As a financial planner, therefore, you have much more to offer an individual than simply financial advice. You can actually serve as a catalyst for one's own growth and development as a human being. Being sensitive to this as you watch your client grow can be almost as satisfying as enlarging the portfolio!

"I can't tell you how many prospects I get each year. I can't tell you how many initial interviews I have each year. I can't tell you what my closing ratio is. I can't tell you because I don't know and I don't care. I'm not in the business of keeping score; I'm in the business of helping people."

—COLIN B. COOMBS, CLU, CFP

Colin B. Coombs, CLU, CFP, has been involved in the financial services industry since 1960. In 1966, Mr. Coombs received his Chartered Life Underwriter designation, and in 1973 he earned his Certified Financial Planner designation. He is a graduate of Occidental College.

His organizational and professional activities include membership in the International Association for Financial Planning; he has served as president of the Los Angeles County Chapter. As a founding member of the Institute of Certified Financial Planners, Mr. Coombs also was its president. Likewise, he was president and founding member of the Warner Center Estate and Tax Planning Council. Currently, Mr. Coombs is an adjunct faculty member of the College for Financial Planning, is a registered principal of an NASD member firm, and is licensed in California for life and disability insurance sales.

Forming the Initial Client Relationship

We all have a tendency to aggrandize our roles and activities in life. The title of this chapter sounds pretty lofty, but it is really all about selling. Selling somehow isn't professional, but "forming the initial client relationship" has a professional sound to it. But let it be said early on; we are all salespeople.

Selling has a connotation of a contest—of winners and losers. Sports analogies are often used in the discussion of selling, and you'll find them in this discussion as well. Selling is often thought of as something you do *to* someone, not something you do *for* someone. For all these reasons, and many others, we are repelled by the thought of being salespersons. I had been a life insurance salesman for eight years before I entered the financial planning business. When I became a financial planner, I wanted to be a professional, so I did the opposite of whatever I was trained to do as a life insurance salesman. It was a foolish act on my part. Fortunately, I was a poor salesman so when I did the opposite of what I had done before, I became successful. In other words, I began to do what I should have done as a salesman and became successful.

First of all, let's define salesmanship. It is the process of discovering what other people want or need and helping them get it. Couldn't this also be the definition of financial planning? It is my contention that financial planning did not become popular because of runaway inflation and taxes. And it will not fade away because inflation and taxation are receding. It grew, and is here to stay, because salespeople of financial products began to ask questions and listen to their clients. Heretofore we all made presentations; we never conducted interviews. We called our presentations interviews, but who did all of the talking?

The key to successfully forming the initial client relationship is an attitude. "My purpose is to help you discover what your financial needs and wants are and then to help you fill them. If you win, I win." This attitude requires that you don't keep score. I can't tell you how many prospects I get each year. I can't tell you how many initial interviews I have each year. I can't tell you what my closing ratio is. I can't tell you because I don't know and I don't care. I'm not in the business of keeping score; I'm in the business of helping people. If I do, I win; if I don't, I lose. It's that simple. This is not to say that you shouldn't be a good salesperson and marketer of your services. You have to be. But if your eyes are on the scoreboard, you'll probably strike out.

Before discussing the process of forming client relationships, we need to differentiate between selling and marketing. Marketing is everything you do to get yourself up to bat. Selling is getting a hit. This chapter is about getting hits—forming client relationships. Also, you must realize that there are at least two parties to this transaction—you and the potential client. You are who you are and the potential clients are who they are. There are some people you just can't relate to or work with, and the reverse is also true. You won't get a hit every time. In fact, you probably get too many now. Have you ever taken on a client you shouldn't have? Don't you have clients with whom you just don't communicate well or who can't communicate with you? The first step in forming client relationships is getting to know yourself. Make a list of the clients you have the best relationship with and those (probably ex-clients) with whom you have (or had) the worst relationship. Now review each client and list personal characteristics—personality, employment, social standing, and any other characteristics you can develop. You will probably begin to see some consistency. You will probably find that they tend to fall into certain age groups, economic groups, employment groups, and social groups. This will give you guidance as to how to target your marketing. But you should also realize that prospective clients are making similar decisions, at least subconsciously, about you. You will intimidate some and make others comfortable; you will seem confident and competent to some and cocky to others. Don't force people to become clients. Remember, you've got to work together for a long time. You will invest a lot of time. You don't want it to come to naught because the client was never comfortable with you in the first place.

Next look around you. Is your office an adequate reflection or extension of yourself? Will prospective clients get an immediate sense of who you are when they walk in the door? Or will they know more about your interior decorator, or your wife, or whoever did your decorating, then about you? If so, start over. You don't have to move or throw everything out or go broke in order to redo everything overnight. But make a start. Maybe all you have to do is move the furniture around. Whatever you do, invest yourself in it. If you don't have any talent, hire outside help. Be sure, however, that your advisor gets to know you well and the message you want to convey to prospective clients. Don't be afraid to override his suggestions. Be involved in the process.

The most important part of the decorating process is the physical layout of your office. Don't build barriers between you and the client. Perhaps you should have a U- or L-shaped desk with a couch facing the open side of the desk. A round table for conducting your interviews is useful. Don't hang sales awards on the walls. That's like inviting the lion into the big game hunter's den. Display only diplomas, plaques, and achievement awards that demonstrate professional achievement and community service.

Now that you have established the proper environment, the next step is the initial interview with the prospective client. The best possible situation is that the client comes to your office. If that isn't happening 75 percent or more of the time, do something about it! Probably all it will take is a change of attitude on your part. If you expect and assume that clients will come to your office, that's what will happen. When clients arrive at your office, your secretary/receptionist should know exactly what to do every time. At our office clients are warmly and genuinely greeted, offered a cup of coffee, and asked to fill out a very brief personal data sheet. The message: This is a business-like, professional office that is glad to see me.

Next, you go out to greet them. Don't let your secretary bring them in; you should personally escort them to your office. The message: You're not some cold, ivory-tower, impersonal advisor. Clients want more than professional advice. They want a caring relationship. They don't get it too many places—maybe not even at home. If you provide nothing else, you will retain clients!

Once they are seated around your interview table, follow a set interview format. Have a consistent opening statement designed to communicate certain precise messages. Ours is designed to communicate our experience, our understanding of the broad concerns everyone has about financial affairs, and our commitment to be client-centered. We say the same thing every time with only minor tailoring to fit the particular prospective client.

An important point to interject at this point is that you should do your homework on the prospective client. Talk to people who may know the prospective client. Talk to your referral source. Talk to others in the same line of business or those who might belong to the same organizations as the prospective client. Do what you can to learn about clients before they come in to see you. At the very least, they will be flattered that you were interested enough to learn about them, but more importantly, you can tailor your comments during the interview to be more personal.

After the opening statement, have ten questions memorized that you can ask during the interview. Remember, you are an investigative reporter at this point. Ask the question; then shut up and listen. Make notes, but ask permission first. The prospective client will be flattered. When your prospect says something you feel is a key point, interrupt and ask that it be repeated. (''You just said something very important. Would you repeat it, please, so I can be sure I got it?'') Let him or her reinforce those points that will solidify your potential relationship. Or you can reinforce them by saying, ''Let me be sure I got that right.'' Then repeat what the client said. Then agree with it. To facilitate this interview process, ask prospective clients to bring in last year's income tax return and a summary of their assets and liabilities. This information will help you ask tons of questions.

Once the interview is completed, move on to a presentation of your services. Again, a set presentation format is critical. However, don't waste the information you gathered in the interview. Tailor your remarks based upon this information. Make your services and the benefits specific to the client. If you don't, prospective clients will quickly assume you didn't hear a thing they said. They will accurately assume that it is a ''canned'' presentation.

The ''close'' is a natural consequence of everything that has gone on before. In fact, that's almost what I say in the presentation: ''The next step is to get together again for the fact-finding interview.'' Then I hand them a list of all the data and documents they have to gather together for this next interview. ''How long would it take you to gather all this data?'' Some will come up with an answer right away; others won't. In the first case I pull out my calendar book and set an appointment. In the latter case, I say, ''This is the hardest part of the process for most people. But my clients tell me that it is often the most valuable part, because for the first time in their lives, maybe, they feel organized. They have everything in one place at one time. But it is also the easiest thing to put off. The best way to get around that problem is to set a goal. Let's select a date two or three weeks from now to get together again. That way you'll have a deadline, OK?'' It doesn't need to be two or three weeks. Ten days to two weeks is plenty of time.

It won't work every time. But nothing does, and if it did, you'd be doing business with a lot of the wrong people. Remember, don't keep score; just keep on helping people.

"It is not my job to persuade the client that my view is correct; only to help him clarify his views and to select a plan that is appropriate."

—FELICE PRICE, CFP

Reading and Understanding Your Client

Felice Price is a Certified Financial Planner and President of Felice Price Financial Services, Inc. She has been involved in financial and estate planning since 1977. Felice is a registered principal with Integrated Resources Equity Corporation and is member of numerous professional organizations, including the Institute of Certified Financial Planners, the International Association for Financial Planning, the American Numismatic Association, and the Southern Alameda County Estate Planning Council. Ms. Price holds a B.A. from Indiana University and has taken graduate courses at the University of Chicago.

In simple terms, the financial planner is a financial "shrink." I view my role in much the same way as the psychologist: to understand and to help clients understand their financial goals and fears, hopes and dreams, and to help them come to grips with the risks and choices they will face along the way.

The process of reading and understanding starts with the first contact, usually on the telephone, and is followed with the get-acquainted meeting. I use this free meeting to evaluate what kind of prospective clients I have and to decide if I will be able to work successfully with them. It is truly a mutual evaluation with the client sizing me up as well. This is my opportunity to eliminate the troublemakers and the "China eggs" (they never hatch) quickly and cheaply before I invest too much of my time or their money.

This get-acquainted meeting is the time to examine the data the client brings—or does not bring. Clients are requested to bring the past three years of tax returns and a completed cash flow sheet. Not many people realize how much is revealed about themselves in an income tax return and a cash flow data sheet.

Let me explain what I look for. In addition to the content, how the tax returns were prepared tells me something. Did he go to a reputable CPA firm, to a franchise tax-preparation firm, or did he prepare it himself? Is she accustomed to dealing with the professionals? Does he look for the cheapest outfit? Does she prefer to do everything herself?

The cash flow statement reveals even more. Some people seem to handle the numbers with ease, but more often some significant problems arise. For instance, on one occasion a husband filled out the data without consulting his wife; he had no idea of how much she spent on food and clothing for herself and the children. That his estimates were not reasonable is not the point at all; the point is that he will probably reach decisions without consulting his wife. Such investment decisions based on his estimates could lead to rather poor planning results as well as marital conflict for the couple.

In another case, a client couple jointly filled out the data in minute detail, and they were so hung up on giving precise numbers that they neglected to allow for unexpected expenses that always arise sooner or later. An investment plan based on their budget would surely fail because the cash flow was unrealistic.

The get-acquainted session is, most importantly, the time to get the prospective client to discuss his goals and risk tolerance. I want to see how realistically the client views the world. If she must have an absolutely safe 24 percent annual return, I know I can not work with her. If he has managed only to save $25,000 in his entire working career, and now he wishes to retire in five years, I know I have a formidable reeducation job on my hands.

If we have agreed to work together, the data session is my opportunity to probe deeply, to test and evaluate at length, and to gather the data needed to build the financial plan and/or investment program. By now we have clarified the cash flow data, and I have given the client a list of other necessary documents: titles to property, company benefit plan descriptions, insurance policies, and the like. Again, if she can not find important documents, this tells me a lot about whether or not she is organized and how much service I must provide.

Nonverbal communication is always important. I am especially aware of my clients' facial expressions, tone of voice, and of what they leave unsaid. For example, once when I explained to a couple a variable annuity with a blue-chip stock fund as the investment vehicle, the husband said he understood it and decided to invest. I was going over the term *fluctuate* when I saw the wife grimace. I knew there was a problem, but I did not know what it was. After all, they had read the material earlier, and I had discussed it entirely with them. The husband understood and had reached a decision. But further probing revealed that the wife had not read the material, did not understand it, and was not about to approve such an investment. We decided to postpone the investment decision to give them a chance to review the material further, discuss it between themselves, and get back to me for a second appointment. They did, and the second time around the presentation went smoothly.

One of the most difficult jobs in working with unsophisticated investors is communicating the concept of fluctuation. I spend a great deal of time on this one concept, because if I fail to make this point clear, I am going to have unhappy, maybe even angry clients. Often, the client believes he understands the term; fluctuate, to him, might mean higher and higher. I try to convey the feeling of a roller coaster instead: exhilarating ups, and gut-wretching downs.

I have a teen-aged daughter, some of whose savings I have invested in a mutual fund. Her perceptions are very enlightening, because she is not afraid to say what she thinks. She does not remember the purchase price, and she is completely oblivious to the increase in number of shares from reinvested dividends. But she does remember the highest price it reached and is constantly comparing today's price with that high. I believe her comments are an accurate reflection of what many unsophisticated clients are thinking but will not articulate. Consequently, I always repeat my daughter's comments and mimic her expressions to explain comfort level with fluctuation.

For mutual funds, I go over the track record and specifically note the worst year or worst period. Anybody can do well in a good market; it is how well the management does in the bad times that counts.

One of the areas I want to develop in detail during the data session is the client's view of the world. This is a process that takes gentle probing, leading questions, and thorough, nonjudgmental listening. If the client is a doom-and-gloomer, he will want his investments in tangible assets, not paper securities. If she is afraid of another Great Depression, she will want guaranteed safety. If they expect rampant inflation, they will want securities and/or tangible assets that will prosper in such an atmosphere. It is not my job to persuade clients that my view is correct, only to help them clarify their views and to select a plan that is appropriate.

Besides listening to clients, I also examine how they have invested in the past. If I see that the most daring investment they have ever had is a bank certificate of deposit, I instantly receive better insight into their risk tolerance than from anything they actually say. I remember a prospective client, a civil service engineer in his mid-fifties who described himself as a sophisticated, aggressive investor looking for an 18 percent annual return. However, in his entire career, he had never invested a cent except in bank CDs. I decided I could not work with him because he would never be happy with the return I could get for him with safety and would never accept the risk inherent in his target return.

The long-term relationship between planner and client must be based on mutual respect and understanding. As you sharpen your skills at reading and understanding your clients, you will be better at tuning into them, better at communicating with them, and better able to cope with the changes in their situation as the investment environment changes.

"One must keep in mind that successful investment is not only measured in terms of gains and losses, but also the pain and suffering the client must experience regarding the investment."

—JOSEPH H. CLINARD, JR., CFP

Evaluating a Client for an Investment Strategy

Joseph Clinard is Executive Vice President and a Director of DESCAP Planning, Inc., and is President of DESCAP Securities, Inc., an affiliated registered broker-dealer. Prior to joining DESCAP, Clinard was the senior officer in Chemical Bank's Private Banking Division on Long Island and has served as a Vice President and Director of Financial Planning for major Wall Street firms.

Mr. Clinard is very involved in industry professional associations and currently serves the Long Island chapter of the International Association for Financial Planning as Chairman of the Board of Directors. He is also former President and the chapter's founder.

A popular seminar leader and published author, Mr. Clinard is currently working on a publication for Prentice Hall. He has lectured at New York University, Long Island University, and New York Institute of Technology. In addition, he is an Adjunct Professor and Special Assistant to the Dean for Financial Planning Programs at Adelphi University. Recently, Mr. Clinard has become a Director of the new Long Island Center for Financial Studies, Inc.

Years ago, I developed a system called *investment cybernetics*, a dual-phased control process of managing investor capital. Today it is still used with much success. It is both a technique designed to accurately measure the fundamental investment goals of an investor and a methodology used to act upon these goals that results in constant reevaluation and redeployment of monies. This article deals with the establishment of the client profile, the necessary first step in handling his funds.

By assigning value-weighted, investment-selected objectives to investment requirements, the risk propensities of the investor can be measured quantitatively. This technique then places the client into one of five profile categories relative to his or her psychological needs and personal investment philosophies.

While it is possible to further subdivide these risk-measurement categories, basically all investors fit into one of the following five fundamental investment descriptions:

- Superconservative
- Conservative
- Moderate
- Aggressive
- Superaggressive

It is not always possible to identify accurately the exact profile of an investor simply because many risk-tolerances are psychologically driven. For example, investors are frequently subjected to mood swings, oscillating between several of these categories. Variables such as the current status of the economy, stock market trends, seasonality factors, personal biorhythms, etc. often heavily contribute to emotion, and consequently, investors will respond differently to questions designed to classify their investment philosophies at different times. Nevertheless, all investors will respond in a way that somewhat reflects the individual level of importance they place upon each of the following four investment attributes:

   I. Investment return (i.e., income)
  II. Investment liquidity (i.e., liquidity)
 III. Preservation of capital (i.e., safety)
 IV. Capital appreciation (i.e., growth)

The investor is then asked to assign an importance-value to each attribute. On a scale of one to five, a "one" is considered least important, while a "five" is considered most important. The exception to this is Category IV (capital appreciation), where the system is reversed and "five" becomes least important while "one" is most.

The purpose of these ratings is to measure the relative consideration level allotted to each attribute. Investment personalities differ, and while investment **income** may be important to some (such as, notably, retirees), it may not be important at all to others (such as young executives). **Liquidity** may be very meaningful to some who might foresee a need for their capital within a short period of time but unimportant to others who may be seeking to invest only a small portion of their overall funds. Relative **safety** of an investment is paramount to the investor unable to afford to sacrifice any portion of the capital, while high-rollers who are wealthy enough to lose it all in their quest for short-term gain tend to place a low value on this category. **Appreciation** is significant to those who look to increase the principal's value through risk-related, open-market operations; yet, while growth of capital is very important to some, particularly the younger set, to others it has little or no meaning at all.

This category pertains to appreciation of the underlying investment value without regard to any compounding of the investment with interest or dividend reinvestment. We reverse the order of valuation here because the value comparisons in this attribute contradict all the others. Reversing them puts this category in sync with the other three attributes. It now becomes possible to analyze mathematically the client's investment profile.

Scoring the values is really quite simple. Since the maximum score per attribute is 5 and there are only four attributes, the highest possible score is 20. Nevertheless, it is not the aggregate score that we are looking for, but a value-weighted score. Accordingly, you must divide the aggregate score by 20, the highest attainable score. This will give you the actual weighted value.

For example, assume that Mrs. Brown, a retiree, assigns a 5 to each attribute. In other words, she places great value on income, liquidity, safety, and little, if any, on appreciation. Mr. Green, her young son-in-law, on the other hand, places the following values on the attributes: 3 on income; 2 on liquidity; 1 on safety; and 1 on appreciation. We can see that Mr. Green requires some income, needs little liquidity, desires risky investments, and seeks maximum appreciation. Consequently, Brown's total score is 20 and Green's is 7. If we then divide by 20, the highest attainable score, we arrive at the following result:

$$\text{Brown:} \quad 20/20 = 1.00$$
$$\text{Green:} \quad 7/20 = .35$$

The next step in the process is to place an investment classification on each investor based upon his or her value-weighted score. Here, experience and professional judgment come strongly into play in order to assign a proper investment profile to the value-weighted score. I have devised a set of suggested values. Nevertheless, different profiles are, of course, possible, depending on an adviser's own degree of aggressiveness or conservatism. These factors assigned to investors result in the following profile characteristics:

Value-Weight Score	Investor Profile
0.00–0.25	Superaggressive
0.26–0.49	Aggressive
0.50–0.74	Moderate
0.75–0.99	Conservative
1.00	Superconservative

Getting back to our example, Mrs. Brown, at a 1.00 weighted average score is considered to be a superconservative investor, while Mr. Green's score of 0.35 identifies him as aggressive. Knowing this, we then structure investment policy so that both advisor and client are comfortable with the ultimate investment selection.

The value-weighted system of quantifying investment objectives is only the beginning. We must next select investment choices depending upon the profile. Below are examples of investment choices which are part of the asset allocation decision process:

- CDs or money market funds
- Speculative stocks and listed put and call options

- Safe, managed investments with good yields
- Aggressively managed investments with good yields
- Balanced mutual funds with moderate yields
- Highest yielding bonds, unit trusts, or mutual funds
- U.S. Government bonds or government mutual funds
- Municipal bonds or municipal bond funds
- Currency or interest rate futures contracts
- Single-payment, tax-sheltered annuities
- Inflation hedges such as precious metals and real estate

The process that leads to asset allocation for a client must begin with the creation of an investor profile, a requirement that allows you to know the client's objectives and risk tolerance. Without that understanding, the chance of successful investment is doubtful. One must keep in mind that successful investment is measured in terms of not only gains and losses, but also in terms of the pain and suffering the client must experience regarding the investment.

The objective of the professional investment advisor is to give his client the best chance for success. But at the same time, it must be done in a way that allows the client to feel comfortable and to sleep nights. By following the strategies outlined in this article, the investment advisor should have greater insight into investor profile, which leads to proper investment selection.

"Comprehensive financial planning . . . is a personalized professional service addressed to the actual needs of clients, whose interests necessarily come first because of the fiduciary relationship between you."

—DALE S. JOHNSON, Ph.D., CFP

How to Create and Communicate the Language of Financial Planning in Your Practice

Dale Johnson, CFP, has been an Account Executive with Merrill Lynch, Dean of the College for Financial Planning, a financial planner, and a faculty member at the American College. He has made significant contributions to the development of both the CFP and ChFC professional education and certification programs. He holds a Ph.D. from the University of Michigan, an M.A. from Tulane University and a B.A. from Rhodes College.

Mr. Johnson is author and coauthor of numerous articles, monographs, and books on financial planning topics, including *Readings in Financial Services: Environment and Professions, Fact Finding for Comprehensive Financial Planning, Professional Financial Planning: Practice and Procedure,* and *Financial Planning Strategies and Techniques.* He is a member of the IAFP and a Director of the Association for Financial Counseling and Planning Education.

Your success in marketing financial planning through your practice will ultimately depend on whether you can (1) assimilate its process, procedures, and delivery methods, (2) provide relevant information and communications support for your clients' personal financial decisions, and (3) develop an appropriate professional discourse and communications envelope to represent and market the planning and implementation services you actually provide. The medium of this projection of your practice image is clear conceptual language.

Everything you do in structuring and managing your practice is fundamentally related to issues of communications and information exchange. What you need, then, is a two-dimensional model on which to base your practice's communications system for the intermediation that you provide between your clients (and prospective clients) and the financial services marketplace. This model includes (1) a verbal description of what the financial planning process includes in your practice and (2) what business and practice structure are in relation to this description.

This model of practice is essentially conceptual and descriptive; therefore, it can be formulated in language and transmitted as a communications image of who you are and what you do. In the absence of a uniformly endorsed definition of planning through either self-regulatory or statutory guidelines, it is imperative that you create and communicate your own.

We will look at how to develop this model by examining its conceptual and technical dimensions. What this process is and what it delivers constitute the language model on which your practice image should be based. From this model, you can develop a marketing strategy that is consistent and compelling on the level of language itself. What follows is a conceptual outline of a model that you should modify and customize for your own needs.

THE CONCEPTUAL AND TECHNICAL DIMENSIONS OF PLANNING

The personal financial management system that planning creates focuses on formulating, implementing, and then measuring the consequences of financial decisions by their effects on taxes, cash flows, and personal and investment net worth. Through in-depth counseling and relevant information gathering, it integrates all planning considerations and implementations in relation to the client's personal concerns, constraints, and financial objectives, both short- and long-term.

Comprehensive planning allocates cash flows and investment capital assets to each client's financial objectives. Success in that process requires complete information about his personal and financial situations balanced against extensive, clarified, and actionable information from the financial services marketplace that you provide.

In this process, you are the facilitator of decision making, not the decision maker. You are the organizer and manager of information and communications and the conductor of an advisory, fiduciary, and planning relationship—the intermediary who brings buyer and seller together through the shopping lists of financial services and products that you design and your clients endorse.

To help assemble, organize, and analyze their personal and financial information for marketing purposes and relate it to basic concepts of personal financial management, both you and your clients will find two simple explanatory approaches useful:

1. Allocational principle of cash flows
2. Production principle of structuring investment capital assets to produce foreseeable cash flows on an ongoing basis.

THE ALLOCATIONAL PRINCIPLE OF CASH FLOWS

This principle allocates all cash inflows of an individual adult to three categories of spending:

1. Life maintenance
2. Taxes
3. Saving and investment

Life maintenance includes everything purchased for use and consumption—such as housing, food, clothing, transportation, vacations, hobbies, entertainment, gifts, publications, and premiums for insurance contracts (a personal capital-expense item). Taxes include federal, state, and local income tax and Social Security tax. Saving and investment includes every dollar from current cash inflows whose spending is deferred for specific financial objectives, life maintenance during retirement, or distribution through estate settlement.

Cash inflows allocated to acquiring assets create the basis of total net worth—the difference between total assets and total liabilities. After all spending for life maintenance and taxes, whatever remains—the net annual surplus of cash—is spent for saving and investment. Successful investment assets create an increasing capital base that produces additional cash flows; reinvestment of these cash flows compounds the growth rate of the capital base, thus increasing net worth over time. This effect is accelerated, of course, if liabilities are held flat or reduced.

This principle creates additional cash for investment by employing tax-reduction techniques that convert dollars otherwise payable as taxes into dollars available for further investment. This effect is also accelerated if life maintenance expenses are held flat or reduced while personal income and other cash flows rise.

Effective personal financial planning begins with an analysis of how cash flows are being generated and allocated. This analysis enables planning to focus on managing and controlling cash outflows related to living expenses, taxes, and investment—the three parts of the allocational principle in which all cash inflows are ultimately spent. This is the essence of cash flow management.

Clients can grasp and utilize this cash flow management principle in every area of their financial lives, thus directing appropriate allocations of cash and investment capital to each funding objective in the spectrum of comprehensive planning. The principle is a handy, succinct, and efficient communications tool for every area of financial focus, pointing always to the sources of dollars going into the client's pocket and the uses of dollars going out.

THE PRODUCTION PRINCIPLE OF INVESTMENT CAPITAL

An investment asset structure consists of all the financial resources that work together to produce a desired amount of money each year. Any organized business consists of several departments, and a client's financial life can be compared to that of a business. Each department requires investment in time or assets to fund its expected production of cash flows. A person's ability to earn money through employment is, of course, a capital-producing asset.

For most persons these departments would include Job, Investments, Social Security, Pension, and Insurance. In a sense, it does not matter which department of the business entity produces the income so long as cash inflows are adequate to take care of annual spending requirements for life maintenance, taxes, and saving and investment. Without planning and proper funding, however, one or more of these departments may not actually produce the desired level of cash inflows as needs arise.

In addition, to remain viable a capital-producing enterprise must generate enough output each year to reinvest itself for capital growth, so that there will be enough cash inflow at every foreseeable point to fund specifically-determined financial objectives at a level consistent with estimated needs.

If one department of the business entity shuts down, the other departments must increase their production to maintain desired levels of cash inflow. When a person retires, for example, the Job department closes and the Pension, Social Security, and Investment departments must fill the cash-inflow gap up to the desired level of take-home dollars. Similarly, if a person dies or becomes disabled, the Insurance department joins the other remaining departments to replace the cash inflows of lost capital production in the Job department.

Personal assets—such as personal residences and automobiles—are of course factored into a person's total asset structure. However, personal assets are not included in the capital or investment asset structure if they are acquired for use and consumption rather than for production of cash flows. Many personal assets can be liquidated for cash, or converted to investment assets, and this may become desirable at some point in the life cycle (as after retirement). One of the purposes of planning, however, is to ensure that clients not have to resort to this extreme measure to supply the dollars needed for their spending program. Except in this contingency, personal net worth—which includes personal assets—is not as reliable a gauge of effective planning as investment net worth, which is the difference between total investment assets and total liabilities.

This production principle of investment capital is the essence of investment planning.

THE ALLOCATIONAL/PRODUCTION PRINCIPLES AND FINANCIAL PLANNING

The relationship between these two principles is integral with the basic thrust of comprehensive planning. They provide the following developed point of view and succinct definition. *Comprehensive personal financial planning is the systematic method for establishing, maintaining, nourishing, and eventually liquidating or otherwise disposing of an individual's investment capital assets to produce desired levels of cash flow for attaining specific financial objectives during the client's lifetime, including the conservation and distribution of estate.*

The basic conceptual framework of this definition will enable you to understand succinctly and explain to your clients, associates, and the marketplace what financial planning is. Cash flow and investment management principles pervade and define the economic consequences of planning options available throughout the scope of this practice field. Indeed, the areas of focus beyond cash flow management and investment planning as such can be considered as areas of increasingly technical and tax-intensive possibilities for acquiring, holding, and ultimately disposing of investment capital assets for the production of cash flows.

In addition, this basic conceptual framework provides the starting point for developing a professional language of financial planning for all of your practice communications and marketing activities, including brochures, promotional materials, and compliance documentation. How much elaboration and procedural detail you add to this definition in your own practice environment will depend, ultimately, on your marketing objectives and capabilities—on the scope of planning services and products you provide. You should have a firm grasp of what the possible scope is.

THE SCOPE OF COMPREHENSIVE PLANNING

Extensive personal and financial information on each client is required to determine the client's current financial position, provide analyses of that position, establish realistic financial objectives, and evaluate and finally choose from among available planning strategies and techniques in order to help the client move in a total, integrated manner from point A (current position) to point B (desired result) in a planning time frame.

The aim of comprehensive planning as a practice is to install an objectives-oriented communications and decision-making model to the technical disciplines of the following areas of typical client needs for planning.

Planning for qualitative, personal client's objectives • Determining each client's most immediate needs, desires, and personal circumstances and developing personal financial objectives based on accurate and complete information on the client's financial resources and prospects.

Cash flow and liability management • Maintaining and enhancing personal cash flows through employment, professional practices, business ownership, and investment, and controlling allocations of expenditure for life-style maintenance, taxes, investment, and debt.

Individual income tax planning • Planning for the reduction of income tax liabilities to increase cash flows for personal spending and create additional surplus dollars for investment.

Risk management and insurance planning • Planning for the protection of cash and assets through sound financial management, control of risk exposures, and cost-effective protection against risks through contracts of insurance.

Personal investment planning and management • Planning and managing the building of a capital base for generating future cash flows by spending current annual surpluses of cash for investment assets, managing appropriate levels of liability associated with investment net worth, and constructing and managing an investment portfolio.

Planning with business interests and professional practices • Planning and managing the integration of personal financial planning objectives and the assets and cash flows of business ownership interests and professional practices.

Compensation and employee benefit planning • Planning for total compensation packages, including the use of qualified and nonqualified deferred compensation plans and the various employee benefits typically associated with corporate executives, other salaried employees, and business owners and professional practitioners.

Planning for economic independence and retirement • Planning the allocation of specific tax-favored investment dollars (in conjunction with social security benefits and employment-related pension and other related plans) to provide adequate capital to generate the cash flows deemed necessary for economic independence and retirement.

Planning for estate conservation and distribution • Planning for the lifetime accumulation and appropriate titling of assets and their distribution with minimal shrinkage of estate values through lifetime and testamentary transfers, according to the dispositive intentions of each client.

These planning areas encompass every conceivable personal financial objective, actionable financial technique, and overall financial strategy. In each area the aim is to apply systematically developed, integrated, and cohesive planning decisions simultaneously, so that they will work together interactively. The planning process itself applies these decisions. Without the synthesizing procedures of that process, these focus areas are mere specialist areas, fragmented and isolated one from the other, both conceptually and in application.

Comprehensive personal financial planning therefore includes the following characteristics:

- It is a personalized professional service addressed to the actual needs of clients, whose interests necessarily come first because of the fiduciary relationship between you.
- It is a systematic method of financial decision making that produces an overall strategy and a shopping list of customer-tailored decisions to help each client achieve specific financial objectives in the planning time frame.
- It represents the blueprints of the client's allocation of cash flows and investment capital.
- It encompasses the total personal and financial circumstances of each client insofar as they can be uncovered, clarified, and addressed through counseling and information gathering.
- It integrates into its own methodology all facets of professional financial services specializations, including the practice standards (or their equivalents) of participating professionals.

The planning process permits you to design a personal financial management system for each of your clients structured to reflect

- Their current financial position.
- The consequences of that position if no further significant financial decisions are implemented.
- Recommendations and decisions for new actions based on specific objectives, and their foreseeable consequences on cash flows, personal and investment net worth, and tax liabilities.

- An overall strategic framework within which specific financial decisions are formulated, understood, measured over time, and evaluated by you, the client, and your peers in other specialist disciplines.
- A marketing plan for financial services and products needed by each of your clients.
- A marketing plan for your practice that supports your role in developing personal financial management systems.

These considerations lead directly to the most emphatic point to be made about comprehensive financial planning: *It is a sophisticated marketing process that matches consumers' financial needs, preferences, and objectives with the appropriate vehicles and instrumentalities for satisfying and achieving them.*

When you employ the planning process to deliver the foregoing definitions, it enables you to accomplish the following essential communications objectives.

- You can relate information about clients to the thought processes and procedural methods (the delivery system) of financial planning.
- You can create a professional language for financial planning that guides you, your associates, the client, other advisors and specialists, and providers of support services (such as software developers and vendors).
- You can delineate the demand for appropriate services and products and match it with supply for each of your clients.
- You can establish the trusted advisor relationship with each client.

Financial planning itself is actually not very difficult to understand. Unfortunately, all too often our definitions of it are. In precise definitions of the process and scope of planning, you will discover the heuristic capacities of language itself to provide intelligible and marketable communications structures for every dimension of your professional practice.

"A client who participates in the decision-making process is far more likely to implement than a client who is spoon-fed his or her recommended actions."

—RICHARD B. FREEMAN, M.B.A.

Motivating Clients to Take Action Through the Financial Counseling Process

Richard B. Freeman, M.B.A., is currently a Financial Counselor with DESCAP Planning in Westport, Connecticut. His previous corporate experience was with Citicorp and Bankers Trust Company in New York City. He holds a bachelor's degree from the University of Pennsylvania and a master's in business administration from the University of Chicago. Mr. Freeman is a member of the International Association for Financial Planning.

INTRODUCTION

Implementation of recommendations is the desired end result of every financial plan. Clients fail to implement for a variety of reasons. Some of the most frequent reasons are that we have failed to get them to accept our recommendations and/or convey a sense of urgency. These failures are often due to the treatment of the ''plan'' as a product to be ''delivered'' versus a counseling process that evolves as the client is taken through it.

The process described below is a counseling approach in delivering a financial plan. It is a very time-intensive approach. I have found it to be very effective in getting clients to take action because they

1. Understand why recommendations are made.
2. Help make the recommendations themselves.
3. See the benefits of the recommendations.

This results in clients taking action because they are comfortable with the recommendations made. They do not need to be cajoled into implementing. They will implement themselves because the recommendations are within their *comfort zone.*

COMFORT ZONE

All clients have a set of perceptions about the various areas of financial planning that impact their lives—tax, investment, estate, contingency, and the like. These perceptions, in turn, will determine how a client *feels* about a particular subject. Does he dislike the stock market because he perceives it as too risky? Does he like bonds because he perceives them as safe? If so, he probably owns bonds rather than stocks because he is comfortable with bonds. Bonds are within his comfort zone. Stocks are outside of it.

Most clients express objectives that require that they move outside their comfort zone in order to achieve the objectives. In the example above, the objective might be growth. Clearly, the client must move outside his comfort zone to achieve growth.

The comfort zone can be viewed in the manner shown in Figure 1.

The heart of the counseling process is helping clients expand their comfort zones in order to help them reach their objectives. A description of the process I use starts below. I hope it will help you help your clients.

PLAN PREPARATION

This step of the process probably starts out much the same as your own. Data is collected and then organized to be ''worked on.'' Some areas of the plan cover black and white issues. For example, pre-1981 wills in a large estate indicate a clear need for new wills. For this planning issue, objectives, observations, analysis, and recommendations are fully developed. Other areas cover gray issues—for example, helping a client decide whether to take an early retirement package when the benefits of doing so are marginal. Here objectives, observations, and analysis are done but no recommendations are made at this point.

The financial plan at this point consists of your analytical backup materials

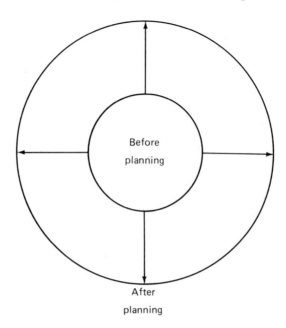

Figure 1 Client comfort zone.

and personal notes covering the planning areas described above. There is no preparation of a binder or notebook. Counseling is a process, not a product. (Summary letters are sent *after* each client meeting.) You are now ready to begin plotting your strategy for moving your client to take action.

MEETING PREPARATION

The first step is to determine where you want your client to be at the end of the process. For each planning area (taxes, investments, etc.), you should have a good feel for the strategies needed to achieve client objectives.

The second step is to think about how the various issues to be covered will be perceived by your client. These are the levers you will manipulate to guide your client through the counseling process. Possibilities include technical/non-technical, disturbing/nurturing, interesting/boring, unemotional/emotional, clear-cut/complex, and so on.

The third and most important step is the determination of the sequence of issues to be covered. It is a creative process, not a static one like the table of contents in a financial plan "product." Like a movie director, you can take a set of events (issues) and arrange them so that your audience is either bored or *excited!* The sequence decided upon will become your agenda for the counseling process.

As an example, a recently divorced client came to me with four major concerns as follows:

1. A desire to help her son buy a house. Should she?
2. An unfocused concern about retirement resources.
3. An unfocused concern about her major investment holding—$150,000 in one stock issue. Emotionally, she was very attached to the stock.
4. A need for an investment strategy.

After reviewing the case, I realized that she was in adequate, but not terrific financial health. She would need to forego concern 1 for now, take action to change concern 3, and would need her hand held for concern 4. To set the agenda, it was helpful for me to consider the following:

- Do I have credibility with the client (e.g., a referral), or did I need to build it?
- Should I begin with what the client is most concerned about, or should I build up to it, leaving it for last?
- Should I begin with what I see as the most pressing issue, or build up to it, leaving it for last?
- Do I need to nurture her, or disturb her to move her to action?

I realized that I needed to show her the weak state of her financial health and the inappropriateness of her current thinking regarding her finances. I would have to disturb her initially to get her to "wake up." I set the following agenda:

1. Retirement Resources

(Disturb, nontechnical issues, clear-cut) Showed her that retirement resources were inadequate to support today's lifestyle in the future. This got her attention and helped her appreciate the seriousness of the next two areas.

2. House for Son

(Disturb, technical tax issues, emotional issues) Showed her that she could not afford it; the house would be in a mediocre area and a poor investment; it also would not do much for her son.

3. Stock Holding

(Disturb, technical tax issues, clear-cut investment issues) Reviewed benefits of diversification, risks in holding single issue, tax consequences of sale, etc.

4. Investment Strategy

(Nurture, interesting, clear-cut, nontechnical) Developed an investment strategy that she was comfortable with.

Careful setting of the agenda for Mrs. Jones was crucial in helping move her successfully through the planning process and implementation. With your agenda set, you now focus on the client meeting itself.

CLIENT MEETING(S) *

Three concepts that will guide you here are education, participation and visualization.

---

*Much of this section represents a refinement of a counseling process developed by Vern C. Hayden, CFP.

Education

Educating clients is something every planner does. Every planner has his or her own way of presenting the basics of tax law, estate law, economics, insurance, and so forth. I offer nothing new here. Understanding the *role* of education in the process is just as important as educational technique.

Clients occupy their current comfort zones largely due to lack of knowledge. They do not understand the financial world that exists out where their objectives lie. So they retreat to their comfort zone.

A process of education will make clients more aware and help them begin to expand their comfort zones. In my planning process, education *precedes* rather than follows presentation of recommendations. This allows the client to become an active participant rather than a passive observer in the development of plan recommendations.

Participation

A client who participates in the decision-making process is far more likely to implement than a client who is spoon-fed his or her recommended actions. These clients are excited!

To see this in action, let's look at client John Smith, a corporate employee who has three medical plans to choose from (A, B, C). John has been in plan A for five years and has expressed no concern about his medical coverage to you. Plan A is the simplest for John to understand and use. After your case review, however, you determine that plan C would better protect John and his family. Plan C, of course, is the most complex and difficult to use.

Standard planning techniques would have *you* recommend plan C to John with comparisons and contrasts involving plans A and B. My process would involve recognition that John is unaware of the issues governing selection of and working with a medical plan (he is uneducated). His comfort zone is the simplest choice—plan A. To begin to expand his comfort zone, I would present the basic issues involved in selecting and working with medical plans (education).

The client begins to ask questions and develop a sense of understanding. He is *participating* in the development of recommendations. The decision-making process you used to choose plan C is beginning to be internalized by the client.

Visualization

When I felt that the client's knowledge base was adequate and his comfort zone expanded, I would present the three options for his consideration, emphasizing the benefits of each. He can then *see* (and understand) the benefits of each plan. If all goes as planned, *he* should say to me, "I think I should do plan C, don't you?" And I say, "That's right; plan C is best for you."

CONCLUSION

The client was able to make the choice because his comfort zone had been expanded to include the recommended strategy. The process by which this was accomplished was

1. Education—he understood why recommendations were made.
2. Participation—he was an active participant in the process.
3. Visualization—he was able to see the benefits of the recommendations.

Using the counseling process creatively can be extremely effective in motivating clients to take action. You probably had a creative, dynamic interchange when you "sold" the client on working with you. The client implemented at that stage—he or she signed a contract with you. The client was *excited!* You did not present your services in the same static manner that most planners use in their planning process. So why stop being creative at the initial interview?

*"It is not the financial planner who figures out and **tells** the people what they should do with their money who is the hero or heroine today. Rather, it is the planner who **sells** them on doing it!"*

—LOREN DUNTON

The Importance of Selling

Loren Dunton is the founder and president of The National Center for Financial Education, a nonprofit consumer organization. Mr. Dunton has played a major role in the foundation of the Society for Financial Counseling, the International Association for Financial Planning, the College for Financial Planning and *Financial Planning* magazine. He is the author of several books on salesmanship and has authored *Your Book of Financial Planning . . . A Consumers Guide to a Better Financial Future,* published by Prentice Hall in 1983, *The Financial Planner . . . A New Professional,* published by Longman in 1985, and *Financial Planning Can Make You Rich . . . And Thirty-Three Case Histories to Prove It,* published by Prentice Hall in 1987. Mr. Dunton has authored numerous magazine articles and frequently lectures on financial planning and education to both consumers and professional groups.

"Salesmanship: the science of making other people want to buy and buy what it is you are selling."

It was over twenty years ago that McGraw-Hill contracted with me to write my first book on "how to sell," or salesmanship. It had been a real surprise some years before when my dictionaries showed no definition for the word "salesmanship." The one above is what I came up with and often used in setting the stage for the sales clinics and seminars I was giving around the country.

To me, salesmanship was, and is, a science, not an art. Like other sciences, it can be taught and it can be learned. You will notice too, that salesmanship is not pushing off on people something they do not want. It is making them want it and if possible, want to *buy* it.

Charles B. Roth, who wrote *Professional Salesmanship* and *Secrets of Closing Sales*, plus more than a dozen other books on selling, became my mentor over thirty years ago. It was he who helped me appreciate salesmanship as something that made the free enterprise system special and workable. Red Motley, president of Parade Publications in the nineteen-fifties, used to say, "Nothing happens until somebody sells something," and this is still true.

It was in the nineteen-sixties, however, that most of my sales consulting was being done with companies in what we now call the financial services industry. Appalled at the lack of professional salesmanship being practiced by mutual fund representatives and life insurance salespeople, I wrote that book for McGraw-Hill and started on a year-long trip around the world with my wife and two teen-aged daughters.

It was on this trip that I was confronted by people disparaging our free-enterprise system and quoting President Kennedy to the effect that 95 percent of our people were dependent upon social security when they retired. While I was conducting research for what I thought would be another book, it became obvious that we were doing an outstanding job in this country in selling people on spending their money. It became just as obvious that we were doing a very poor job of selling people on putting enough money aside for their futures.

Part of the reason for this lack of saving for the future was that salespeople from the insurance industry were disparaging investments, and the securities salespeople were disparaging insurance. Bankers, of course, were telling people to keep their money in the bank at a passbook interest rate that was not even keeping up with inflation. But the other part of the reason was the ineffective salesmanship being practiced in the various segments of the financial services industry. In my opinion, only the credit unions were really looking after Mr. and Ms. Average American, and at that time not enough people could belong to them.

The only good salesmanship being practiced—that I could find, anyway—was by the dually licensed mutual fund and insurance salespeople. Many of them had been chased out of the insurance industry for selling funds, but they were the real pioneers of the financial planning profession.

They were effective partly because they knew how to sell.

A lot of them still do, but in the nineteen-seventies many of them became Certified Financial Planners and, in too many cases, started acting like "professionals." Some of them even started acting like accountants or practitioners to other people's financial health. This was especially true of the newer people who started entering this new and growing profession. While some of the old-timers had forgotten how to **sell,** most of the newer people never did know how. Most of them, in fact, were not aware that the ability to sell is what would determine their degree of success in their new profession.

Many of the much-admired leaders in the profession went into fee-only financial planning and succeeded partly because they were so effective at selling their services. They had learned how to sell when they formerly had **sold** financial products, and it stood them in good stead when they "graduated" to selling only their services.

Unfortunately, perhaps, the people coming into the profession and attending the talks and seminars given by those pioneers at the various professional conferences and meetings saw only how proficient they were at preparing financial plans for their clients and what a helpful professional service they were providing. What they did not see often enough is the quality of salesmanship demonstrated by these leaders. In fact, some of those leaders did not even realize how good they really were.

Whether the new people coming into the profession went into fee-only planning, fee-plus-commission planning, or commission-only planning, there has been too little emphasis, and for too long, on the importance of successfully motivating people to do what you (and often they) know they should do. And that is to plan and to prepare for their financial future.

During the late nineteen-seventies and early nineteen-eighties, there was even a strong contingent in the financial planning movement that believed "selling" was unprofessional. They even winced a little at "motivation." The public was being exposed to powerful and convincing salesmanship to get them to **spend** their money but was also exposed to reluctant, very poor and amateurish salesmanship when it came to getting them to put money into savings, insurance, investments, or financial planning advice, with some notable exceptions, of course.

The science of selling has never been more important in this society. As a matter of fact, it is vital if we are to help people have a better future. But they need to plan and prepare for it. The forces in our society trying to influence people to *spend* money are using very powerful salesmanship in a variety of ways.

If the financial services industry expects to get a logical share of the consumer's discretionary dollar, it is going to have to **sell,** not just **tell.** It is the financial planner who can play the key role. But it is not the financial planner who figures out and **tells** the people what they should do with their money who is the hero or heroine today. Rather, it is the planner who **sells** them on doing it!

Perhaps I go a little overboard in stressing the importance of motivating your clients. But there is a reason. Let me explain. A few years ago, I had a challenge thrown at me by a national TV financial talk-show host. He made it sound as if this were something of which financial planners should be ashamed, and he almost choked when I said, "Yes, and isn't it fortunate for us that they do?"

As the interview went on, he gradually realized that buying more insurance or investing in a mutual fund is something a lot of people are awfully glad they did. He also admitted later that for every person who regrets even buying a shady tax shelter, there were probably ten or twenty individuals who invested in good ones—and are grateful.

Now that I am in my sixties, with more years on which to look back than ahead, my perspective has brought a new clarity, and more than a few regrets. Oddly enough, however, my moments of regret dwell far more on the stocks I did not buy, the extra insurance I did not take out, the mutual funds in which I did not invest, and the money I spent instead of putting into investments.

So where did this interviewer's feelings come from? What conditioning was he exposed to that made him categorize as negative the fact that financial planners want to sell us something?

Forty years ago, Harold Dill sold me a lot of cash-value life insurance. Twenty years ago, we cashed it in, along with some stocks we had, and took our two daughters on that year's trip around the world. The money we put into insurance, with Harold's insistence and the forced savings feature, would probably have been spent in Reno, or on another new car—exactly where much of our other discretionary income went. When we got ready to take that trip around the world, we were very glad Harold had tried to sell us insurance—and had succeeded.

Oh, I do have regrets, too, of course. I especially resent the mutual fund salesman who called on me when I was 28 years old, unmarried, and making far more money than my friends. That is, I regret the fact that he did not know how to sell—or did not try hard enough.

Even though I could have easily afforded it, I fluffed him off when he tried to sell me a hundred-dollar-a-month mutual fund investment program. I thought I was smart because I had not let him talk me into anything.

Last year, forty years later, just out of curiosity, I wrote to the Investment Company Institute in Washington, D.C. and asked them to figure out how much those mutual funds would be worth to me if that fund representative had been a better salesman and I had maintained a hundred-dollar-a-month investment program, which I could have easily afforded to do.

Over a million dollars! Yes, even with a sales charge deducted! All for $48,000, a little financial self-discipline, and the time-value of money. Why did that salesman not tell me then about the dollar-cost-averaging? Or why did he not talk about the time-value of money? And the tremendous power of compound interest? Why did he not use a financial planning approach and really sell me on looking ahead?

Maybe somebody taught him that his job was to **tell** people about mutual funds. Oh, if only some sales trainer had made him realize he did not help people when he told them something, but only when he sold them something! And then showed him *how* to sell!

Yes, from my experience, most financial planners want to sell you something. At least they know you should be putting more of your money aside for the future—either in the bank or into some investments or insurance.

But for the most part, and admittedly with some exceptions, those mutual funds, or that insurance, or those tax-sheltered investments they might try to sell you will be far better for the person you will be when you are my age. Far better than the new car, the seldom-used personal computer, the too-many 40-dollar dinners, or the too-high liquor bills somebody else will have sold you.

So, when a financial planner tries to sell us something, we might be smart to say, ''Yes!''

At least the odds are in our favor!

There you have it. My very personal reasons for feeling that financial planners should attach more importance than many of them do to motivating their clients and prospects.

People need to be **told.** But in today's economy, when it comes to savings, investments and insurance, they need even more to be **sold.**

"Becoming competent in dispensing sound financial advice, and maintaining that competence by keeping current with the latest developments in the field is, without question, the best way to service our clientele."

—RONALD P. HOGARTH, CLU, CFP

Servicing Your Client After the Plan Is Written

Ron Hogarth has been involved in the financial services industry for over 15 years. Starting with Travelers Insurance Company, he progressed through a three-year agency development program which resulted in a Travelers agency. Later he teamed with another agent to form an independent agency, which began offering general financial planning as well as estate planning. Eventually the financial planning activities overtook insurance operations, and Mr. Hogarth exclusively converted to a financial planning firm.

Merging with two other financial planners, Mr. Hogarth is one of the founding partners of Bretschneider & Associates, Inc. where his primary responsibility is for plan generation and client servicing. Ron is a Chartered Life Underwriter and Certified Financial Planner. He holds life, health, and casualty insurance licenses and is a NASD registered representative.

In related activities, Mr. Hogarth is a past president of the Delaware Valley Chapter of the IAFP and past officer of the Bucks County Estate Planning Council. He is on the adjunct faculty of New York University, where he has taught courses in financial planning practice management, and also at Bucks County Community College, Newtown, Pennsylvania, where he presents courses and seminars on financial planning.

Client servicing is the most important component in securing the successful future of a financial planning firm. Financial planning is a service industry. Whether you realize it or not, you are constantly selling service. It may be advice, products, arranging ancillary services of allied professionals, or just making your clients feel confident that you are concerned about them. How well you do this will directly affect the willingness, and even enthusiasm, of your clients to refer you to others as well as to continue their relationship with you. A loyal clientele, who readily make referrals, is the concrete foundation of a solid financial planning practice building for a successful future.

When I teach financial planning "practice management" at New York University, I always ask my students what they consider the most important ethical standard for a financial planner. I inevitably receive answers such as: obey all laws, keep the clients' interests above all else, be truthful, and so on. These, of course, are fine upstanding qualities, but the answer I really wanted, besides its ethical application, is also of preeminent importance in client servicing. That answer: to develop and maintain professional competence.

Financial advice is the service we sell as financial planners. Becoming competent in dispensing sound financial advice and maintaining that competence by keeping current with the latest developments in the field is without question the best way to service our clientele.

Assuming that you are recognized as a competent financial planner, let's explore some specific tactics that will continually remind your clients of your competence and which will also bond them closer to you as their financial counselor.

The first tactic I would like to discuss is simply being available to your clients. This is such a basic concept, yet if it is not heeded, it can be the source of endless frustration to clients. I have on a number of occasions heard the complaint that professionals are hard to reach. This may be an undeserved generalization for many, but it does emphasize just how important availability is to most clients. In fact, I have had a few clients tell me that they left their previous advisors not so much because of bad advice, but because they had a hard time getting in touch with them. Their loss was my gain, but what a foolish way to lose a client.

Good availability to a client is simply a matter of common sense and courtesy. Nobody likes to be put off, so when a client calls, take the call, even if it may be a bit inconvenient at the time. When you have been out of the office, return the phone calls of clients as soon as possible. It will be tremendously appreciated. Try to avoid distractions when talking with your clients, either personally in the office or on the telephone. It is most satisfying to feel that you are all-important. One other point on this subject. I have known some planners who will only meet clients at their offices. While this does have the merit of engaging the client in the planner's controlled and familiar environment, it can often be very inconvenient to the client, who must always travel to the planner in order to meet. In my opinion, availability means accommodating the client, and that may mean meeting somewhere convenient to the client rather than to the planner.

Beyond the general aspects of being available to clients, let's discuss some specific servicing items.

The first specific opportunity for servicing a client once the plan is completed and delivered is implementation. It is important that you provide effective assistance with placing the financial plan in action. This is true whether your compensation is fee only or fee plus commission. In fact, I think it is especially important if you receive a commission on products. The client should rightfully expect and receive thorough help in selecting and processing the appropriate products for that commission. It is here, during the implementation process, where you convert your ideas and recommendations into results and, after all, results are what the client is buying.

Clients are naturally responsible for actually executing the financial plan recommendations and utilizing your assistance. However, people are busy, and even well-intentioned folks can often use some nudging to keep the implementation procedure going. To accomplish this, I have found a regular progress report to be effective.

I use a quarterly reporting frequency for this purpose. The report is simple; it summarizes the financial plan objectives and then lists each recommendation for accomplishing those objectives. The report supplies a check-off space to indicate which recommendations have been completed and which are yet to be done. Space is provided for comments, where I can urge the client on with my suggestions concerning which items should be implemented next and when. Also provided with this quarterly progress review is a summary of the performance of the client's investments.

This service makes the financial plan come alive. The client regularly sees how well his or her objectives are being fulfilled and is constantly reminded that I care about the success of the plan and that I am always ready to help. In addition, it serves as an early warning system to spot any implementation problems or recommendations that aren't turning out as anticipated. This in turn allows for early correction before a problem develops into a matter of significant disenchantment on the part of the client.

The method for the most frequent organized communication with clients is a monthly newsletter. The newsletter accomplishes three key items in servicing clients that enhances your position with them. It helps inform and educate the clients on financial matters which should be pertinent to their planning. This in turn helps keep their level of financial interest high. Finally, they are constantly reminded that you are the one to serve them.

I believe it can be a mistake to underestimate the effect a good newsletter can have on marrying clients to the planner. It provides you with twelve contacts a year with all clients to which they could respond with inquiries that may result in even more business. It provides the opportunity to showcase your firm and the accomplishments of its personnel. This can create the feeling of a personal relationship with your firm. It can be used to describe various financial products that you consider very good at any given time. All this contributes to establishing the image of you as a good, conscientious friend, and friends do not like to part company.

Probably the most prevalent client-servicing practice in financial planning is the annual review, and properly so! Financial affairs are dynamic, not stagnant. A comprehensive review of the previous year's progress in relation to accomplishing the client's objectives is a minimum servicing requirement. The annual review also offers an excellent opportunity to become current with a client's attitude about the original planning objectives. This will help determine if any planning strategy changes are warranted. You can also check if any significant financial activity on the part of the client has escaped your notice. In short, an annual review is such a primary servicing function that it needs no further justification.

There are a few other touches I like to use as part of client servicing which I hope will further personalize my relationship with them and solidify their loyalty to me. Upon acquiring new clients, I send a letter welcoming them to the firm and reiterating that I expect to earn the trust they have placed in me to advise their financial affairs. This is to reinforce the decision they have just made to do business with me and to demonstrate immediately that I care about them. Sending birthday cards and season's greeting cards is a nonbusiness social method to remind clients that you are there for them when financial matters need attention. Finally, a few months after the plan is complete and implementation is in progress, I send clients thank-you letters for doing business with me. In these letters I tell them how important they are to me and my business and that I will make every effort to live up to their expectations. I hope all this will make them feel that they are now a vital part of a growing operation, because now I take the opportunity to ask them to refer me to others. I note that it is the most important manner in which my business, the one that they are a part of, will thrive and expand so that even better service can be offered in the years ahead as we continue our relationship.

Chapter II

Developing Your Client Base: Marketing Your Practice

James A. Barry, Jr., CFP
Anne M. Lieberman, CFP
Michael A. Darany, CFP
James Miller, Ph.D.
Lee Rosenberg, CFP
Lindsay K. Wyatt, AFP
Vern C. Hayden, CFP
Murray Iseman, CLU, M.S.F.S.,
ChFC, M.S.M.
Laura Waller, CFP
Lisbeth Wiley Chapman
Lewis J. Walker, CFP
John E. Sestina, CFP, ChFC

"People have a tremendous way of procrastinating, putting things off, not getting things done. Our job is to guide them, direct them toward financial freedom."

—JAMES A. BARRY, JR., CFP

Getting Your Message Out to the World: The Essence of Marketing

James A. Barry, Jr., is the founder and Chief Executive Officer of The Barry Financial Group/Asset Management Corporation in Boca Raton, Florida. Prior to forming his own company, he was Senior Vice President of Putnam Group.

Mr. Barry is a member of the Institute of Certified Financial Planners, has been admitted to the Registry of Financial Planning Practitioners, and has been quoted in numerous national publications. He is the author of *Financial Freedom, A Positive Strategy for Putting Your Money to Work.*

In addition to his national television and radio guest appearances, he was the contributing business editor and financial talk-show host of his own weekly radio show for more than two and a half years. He is presently hosting a live television program and a radio call-in show and is also a well-known national lecturer, speaking at national conventions and association meetings.

Mr. Barry is a founder of the Gold Coast chapter of the International Association for Financial Planning and is affiliated with numerous other professional organizations in South Florida. He has also served on the adjunct faculty of the College for Financial Planning.

We as financial planners could have the greatest invention since the jet airplane, but if the world does not know about it, what does it matter? Marketing and selling are two of the most essential ingredients in building a successful financial planning practice. Please keep in mind that our job is to get people to do things that they would not do under what they perceive to be a rational set of circumstances. People have a tremendous way of procrastinating, putting things off, not getting things done. Our job is to guide them, direct them toward financial freedom.

I would also like to point out that you are selling all the time. Every morning you wake up you are selling your spouse, you are selling your children, you are selling your business associates, selling your next-door neighbor on concepts and ideas. It's just a natural course of events. So why should we not be selling and marketing constantly in the financial planning arena?

SEMINARS

Any time you can have the undivided attention of a group of people for one or two hours, you save a lot of prospecting time. Please remember to keep in mind that when you give a seminar, you are not there to educate; you are there to disturb people—to make them aware that they have a problem. There are three basic selling grounds in people's minds. One is in the enemy's camp—that's coming into your office; a second is going to their place of operation—that's their ground; the third is neutral ground, which is a seminar. They feel they are lost in the audience, but if you are good at disturbing and uncovering needs, you might very well end up with a client.

There is a very definite sequence of events that must take place at the seminar. First is to uncover the needs that people have, whether they realize they have needs or not. Next is to disturb them so they realize that they have a problem today, not tomorrow. If they think the problem can be solved tomorrow, that is exactly what they will do—procrastinate, put things off, and not get things done. The third task is to solve their problems, but not at the seminar. Solving their problems takes place in your office.

The key in running a seminar is to be absolutely prepared, to leave nothing to the imagination. Think of yourself as being on a Broadway stage; you are an actor, and first impressions are lasting impressions. In our organization when we run a seminar, we have a three-screen, six-camera rear screen projector. There is a three-minute opening that absolutely grabs the attention of the audience, and there is a closing of the program that leaves a lasting impression. The middle part of the program is the actual presentation itself. We use 35 mm slides; we have the ability to have them fade in and fade out on the screen; we have a wireless microphone and a wireless control for the 35 mm slides so that I can walk through the audience and communicate with the audience without worrying about stumbling over any wires and controlling the projector. We have a professionally designed brochure that each participant receives, that tells the attendees what we intend to cover at the seminar. It includes a mini data sheet, incorporated right within the brochure, that is helpful to us for our first meeting within our organization after the seminar takes place. People from our staff attend each program so that we have complete registration. We know where the attendees have come from; we know what sources have brought them there (whether it be newspaper ads, radio programs, television programs, or other advertisement). When a person requests an appointment with our company as a result of a seminar, we are able through computerization to track that prospect right through to his becoming a client and later to determining exactly what business he has generated; indeed, we can track everyone who attended that seminar who requested our services.

PRIVATE SEMINARS

We have an annual event in our company for clients; once a year, all day long, there is a workshop that starts at 8:30 A.M. and runs through to 4:30 P.M., with wine and cheese at the conclusion of the program and break-out sessions within the program. We invite all the money managers that we work with, as well as attorneys, CPAs, and professional people. Lunch is included. Each of our clients can invite a friend into that special annual client workshop. This provides tremendous public relations for our firm, as well as giving me the opportunity to get up in front of a good portion of clients and give them our viewpoints of the year and the future, to tell them what our company is doing, and so on. Some nationally recognized speakers attend this program. This project is assigned to a person on our staff who in turn heads up a committee to make sure that nothing is left to chance at this all-day annual event for our clients. We have a slogan for this seminar—"Be a Friend . . . Tell a Friend about our programs."

NEWS MEDIA

The news media can either make you or break you. You have to be able to reasonably control the interviews with the news media. One way is to have press releases prepared on company stationery—give ideas to the news media. How do you build that list? Easy. Read publications like *Money* magazine, *Newsweek*, and *Forbes*, and track down the person who wrote the pertinent article. If you like the article, you write to them, tell them how much you enjoyed the article, and introduce yourself as one who is in the financial planning business. Then you say, "I am enclosing some information that might very well be of some interest to you. From time to time I would like to send you some of my ideas." You build a list of these media people.

It is important to have a rapport with your local newspaper editors, business writers, and special event writers. Invite them to one of your seminars. Let them see exactly what you say to the public, how you operate, how you handle yourself, and what your philosophies are. Invite them out to lunch; tell them how long you have been in business and what your background is. If you have staff people, let writers have the freedom to interview some of them. The news media can be used also for all kinds of other public relations for your firm at no charge. Each time you accomplish something of importance, let the news media know through a press release. Examples include completing your CFP program or parts of your CFP program, acquiring real estate or life insurance licenses, establishing a paraplanner program, and the like.

ASSOCIATION MEETINGS, GROUP MEETINGS, PREFORMED GROUP MEETINGS

The opportunities in this area that we don't take advantage of are mindboggling. The American Association of Retired People, the Chamber of Commerce, the Jaycees, and many other groups all meet regularly. In Boca Raton,

Florida, where I live, there are about 185 different associations and nonprofit organizations that meet once a month at various locations. That is a whole marketing program in itself.

SPEAKERS SERVICE BUREAU

We have put together what we call a Speaker Service Bureau. We provide speakers locally to a variety of associations; these speakers come from our staff. These staff members are able to talk intelligently about certain subject material that might be important to that association. Examples are social security changes for retirees, pension profit-sharing programs for the closely held corporation, financial planning in general, the stock market, and interest rates. Let associations know that you have a speaker bureau that is available as a community service within the area where you live.

RADIO AND TELEVISION

I have hosted radio programs for about four years—radio talk shows in which people call in through 800 numbers and talk to me about their financial problems. We have recently produced a television program called "Talk about Money." It is shown live each Sunday morning from 9:30 until 10:30 with different guests each week from various areas of the business and investment arenas. Viewers have the opportunity to call in with questions through the use of an 800 number. We are planning to cover major market areas throughout the country with this program. Radio is a tremendous way of communicating with the masses of people. People love to communicate, to talk to you by radio. They feel that they are lost in the crowd, that you are not going to zero in on them, that they are anonymous. When you do radio you must have patience and empathy in order to relate to that person's feelings and to put yourself in his position. You must also learn to communicate in words that they can relate to. They do not understand the price-earning ratio of a stock or the international monetary fund. You must talk in words that they understand; otherwise, you are going to confuse them. They will lift the rug up and sweep the problems under; they will not address them; they will procrastinate, because you have not done an effective job of getting them off dead center through communication. Television programs are entirely different. Radio gives you more time normally to answer the question that is posed to you. Television is not that way. It is very quick; time goes by awfully fast, so you have to be concise, yet very effective with your words.

NEWSLETTER

We publish a newsletter called "Financial Issues." This newsletter goes out on a bimonthly basis to all our clients. It gives me the ability to communicate with people about my philosophies, about our company, about our upcoming seminars, about promotions within our company and designations that we are receiving, and the like. The newsletter also is regularly sent to other people who are not clients of ours, so that they get an idea of just who the Barry Financial Group is.

ARTICLES OF INTEREST

From time to time, normally on a quarterly basis, we do a special article of interest to our clients. It might very well concern what's happening with the energy area, or what might be happening with the real estate market—something that they have been reading a lot about. We want to provide them with the right input, but in an in-depth fashion. We call this a "white paper."

WRITING COLUMNS FOR MAJOR MAGAZINES

I write for two major magazines, one of which goes to executive directors of associations. These monthly articles are read by a targeted market. In turn, I receive speaking engagements for a fee. The other magazine, a "glossy" type, goes to high-income people who normally have accumulated wealth or are professionals. The point I am making is that you can pinpoint the type of market that you want to reach by determining the magazines that they read. If you would like to write for one of these publications, go after it. Talk to editors; tell them what you do and how you do it, and ask them for the opportunity of writing articles.

SUMMARY

There are three kinds of people in the world. There are people who make things happen, those who watch things happen, and those who scratch their heads and wonder what's going on. If you are determined to be the first kind of person, remember you travel a very lonely road. Most people are not going to travel that road with you, and the great majority who are not traveling the road with you have to find excuses for why they are not with you. Believe in yourself. Don't be the person on the elevator on a Monday morning who says, "Where did the weekend go?" or the person who on a Friday afternoon says, "Thank God it's Friday." Be committed and become the marathon runner within the financial planning business.

"If you understand the marketing concept, then you realize that the most powerful marketing tool of all is the simple ability to put yourself in the client's seat and evaluate everything you do from that vantage point."

—ANNE M. LIEBERMAN, CFP

Market Planning: Planning for Your Own Success

Anne M. Lieberman, CFP, is Director of Lieberman Associates in association with Lawrence A. Krause and Associates Inc. Prior to her current employment, Ms. Lieberman occupied upper-management positions in another advisory firm and was Vice President at the Bank of America. She holds a Master of Business Administration degree in operations research. She is an adjunct professor at the University of San Francisco, instructing financial professionals.

With Lawrence A. Krause, Ms. Lieberman coauthored the book *Marketing Your Financial Planning Practice.* She also coauthored (with J. Edson Clinton) *Mastering Money;* both books are published by Longman Financial Publishing, Inc. In addition, Ms. Lieberman has had articles published in the *ICFP Journal* and was a contributing author to Loren Dunton's *Financial Planning Can Make You Rich and 33 Case Histories to Prove It.*

She has received the Financial Writers Award of the *ICFP Journal.*

Ms. Lieberman has appeared on both radio and television and has been quoted in *San Francisco Business Journal, The Financial Planner . . . A New Professional, Changing Times, Parenting,* and *Motivator* (published by the National Center for Financial Education). Her professional organization membership includes the International Association for Financial Planning and the Institute of Certified Financial Planners.

PLANNERS RARELY PLAN

According to the old saw, the cobbler's children go barefoot. Likewise, attorneys die intestate, doctors let their own medical problems go untreated . . . and most of the planners I know don't have plans—personal financial plans, business plans or marketing plans. All of the above have the same excuse—they are too busy, like the cobbler, making shoes for other people's children.

If you could see into the future . . . would you still be too busy? Numerous studies of corporations have shown that companies with a formal planning function, such as a strategic planning group or department, are more profitable than firms that have no formal planning mechanism. Given that, we plan for others and see the results, why don't we plan for ourselves? I suspect the answer is "lack of time and lack of knowledge."

The purpose of this chapter is to take away your excuses. You already know how to plan. You simply need to learn how to trace personal financial planning back to its roots in business planning. I'm convinced that the "lack of time" excuse will take care of itself when you see the benefits of planning.

The pages which follow cover some key concepts and describe the process of constructing a plan. The article ends with an outline that will help you to construct your own plan.

THE MARKETING CONCEPT

It is imperative, whatever your level of knowledge regarding marketing, to understand the meaning of the "marketing concept." Marketing is not so much a theory or set of techniques as it is a point of view. If a firm has a marketing view, it directs itself toward satisfying consumer wants or needs. And if a firm truly has a marketing orientation, this viewpoint pervades it—it is part of the thinking and behavior of every member of the firm. This is in marked contrast to the common notion that a firm makes a product (or service) and finds a clever way to foist it on an unsuspecting marketplace. If you understand the marketing concept, then you realize that the most powerful marketing tool of all is the simple ability to put yourself in the client's seat and evaluate everything you do from that vantage point.

SEGMENTATION

The marketing techniques that you select will depend upon the segment(s) of the market you are trying to reach. Imagine, for example, that your objective is to handle corporate cases. You wish to be "the" planner or one of the planners recommended to all of the executives of a corporation. Each executive will receive financial planning as a corporate prerequisite. To accomplish this you would need a marketing plan which includes a strategy to gain access to the corporate decision maker. You would probably make a formal presentation to a managing committee or other decision-making body. You would need a strategy for that presentation and for the discussions that would follow. In contrast, if your market were physicians, you might attempt to publish an article in *Medical Economics* or to speak before the county medical society.

"Segments" are portions of the total market for your services. A segment has two characteristics—it is identifiable and reachable. It may or may not be profitable. A desirable market segment is

- *Identifiable.* You have to be able to define who belongs in the segment and why. You must understand enough about their problems, attitudes, and behavior that this knowledge will guide you in structuring the environment of your office, your interaction with clients, the financial plan, and other products and services.
- *Reachable.* It is not enough to understand the segments and their needs. You must be able to reach them; otherwise you won't have a chance to serve those needs. You need to know what they read, what topics are of interest to them, where they congregate, and what messages about your service appeal to them, along with various other bits of information that will enable you to reach them in two senses: to get your message in front of them and to communicate it in a way that touches them.
- *Profitable.* No matter how good a job you do in identifying and reaching segments of interest to you, it will do you no good if you cannot stay in business. Therefore, the segment or segments at which you aim your practice must provide enough revenue to make it worth your while to stay in business.

INTERNAL RESEARCH

The most useful starting place for a marketing plan is your own internal data. If you are not collecting useful market data and analyzing it, it is time to revise both your data questionnaire and your priorities! If you cannot answer the following questions now, you have work to do:

- What is the profile of your average client?
- Is the average the same as a few years ago? If not, how is the average client different?
- Who or what are the five major referral sources for your clientele?
- What geographic area is your office serving? Has it changed in the past few years?
- If you were to divide your clients into the most profitable and least profitable 25 percent of your client base, how would they differ from each other?
- Is your average client looking more like or less like that profitable 25 percent than he or she did last year?

THE BENEFITS OF MARKETING PLANS

Corporations experience a number of benefits from involvement in planning. Some of these will benefit all financial planning firms; others will benefit primarily multiplanner firms. These benefits include:

- *Identification of future changes.* People are surprisingly good at perceiving the nature of developments if they simply make a disciplined effort to look ahead.
- *Readiness to meet changes when they occur.* When changes do occur, the forward-looking planner will often find that he or she had already

considered the actions and counteractions that would be useful under new circumstances.

- *Cool-headedness under pressure.* Forethought can keep a planner from responding hastily and making erroneous decisions when difficulties arise, as they inevitably do at times of transition.
- *Coordination of activities within the firm.* When goals and strategies are articulated, each member of the firm is clearer about how his or her activities contribute to the overall objectives of the firm.
- *Reduction of conflict among members of the firm.* When company goals are unknown, individuals substitute their own goals for those of the firm; these goals may not be in the firm's interest. With members of the firm pursuing their individual goals, chances of conflict are far greater than when there is agreement on a single set of goals which all firm members will pursue.

THE CREATION OF A MARKETING PLAN

To derive the benefits of planning, the process is very similar to personal financial planning.

1. You must establish your goals within a clear statement of the mission of your firm.
2. You perform a situation analysis.
3. You then establish marketing objectives and settle on the appropriate strategies for meeting them.

The plan should be committed to writing, and you should establish procedures for monitoring and updating the plan. The monitoring and updating process should include contingency planning for possible developments within the firm or outside of it. (Sounds familiar, doesn't it?)

Situation Analysis

This section of the marketing plan is analogous to the "current" scenario for a personal financial plan. It looks at where your firm is today and how it got there. This is the place to bring in the internal research described above. Financial results on a monthly or annual basis belong here, too. The situation analysis should contain an assessment of the environment: Is it static or dynamic? If dynamic, what is changing and how? The environment includes the competition. Can you feel the presence of competition? If so, in what way?

The hardest part of a marketing plan is within the situation analysis. It is the subsection in which you take a critical look at your company's strengths and weaknesses. This is very important, because whatever weaknesses can be fixed should be fixed. All marketing strategies should play to the firm's strengths and avoid its weaknesses. Thus, this assessment is the underpinning for the rest of the plan and should be done with as much objectivity as possible. Depersonalize the weaknesses so you can see them clearly. If you tend to gloss over the negatives, go to your own best critics for a broader perspective.

In reviewing and analyzing your situation and assessing the strengths and weaknesses of your firm, you should look at:

- *Image.* How are you perceived by your clients, the general public, and your colleagues in the profession?
- *Nature of your business.* What services do you offer? What is the profitability of various services?
- *Adoption of technology.* How do you compare with other firms in the adoption of technology? Are your operations as efficient as the competition's?
- *Do you have the right skills available?* Are you keeping the skilled people you have, or is turnover a problem?
- *Location.* Are you in a location that is convenient to your desired clientele? Are you in a community with growth potential?
- *What is your client base?* Is it full of deadwood? What do the highly profitable clients look like in terms of demographics and referral source?
- *Who is your referral base?* Where are your clients coming from? Are you managing your referral base? Do you keep track of referrals sent versus those given?
- *Can you grow by expanding service to existing clients?*
- *Advertising and PR.* What have you done? How is it working?

Planning for the Future

When you have completed your situation analysis, you will know more about where you are today than you have ever known—like a client who sees a balance sheet, cash flow statement, and tax estimate for the first time. Now you are ready to decide where you want to go; you are ready to set marketing objectives. Here you can address income, sales, profits, billings, staffing, and technical capabilities. For each objective, you must develop strategies for achieving the objective and put into place any procedures or policies that are needed to support the strategies.

From here, you must develop a marketing program that shows what work is to be done, by whom, where the budget will come from, and how you will measure the results and modify the strategies, if necessary. The plan should contain milestones which indicate what actions are to be taken by what date and what results are expected. Do some contingency planning to develop alternative strategies to implement if the first-round approach does not work. The plan will need periodic updating, at least annually. (Relax; the updates take far less time than the original plan.)

In the paragraphs above, we have briefly described a process that deserves a bit more attention now that you have the overview. Let's take a closer look at each of the remaining steps.

Set Objectives

Workable objectives are very specific and are measurable. They should be attainable, but you should have to "stretch" to meet them. If you have a number of objectives in your plan, it is important that they not conflict with one another.

Objectives have to do with entering new markets, offering new services, expanding the services utilized by existing clients, taking advantage of a new market opportunity, increasing total revenue per client, eliminating deadwood from client base, and the like.

An objective might be to increase this year's total fee and/or commission revenue by 15 percent over the previous year.

Develop Strategies

Strategies focus on the target markets and encompass all of the aspects of marketing: product design, pricing, location, advertising, promotion, and sales, as well as market research. Don't forget operations. Operational changes may be used to improve the quality of client service and the intensity of follow-up. These can have a profound effect on profits as they increase your retention of clients and the amount of business you harvest from existing clients.

Strategies are ways of applying the resources of the firm—people, time, money, skills—to achieve the objectives. They should always involve a schedule for implementation which is designed to achieve the objective within the stated time period.

Our objective is to increase total revenue by 15 percent this year. Our first strategy involves bringing in additional clients.

Our situation analysis has told us that, among our client base, the entrepreneurs have been the most profitable. A demographic analysis of the area indicates that the entrepreneurial segment in our market area is very large, and we have barely touched it. There is definitely untapped market potential. Further, research we have read confirms our own instincts (and internal data) about working with entrepreneurs: They are accustomed to making their own decisions. Although they have numerous advisors, it takes much longer to earn their trust than it does to earn the trust of other segments. They will not lean on you for advice until you earn it. You can earn it by being sensitive to the unique problems entrepreneurs face—balancing between investing in their own businesses and building capital outside of it; making an orderly transition of ownership and control when they are no longer willing or able to operate the business, and so forth.

Our situation analysis has shown us that we are at ceiling capacity, and the added clientele cannot be served by our existing staff. We must make operational improvements or add more staff. We definitely would prefer the first alternative, so part of our plan will involve making operational improvements to increase our capacity.

Develop a Program

Programs are the game plan for each strategy. They include the tactics. The action programs show who is responsible for various action steps, what resources are available and what must be produced by when. The "what must be produced by when" are the milestones. These should be concrete, *deliverable* items, rather than just actions.

The marketing program is not completed until it is budgeted, staffed, and scheduled. In addition, the system for measuring results must also be in place. For our market expansion strategy, we might decide that we wish to appear in three publications of interest to entrepreneurs or of general interest. In the articles we will discuss subjects we have identified as dear to the hearts of entrepreneurs. On our next three radio invitations, we will suggest that the host devote some of the time to topics of interest to entrepreneurs. We will hold a seminar on tax reduction for the business owner at a time and in a location accessible to entrepreneurs. We will develop a mailing list of successful entrepreneurs in the service area of our office and use it for seminar invitations and for recycling the media coverage. We will time these events so that at least one event—appearance in print, appearance on the radio, a seminar, or a mailing—occurs once each month for the first nine months of the year.

To implement this program, someone will have to identify the publications by doing some media research. Someone will need to home in on the topics most likely to be of interest to entrepreneurs, someone will have to find or develop a mailing list, and someone will have to design the seminar. "Someone" should have specific responsibility for each of these assignments. Responsibility involves delivering the various elements of the program on time and within budget. Finally, someone must count the clients who mention having seen one or more of the articles, having heard the radio show, or having attended the seminar, as well as counting the number of people from the target segment or segments who arrive at our door. This is the only way we can do a cost/benefit analysis to see if we got our money's worth—the ultimate measure of the program's value. (Whew! Someone is very busy.)

We have left until last the single most important factor in developing a marketing program. A marketing program lets you make mistakes on paper. When you compare your budget for achieving the results with the anticipated results, if the increased revenues don't substantially exceed the increased costs, you scrap the program. In fact, we would suggest that, if your estimates of cost and benefit don't add up to a $3 increase in revenue for each $1 increase in cost, scrap the program.

Develop Contingency Plans

A contingency plan is a strategy, complete with program, to be utilized if the first plan of action does not produce the desired results. Where our strategy is increased penetration of the entrepreneurial market through media exposure, seminars, and direct mail, a contingency plan may involve eliminating one medium and expanding activity in another based upon early results. Experience with various tactics may indicate that some have a far greater payoff than others.

SAMPLE MARKETING PLAN OUTLINE

    I. SITUATION ANALYSIS
        A. Products/services. What do we currently have (plans, modified plans, carefully selected investments, manufactured investments)? What products/services have we considered developing?
        B. Market segments. Which ones do we serve or intend to serve?
        C. Clients. How many, demographic profile, referral source.
        D. Company strengths and weaknesses in marketing, finance, information systems, policies, procedures, management.
        E. Basis of competition. What do clients seek in a financial planner? Who is our competition? Do they have more of what clients look for?
        F. Key success factors. What has given us our market position to date?
    II. ANALYSIS OF THE PROFESSION
        A. Size and growth rate.
        B. Key growth factors.
        C. Cyclicality/seasonality, if relevant.
    III. MARKET ANALYSIS
        A. Market scope, size, and distribution.
        B. Market segmentation. What segments are of interest to us? What is the size of the segments in our market? How are they dispersed geographically? Are there identifiable segments in the current client base? Do we wish to penetrate other segments?

    C. Market demand changes and trends. Is the market we serve growing? Are there new segments emerging? What are the current desires of the segments we serve? Are the desires of the segments we serve changing?

    D. Sales tactics. How do we intend to sell our services to various segments?

    E. Distribution channels. How do we intend to serve markets—multiple offices???

    F. Pricing. How do we compare?

    G. Promotion and advertising. Direct mail, paid advertising, public relations activities to date. Are we gaining access to the promotional channels which best reach our market? Is the relationship between the cost and benefit favorable?

    H. Who is/are our competition?

    I. What are our market share and sales? Sales forecast.

IV. MARKETING GOALS, STRATEGIES, AND TACTICS

    A. Goals. Pick your measure—revenues, net income after taxes, number of employees, product sales, numbers of clients, and the like.

    B. Key performance indicators. Use to track achievement of goals; may be financial or nonfinancial.

    C. Milestone schedule. Key events, such as hiring of personnel, purchase of equipment.

    D. Plan assumptions regarding the economy, industry, market, outside influences.

    E. Red flags. Problems which cannot be overcome in the business plan.

    F. Company strengths to exploit.

    G. Company weaknesses to overcome.

    H. Market opportunities to exploit.

    I. Strategies. List possible strategies.

V. MARKETING PROGRAMS

    A. Company thrust and business strategies. Timing, responsibility, tactics, estimated cost, source of funds.

    B. Impact on or resources needed from: market, product, technology, operations, finance.

    C. Mechanism for feedback and control of program.

    D. Contingency plans for use if program falls short of desired results.

    E. Cost/benefit analysis. Is program likely to return revenues in excess of expenditures by three to one?

    F. Develop milestone schedule, assign responsibilities.

    G. Communicate program.

Marketing Your Financial Planning Practice: How to Turn Your Image Into Profit. Lawrence A. Krause and Anne M. Lieberman. Copyright 1986, Longman Group USA. Reprinted and excerpted by permission.

"Your 'company look' should give an immediate feeling of trust and confidence."

—MICHAEL A. DARANY, CFP

The Look of Your Company: A Basic Recipe for Success

Michael A. Darany, CFP, is President of The Consortium Group, a Miami-based financial services corporation. He is also Branch Manager of Investacorp, Inc., his broker-dealer. Mr. Darany has been involved in the finance industry for more than twenty years.

A well-known speaker throughout South Florida on the subject of comprehensive financial planning, Mr. Darany has appeared as the keynote speaker for various investment clubs and civic organizations. In 1986, Mr. Darany had several articles published in the IAFP's *Outlook Magazine.*

In January 1986, Mr. Darany was the chairperson of the South's largest financial planning symposium and exhibition held at the Fountainbleu Hotel in Miami Beach. His other professional affiliations include the office of Vice President of Programming and Board Member of the International Association for Financial Planning's South Florida chapter and membership in the Institute of Certified Financial Planners, the Dade Association of Life Underwriters, the National Financial Advisory Panel, and the National Association of Tax Practitioners.

If you are not prepared to pay for outside advice in the form of professional marketing, public relations, or advertising professionals to come and design your identity, then the following pages are for you.

BASIC ELEMENTS OF YOUR COMPANY PERSONALITY

1. Company name and what you do.
2. Who you are (credentials).
3. Logo.
4. Company calling cards/stationery.
5. Public accessibility (Yellow Pages ad).
6. A company brochure covering the following: corporate philosophy, the financial planning process, company history, biographies of management and principals, and services rendered.
7. Proposal or presentation folders and inserts (inserts can be used separately).
8. The financial plan itself/the package of the financial plan.
9. Personal appearance.
10. Automobile.
11. Summary.

IN THE BEGINNING

I am sure you can remember the last time you made an important decision involving a great deal of money for a long-term commitment. All of the elements just listed, whether you realize it or not, helped determine with whom you ultimately dealt. For your commitment, whomever you choose had better know their business and meet your expectations of a successful individual in that field.

The clients' need to seek help from a professional is one that is motivated by internal as well as external forces. The internal forces are the financial pressures that clients begin to notice exist in their particular situation for which they have not found the time to resolve, or have not been able to resolve alone. They realize that if help is not sought, the family's ability to handle those pressing financial matters lessens with time.

The external forces that motivate the potential client are those continuing ads in the media (newspapers, magazines, radio, television) and close friends describing their recent investments. Sometimes it is a tragic motivation, when someone close dies or becomes disabled, for instance, which initiates the search; the client now begins the quest, the analysis of whom to go to.

They begin to look for those familiar signposts that somehow tell them, "This person is the person with whom I want to work." If they have not been referred to someone already, they begin by seeking out a source of professionals, usually through the Yellow Pages. (If your ad is not there yet, get moving.) The following is an example of how your ad might read:

```
CONSORTIUM GROUP THE
    FREE FINANCIAL CONSULTATION
            SUITE 106
    REGISTERED INVESTMENT ADVISOR
    11430 N. Kendall Dr .......... 596-3650
```

The ad should include your name, company name, credentials, address, and a brief description of services; it should offer a complimentary initial consultation.

CHOICE OF COMPANY NAME

This is an important decision to make. As in naming your kids, the name of your company will affect future success. Although many practitioners may disagree, I believe that from a goodwill standpoint, if in the future you want to sell your firm, it will be easier to sell with a name that is not your own or someone else's surname.

WHO YOU ARE (Credentials)

You should have the proper credentials with which to begin before going out on your own. It is possible to begin without them, but not very sensible in this day and age. The emphasis by the professional guilds, not to mention the incredible body of information and experience you must possess, tells the intelligent planner that help is needed, even as a seasoned practitioner. You should have some kind of support from those established professionals while taking the time to attain your designations (CFP, CPA, ChFC, etc.) to prepare you for what you're going to be faced with in terms of responsibility, work load, and liability.

LOCATION OF OFFICE

When determining the location of your office, consider the area you would like to "target market" for the clientele you are seeking. Some planners prefer being downtown in the hub of business activity, where they can be constantly in touch with new sources of prospects. Others prefer being in the suburbs, where clients can have evening hours available for appointments. Think of your future plans for growth when determining the terms and conditions of your lease, so that it suits your requirements in order to avoid any unnecessary moves.

THE OFFICE ENVIRONMENT

The sooner you can convince your clients to come to your office, the better off you will be. Not only is it a psychological edge to have them at your office, but you also get a chance to show them a little more of who you are.

Make sure that your office has the appearance of success and organization. If it looks shabby and files are everywhere, the confidence you may have built on the phone or at the meeting outside your office could all be lost. Invest some well-spent dollars on your interior decorating and equipment so that you can operate efficiently. Our business is a giant, continuous paper shuffle. Without the proper equipment (computers, file systems, software, etc.) and office help, keeping up with the responsibility of our profession is nearly impossible.

COMPANY IDENTITY

The first impression when meeting someone is a lasting one. This impression extends itself to your correspondence as well. I'm referring to your company logo, company cards, stationery, company brochures, and general promotional material.

All of us have this feeling of who we are and how we want the public to perceive us. We want to be known as conscientious business people with above-average ability and integrity who can get the job done—people with answers to the questions that are asked, people who can be relied upon to give a clear explanation that is understandable to a client with limited knowledge of financial matters.

Your "company look" should give an immediate feeling of a sense of trust and confidence. I have seen it expressed in many ways by the big "mega" financial companies, but most of us don't have the resources to invest in a massive ad campaign, nor do we need that for our practices, at least in the beginning.

LOGO

The way your logo is presented is as important as the logo itself. A well-thought-out, attractive logo should tell at a glance what you do and how you feel about what you do.

Picking the right type of paper stock for your business cards and stationery is something that the successful business person will recognize immediately. A logo can be a very important thing to a firm. It is a way for people to remember your firm. It can be modern, abstract, traditional, institutional; it all depends upon the image you would like to project. Having a company motto or watchword to enhance your logo expands on "the identification" of your firm with the public as well as your colleagues. However, be ready to live up to it.

Be careful of acronyms that relate to something other than what you desire to project. For example, Diversified Underwriters Money Management Investment Enterprise Systems, Inc. in acronym form spells out DUMMIES, Inc. An unwitting mistake like this certainly is one to avoid.

COMPANY BROCHURE

Now that you have your cards and stationery, a nice company brochure can really make the difference. Your brochure should explain the financial planning process as prescribed by the profession and handled by your firm. There should be a section on compensation for financial planners that explains how your firm is compensated and why. A brief history of the firm and its philosophy should be included. The last page or back page should list the various services performed. The brochure will speak for you when you're not there; it is an ambassador of goodwill wherever it goes. As it is reviewed, the reader should get an image of the firm and the principals in the best possible light.

COMPANY FOLDERS

An 8 X 10-in. pocket folder with the company name and logo on it which opens up with a letter of greetings, the company brochure, and various information for thought inside can convince prospects of your ability as a firm to assist them in their affairs. That is the type of packaging needed to complete that external look. It is that window to the company that allows potential clients to browse privately.

Now, if you have all of the things described herein, the company should look and be ready to handle the type of clientele you desire. All of this helps to assure the public that you know your business and have taken the time to learn your profession from the technical to the administrative side.

Finally comes the ultimate truth. The client is convinced. The brochure you mailed was impressive after the yellow pages motivated a call. The individual has made an appointment and has agreed to become a client. After the fact-finding analysis via your conferences with them, the client is awaiting the final plan results. Everything has gone well; it's been an enlightening experience. At this point, the final look, the result of all the work, comes together!

THE FINAL WRAPPING

The organized way you present their financial plan and its contents are very important to the future of your relationship with your clients. When they are handed that plan for the first time, you must remember that *that is the story of their lives*, past, present and, we hope, a glimpse into the future. You should take special care in what you hand them. Going to a little expense to put the plan in a special binder will be very much appreciated by your clients. It makes very little sense to go to all the trouble of designing the look of your firm and to stop short when it comes to the very product you manufacture.

Make sure that your plan is well organized with a well-defined table of contents so that your clients can sit by themselves and find the information they need. Once found, make sure the information is presented in terms that are as nontechnical as possible for easy reading.

PERSONAL APPEARANCE

Looking successful is what we have been writing about. Let us not forget that personal attention to our wardrobe, hair, nails, and so forth is also essential. Knowing you look good has as much to do with your attitude about success as does your knowledge of the trade. It not only attracts your clients to you but everyone else with whom you come in contact as well. If you don't feel comfortable about fashion and what to wear, ask for help from your spouse or a friend. If you know you look as good as you can, you will feel much more confident in yourself, and it will show in everything you do.

Provide in your budget money to keep yourself consistently looking good. Try to stay in shape. This is a tough one for a great many of us. However, if you can discipline yourself, it actually aids you in all of the other thought processes of the body. Fitness will enable you to go that extra distance in competition with your colleagues or to meet that deadline for that client without suffering an amplified amount of anxiety caused by lack of good physical condition.

YOUR TRANSPORTATION

This is a subject I believe to be very important because it can make you feel good. I have been driving an American luxury car for a number of years. Many of you may prefer a foreign car or perhaps a smaller car. Whatever you choose, remember that it speaks for you. The car you choose does not necessarily have to be brand new, as long as it is clean and in good working order. Remember your target market and what they are driving. There needs to be an "identification bridge." Whether it is your car, clothes, office, appearance, or the like, it's essential that the bridge be established.

SUMMARY

The description of these elements has been brief in the interest of space. The subject of market identity is a vast one that *must be understood*. It needs to be reviewed regularly for the sake of your success. By putting this recipe to work, you give yourself the best opportunity and will be a credit to your fellow professionals.

"Current and potential clients are interested in your knowledge, skills, experience, abilities, products, and services only insofar as they can see clear benefits for themselves."

—JAMES MILLER, Ph.D.

James Miller, a graduate of Yale with a doctorate from Princeton, was an assistant professor of comparative literature at the University of California, Berkeley from 1972 to 1978. He entered the investment arena in 1979 as a stockbroker with Drexel Burnham Lambert, where he created and promoted investment and financial planning seminars.

In 1981, with Loren Dunton, he helped establish the nonprofit National Center for Financial Education, serving as founding executive director. In 1982 he joined Consolidated Capital Companies, where he was vice president of publishing and editor in chief of the *Digest of Financial Planning Ideas.*

In 1986, Miller founded a marketing consulting firm, Financial Information Group. Clients include financial services firms in securities, insurance, financial planning, and banking. The Group creates a full range of marketing strategies and materials and publishes a newsletter, *Financial Marketing.*

Dr. Miller speaks on marketing issues to conventions and meetings of financial professionals and frequently publishes articles in professional and trade publications on financial services marketing strategies and trends.

The Golden Rule of Marketing Financial Services: Integrity Creates Profits

The new tax act and a host of structural changes in the financial services industry will make the future exciting but trying. It may also be the time in which increased competition compels financial services firms to adopt the marketing practices already standard in other industries.

THE ABUNDANCE OF OPTIONS IS CONFUSING

Few financial professionals take the time to devise a broad marketing program that seeks to identify unmet needs in the marketplace and then develop strategies to meet them. Instead, they stick to familiar ground and try to sell what they know and find comfortable. It is easy to understand why.

Consider the number of potential target markets—not just broad categories like executives or retirees, but subgroups more narrowly defined by business type (automobile dealers or retail merchants), common needs (parents of college-bound children or divorced women), interests (golf club members or tennis fans), or combinations of criteria (homeowners who live in certain zip codes and have established UGMA accounts or Clifford trusts). If you multiply the number of potential target markets by the number of special services or products you could offer, and then multiply the result by the number of communications alternatives (such as radio advertising, speeches, direct mail, telemarketing, or seminars), you might just find yourself faced with options with no way to choose among them.

No wonder many financial professionals are at sea when it comes to making marketing decisions.

SIMPLIFY DECISIONS WITH A "GOLDEN RULE"

Achieving your marketing goals in the financial services industry needn't be complicated. In fact, when you let one rule guide you, financial services marketing becomes much simpler. The rule? *Organizational integrity creates profits.* The successful firm is one that coordinates all its activities into a unified plan of action that is based on identifying and meeting the needs of present and prospective clients.

In contrast, a firm lacks this type of organizational integrity if its owners or managers keep their focus inward on their current skills, staff, and services. If you think your goal in marketing is to sell what you've got, you are making a fundamental error that will limit the growth and health of your business.

Current and potential clients are interested in your knowledge, skills, experience, abilities, products, and services only insofar as they can see clear benefits for themselves. The starting point of your marketing plan, then, has to be to determine the nature of the *demand* for financial services in your marketplace.

CLIENT NEEDS ARE THE STARTING POINT

The firm that markets effectively—that bases decisions on knowing and responding to what clients want—stands out as the firm with organizational integrity. Its cycle of delivering services begins with identifying client needs and ends with meeting them. For this firm nothing is more important than perceiving and responding to clients' needs, even to the point of making fundamental changes in how the firm is run.

WHO ARE YOUR CLIENTS AND WHAT DO THEY WANT?

You can collect information about current and potential clients from a variety of sources. Start by using your client records to sort your clientele into categories—by age, sex, profession, income, portfolio size, risk profile, investment products, commissions or fees generated, personality types, or other groupings significant to understanding who they are, what their needs are, how they already fit into your business, and how they become your clients.

Next, you can buttonhole clients, survey by phone, mail questionnaires, hold focus groups, buy research, or hire a consulting firm. Whatever your means, you need to uncover responses and attitudes that you won't find in your office records:

- What do current clients like most—and least—about your services?
- How do current clients perceive your firm compared to your competition?
- How do potential clients perceive your competition?
- What do potential clients *want most* from a financial advisor?
- What do potential clients *expect* from financial advisors?
- What are the greatest financial concerns of current and potential clients?

Collecting this information will take time, energy, and money, but you must create a detailed picture of the needs, desires, fears, expectations, experiences, demographics, and finances not only of your current clients but also of identifiable groups of potential clients in your market area.

Once you have made the investment of discovering the needs of current and potential clients, you will have an advantage over most of your competition. Few small to medium-sized firms do market research, and the marketing support of major national firms is based on national statistics, not an in-depth knowledge of your clients, community, and local business atmosphere. If you take the time to understand the unmet needs of your current and potential clients, you will be able to assess yourself and your practice against your local competition and identify areas of opportunity: unfilled local market niches.

EXAMINE YOURSELF AND YOUR COMPETITION

If this first phase of establishing a marketing program is time-consuming, the second phase can be both painful and exhilarating. You will need now to face up to your firm's weaknesses in meeting needs and desires of clients. That can be uncomfortable, but the other side of the coin is that you will also be identifying your own strengths and other firms' weaknesses. Give equal attention to your firm's plusses and minuses—both will enter into your marketing decisions.

DEVELOP AN INTEGRATED MARKETING STRATEGY

Creating a marketing strategy entails choosing one or more target markets, selecting an appropriate system of communication and delivery, and modifying your business to deliver new services or products. You don't want to twist yourself into a pretzel to accommodate market needs entirely foreign to you—the way you run your practice should fit your background, skills, and taste. But you should consider any reasonable changes that will enhance your ability to serve your market.

In addition, you must define your market position: *what* your products and services are, *whom* they will benefit, and *how* you want prospective clients to perceive your firm in relation to other firms. With market position clarified, you then can identify the marketing "hooks" that capsule how you surpass the competition at meeting client needs.

Once you have defined your market position and hooks (e.g., "we're the firm that excels in estate planning" or "we know more about mutual funds than anyone else in town"), the selection of your communications vehicles becomes much easier. When your message is clear and on target—because it is based on solid research into the needs, fears, and expectations of your local market—almost any medium will work. Your task is simply to test several options to find which proves to be the most cost-effective.

Throughout the many decisions, let the needs and desires of your clients guide you. With these as a reference point throughout your planning, you will create a marketing program with organizational integrity.

The financial services marketplace recognizes and rewards organizational integrity in the delivery of services. Client appreciation quickly translates into increasing responsiveness to marketing efforts—and a growing business.

"Advertising is the single most impactful marketing device available that you can use to 'talk' to your target audience."

—LEE ROSENBERG, CFP

Advertising Your Financial Planning Practice

Lee Evan Rosenberg is a principal of ARS Financial Services, Inc., a firm specializing in personal financial planning. He is a Certified Financial Planner, a Registered Investment Advisor, and a Registered Representative with the National Association of Securities Dealers. His knowledge and experience in both investment and retirement planning have led to frequent appearances on national radio and television programs as well as interviews in many industry publications. Rosenberg personally conducts extensive seminar programs for many Fortune 500 companies and continues to lecture on financial planning for some of New York's largest banks.

A member of the Institute of Certified Financial Planners, Mr. Rosenberg serves on the Board of Directors of the Long Island Chapter. In addition, he serves on the National Speakers Association's New York Chapter. He is also a member of the International Association for Financial Planning and is listed in *Who's Who of Financial Planning.*

In today's competitive marketplace, consumers are no longer surprised to see just as many advertisements for doctors, lawyers, and other professional services as they would for retail stores. In fact, not only is a professional's advertising accepted by the public, it generates considerable interest because it is the only way for people to learn about the availability and benefits of a particular firm.

This is especially true for financial planning practices. Although the public is becoming more familiar with the benefits of financial planning, they are less likely to know how to go about finding the right planning firm. Unlike doctors and lawyers, not everyone has a financial planner to whom a friend can be referred.

That's why advertising is the single most impactful marketing device available that you can use to "talk" to your target audience. In fact, like a retail store, if you don't advertise, do you know what happens? Nothing. Nothing happens, and that's the worst fate for any business.

For this reason, I strongly believe that advertising, be it in the local newspaper, through direct mail, on radio, broadcast TV, or cable TV, serves so many important functions for a growing financial planning practice:

- Advertising announces, via the widest means available, the very existence of your firm as well as all of the particulars of your business—location, hours, services, benefits, expertise, and the like.
- Given the proper "creative" (copy and headlines) your advertising messages can uniquely reinforce the name of your firm as well as your own particular philosophy and expertise.
- Utilizing the right creative design along with a good and consistent advertising concept will result in establishing your firm as a "brand name" in what right now is a very faceless environment. Being a brand name means that consumers will gravitate to you because your name is safe and familiar, even if they've never had any contact with you or don't know anyone else who has either.
- In other words, the right advertising message, consistently presented, will generate tremendous awareness of your practice, subsequently bringing in qualified, prospective clients.
- Advertising does yet another important thing: It brings people to you. Unlike insurance and other salespeople who depend on home solicitation, advertising your practice will generate leads that come to *your* office. Just like doctors and lawyers, consumers will be calling *you* for appointments—and that, in itself, establishes the proper environment for a professional client relationship.
- Finally, advertising to consumers has a dual function, in that it serves as an excellent recruiting vehicle. CFPs, or individuals who are studying for their certification, will hear your messages and contact you regarding employment opportunities. This can be a tremendous advantage to a growing firm.

If you are now developing an advertising effort, or are considering the possibility, there are a variety of tactics which I have used for my firm that have helped make our advertising expenditures not only worthwhile, but extremely profitable. This year, in fact, our firm realized a three-to six-dollar return for every dollar spent!

Here are several recommendations for advertising your financial planning practice, whether it is a brand new firm or one that is already established.

1. Through your own creation, or with the help of a professional advertising agency, develop an advertising logo and slogan that can become your unique signature. This "slogo" should appear in all of your advertising so that it quickly becomes associated with your firm's name.

2. Determine in your market which are the most effective media available to reach the right target audience—the consumers who will potentially have the greatest interest in financial planning. In our experience those are the people who tune in to the "all news" radio stations, the business pages of the local newspapers, the financial advice programs, and the like.

The key is to go *where* your target audience is *when* they are in the right frame of mind to receive and be open to your message about financial planning.

3. It is also important to take advantage of as many different media outlets as possible. This will give your message the greatest reach as well as give you the opportunity to take advantage of the benefits of the different media. For example, you'll find that newspaper advertising provides you with enough space to tell your story while giving the consumer something to clip and save. Radio's immediacy offers the ability to deliver a timely message. Cable TV enables you to deliver your message in a targeted programming environment. Broadcast TV gives you tremendous coverage and credibility.

In our market, the largest suburban area outside New York City, we have found that the combination of radio, cable TV, and newspapers is extremely impactful for us. Cable and radio, with their highly specialized programming, allow us to target our message to the right audience. Newspapers, with their shotgun approach, help us reach the masses, quickly and cost efficiently. And this year, we anticipate moving into broadcast TV to broaden our reach and provide the ultimate in credible exposure.

4. Equally important as the variety of media is the frequency with which you advertise. This does not mean you have to be out there every day, but the more you have your name in front of the public, the more activity you will generate.

5. It is also important to make your advertising messages timely. By using different and relevant copy on a frequent basis, you will be more likely to capture consumers' interest, even if they have read one of your ads before. It is important to have something to say that reflects the interests and the needs of the public at the time. For example, when the new tax laws went into effect, our firm was right there with advertising that addressed people's concerns about those laws. Anticipating those types of events and planning advertising that speaks to those issues will guarantee that people will pay closer attention to you.

At the point that your advertising efforts are generating satisfactory results and that your firm is equipped and able to handle the new caseloads, you may want to explore more sophisticated means of marketing that will surely elevate your practice to its next revenue plateau.

Specifically, the areas that you should consider moving into include (1) conducting financial planning seminars, (2) establishing a local advertising cooperative with planners in noncompeting locations, and (3) hiring a professional public relations firm.

Here are the many ways you can expect to benefit from these special efforts:

FINANCIAL PLANNING SEMINARS

- Your advertising messages will have something specific and tangible for consumers to respond to.
- Your firm will be perceived as a "big" operation.
- Your firm will be established as a credible resource for financial planning in your community.
- Seminar attendees will be an excellent source of qualified leads and prospective clients.
- Nonattendees will be inclined to call for information about your services, just on the basis of an ad for a seminar.
- Seminars generate free publicity in local media.

LOCAL ADVERTISING COOPERATIVES

- Pooling advertising and media dollars with other financial planning firms based in geographically noncompeting areas will help you create a sizable advertising budget that can give all of the participating firms in the cooperative greater leverage for their money.
- By creating a special name for the financial planning alliance, advertising can run under this "umbrella" name, listing all participating firms and locations, giving the appearance of a very large, professional organization.
- Consumers can call the participating office nearest them, or a special "hotline" can be established, so that leads can be appropriated to the proper firm.
- Consumers will be impressed with this level of professionalism and will be introduced to financial planning in a way that will stimulate confidence in the field.

PUBLIC RELATIONS FIRMS

- Public relations firms, or consultants, should have the ability to generate considerable positive publicity on radio, TV, and in the newspapers for your firm.
- They should be able to secure speaking engagements for you at local events, none of which you should ever turn down!
- They should be able to provide you with guidance and direction on how to keep your firm's name in front of the public—even when you're not running any advertising.

Since our firm has opened its doors, we have allocated an average of 15 to 20 percent of our annual revenues to advertising and marketing. There is no doubt that this strong commitment to professionally marketing our practice has been one of the key reasons that we have grown into one of the largest independent financial planning firms on Long Island. And that commitment to communicating with and educating the public will continue.

Although our clients' referrals now contribute greatly to our growth, we recognize that only through the development of brand-new clients can we hope to continue growing at such a dramatic pace.

Earlier I pointed out that when a business doesn't advertise, *nothing* happens. Fortunately, when a business, like a financial planning firm, does advertise, *everything* can happen! The phones ring. The date books fill up. The conference rooms and computers stay busy. And that's as it should be. We CFPs provide such an important service to so many people that it would be a shame to keep what we do a secret. Get out and advertise!

"Create a reason for people to contact you after your speech. One way is to offer them a written report you've prepared on the subject of your talk. Don't have the report available at the meeting; it should be something you have to mail later."

—LINDSAY K. WYATT, AFP

Public Speaking as a Promotional Technique

Lindsay Wyatt, AFP, is President of Wyatt Investment Advisory, Inc., a registered investment advisory firm in Atlanta, Georgia, specializing in the middle-income market. She also provides communications consulting to the financial services industry. Prior to opening her practice, she served for five years as Director of Corporate Communications for Financial Service Corporation (FSC), where she established FSC's quarterly magazine, *Financial Strategies*, as one of the country's leading financial planning publications and served as its editor in chief. She contributes a regular column to the magazine called *Promoting Your Practice*.

Ms. Wyatt holds a B.A. in business administration from the University of Maryland. She is a member of the IAFP, where she is Director of Public Relations, and is a member of the ICFP. She is also former President and current Director of the International Association of Business Communicators, Atlanta chapter. Ms. Wyatt is a frequent speaker at workshops and conferences for financial planners on subjects related to financial planning and promotion and publicity.

If you're a good public speaker, you have a powerful promotional tool at your fingertips. Public speaking can help you:

- increase your credibility and visibility in the community.
- position yourself as an expert in your field of endeavor.
- attract new clients.
- improve your ability to communicate in general.
- be a better salesperson.
- make more money.

If any of these benefits appeal to you, consider using public speaking as a way of promoting your financial planning practice. To use it effectively, start the same way you'd start any marketing effort: by identifying your target markets.

Think of potential audiences for your message, then find gatherings where those people can be found. The kinds of groups that might be interested would include:

1. Professional associations with regular meetings at which speakers make presentations. Check your library for a directory of associations, or look in your local Yellow Pages telephone directory for ideas.
2. Neighborhood associations in neighborhoods where the home value and average income level identify the residents as good potential clients.
3. Service clubs such as Rotary, Lions, DAR, Junior League, League of Women Voters, Jaycees, and so forth.
4. Business clubs and associations.
5. Churches.
6. Schools and universities, especially those with adult education programs.

Once you've targeted the groups you'd like to talk to, get in touch with the program chairman (sometimes called program director or vice president/programs). Contact the person by telephone, and ask for a mailing address. Explain that you're a specialist in personal financial planning (or whatever) and are available for speaking engagements. Say that you'll send some background information and a list of presentation topics for consideration.

Then send that person your materials. They should be the same materials you might include in a media kit: a professional-quality black and white photograph (in case they plan to promote your speech in their newsletter), a well-written biography, a couple of paragraphs on what you plan to talk about (with a catchy title), and any reprints or other background material you wish to provide for reference.

Some planners spend the time and money to create a brochure or flyer specifically to market themselves as public speakers. It lends impact and credibility and needn't be expensive to do. But it must be well-written, in a way that will attract the interest of a variety of audiences.

A week or so after you send out your materials, follow up by telephone to see if there is any interest in your proposal. At this point, you can reinforce the fact that your presentation will be tailored to the needs of the specific group.

Needless to say, you must know something about the group to be able to do this, and have a couple of examples in mind when you call.

MAKING THE MOST OF YOUR APPEARANCE

The value of a speaking engagement doesn't stop at the point of reaching the eyes and ears of those who are physically present at your talk. Here are some suggestions for making the most of your appearances:

Capitalize on the publicity value of your appearance by sending out press releases about the event. Sometimes the person or organization who booked you will do this automatically; if not, you should do it yourself.

If the organization has a newsletter, ask if they plan to run a story about your program. If not, offer to contribute one. This will help you to reach members who might not actually attend your talk, but who are potential clients.

Invite media representatives to your talk (first asking permission of the organizers). They probably won't attend, but it will give you a chance to follow up with a copy of your speech and a press release, and is a reinforcement of your value as a news resource.

Create a reason for people to contact you after your speech. One way is to offer them a written report that you've prepared on the subject of your talk. Don't have the report available at the meeting; it should be something you have to mail later. That way you can obtain valuable names and addresses to add to your prospect list.

Make further use of the report by sending it to other people you might have on your mailing list, with a note saying, ''Here is some information I thought you might be interested in.''

Finally, follow up on audience interest. Contact leads while they're still hot. Be ready to send your materials quickly to those who request them. Plan ahead!

ADVANCE WORK

Your advance work doesn't end with obtaining a booking. Your next few steps are critical to your success. They include: analyzing the audience, analyzing the occasion and the setting, and establishing the objectives for the speech.

The best source of information about the speaking engagement (including audience, occasion, and setting) is likely to be the person who engaged you. Start with her or him for all the relevant information that may be available.

Here are some questions about your audience whose answers will help you to make your speech more effective:

- How large a group will there be? Who are they? What do they expect to hear, and what do they hope to get out of the speech?
- Is there anyone in the audience who should be mentioned in the speech? An outstanding sales representative, a dedicated volunteer, or someone else who deserves recognition or honor?
- Have there been recent current events—either within the country, region, or community—that could or should be alluded to in the speech?
- Are there any local sensitivities or customs that should be addressed or avoided?
- What are the special interests of the audience?
- Will there be a question and answer period? What are likely questions?

Likewise, ask questions about the occasion and the setting of the speech:

- What events or speakers precede or follow your talk? Is there any danger of overlap?
- How long are you expected to speak? Is it a breakfast, luncheon, or dinner address? A keynote speech? A seminar session?
- Where is the speech to be delivered, and at what time? What equipment is available? Are you expected to bring your own equipment? Is backup equipment available?
- Are you expected to provide copies of the speech for later distribution?

After you've learned the essentials about the audience and occasion, establish some specific objectives for the speech:

- Why have you accepted the speaking engagement? What are you trying to do? Instruct? Sell an idea? Sell a product or service? Motivate the group to take a specific action? Correct a misconception? Change a point of view?
- Write down your objectives. Exactly what do you want the audience to remember and take away with them at the end of the speech?
- Decide what one key thought you want to leave with your audience. Try to summarize it in one sentence. This will be the core around which you build your speech.

WRITING THE SPEECH

The next step in the process is the actual researching and writing of the speech. Many excellent books have been written on the art and science of speechwriting, and this brief chapter can't begin to cover the subject exhaustively. But it can offer a few pointers about structure and approach.

Start with structure: A good speech is like a play with three acts—opening, middle, and closing. The opening has to get the audience's attention and generate some interest in what you're going to say. The middle should be the meat of the speech, and build logically to your conclusion. The closing should be a powerful summing-up.

Before you actually start writing your speech, focus again on your central message. What's your point? If it isn't clear to you, it certainly won't be clear to your audience. Boil your message down into three or four main points, and use those as the beginning of your outline.

The structure of your speech should be simple and logical. Whether you use a chronological, cause-and-effect, or problem-solution format, don't make it too complex to be grasped by a listener. The same goes for language: Use short words and short sentences.

There is an old show-business truism that is helpful to keep in mind when you're writing your speech. Nothing is duller to an audience than a fact; nothing is more interesting to an audience than an emotion. If you must state a fact, wrap it in an emotion.

Example: If you were to start a speech with, ''The American educational system is not performing with optimum efficiency,'' it might be a statement your audience would agree with—but it's dull. However, suppose you began like this: ''Look at the person seated on your left, and the one on your right. If you were a cross section of America, one of the three of you would be illiterate.'' That's much more likely to capture your audience's interest and attention.

72

Chap. II / Developing Your Client Base: Marketing Your Practice

The example above also illustrates another point: If you must use statistics, humanize them. Put them in terms that create word pictures in your listeners' minds. Give the audience information that they can relate to their own lives and experience.

Finally, be brief. A speech shouldn't run more than 20 to 30 minutes (unless, of course, you're teaching a class or leading a workshop). If you've been assigned an agenda slot with definite beginning and ending times, *keep to those times.* If you practice your presentation, you should know how close you'll be to the allotted time and when you need to add or delete material. Rehearse until you're familiar with your own pace and can estimate your time correctly. Be sure to leave time for dramatic pauses, sips of water, and audience questions.

Should you speak from an outline, or a fully written script? It depends on what you're comfortable with. The danger with speaking from a script is the tendency to read it and for that to be apparent to your audience. They need eye contact and involvement from you—you need to talk to them, not read to them.

One technique that works well for many speakers is to know the opening and the closing of the speech cold, but to work from an outline in the middle. The outline keeps you on track and building toward your conclusion, but is loose enough that your remarks will feel free-flowing and spontaneous.

Become a collector of interesting facts, anecdotes, metaphors, and comparisons. Use these where appropriate to spice up your speeches. You may be speaking about a serious subject, but that doesn't mean your speech must be devoid of entertainment value. Mentally put yourself in the audience: Is anything I'm saying memorable or interesting? Am I painting word pictures, or just relating facts? Keep in mind that this is the age of video—audiences are sophisticated at judging speakers, and you'll have to be good to keep their attention.

STYLE

The "style" aspects of public speaking include such things as body language, humor, and appearance. They can significantly enhance—or detract from—the impact of your speech. Here are some points to remember.

Humor is serious business and should be used wisely. Avoid humor that has any possibility of offending someone in your audience, unless you are charging the audience's emotions intentionally to make a point, or as part of your technique. Keep the audience on your side.

Vary the pitch and volume of your voice as you would in a conversation. This is another reason not to read a speech from a script, because readers have a tendency to lapse into a monotone. Practice projecting your voice with depth and resonance.

Use gestures that are natural to you, but don't feel you have to gesture if you are normally still. Be careful of unnecessary or fidgeting movements, such as pulling on your earlobe or jangling keys in your pockets—they convey nervousness to your audience.

Dress up for the occasion. Audiences expect speakers to be polished and "respectable" and will react negatively if you are poorly dressed.

Finally, watch your posture. Don't slouch or prop yourself up on the lectern. If you can, use a lapel microphone and get out from behind the lectern altogether. It's a way of interacting with your audience and improving eye contact and involvement.

THE QUESTION AND ANSWER (Q&A) PERIOD

The question and answer period at the end of your speech can be rather frightening. What if there are no questions? How do you control a Q&A period? What if someone shoots you down, or asks you something you don't know the answer to?

One way to ease apprehension about Q&A is to rehearse. Practice by having someone read or listen to your speech and ask you the kind of questions that might be asked by your audience.

Always have extra material prepared to fill time if there are no questions (or very few) from the audience. If you say, "What are your questions?" and get no response, you have several options. You can say, "Well, we have 10 minutes left and during that time I'd like to tell you about an issue that is related to what I've been talking about," and proceed to talk for the remainder of your time. Another technique is to say, "If there are no questions, let me respond to a question I have often been asked in the past." That may stimulate follow-up questions from audience members.

You can also elicit questions by researching your audience in advance and by knowing what their "hot buttons" are. You can then suggest topics the group might have questions about by saying, "People like you, who are involved in ———, might be concerned about issue A. Does anyone have a question about Issue A?"

If you know your subject and have prepared your speech well, you should be confident about handling questions comfortably. The time may come when someone asks you a question you can't answer—but in such a case, simply tell the truth. "I don't know" is an honest response, not a failure, so don't hesitate to use it. You may, if you like, follow it up by suggesting a possible resource, or offering to get the individual's name after the meeting and to call later with the answer.

Likewise, if you're asked a question that you're not willing to answer because of policy or sensitivity, simply be honest. Say, "I can't discuss that at this time."

Hostile or challenging questions from audience members are rare, but they do occasionally crop up. Rehearse so that you'll be comfortable dealing with them, and then forget about it. You're in control.

DEALING WITH STAGE FRIGHT

According to *The Book of Lists*, speaking in front of groups ranks as our number one national phobia. And nervousness, or stage fright, doesn't just happen to amateurs. A show business friend tells me that even Sir Laurence Olivier—known as "the most accomplished actor in the English language"—has a case of what he calls "nerves" before making an entrance on stage.

Being a little nervous isn't necessarily all bad. That extra shot of adrenalin can give you an extra sparkle. It only gets in the way if you are so unsure of your material or presentation that the fear destroys your concentration.

Which brings us to the good news: There are some things you can do about stage fright. First of all, get to the speaking location early and familiarize yourself with the place. This is especially appropriate if it is a place you've never been in before. Get up on the stage and walk around on it. Locate the lectern, test the microphone, and figure out how to operate the controls to the slide projector. Plan how you'll enter and exit the room, and practice a couple of times until you're sure you won't be stumbling over microphone cables. If there are stairs up to the stage, walk up and down them a few times. Believe it or not, this simple reconnaissance will make you feel at home and boost your confidence enormously.

Another way to quell stage fright is simply to practice—the more often, the better. Join Toastmasters International or take a class in public speaking. Teach a Sunday school class. Chair a meeting or speak to a service organization. The more you speak, the less fearsome it will be.

If you understand your audience, you'll be less likely to be intimidated or frightened by them. When you're researching your speech, do a little research on the people you'll be talking to. Who are they? What are their concerns, their ''hot buttons?'' Familiarity, in this case, will breed comfort.

Finally, you may be nervous because you're not sure of your material. If you don't know what you're going to say or haven't decided what order to say it in, you have every right to be terrified. Do your homework!

USING VISUAL AIDS

Visual aids—slides, overhead transparencies, flip charts, blackboards, whatever—should be used only when they can materially help the audience in understanding your message. Too many speakers use visual aids to aid themselves rather than the audience. They'll fill a slide with the outline of an hour's worth of material and then put the audience to sleep. (Why should they listen if they know how the story ends?)

Slides or other aids should highlight your talk, not reveal the details. Keep them as simple as possible. Use brief phrases and incomplete sentences—keep your audience from knowing your complete thought, or they'll be reading it before you have a chance to say it.

Make sure that anything you project is easily visible from all parts of the room. Check it out in advance by sitting in various seats in the audience and having someone change slides for you. And here's an inviolable rule: **Never** produce overhead transparencies or slides from a typewritten page. They cannot be seen by audiences of more than two people, and even then the audience has to be seated within three feet of the screen. If you're going to use visuals, pay what it takes to have them professionally produced.

Rehearsal is doubly critical if you plan to use visual aids with your speech. Rehearse until your timing is right and your visuals appear as a fully integrated part of your presentation. Before your speech, hold a ''technical rehearsal'' in the room where you will be speaking. Make sure the equipment works and that you can operate the slide projector from the lectern (or that you can walk comfortably to the overhead projector). Find out how the lights work, and assign someone to operate them at your signal.

MAKE IT WORK

Public speaking can be an effective method for increasing your visibility and enhancing your professional credibility. It can be—if you do it well. Allow yourself enough time to prepare and practice thoroughly before you attempt this type of promotion. The effort will pay off.

This article was adapted from Ms. Wyatt's book, *Financial Planner's Guide to Publicity and Promotion* (Longman Financial Services Publishing, 1986).

"The key is to have an opportunity to build your credibility and develop some sense of relationship, trust, and desire for your services."

—VERN C. HAYDEN, CFP

How to Give Successful Financial Planning Seminars

Vern C. Hayden, CFP, is considered a pioneer of the financial planning profession, having started his first practice in San Rafael, California, in 1968. Presently, he is a Registered Principal of the NASD and is affiliated with the Westport, Connecticut, branch office of DESCAP Securities, Inc. He holds a B.A. from Wheaton College in Illinois.

Mr. Hayden has authored *Money: Use It or Lose It*, and a training manual for financial professionals entitled "The Common Sense Process of Financial Counseling," as well as various professional articles. He has appeared on several national media programs and has been quoted in many major publications. He is a popular speaker at professional conferences.

Hayden has served as a consultant to many companies and individuals in the financial services industry. He also serves on the advisory board for the graduate degree program in financial planning at Golden Gate University in California, the advisory board for the Certified Financial Management program at Iona College in New York, and is a founding program coordinator and advisory board member for the financial certification program at the University of Bridgeport in Connecticut.

Hayden is former president and director of the International Association for Financial Planning, North Bay chapter, California, and is Founding Chairman of the International Association for Financial Planning, Westchester/Rockland chapter, New York (1987). He is a member of the Institute of Certified Financial Planners and was one of the first twelve planners to be admitted to the Registry of Financial Planning Practitioners.

Building and maintaining a successful financial planning practice assumes two crucial points. First, that there are professionally skilled people with adequate resources to perform the practice of counseling clients and second, that you have the capability of obtaining new clients.

The central issue of your marketing strategy addresses the second point: How are you going to obtain the number of new clients you need in order to achieve and maintain profitability? The purpose of this chapter is to enable you to master one marketing tool that assures your survival and prosperity. In terms of effectiveness, the four best ways of getting new clients are:

1. Referrals • Referrals are obviously powerful because they come from a satisfied client or successful relationships with attorneys, accountants, and other people who serve as important centers of influence.

2. Sponsored seminars • There are seminars sponsored by homogeneous groups such as associations and charities that are endorsing your seminar and therefore your services. Typical examples are medical and dental associations, a corporation, a church, a university or college, a hospital, and various charities like the Red Cross or a home for delinquent kids. In effect the sponsoring organization is saying, "We are bringing in some real professionals that you should use if you have a need for financial planning." Needless to say, these are powerful seminars with the highest degree of benefit.

3. The nonsponsored targeted seminar • This kind of seminar is targeted (but not sponsored) at a specific group. For instance, you may decide to target a seminar for small business owners, members of a country club, or accountants. While these are highly focused seminars, the number of potential attendees is generally less, so fewer people are at the meetings. However, these will probably be more affluent people, so a more profitable clientele may result.

4. The public seminar • The public seminar is composed of people from the general public in a particular community that you would like to have as clients. The primary purpose of this chapter is to discuss the public seminar in more detail. It is this marketing tool that, if mastered, can assure your survival and prosperity.

Table 1 presents figures corresponding to the different aspects associated with the three types of seminars outlined.

TABLE 1

One-Time, Two-Hour Seminars

	Sponsored	*Targeted*	*Public*
Number of attendees	60	50	97
Number of prospect units (P.U.s)*	40	30	67
Number of P.U.s requesting an interview	26 (65%)	15 (50%)	40 (60%)
Number who become clients	16 (62%)	8 (53%)	18 (45%)
Average revenue per client	$2700	$3000	$2500
Total revenue	$43,200	$24,000	$45,000
Cost per seminar	0	$2500	$4000
Profit per seminar	$43,200	21,500	$41,000
Cost per client	0	$313	$223
Profit per client	$2700	$2687	$2277

*Couples count as one.

THE PUBLIC FINANCIAL PLANNING SEMINAR

The most effective seminar is the sponsored seminar. The problem is that it takes time to develop the relationships needed to find a sponsor. There may also be a limited number of possible sponsors available. The same is true of referrals—it takes time to develop the relationships to get them. The only marketing vehicle that gives you total control, buys the time necessary to develop other relationships and has a high degree of predictability and profitability is the public seminar. That is why it is the primary thrust of this chapter.

WHAT IS A GENERIC PUBLIC FINANCIAL PLANNING SEMINAR?

It is an educational and motivational marketing meeting composed of new prospects whom you want to become clients on a favorable basis. The key is to have an opportunity to build your credibility and develop some sense of relationship, trust, and desire for your services. To put it more succinctly, the seminar has seven objectives:

1. To build trust and credibility.
2. To disturb the audience with respect to current issues and conditions that affect them.
3. To educate them about the process of financial planning and how they can benefit.
4. To motivate the attendees to do financial planning, using your services.
5. To enable you to demonstrate your professionalism and distinguish you from other perceived competitors.
6. To convert as many members of the audience as possible to clients.
7. To achieve a high degree of profitability.

These last two points are obviously the ultimate objectives.

There are also seven reasons why this kind of seminar works effectively:

1. The attendees have made a conscious decision to participate in the seminar. In a sense they are volunteering on behalf of themselves to join in the experience for their own benefit. This kind of self-determination is a powerful motivator.
2. The seminar is relaxed and informal. People do not have to dress up or worry about whom they have to impress. The casualness of the event makes people more receptive to the event.
3. The participants are keenly aware of their own needs and financial concerns. They are attending with the hope that their needs and concerns will be addressed.
4. The people are relieved to see many others attending the seminar, because it confirms that at least some of their feelings are shared by others. They are not alone in their dilemmas.
5. There is an overall perception that they are attending in order to learn something. The educational aspect has to be genuine.
6. The people can be as anonymous as they want to be, so the experience is perceived as nonthreatening.
7. People are confused. They don't have the time, resources or background to know and sort through all of the different pieces of financial

information. They are looking for ''information filters'' in the form of professional help. You are there to convince them of your professional competence to provide it.

HOW DO YOU ORGANIZE A SEMINAR?

First you must decide what kind of seminar you are going to conduct. We are assuming a one-night, two-hour generic public financial planning seminar.

Second, you must organize it into three stages:

1. The planning stage—before the seminar.
2. The presentation stage—what happens at the seminar.
3. The postseminar follow-up actions.

It is important to realize that in this marketing role you are a professional in a different sense than you may think of yourself. You are now a producer, director, and performer. Do not make the mistake I did in the early years by thinking you can intuitively, instinctively, and spontaneously perform these roles. They require dedication, hard work, and training. If you can, seek a successful mentor. I chose three. One will always be the best, and as a matter of professional courtesy, I wish to acknowledge her and thank a very great lady: Venita Van Kaspel.

At this point we will discuss some general comments about the most important issues of the three stages.

Stage 1: The Planning Stage

Type of seminar • An effective seminar needs to be planned eight weeks in advance (see Table 2: Task Flow/Checklist). The first decision relates to the kind of seminar to conduct. As mentioned, we are assuming that a decision has been made to do a one-night, two-hour generic financial planning seminar. I have experimented with seminars that last from four nights down to one night. Several three- and two-night seminars were done. They were all successful, so we are comparing only degrees of profitability. After doing several one-night seminars, it became clear to me that they were the most profitable and were the most manageable. Comparing the one-night seminar with a three-night seminar, we found that the one-nighters were more profitable on the low side and not as profitable on the high side as a three-night seminar. However, if three different one-night seminars were held, they were significantly more profitable than one three-night seminar. In addition, the lower development costs, significantly less time, greater simplicity, and the increased public relations advantage convinced me to stay with the one-nighters. For further thought on this subject please review Table 3.

Location • The best locations are places like a university or college campus, libraries, historical museums, civic centers, and high schools. These are noncommercial settings where people go for educational or cultural events. There is also an implied endorsement, since the location is identified in the invitation. A local Holiday Inn does not afford these advantages.

The invitation • The invitation is a foldover about the size of a wedding invitation, and it contains a reply card. On the front of the invitation is the title of the seminar, the two speakers, and the place and time. On the inside left-

TABLE 2

Task Flow/Checklist for Financial Planning Seminar

# of Seminar 1

Seminar Date: 9/17/85   Time: 7:30–9:30   Facility: Scarsdale Library   Guest Speaker: Ray Planne

Task	Planning Weeks								Date Task Completed
	1	2	3	4	5	6	7	8	
A. Planning stage									
1. Select date	•							S	
2. Identify/order mailing list	•							E M	
3. Determine mailing size	•							I N	
4. Identify, visit, & commit facility	•							A	
5. Prepare/design invitation	•							R	
6. Prepare/design handouts	•							W	
7. Identify guest speaker	•							E	
8. Prepare/design visuals		•						E	
9. Identify equipment			•					K	
10. Design signs				•					
11. Speaker system	•								
B. Implementation stage									
1. Acquire mailing list	•								
2. Obtain envelopes		•							
3. Print invitations, reply cards, maps			•						
4. Address & stamp envelopes			•						
5. Contact post office			•						
6. Stuff & seal envelopes				•					
7. Mail invitations					•				
8. Deposit to facility				•					
9. Insurance coverage		•							
10. Verify guest speaker	•								
11. Verify facility person		•					•	•	
12. Sort incoming cards						•	•	•	
13. Enter names on control sheet						•	•	•	
14. Assign receptionist						•		•	

TABLE 3

One-Night vs. Three-Night Seminars

	One 3-Night Seminar		1 Night	1 Night	1 Night	Total Composite
	High	Low				
Number of attendees	97	40	97	97	97	291
*Number of prospect units	67	30	67	67	67	201
Number of prospect units on 3rd night	60	27	**NA	NA	NA	NA
Number of P.U.s requesting interview	48 (80%)	22 (80%)	40 (60%)	40 (60%)	40 (60%)	120 (60%)
Number who became clients	29 (60%)	14 (60%)	18 (45%)	18 (45%)	18 (45%)	54 (45%)
Average revenue per client	$2500	$2500	$2500	$2500	$2500	$2500
Total revenue	$72,500	$35,000	$45,000	$45,000	$45,000	$135,000
Cost per seminar	$5000	$4000	$4000	$4000	$4000	$12,000
Fees from seminar @ $30 per person	$2910	$1200	NA	NA	NA	
Net cost	$2090	$2800	$4000	$4000	$4000	
Profit per seminar	[$70,410]	[$32,200]	[$41,000]	[$41,000]	[$41,000]	[$123,000]
Cost per client	$72	$200	$223	$223	$223	$223
Profit per client	$2428	$2300	$2277	$2277	$2277	$2277
Variance in cost per client	$151/23 less per client		$151/23 more per client			
Variance in profit per client	$151/23 more per client		$151/23 less per client			
Variance in profit	[$52,590 to 90,800 less]					[$52,590 to 90,800 more profit]

*Couples count as one.

**Not applicable.

hand side is a short biography of the two speakers. The biographical points are simply listed under the names. On the right-hand side is a list of high-interest questions that the seminar is designed to answer. On the back side it is optional, but helpful, if you can list your accounting firm, law firm, and banking relationship. If you don't have significant relationships with these entities, then leave the back page blank. The point is to borrow credibility whenever it is feasible.

Number of speakers • You or another financial planner should be the primary speaker. The only other speaker should be a local estate-planning attorney from a recognized law firm. Again you are borrowing credibility. The attorney is not paid to do this, because he/she will undoubtedly get business from the seminar. The financial planner speaks for $1\frac{1}{2}$ hours, and the attorney for a half hour.

Content • The presentation is organized in four half-hour segments. The first half-hour contains introductory material and an overview of the seminar. The core of this time period relates to how people can organize their financial lives around six main areas: cash flow planning, tax planning, investment planning, retirement planning, contingency planning, and estate planning. A short general explanation is given for each area, an overhead slide being used for each.

The second half-hour covers tax-planning ideas. The third half-hour the attorney discusses estate-planning ideas. The last half-hour is for a discussion of investments and the close. Rather than discuss specific investments, I simply teach them how to use an investment decision-making model. Using this technique not only gives them a useful tool, it also assures them that you are not giving a product pitch.

Humor and telling stories • It is very helpful if you can tell an occasional story and inject an element of humor into your presentation. Humorous stories should tie into a particular point; this will also help people remember your point. The secret to doing this is finding good stories and hours of practice in telling them.

Refreshment • It is not absolutely necessary to provide refreshments. Where it is convenient, coffee, tea, and cookies add a nice touch. Never serve alcoholic beverages.

Visuals • The only visuals I use are overhead slides. They are more informal and less slick, and they make it easy to write on blanks in making an occasional point.

Handouts • Handouts fall into three categories: The first includes information about me and/or my company, including any third-party articles and the like. The second category includes worksheets, financial tables, and data. The third category is simply an evaluation sheet. This sheet becomes the closing mechanism. It asks for feedback as to what they liked the most, the least, and any other comments. In the middle of the page is a place for their name, home and office phone numbers, and the best time to be called for their appointment. This appointment is positioned as the second part of the seminar and is an exploratory, get-acquainted meeting. The bottom part of the evaluation sheet is a place for names and addresses of other people who they think would like to attend a future seminar. (See "Evaluation" form, p. 86.)

Amplification system • Purchase your own portable loudspeaker system. Many facilities are not properly equipped for sound. Your portable should come with a wireless lavaliere mike and operate from a rechargeable battery. The cost is about $1000. You may find the following information useful.

Lectronsonics, Inc.
P. O. Box 12617
Albuquerque, NM 87195
505-831-1010/800-821-1121

Freedom Mike System 831 AV4
FM-AV #4, 33.40 MHZ
M116 microphone
M30 transmitter S/N: 31795
FM 831 Sound System SN: 30749
CC-831 Case
$1000 approx.

Sending the invitation and follow-up • The envelopes for invitations are hand-addressed. Most people open hand-addressed envelopes. After experimenting with various mailing lists, I feel that a reverse directory works the best and is certainly more economical (about $250 a year versus $50–60 per thousand for a rented list). The directory lists names and addresses by street headings. Simply pick the up-scale part of your community and mail 5000 invitations. The response should average about 2.5 percent. (See Table 4.) The invitations should be mailed, first class, three weeks in advance of the seminar. Allowing time for final design, printing, ordering envelopes, addressing, and so forth requires about five weeks prior to the mailing.

As replies are received, confirmations should be mailed. Two days before the seminar, each person should be called to reconfirm his or her attendance. At least two alphabetical lists should be prepared for checking in attendees at the seminar.

Stage 2: The Presentation of the Seminar

Arrival time at the facility should always be at least one hour before starting time. If it's the first time you have used a facility, it's a good idea to arrive one and a half hours early. The seminar starts at 7:30 and ends at 9:30. You will need at least one and preferably two receptionists at a check-in table. As they check people in, they give them the handout.

It's all right to start about five minutes late if people are still wandering in, but you should still finish on time. The actual presentation is made as we discussed earlier.

At the end I give people three to four minutes to complete the evaluation sheet and then close with a final story. Then they are requested to hand the evaluation sheets to me and the receptionists on the way out. Always try to work your way to the back of the room so that you can say goodnight to the people as they hand in the evaluations.

Stage 3: Follow-up

After the seminar you should have several requests for appointments on your evaluation sheets.

Either you or your secretary can make the call. The results are slightly higher if *you* call. Remember, the only purpose for the call is to make the appointment. For example, "Hello, Mr. Roberts, this is Rich from the seminar at the high school the other night . . . I was just calling to arrange for your appointment time . . . " Once the appointment is made, a new client file should be set up and a confirmation/data letter sent. Along with the letter we send a very short simplified data sheet. The purpose of the data sheet is to get clients in-

TABLE 4

Mailing Lists' Response Rates

List Name	Poll of Response Percentage
New York Affluential Individuals	2.6%
American Management Association	2.4%
Prime Investors	2.2%
Forbes	2.0%
Affluent Multi-Buyers	1.8%
Tax Shelter Purchasers	1.8%
Reverse Directory	2.5%

Cost: $55–$65 per 1000—one-time use Reverse directory—$350./year

volved before they come in. It is then used to help guide the discussion in the first interview.

The day prior to the appointment time your secretary should call to reconfirm. The first meeting with the prospective client is called the data/concept/commitment meeting. Its purpose is to get a new client. Consequently, your attention should be directed at both subjective and objective information. The briefing to start this meeting is as follows:

> ''You are probably wondering what to expect over the next few minutes, so let me clarify the purpose of this meeting. Probably the most important thing is for me to gain as much of an understanding of you and your financial concerns as possible—consequently, I'll be asking you some questions and taking some notes, but mostly listening to what you're saying. When we finish, I'll give you some feedback as to, first, whether I think we can help you, and second, how the planning process works. Finally, I'll give you an idea of what our fee is. . . . ''

From that point you will, we hope, have a new client who will eventually give you some good referrals and allow you to cut down on the number of seminars you need.

The appendix that follows contains information for your guidance and is self-explanatory.

Above all, I wish you success and profitability in your practice.

APPENDIX

Comments About Subjective Analysis of Seminar Type

This analysis (see Table 5) is based primarily on my personal experience in giving over three hundred seminars covering about fourteen years. It also includes some feedback from others who have given seminars. Therefore, it must be considered subjective and intuitive. The higher the number, the more favorable the rating. Therefore, the number 1 represents the lowest rating and the number 3

TABLE 5

Subjective Analysis of Seminar Type

	Kind of Seminar			Number of Nights Per Seminar		
	Sponsored	Targeted	Public	One Night	Two Nights	Three Nights
Cost per event	3	2	1	2	1	1
Development costs	2	1	2	3	2	1
Control	2	3	3	3	2	2
Predictable	3	2	3	3	3	3
PR benefit	3	3	3	3	2	1
Profits	3	2	3	3	2	2
Time & preparation of delivery	3	1	2	3	2	1
Time it takes to get a client	3	2	2	2	2	3
Ease of getting attendees	3	1	2	3	2	1
Totals	25	17	21	25	18	15

represents the highest rating. The categories are rated relative to each other. For example, a 3 is assigned to a sponsored seminar for the cost per event, because the sponsor pays most of the costs. In contrast, the public seminar costs relatively a lot more, because you are paying for all of the costs.

According to this analysis the overall most effective seminar to give is a one-night (25) sponsored seminar (25). Relatively speaking, the least effective is a targeted (17), three-night seminar (15).

Comments About One-night Seminars Versus Three-night Seminars

The model shown for the three-night seminar (see Table 3, p. 80) shows high performance figures and lower (perhaps more average) performance figures. The model was developed from both personal experience and information from other people doing seminars. The percentage of attendees who return for three nights and come into the office for an interview and become clients is higher, because the assumption was made that a fee was charged for the three-night seminar. Without the fee these percentages would all be lower. However, the fee acts as a qualifying device for first-night attendees; it is logical that there would be fewer attendees for a nonfee, one-night seminar.

It is interesting to note a paradox between the two models: It is possible to have a higher profit from a one-night seminar, even though the cost per client may be more.

While none of these models are a result of an analytical/scientific/academic research project, the assumptions are derived from extensive practical experience. It is this experience that caused me to decide to dispense with two- and three-night seminars and use the one-night format.

Seminar Content—Two Hours

    I.   *Opening*
        A. The confusion over money
        B. The reasons for doing these forums
        C. Like to get to know you better—questions
        D. How to go about organizing yourself financially:
            1. Cash flow planning
            2. Tax planning
            3. Investment planning
            4. Retirement planning—financial independence
            5. Contingency planning
            6. Estate planning
        E. Discuss three of these arenas in more depth:
            1. Tax planning
            2. Estate planning
            3. Investment planning
   II. *Tax Planning:* How to develop a strategy
  III. *Estate planning:* Attorney
  IV. *Investment planning:* Demonstrate decision-making model
    V. *Close:* Questionnaire, Evaluation sheet

TABLE 6

Average Seminar

Item	Costs (dollars) Per Unit	Total	Revenue	Number	Percent	Profits	
Facility	—	200.00	Number of mailings	6000		Total costs	$ 4,224.70
Insurance	—		Replies	129	2.3%	Total revenue	$45,000.00
Invitations	0.06	360.00	Attendees	97	75	Profits	$40,775.30
Reply cards	0.065	390.00	Client units	67			
Envelopes	0.08	480.00	Requesting interviews	40	60		
Addressing Stuffing	1.75	1050.00	Actual interviews	30	75		
Receptionists (2)	25.00	50.00	Clients		45		
Refreshments	1.00	120.00					
Signs	2.50	7.50	Counseling fees	$1000			
Handouts	1.20 (p.c.)	144.00					
Postage	0.22	1320.00	Commissions Securities	$1000			
Police/student parking guides	20.00	60.00	Inspections	$ 500			
Confirmation letter and env.	0.14	16.80	Total per client	$2500			
Postage	0.22	26.40	Total revenue per seminar—$2500 × 18 = $45,000				
Total	52.24	4224.70					

Sample of an Evaluation Sheet

EVALUATION

1. In order to help us serve you better, please give us your response to the following:

   Of the material covered during these sessions:

   A. Which subject did you find most interesting?

   _____

   B. Which subject did you find least interesting?

   _____

   C. How can we make future meetings more helpful?

   _____

   D. Please give us your overall appraisal of the value of this financial forum.

   _____

2. Name _____ Phone: Home _____
                                                       Office _____

   Best time to call _____

3. If you would like us to send an invitation for a future meeting to any friends or business associates, please complete the following:

   Name: _____

   Address: _____

   Name: _____

   Address: _____

   Name: _____

   Address: _____

''How to Give Successful Financial Planning Seminars'' is printed here by the author's permission.

"Make no attempt to sell during the seminar. Remember, it is an educational experience. Your objective is to discover problems, to stir up your guests, and to establish credibility."

—MURRAY ISEMAN, CLU, M.S.F.S., ChFC, M.S.M.

Establishing Credibility Through Seminar Selling

Murray Iseman is President of U.S. Equities, which is a wholly owned subsidiary of the USLICO Corporation. He is the past chairman of the LIMRA Advanced Sales Committee and currently the chairman of the Eastern Agency Officers Association. Murray has conducted numerous financial planning seminars around the country.

He has a bachelor's degree from Rider College and has done graduate work at Temple University. He holds a master's degree in financial sciences and a master's degree in management from the American College. Mr. Iseman is a CLU and a member of the first graduating class of Charter Financial Consultants. He has taught advanced estate planning for the American College and estate planning at the University of Virginia, and he was an instructor of income taxation at Montgomery College. He has made presentations before many industry groups, including estate planning councils, CLU chapters, agents' associations, an American College workshop, and company conventions. Murray writes a column for a monthly financial planning newsletter, and his articles have appeared in industry publications. He is listed in the current edition of *Who's Who in the East.*

No one can argue against the merits of seminar selling. I am continually amazed that so few planners use this proven technique to help build their practice. It provides the opportunity for multiple sales resulting from just one initial presentation. It casts the financial planner as an educator, not a salesperson, which is comforting to most prospects. There are many paths leading to successful seminars. The path I will outline works for me. It is the result of a twelve-year evolution from hundreds of presentations. While you may find it awkward to copy this exact approach, it should provide you with a starting point.

SPEAKING SKILLS

Some of us are very comfortable in a one-on-one sales situation but are intimidated when addressing groups. I can personally assure you that this uneasiness (or fear) can be overcome. Consider joining your local chapter of Toastmasters. You will gain experience by practicing your own presentation as well as observing your peers and the critiques that follow. Borrow or rent a video camera and tape yourself. You can practice by yourself or to a live audience consisting of family or friends. But prepare yourself for a humiliating experience! You are your own worst critic. Your voice will not be recognizable to you, and nervous mannerisms will be exaggerated. Many professional speakers find it difficult to practice alone. They need audience feedback to reach their optimum performance level. Even after conducting many successful seminars, you should still arrange for periodic taping. Even after years of public speaking, you may acquire bad habits such as rattling pocket change, moving too much, or repeating key words too frequently. You will know that you are ready when you are able to employ eye contact, moderate your voice, use pauses between points, utilize summary sentences, effectively use humor, and eliminate the ''ums,'' ''you knows,'' ''uhs,'' and ''as I said befores.'' Very few of us are effective memorizing a text. Consider using three by five file cards containing the pertinent points.

TARGET MARKETS

Once you are comfortable with your style of delivery, you must identify the audience that you wish to target. Most practitioners are aware that they should seek a market that has the need and ability to purchase their products. It is important that you are comfortable with your audience. (For example, some choose to work with doctors, while others are either resentful or intimidated by the medical profession.) Consider narrowing your areas of concentration. I know planners who specialize in members of the clergy, retired airline pilots, single parents, alumni groups, independent women, retired couples, GM dealers, chiropractors, and parents of college students. Many charities and community groups are always seeking speakers. The United Fund, Red Cross, Salvation Army, church auxiliaries, homeowners' associations, and travel groups are usually receptive to a quality financial planning seminar.

Your audience should be homogeneous in order to help focus on its needs. A clergyman has no interest in business transfer problems, and retired people are not saddled with educational requirements. Invite spouses whenever possible. It will pave the way for your sales efforts. The spouse can become your best center of influence.

SELECTION OF ATTENDEES

Direct mail to selected zip codes is not productive or economical. Low response rates require a huge saturation in order to net an acceptable number of positive replies. A third party endorsement will greatly improve your response rate. Determine those groups, clubs, and associations that relate to your target market. (Example: Target—single parents/groups; contacts—Parents Without Partners, church singles associations, dating services.) Ask the group to announce your seminar. You must assure them that there will be no selling at the seminar. Consider charging admission and donate the proceeds to your sponsoring group. Seek a few moments on their meeting program to promote your seminar. Place ads in their newsletter. Association backing may even entitle you to free announcements on radio and television. Place notices in the local newspaper's business section. You may wish to consider using an established accountant, trust officer, or attorney as a cospeaker. Assign this professional a 15-minute segment to discuss his or her area of expertise. Professionals will invite their own guests, so you then have an entree to that client base.

SITE SELECTION

I have conducted meetings in all types of settings, from a private recreation room to a country club. Your site should be easily accessible and offer ample parking. Hotels, restaurants, schools, and community centers are the most common facilities. Hotels can be expensive, but they are often open to negotiation. Meeting room charges can be waived if you are generous with refreshments. If you decide on a hotel, inspect the room. Is it easy to find? Is it noisy (i.e., loud fans, near the kitchen)? Who will be using the neighboring rooms? Is a microphone necessary? Are there posts obstructing the view of the podium? Will the size comfortably accommodate your group? Is a larger room available if your response rate is greater than anticipated?

Insist on classroom-style seating (rows of tables with chairs). Don't supply more seating than what you expect. Thirty attendees occupying sixty chairs gives the illusion of many no-shows. Have a table and chair outside the entrance. Ask attendees to sign in and issue name tags with their first names only. Provide refreshments prior to the meeting to limit interruption by stragglers when your seminar begins. Make sure that the hotel lists your seminar, using the same sponsoring name that appears on the invitation. This will appear on the bulletin board of the daily activities by the reception area.

Restaurants usually offer private rooms at no cost if you order a minimum food service. Make sure that there is a completely closed-off area away from the kitchen. Food should not be served during the presentation. You obviously do not have as much control or privacy in a restaurant as you would in a hotel.

Many communities rent out classrooms in the evening. The rates are reasonable, parking is usually sufficient, and there is rarely any activity to disturb your meeting. Make sure that the chairs are ample size for an adult. (Adult attendees squeezed into third-grader seats have a low attention span.) Classrooms lack commercialism and are less threatening than a hotel or restaurant. Determine the school board's position regarding refreshments. If they are allowable, hire someone to distribute them. Your professionalism is undermined if you attempt to act as a waiter.

Community halls such as the VFW, apartment complex auditoriums, and fire stations may also have potential. Temples and churches may also make rooms available. Make sure these have little religious decor in order to avoid turning off nonmember attendees.

MEETING TIMES

This is the most controversial subject among seminar presenters. Most will agree that you should avoid competing with major sporting events, presidential addresses, popular late evening soap operas, back to school nights, ethnic holidays, and similar seminars.

I prefer Tuesday, Wednesday, or Thursday evenings at 7:30. Mondays and Fridays often conflict with people taking long weekends or preparing for or recovering from long weekends. Starting at 7:30 gives most people sufficient time to have dinner and get out of the house before being sidetracked. The seminar concludes before 9:30, so it doesn't become a "late night." Consider serving refreshments from 7:30 to 8:00. Begin the seminar promptly at 8:00 P.M. Allow for a five-minute stretch at 8:45 and conclude at 9:30 sharp! *Never* run beyond your scheduled time. End when you promised, allowing the opportunity for attendees with prior commitments to leave. You can allow questions and answers and resume refreshment service at the meeting's conclusion.

I have seen seminars run on three successive evenings, three Tuesdays in a row, on Saturday mornings, and for three-hour durations. Some planners are productive using these techniques; I am not.

ADMISSION POLICY

The majority of financial planning seminars are free. I fear some people judge things by what they cost. (Many quality sedans are avoided by luxury car buyers because they are too inexpensive. I overheard two people arguing over whose lawyer was better. The issue was finally decided by which one charged the most!)

Everyone knows there is no such thing as a free lunch. Attendees may expect to be badgered by pushy sales representatives if they take free information. Charging a modest fee makes guests feel less obligated. Receptiveness to your sales efforts should come from the credibility and respect that your presentation has earned for you. I do not feel a $10 per head or $15 per couple fee will discourage serious attendees. They are getting refreshments and information for their money. However, the seminar should not be viewed as a profit center. Donate the proceeds to either the sponsoring association or a local charity. As an alternative, have your invitees make out a check payable to their favorite charity and turn it in as an admission ticket.

If the fee situation is still objectionable to you, there is yet another approach. In your announcement, indicate that there is usually a seminar fee. However, the sponsoring organization is either paying it or has managed to get it waived.

ANNOUNCEMENT LETTER

Now that all of the logistics have been decided, it is time to prepare the announcement. Use the sponsoring association's stationery wherever possible. Be brief, use headings, and underline. List the title of the seminar, the location, and the time in bold print. Also state the concluding time. You may wish to use an odd time, such as 9:35. Prepare an agenda to arouse interest or use questions that will be answered during the presentation. Your biography should appear on a second separate page. The biography helps establish your credibility. Here is where education, teaching experience, designations, association memberships, published articles, and professional (not sales) accomplishments come into play. "Insurance agents" and "stockbrokers" will not attract a following. "Financial planners," "consultants," "counselors," and "tax advisors" have a better chance of appealing to an audience. But these titles are meaningless if you have no "icing on the cake."

If you are not comfortable with your current biography, consider: writing a column for the neighborhood newspaper, teaching adult evening classes, volunteering as a career advisor at the high school, arranging for radio interviews, publishing announcements about your professional achievements in the society page, and speaking at a local Jaycee meeting.

The third page of the announcement letter is divided into two portions. The upper segment repeats the time and location. Your attendees return the lower half advising of their decision to attend. This half must include their phone number. You may add another statement in which prospects may indicate that although they can't attend the upcoming seminar, they would like to be advised of subsequent sessions. Be sure to indicate an RSVP date.

It is imperative that all attendees be contacted 48 hours before the seminar. You will lose at least 25 percent if you fail to do this!

PRESENTATION

Your presentation should exhibit total mastery of the subject content. Try to anticipate and encourage questions. But do not lose control and allow yourself to be sidetracked. You can discuss a lengthy personal question after the meeting's conclusion. Avoid the use of transparencies. They require a darker room, making note taking difficult. They keep you chained to the projector and don't lend themselves to a professional presentation. You should make liberal use of 35 mm slides that are professionally prepared. Consider a blue background with yellow print. There shouldn't be more than four to six lines on any one slide. Use a battery-operated pointer arrow to accentuate your material. Prepare hard copies and use them as handouts immediately before the seminar. The paper copy can have much more detail than the slide, which should only act as a summary. This avoids reading verbatim material that is in the hands of your audience.

Your opening comments will set the mood. Reassure your group that they are welcome to interrupt if they have a question, and stress informality. Begin with a humorous story. Choose one that you have seen work at other meetings, or purchase a book containing funny anecdotes. Keep the story brief. The longer the dialogue, the higher the audience's expectation. Avoid ethnic humor or anything else that may be offensive. (You can always poke fun at yourself.) A joke that is considered clever in New York City may be insulting in Butte, Montana. You should frequently summarize your points. This helps your attendees keep pace with your delivery. Interspace your slides with offbeat pictures. I've used photos of babies making faces. An infant sticking out his tongue may be the reaction to the latest wave of tax reform.

Put your personality into the presentation. Make eye contact with your audience and sense their mood. Be prepared to make adjustments to your talk. If you discover a high interest level in a particular concept, elaborate. Don't cut it off in an attempt to complete your talk. Time your seminar to end before the prescribed deadline. Ending early is not a crime—running late is. People frequently time their attention span to peak at the cut-off point. Keeping your audience after that is counterproductive. If you are concerned about ending too soon, consider using extra slides that do not have accompanying hard copies. This will provide filler material if needed.

Make no attempt to sell during the seminar. Remember it is an educational experience. Your objective is to discover problems, to stir up your guests, and to establish credibility. Many of your concepts should not suggest the purchase of products. They could include proper use of credit cards and their fees; sale and lease back of elderly parents' home; split dollar and bonus plans for existing life insurance policies; examples of the marginal tax bracket; the TED spread (a little-known commodity arrangement using T-bills and Eurodollars); employment of family members; the deductibility of mortgage interest; the granting of a second trust as an investment device; and equity sharing. Discussion of these topics shows that you are not merely trying to hype your own products but are able to integrate them into an overall financial plan.

Guests should be given a questionnaire when they enter. The critique will identify the good, the bad, and what was missed. Ask how the presentation could be improved. Have items rated 1 to 5 and have them circle and check off appropriate statements. Request names of referrals who should be invited to subsequent meetings. Signatures are optional. Obviously, those who sign and express interest in a particular item are prime prospects.

Use the time after adjournment for questions. Circulate in the group if no formal question is asked. Invite your attendees to enjoy the remaining refreshments.

You or your office should contact every guest within three days of the meetings in an attempt to get an appointment. Don't wait too long, or your efforts will not be rewarded. They may instead refer back to existing advisors, who will try to downplay your ideas and resell themselves.

Seminar selling works! But you must make a commitment and see it through. As with any skill, it improves with practice.

"A strong personal reputation and the word of mouth that goes with that in many ways outperform all other efforts undertaken in working with the media."

—LAURA WALLER, CFP

Laura Waller, CFP, is President of Laura Waller Advisors, Inc. She received her B.A. from Sophie Newcomb College in 1966 and her M.A. from Tulane in 1968. She is a well-known speaker who has lectured for the Coca-Cola Company in Houston, the Anheuser Busch Company of Tampa, the 3M Sector Group of Tampa, The West Company of St. Petersburg, among others.

Ms. Waller's professional affiliations include membership in the Institute of Certified Financial Planners, where she has served as president of the Tampa Bay chapter, and in the International Association for Financial Planning, where she is currently President of the Tampa Bay chapter. She is also a member of the Network of Executive Women, the Florida West Coast Employee Benefits Council, the Greater Tampa Chamber of Commerce, and the League of Women Voters.

Waller has appeared in *Who's Who in American Women,* and *The Wall Street Journal, Money Magazine, USA Today, Sylvia Porter's Personal Finance Magazine,* and other noteworthy journals have quoted her. In addition, she has been a commentator on Tampa's CBS TV affiliate, channel 13.

How to Obtain Media Coverage and Work With the Media

With the advent of *Money magazine, USA Today,* and other financial publications, finance, business, and investments have become an important part of middle-class America's life. With this popularization of finance has come the positioning of financial planners as the knowledgeable experts in the field.

The questions remain:

- How can you get the media to begin calling you?
- How can you get your name before the public at large?
- How can you best work with the media when they reach you?

Perhaps you are asking "Why all the bother?" By having your name mentioned in the media, a certain amount of credibility is obtained if it is a favorable article. Clients and prospective clients see this media attention as outside recognition of the validity of your opinions and your work. It is also perhaps the least expensive way to seek new clients. In our office, a record is kept of how each client learned of the firm. In looking back over our records, it is common to find that prospective clients call our office after having multiple exposures to the firm or to the planners in the firm. By far the greatest number of clients have seen something mentioned about our firm in the newspaper prior to calling.

MAJOR DOs AND DON'Ts WITH THE MEDIA

1. The media are usually on a deadline. When the media call, if possible, have them put through to you. Timeliness is a major factor. Return calls promptly. Be available. Be able to respond quickly. It usually does little good to call a reporter back three days after the first contact to ask what the story is about. It is imperative that your staff be instructed to put the media through if possible.

2. *Always* be honest with the press. If you have no comment or expertise on the subject, tell the person calling. Never tell lies. If by chance you have given bad information to the press, call them back immediately and apologize. You gain immeasurable credibility with the media by being honest.

3. Referring the media to a colleague who can be of help on a specific topic will increase your position as a valued resource person.

4. If you state something to a member of the press, it is available for publication. Don't tell the press something and then ask if it can be "off the record." The best rule is not to say something unless you are comfortable with having that comment published.

5. Deal evenhandedly with reporters. Helen Huntley of the *St. Petersburg Times* cautions against ever playing two competing reporters against each other. This tactic can backfire and ruin your relationship with either or both reporters.

6. When the media call, find out about the subject of the article. Then inquire about the reporter's deadline. Ask whether you can call the reporter back after you research the subject and organize your ideas in a cogent fashion. If possible, try not to talk off the top of your head if you can avoid it. Of course, if the reporter is on a close deadline, then you will need to present your ideas immediately.

7. Try to be quotable. Jeff Smith of the *Tampa Tribune* states that he will usually pick the comment that is most colorful. Instead of saying, ''It is a good time to buy bonds,'' think about what would make your response more interesting to a reader. There is a better chance that you will be quoted if you state, ''Buy bonds, but remember to actively monitor these investments. Bonds are sensitive to interest rate risk. In periods of rising interest rates, bonds tend to be discounted.''

Make your answers short and to the point. Use comparisons that are colorful and attention-getting if possible. For example, when asked about ways around the kiddie tax, a response that begins with, ''Aside from each of us adopting a 14 year old, . . . ,'' will garner more attention from the reporter and be of more interest to the readership than a bland statement of the tax facts involved in income shifting.

Tell about a personal experience. Consider which is more interesting—''Clients need to purchase adequate personal liability umbrella policies'' versus ''A recent accident in Tampa resulted in a multimillion dollar settlement against the father of a teenage driver. Only the father's house was protected against the claims of the creditors. This is why we as planners recommend adequate umbrella personal liability policies for our clients.''

8. Give objective advice. Don't push a proprietary item. If you are asked to give specific investment recommendations, try to think of a recommendation that could benefit the majority of the readers. Remember, the public tends to take what is written or spoken by experts as gospel and applicable to themselves.

9. Feel comfortable with the fact that you will not always be quoted. Sometimes, the local press will call just because they need to come up with a list of items to put in a box on the front page of the business section. The fact that you were called and were able to supply information means that you are developing a long-term relationship with the media. These relationships are rewarding over a period of time. An additional benefit of developing a strong relationship with a member of the media is that the media share resource people with their colleagues. Your network of media contacts will grow.

10. *Never* say something bad about a peer. It reflects poorly on your field, on you, on your colleagues—on all of us.

11. Always send a follow-up personal thank-you note to the media person who quoted you.

12. Never co-mingle your advertising with working with the media. Mentioning to a reporter that you should be quoted because you are a major advertiser in the paper will not elevate you in the eyes of the media.

HOW TO GET COVERAGE

1. If you decide to hire a public relations firm, inquire about their firm's approach to the media. Members of our local press have stated that receiving a phone call from a PR firm promoting someone often does not lead to positive results. Perhaps the most effective way for a PR firm to be of help is in assisting you in your approach to the media.

2. Quite a bit has been written about putting out press releases. Certainly there are excellent publications that can help you to develop a press release format. However, it is questionable how effective press releases really are. The media are skeptical about receiving multiple press releases about an individual put out by the individual. Reporters have told us that long dissertations received from planners discussing the status of the market and the like usually are tossed into the waste basket.

3. Get involved in your professional organizations, such as the ICFP, the IAFP, and the like. Those organizations often issue press releases about positions held by their members. A press release from a third party will get more credence with the media than your issuing your own press release will achieve. The press often looks to the directories of these associations for resource people.

4. Send a letter to the local media—reporters, business editors, and television business commentators—introducing yourself, telling about your background and your areas of expertise. Don't expect an immediate response to this letter. Most of the business media do file these letters for future reference when the need for a resource in your area becomes apparent.

5. Send an idea for a story to a reporter or a television business commentator. It can be helpful to send such people a copy of an article that has appeared in a magazine, saying that you feel this has local interest. Eventually that reporter will look to you as a source of topics and potential quotes.

6. Listen to the radio and television to gain familiarity with the different shows. If a show deals with topics that are within your realm of interest, offer to be interviewed. One of our local television channels announced in the paper that a new talk show was beginning. A letter to the host offering to be interviewed on last-minute tax ideas led to an invitation to appear approximately four months later.

7. Consider writing an article for submission to one of the neighborhood papers or a local business weekly. The major daily newspaper in your area may be more difficult to approach. Smaller neighborhood newspapers are often looking for articles to print.

CONCLUSION

You can become a valued resource for the media. There are simple guidelines to follow, as mentioned in this article. Above all, thoughtfulness and honesty are the most valuable tools in establishing and maintaining a positive relationship with the press. A strong personal reputation and the word of mouth that goes with that will in many ways outperform all other efforts undertaken in working with the media.

"A well executed public relations program in your community will build a perception of excellence, of availability, of competency, and, of course, trust."

—LISBETH WILEY CHAPMAN

Public Relations in Your Community

Lisbeth Wiley Chapman is the former editor of *Financial Services Times* newspaper, a trade publication for financial planners published in Newton, Mass. She was start-up editor for the first 20 issues of the monthly, 76,000 national circulation publication, directing editorial content, and working with freelance writers and contributors. During her editorship the newspaper doubled in size.

Chapman was formerly director of public relations for Confidential Planning Services, Inc., the international network of financial planning firms based in Middletown, Ohio. She was editor of "Networker," the company's internal newsletter, and wrote press releases, news stories, feature stories, advertising copy, and marketing material for the company and its 150-plus affiliates.

Chapman co-presented a 12-city seminar tour "Public Relations for Financial Planning" and helped develop the workbook and slide show that was used in conjunction with the seminar.

Chapman also was on the faculty of the School of Journalism at the University of Missouri-Columbia for seven years from 1977 to 1983, serving as coordinator for continuing education in the Business Journalism Department. She is a graduate of the University of Maine and completed her master's degree in journalism from the University of Missouri.

She is currently directing public relations for Putnam Companies, Inc., Boston, Mass.

Public relations, in its most basic terms, is any communication that is not paid advertising. For service-oriented professional financial planners, public relations in your community can have more impact and give you greater return than paid advertising. At the very least, consider public relations as the very best free advertising you can obtain.

Promoting a professional service is a vastly different enterprise than promoting a product. The difference is the ingredient of trust that has to be earned by professionals such as doctors, lawyers, accountants, or financial planners.

For a financial planner, prospective clients' belief system is built from the knowledge they have of you as a person, their knowledge of you as a visible contributing member of the community, and their respect for the people with whom you have worked. A well executed public relations program in your community will build a perception of excellence, of availability, of competency, and, of course, trust.

Public relations is just what the words say—going out and relating to the public. Five public relations programs to consider include speaking opportunities, workshops/seminars, press releases, newspaper columns, and newsletters.

SPEAKING OPPORTUNITIES

Every chamber of commerce in every town in America has a list of its service clubs and organizations. It can be yours for the asking. Develop a form letter (that you personalize for every group, of course) that suggests three or four generic financial planning topics that you or someone from your office would be delighted to speak about. Suggest that the program chairperson give you a call, or indicate in your letter that you will be following up the letter with a phone call shortly.

Make sure that you do follow up. Find out whether the organization has had any presentations on financial planning. If yes, find out which of your competitors spoke. If you know enough about your competition, you can then suggest an idea or topic that would be substantially different. If the organization has not had a planner speak, but is hesitant in fear of the talk's becoming a sales presentation, smoke that out in advance and assure the program chairperson that you are capable of presenting topics such as controlling taxes, issues of small business planning, estate planning, or retirement planning. All you ask in return is permission to leave some business cards and firm brochures in the back of the room should anyone be interested.

Do not hesitate to accept invitations to less well-known or prestigious groups in your community. You should take any and all opportunities to present yourself and your competent knowledge on financial planning topics in public. Never forget that in many families it is the wives who worry about security issues and lobby their husbands to do something about financial planning.

Many planners have told me that they cannot get a spot on the program for the civic groups of their choice. They say such organizations shun their requests because of the fear that the presentation will become a sales pitch. This is a universal problem, caused by enthusiastic planners taking all their years of sales training seriously and asking for the sale at every opportunity.

Do not sell at a public speaking opportunity. Set the stage for a sale by impressing the audience with your knowledge, your personality, your willingness to get back to them if you don't know the answer, and your invitation to the group to contact you later. You are speaking in order to leave an image, a perception of yourself and your competencies. Don't sandbag your best efforts.

A clever West Coast planner, who also was having trouble getting speaking engagements, sent a letter to every organization offering to fill in if any of their regular speakers cancelled at the last minute. His office was conveniently located in the downtown area, and he knew that he or someone from his office could rearrange their schedules to help a desperate program chairperson at the last minute. His office was called about once a month to rescue groups whose speakers had cancelled.

WORKSHOPS AND SEMINARS

If workshops and seminars fit into your marketing plans, they can be wonderful public relations efforts. To cut down on spending your own advertising or direct mail dollars to gather the audiences, work to develop a seminar in cooperation with another organization that can invite the audience for you. This approach has been successful for planners working with college continuing education departments, church stewardship committees, charitable organizations, medical societies, banks, and corporations.

When the workshop or seminar is organized in this fashion, the financial planner receives the credibility of the sponsoring organization. In effect, you have jumped on a respected bandwagon, and now you must keep your end of the bargain.

In a seminar setting, planners must work behind the scenes to make sure that the environment of the seminar is comfortable and professional, that the content of the seminar will educate and stimulate the audience, and that the follow-up strategies are carried out with dispatch and sensitivity.

Check out each meeting room ahead of time for temperature, noise distractions, lighting, comfort of seating, and comfort for writing. Check for any other meetings that might be going on at the same time as yours and what their noise levels might be like. Try to insulate your seminar attendees from unnecessary disturbances or noise.

Make sure that the material you present can be followed along by the participants in a workbook of some kind. The participants need material that they can mark up as you speak and material that they can go over again at their own speed at home.

Adults cannot continue to learn if they're kept in the same position for more than 40 to 60 minutes. Even if it's only a stretch break, let them stand up and move around for as little as two or three minutes to give them a break. Their concentration will improve, and they will likely assimilate more of the points you are trying to get across.

Do not leave the follow-up strategies to a clerk. Assign each participant at the seminar to someone in your office. Make sure that the prospect is called and that particular questions they may have raised during the seminar are answered. Remember, these people have been in a room with you for one or two hours. If you did your job well, they know that you are competent and professional and have a lot of information they need. Don't let this prospect get away.

PRESS RELEASES

Press releases are the most useful and yet most underused public relations device available to financial planners. A press release is your opportunity to get editorial mention in your local, weekly, county, or regional newspaper and possibly even your large metro papers. A press release takes very little time and less money and can give you some of the best public relations returns.

Many planners believe they have no news generating from their offices that would justify a press release. That simply isn't true. Press releases are appropriate when: the office has a new building or address, the company undergoes a name change, the office hires a new employee, new services are being offered, a principal in the firm is elected to association or public office, associates or principals in the firm are speaking to organizations, the firm is presenting public seminars, a joint business venture is underway, and many other instances.

There is no mystery to a press release, either. Simply keep your material to no more than two pages of $8\frac{1}{2}$ by 11-inch paper. Always double space. Place your name, address, and work and home phone numbers under the letterhead of your company. Follow the who, what, when, where, and why format that you learned in high school journalism. Make sure that it is clearly typed with no misspellings or typos on the page. Make sure the contact person's phone numbers are correct.

Develop a mailing list of all the newspapers in your area, as well as radio stations and television stations. While it is unlikely that most electronic media will use your press releases as news stories, they are still worthwhile sending. They may have a "business briefs" program. Nonetheless, they will continually have your name on their desk, and after a while if they are looking for a financial planner to quote, your name will come to mind.

The last paragraph on every release should be the same, release after release, and that paragraph should say what your company does in 25 words or less. If you do not have that paragraph, stop reading this chapter and sit down right now and jot down on a piece of paper one paragraph that would explain to someone what your company does.

NEWSLETTERS

If you do not write and distribute your own newsletter, and many planners do, then consider subscribing to a service that allows you to customize the letter. Such regular mailings to the centers of influence in your community, as well as to the media and to prospects, have the effect of piquing people's attention and moving them to ask questions. This can only stand you in good stead.

Newsletters make you look good. They establish you as a recognized and accessible expert (every issue has your name, address, and phone number in plain sight). It is also a great way to make existing clients feel loved—and keeping loyalties is very important. Given the increase in competition for your client, you must never put yourself or your practice in the position of looking as if you don't care about the client. Don't be a "one plan, fees and commissions, bam-never-see-them-again" type of planner.

Use the newsletter (filled with news) to keep your existing clients up-to-date on new products you are particularly impressed with, trends that you have noticed, and reasons for their calling and perhaps doing more business.

NEWSPAPER COLUMNS

The idea of starting a newspaper column for your local newspaper should not be discounted as "impossible" or "too much for me to handle," because it is both do-able and possible. Many planners have connected with news media outlets and offered a public service of generic information on financial planning. The key is to find the right newspaper, one that will benefit from your efforts.

A profile of a good newspaper to approach is one that currently is running little or no information on personal financial planning or planning for businesses. This can be a county, weekly, or suburban newspaper. In many cases newspapers that use a lot of syndicated or wire copy—all of which they have to pay for—may be interested in having you write copy for them in return for your name, address, and phone number at the end of the column for further information.

Yes, it's a lot of work, but it certainly can be done. The benefits are great. You become a recognized expert; you discuss topics that raise questions in people's minds; and your name is attached to the information. Do not agree to do it without your name and phone number in the credits.

Metropolitan editors of large newspapers are worth some effort also, but for a different purpose. These business and finance editors have adequate staff to regularly generate their own stories. However, you want to make yourself an accessible expert. Introduce yourself to them by describing the solutions to financial problems that you can speak about and topics about which you would be an available source. They may not use you right away, but if you are gently persistent in letting them know you exist, don't be surprised when they send a reporter to interview you.

THE SATISFACTION OF PUBLIC RELATIONS

The best part of public relations in your own community is the satisfaction you will get when people mention that they enjoyed your speech, saw your name in the newspaper, or caught the news show where you were quoted. Even more satisfying will be the people who will call you for an appointment because they heard you or saw you or read a quote in the newspaper.

In order to develop the perception of excellence and professionalism you must provide excellent and professional services. Then people must know about you, that you are available, competent, and trustworthy. Good public relations is truly the backbone of a successful financial planning practice. So be visible and go for it—and good luck.

"If you are in the information business, how well you communicate with your clients (customers) may well spell the difference among success, mediocrity, or failure. Creativity in communications will help you stand out from your competitors."

—LEWIS J. WALKER, CFP

Your Own Financial Planning Newsletter: A Key Marketing Tool

Lewis Walker, CFP, is President of Walker Capital Management Corporation, an Atlanta financial planning and investment advisory firm. Mr. Walker holds a degree from Georgetown University School of Foreign Service and an MBA from the Northwestern University Graduate School of Management. He has taught financial planning courses for both the College for Financial Planning and the American College. Mr. Walker has frequently conducted seminars and workshops on financial planning and investment topics around the United States and abroad. He often appears on radio and television and has been quoted by major publications including *Money, US News and World Report, Medical Economics, The Financial Planner, USA Today,* and numerous others. He is a contributing author to *Your Book of Financial Planning: The Consumers Guide to a Better Financial Future* and has been profiled in *The Financial Planner: A New Professional* by Loren Dunton.

Mr. Walker has served as Chairman of the Georgia chapter of the IAFP and has been admitted to the Registry of Financial Planning Practitioners. He has also served as president of the ICFP and on the National Board of the IBCFP.

Some financial planners do not like to think of themselves as selling a product. "Professionals do not sell," they might retort, given the suggestion that precepts of sales and marketing should apply to them.

And yet, in today's increasingly complex and competitive world, if you don't market, you will perish.

It may be useful for you to visualize your product not as "financial planning" but as "information." In essence you are an information broker. You study, read, attend courses and seminars, go to meetings, network, and consult, all in an effort to build your inventory of ideas. The way that you formulate, distribute, and apply your ideas in a professional context will be labeled "expertise." If you improve your expertise and communicate that know-how to a targeted audience with the need for and ability to buy your ideas (demand), the odds are high that you will sell (supply) at profit more ideas than your competitors.

If you are in the information business, how well you communicate with your clients (customers) may well spell the difference among success, mediocrity, or failure. Creativity in communications will help you stand out from your competitors. Communications of various types are essential to the marketing process. An effective client newsletter can serve that objective well.

The marketing process can be visualized in terms of four distinct activities:

1. Attracting the prospect.
2. Closing the sale (a signed advisory contract with a check attached).
3. Production of and delivery of the product (writing and presenting the plan).
4. Service after the sale (follow-up, monitoring, future planning activities).

A client newsletter is most useful at stage one and even more important during the long-term relationship in phase four.

Before signing on, a potential client wants to know something about you as an advisor. You may be a highly proficient planner. You may consider your plans to be superior to those of your immediate competitors. But consumers cannot "experience" a financial plan up front. They cannot "sample the plan" before buying. A financial plan is a classic intangible. The plan will be purchased based on what Harvard professor Theodore Levitt calls, in his book *The Marketing Imagination*,[1] "surrogates for tangibility."

They will buy you as a planner based on the signals that you send—a positive demeanor that speaks of confidence, professionalism, and expertise. You will be judged by your mode of dress, office decor, graphics, telephone manners, and visible staff support. Graphics are very important because stationery, business cards, and other printed items often precede even a personal meeting. Key messages, critical to the buying process, are communicated before you even say hello.

Recognizing that the selling of ideas should be part of a well-thought-out, creative, and fully integrated marketing process is the first step in visualizing the importance of a client newsletter as a key element of a marketing plan. If you elect to do a newsletter, do it right. Spend the money and spend the time to make it first class, on the assumption that you are trying to project a first-class image.

[1]See *The Marketing Imagination*, by Theodore Levitt (New York: Free Press, 1986), Chapter 5.

This writer has published a client newsletter for a number of years and considers the effort (it does take effort!) to be highly successful and rewarding. There can be psychic rewards in creating your own newsletter (it can be fun) as well as those gains associated with client-related results.

If you don't have the time, talent (don't sell yourself short), or inclination to do a newsletter, you could buy one. There are a number of fine newsletters that allow you to overprint your name, address, phone number, and perhaps, a message. The plus is that it beats doing nothing at all. The negative may be in the fact that it is too easy. The ideas are not yours. The client may be getting similar newsletters from other professionals or other organizations. Besides financial planners, newsletters may be sent out by stockbrokers, insurance agents, accountants, bankers, associations, educational institutions, nonprofit organizations, charities, and even some mutual funds. Will your newsletter stand out? Will it be seen as unique? Creative? And above all, useful to the client?

You may publish your newsletter as infrequently or as often as you like, but quarterly would be minimal if you wish to stay in front of the client. Monthly would be a feasible maximum, or perhaps eleven times a year with a combined issue in the July-August time frame.

If you buy a "canned" newsletter, perhaps you could insert a page or two of your own as a supplement. But on the assumption that creative marketing requires creative thinking, the balance of this chapter will concentrate on the creative approach—how to publish your own newsletter.

WELCOME TO THE IDEA FACTORY

First decide what you want to accomplish with your newsletter. Think about the target audience. What are their interests? How sophisticated are they? What style of writing or format are they likely to respond to? What style best reflects your talents, your practice, and the image of your firm?

Format is important because you want your newsletter to stand out. Visual impact as well as readability are factors. If your firm has a logo or a distinctive graphics style, these should carry through on your newsletter. A talented graphics designer can be invaluable in attaining the right look. Just as you would expect a client to pay a fee for quality work, you should be willing to spend the dollars to get some advice as to design, format, and approach. Your newsletter can become your signature, and style and cachet are major components.

Format should also facilitate ease of production. Computers, desk-top publishing programs, and word processors have all but eliminated typesetting. Laser printers or other letter-quality machines can produce high resolution text. In-house two-color or multicolor printing is becoming more affordable. Or you can send the camera-ready text to a printer for production with a two-color masthead or other designs.

You could employ a straight letter style, or use a more elaborate design, for insertion into an envelope. With an envelope, the newsletter arrives in good shape, and that is a positive. A negative is higher cost and more labor.

Some planners use a self-mailer in a format that allows easy application of a computer-generated label and smooth insertion into a postage machine. Be sure to use heavier paper so that the newsletter will hold together in the mail. You could test-mail copies to yourself to monitor the quality of postal service.

Use first-class postage. You want your message to be first class, so have it delivered that way. Lower classes of postage look cheap, take too long, and the odds of damage to mail increase. You can pack a great deal of information into a format that weighs one ounce or less to keep costs under control.

If spouses tend to be key decision makers within your client base, you might wish to send the newsletter to the home address. But there also are solid reasons to send the newsletter to a business address. The likelihood of pass-on readership increases. Copies left on desks or tables may be perused. Photocopy machines are available to those who wish to save an article.

SERVICE AFTER THE SALE AND AS A PUBLIC RELATIONS TOOL

Once you have a client, you must stay in touch. While you need personal contact at appropriate times, clients still appreciate a newsletter. It reaffirms that you are still out there, thinking creatively, learning, growing, and keeping your eye on the big picture in their behalf. And you will be surprised at how often they will call you, responding to an idea in your newsletter.

Use the newsletter as a public relations tool and as a prospecting device. Send copies to local radio and television newsrooms or reporters. Send copies to newspapers and magazines and to business and economic writers and editors. An effective newsletter can lead to quotes, media appearances, and even national exposure.

WHERE TO GET IDEAS

Ideas are everywhere. As a planner you have to read, listen to, and assimilate a tremendous amount of information. You will see ideas in other newsletters, books, journals, magazines. Often these inputs are fragments of larger ideas. Maintain a clip file. Store up thoughts and data until a bigger picture emerges. The creative communicator is one who can see a mosaic when others can see only scattered pieces.

Clients have a similar problem. They get all sorts of data thrown at them. They want an advisor who can sort it all out, make sense of it all, and translate it into understandable "action ideas." Seminars are great sources of material. When you attend an educational event, take good notes. Be thinking about an article. When experts speak, listen. By quoting leading figures, you gain by association. Clients are pleased to know that you are learning from the best. When you travel and invest time and money in education, tell your clients what you have learned in your newsletter. As to topics, possibilities are limitless. You can talk about economics, investment trends, specific planning strategies, case study examples, or interviews with fund managers, money managers, or others. By covering a breadth of topics, you can show that you are a multifaceted generalist.

Perhaps the greatest dividend from a client newsletter is the personal gain. If you are going to write a newsletter, it compels you to seek ideas. It forces you to think. Space constraints mandate concise communications. By doing your own newsletter, you will develop your writing skills and your overall communications techniques. Such talents will serve you well in all facets of your practice.

As to the task of writing your newsletter, some final tips. Eighteenth-century author Samuel Johnson, the greatest English writer of his day, said this about writing as a discipline: "Composition is for the most part, an effort of slow diligence and steady perseverance, to which the mind is dragged by necessity or resolution." Give a great deal of thought to your themes before committing words to paper. Mull over articles. Write them in your head first. Once you have a draft, apply appropriate doses of critical revision. And proofread the final text over and over. Have people who neither wrote nor typed any of the text read it. Mistakes and typos are easier to see if you don't know what the message is.

The costs to produce a newsletter vary substantially with volume, format, frequency, and the like. With a creative approach, costs can be held to efficient levels. As a ''cost recovery'' item, we take several approaches on our newsletter. It goes to fee-paying clients on retainer at no added cost as part of their annual fee. A growing list of subscribers, nonclients, other financial planners, academics, and other consultants are subscribers at $30 per year. A complimentary subscription list is maintained for key members of the electronic and print media. Quotes in other newsletters and national magazines, journals, and newspapers have resulted.

In the 1967 screenplay, *Hud,* Cool Hand Luke diagnosed a problem as ''a failure to communicate.'' Expert financial planners with effective communications skills will avoid problems and create opportunities. The written word is powerful indeed!

"The key to marketing and surviving as a fee-only financial planner is to market the concept of fee-only planning."

—JOHN E. SESTINA, CFP, ChFC

John Sestina, CFP, ChFC, is Vice-president of SMB Financial Planning, Inc., a fee-only financial planning firm. Mr. Sestina holds a bachelor of science degree from the University of Dayton and a master of science in financial services from the American College in Bryn Mawr, Pennsylvania. He holds memberships in the International Association for Financial Planning, the Institute of Certified Financial Planners, the Society of Independent Financial Advisors (SIFA), and he has been admitted to the Registry of Financial Planning Practitioners. Mr. Sestina is also former president of the National Association for Personal Financial Advisors and was named outstanding financial planner of 1982 by the SIFA organization.

A frequent speaker and seminar leader, Mr. Sestina has spoken for many business and professional groups nationwide. He teaches at Ohio State University and has taught at Franklin University and Columbus Technical Institute. Mr. Sestina is regularly quoted in many national publications and has frequently appeared on television and radio talk shows, including his own weekly financial planning segment on a local radio magazine show.

How to Market and Survive in a Fee-only Practice

No matter what business one attempts to build, marketing is the key to success or failure. Seventy-five percent of all new millionaires emerging in our society today owe their status to how they marketed their products and services. They either marketed something common uncommonly well or marketed something uncommon to a common audience.

The key to successful marketing in today's marketplace is to find something unique or unusual to attract the public's attention. In addition, the ability to coin ''buzz words'' will also draw attention. In the recent past, financial planning has qualified for such a description.

However, as the consumer becomes more familiar with financial planning, new, more interesting buzz words and techniques will be necessary to continue to attract the public's attention to an individual financial planner's business. In the new marketplace of financial planning, ''fee only'' is one of those buzz words. The key to marketing and surviving as a fee-only financial planner is to market the concept of fee-only planning.

In marketing the fee-only concept, the fee-only planner should market only positively, not negatively. The public is attracted to positive and repelled by negative. As a result, there is no value to the fee-only planner in demeaning the commission-only or the fee-basis planner. The most positive approach is to present to the public who and what you are and let them determine which type of planner they prefer. Some indeed will prefer one of the other types of planners. However, it is not your mission to convert the world, but rather to work with those clients whom you can help and with whom you can build a relationship. It is your mission in marketing yourself to inform the public that there are different types of planners so that, as better informed consumers, they can make what they perceive to be the right choice for them.

In informing consumers, it is important that they understand the vocabulary of the industry. Consequently, an explanation of the three types of compensation that planners receive would be helpful to them. The three types, of course, are commission-only, fee-basis and fee-only.

Part of your ability to inform will revolve around your clear understanding of differences and advantages that you perceive you offer. If the public is researching the difference among various planners, you should be able to teach them how to evaluate the costs of each of these planners. Teach the consumer to have each type of planner disclose all costs associated with the relationship that he is undertaking. Perhaps the disclosure form developed by NAPFA (The National Association of Personal Financial Advisors) would be helpful to you and the consumer. Presumably you can demonstrate how your services are indeed less expensive than the other types of planners'. You need to know that this is true for the specific kind of client you choose to serve. Your competition will be telling clients that you are more expensive. Therefore, it is critical for you to understand the cost differences and to be able to communicate these differences to your prospect.

Teaching consumers cost differences is only a part of your marketing arsenal. Whether it is true or not, another unique advantage you have to market as a fee-only planner is objectivity. There is a perception on the part of the public that someone who works strictly for a fee is more objective than someone who does not. As part of your marketing opportunity you should promote that feeling. You can promote the fact that other professional advisors, such as CPAs and attorneys, operate on a fee-for-services basis. By so promoting, you put yourself in the same category as these other professionals. Such promotion, by the way, is not limited to your prospective client, but also includes those companies and individuals who provide products and services your clients will need. Because you are not selling a competitive product, these providers may refer clients to you. In addition, because you do not expect to participate in the commission, some will refer you clients, realizing that they need only sell you. If they sell you, you recommend their product or service to your clients and they make the same money in less time. Finally, the other professional advisors to whom you are trying to compare yourself may be more willing to refer you clients, as they also perceive no conflicts of interest. Remember, your marketing should include other advisors as well as prospective clients.

Less expensive cost and perceived objectivity alone will not market your firm on a long-term basis. In the end it will be your ability to deliver a top-notch, high-quality service that will be your ultimate marketing tool. In fact, many planners fail for lack of skill, not because of the way they charge for their services. In this area again it is the perception of the client and other advisors. Therefore, if you bring any credentials from your previous profession that have carryover value, promote them. If not, then you must acquire credentials in this profession as in any other. As you achieve those credentials, you have something to promote.

Even credentials do not assure competence. So once again you must be able to deliver. In the area of delivery you have another advantage that you can promote to your prospective client and his advisors: Because you operate on a fee-only basis, you are not out to replace any of the existing advisors. Remember, the client has some excellent advisors who are providers (insurance, securities, etc.). Many planners assume that the existing advisors are incompetent or represent the competition. You, of course, are neither, and you should market that fact to both the client and his advisors. Another area of advantage you have in regard to delivery is implementation. Because the fee-only planner can work with all advisors and providers, he should be in the best position to implement. You may have to deal with an archaic perception that implementation is the placement of product. But minimal discussion should eliminate this lack of perception. You can market the fact that because of your unique position, you can be approached by everyone who has a product or service. As a result, you can choose from this greater selection to the benefit of your client. You should be more current because of this position, as everyone will approach you with each new concept that may be applicable. Once again, this is possible because you are not competing or looking for a share of the commissions.

The success of your practice will depend on your ability to market these unique features of a fee-only practice. The mechanics of marketing are well-known. But you must have something to market when you use the conventional methods of marketing.

The conventional methods of marketing are listed only as a reminder of the avenues for you to pursue:

Personal impression
Association with others
Volunteering your services
Public speaking
Writing articles
Seminars
Teaching courses
Electronic media (radio, etc.)
Hiring a public relations firm
Hiring someone to market for you

Remember to market yourself. Marketing in general as it relates to financial planning is really public relations, not advertising. In my opinion, advertising does not work; public relations does.

I hope you find these considerations helpful to your marketing success. Without a doubt, if you cannot market, you cannot survive.

Chapter III

Planning for Planners

John C. Sweet

Aivars Ziedins, M.S.F.S., CFP, CLU, GRI, ChFC

Raymond A. Parkins, Jr., Ph.D., CFP, ChFC, CLU

Martin J. Cohen, CFP

Eileen M. Sharkey, CFP

Glenda D. Kemple, CPA, CFP

Andrew M. Rich, CFP

James J. Burke, CFP

Jerry L. Frechette

William C. Heath, CFP

Jeffrey L. Seglin

Deborah Danielson, CFP

Robert J. Oberst, Sr., Ph.D., CFP

Carol A. Sandstrom, CFP

Leo R. Burns, CFP

"Few independent planners and planning organizations will survive if they do not soon reorient themselves to being business people first and financial planners second."

—JOHN C. SWEET

Do You Need a Business Plan?

John C. Sweet is the president of John C. Sweet & Associates, a business planning and marketing management firm based in Wheaton, Illinois. He works with financial planners and planning organizations, securities broker-dealers, accounting firms, insurance agencies, and real estate syndicators to help clients develop their own strategic and operational business plans, marketing plans, and management and organizational development projects.

John is a graduate of Wheaton College, Wheaton, Illinois, with additional work at Stanford Graduate School of Business. He is a frequent speaker and seminar leader and is a continuing education instructor for the College of Financial Planning in Denver, Colorado.

He has authored a variety of articles on business planning and marketing, including one in the March, 1987 issue of *The Stanger Register.* His activities were featured in a story in the November, 1985 issue of *Financial Planning* magazine in the Practice Management section entitled, "The Planner's Planner."

The purpose of this article is to discuss what I believe to be a crucial need for independent financial planners today: the need to start using generally accepted strategic business planning techniques as the mechanism to successfully managing their businesses now and into the future.

Other industries have relied on the classical planning process for years to help ensure profitability and growth. It appears to be time for those in this industry to do likewise.

The operation of an independent planning enterprise in this rapidly changing, highly technical industry is one of the toughest challenges an individual can accept.

Surprisingly, however, very few of the financial planners with whom I have come in contact have developed their own formal strategic business plan. Consequently, many are hurting and somewhat fearful about their business and personal futures.

Here are four observations I can safely make about the state of the planner today:

1. The independent financial planning business is not a place for the meek, the immature, or those who wish to take it easy.
2. Many planners, whether successful or not, are currently frustrated or even "traumatose" (my word for emotionally immobile) because they don't really understand or feel able to control their environments.
3. Few independent planners and planning organizations will survive if they do not soon reorient themselves to being business people first and financial planners second.
4. The spoils in this business will go to those who are able to plan, organize, direct, and control their futures rather than reacting to them.

Yet most financial planners, many broker-dealers, and quite a few sponsors whom I have encountered have a built-in aversion or inability to plan for themselves even though they promote the need for others to plan.

There seem to be several reasons for this condition:

1. Done correctly, whether in-house or with a third-party consultant, the strategic planning process can be both difficult and time-consuming.
2. Both success and failure can discourage the commitment to an ongoing planning process.
3. The procedure can be painful, since honest assessments must be made about personal skills and deficiencies.
4. Ego. What do I need a plan for?

A planner may be strong in technical knowledge, but a weak communicator; good in one-on-one situations, but a poor public speaker; a good salesperson, but not really a marketer. Bad news is often hard to admit. Soul searching is always tough.

I frequently hear questions such as, "Who and where is my market?" "How much should I charge?" "Do I need a partner, or should I dissolve my partnership?" "How can I make more money?" "How should I grow?" "How do I stay independent with the demands put on me by local, state, federal, and industry regulations, clients, creditors, tax law changes, market conditions, economic cycles, and family demands?"

These questions come from planners, broker-dealers, CPAs, and sponsors alike, whose businesses are evolving in a piecemeal, patchwork way.

The strategic plan is a necessary and powerful tool that by nature answers these kinds of questions. A good business plan provides a track to run on and serves as a blueprint for the future. (Ever try to build a house without a blueprint?)

Ideas are not business plans! Budgets are not business plans! Sales objectives are not business plans! Rather, a strategic business plan includes specific elements such as statements about the purpose of the business and opportunities for growth. It states objectives in terms of what you want to do and strategies about how you are going to accomplish the objectives. It assesses strengths and weaknesses of the people and the business.

A good plan provides views of trends in the industry and competition; it positions the business to operate effectively and efficiently in the future.

Further, a well-written, long-range plan will always define in detail a one-year action plan that allocates money and people resources in areas of marketing, personnel, facilities, equipment, and finance. In the one-year business plan, the accountabilities and timing requirements of all projects must be assigned so that activity can be monitored and controlled.

One of the key benefits of successfully employing the planning process is emotional liberation. Additionally, having a formal plan enables others—a spouse, a banker, vendors, employees—to view the business and understand its direction and how they might contribute.

Having a business plan will greatly help develop management skills, because it generates a new understanding of what needs to be done, by whom, and when. A strategic plan ties it all together.

There is no formula for management that guarantees success. However, strategic planning is a time-tested fundamental that will significantly improve the probabilities for survival on a profitable basis.

The following outline describes how you can write a three-year strategic and a one-year operational plan. The plan elements follow a logical sequence of thought that takes you from the long-term, visionary side of your business through the details of a one-year action plan.

STRATEGIC BUSINESS PLAN OUTLINE

1. Charter

Write a two- or three-paragraph statement of the mission or purpose for you and your business. What is your business about, where do you operate, and what is your philosophy of doing business? Everything in the business plan should support this "reason for being."

2. Long-Term Objectives

State what it is you want to do in the areas of finance, marketing, personnel, facilities, and equipment. Use a three-year horizon. A few examples:

- *Finance.* Gross income, expenses, net income.
- *Marketing.* Segmentation of clients by income, profession, and investable assets. Who are you working with now? Who do you want to work with, and how many clients are in each category? (Strategies will dictate

use of devices to grow each client base, for example, brochures, telemarketing, seminars, referrals, public relations, and the like.)

- *Personnel.* Hiring, training, policies, procedures, terminations, promotions.
- *Facilities.* Location, space requirements, decor.
- *Equipment.* Computers, telephone systems, typewriters, copiers.

3. Long-Term Strategies

Follow each objective with a statement of how you will achieve it. These statements should allocate three resources: people, money, and time. They dictate the management style you intend to use to manage the resources.

4. Industry Analysis

Write your observations about trends in the industry regarding: (a) services and products, (b) changes in tax laws, (c) regulatory changes, and (d) market conditions and interest rates. State other issues that will affect your business, but over which you have little or no control. Assumptions about these environmental issues affect your one-year action plan.

5. Market Analysis

Review and segment your clients in terms of (a) geography—where they are; (b) demographics—how much they make, size of family, social class, and work status; (c) psychographics—lifestyle—how they live. Analyze each market segment to see if it is profitable, or how it can be made profitable.

6. Competitive Analysis

Who is doing business like you in your area? Are they doing some things better? Are you doing things better than they? Is there a gap or two in the marketplace that you can explore?

7. Strengths and Weaknesses

Your strengths are the strengths of the business; your weaknesses are the weaknesses of the business. List four to six strengths—the things you want to lead with; then list four to six weaknesses—the areas that you need to improve or plan around.

This is a really tough section, since it requires an honest evaluation of yourself and your business.

8. Critical Issues

Acknowledge potential problems or weaknesses that may preclude successful completion of an objective. Any issue that can disrupt your plans is a critical issue.

9. Action Plan (Operating Plan)

Following the sequence in these long-term objectives and strategies, state specific projects and activities that must take place in the next 12 months. List each project in order, fully describe each project, assign individuals to the tasks, and put them in a time frame by fixing start and completion dates. The whole plan comes alive in this section.

By far the most exciting aspect of the business planning process is the implementation phase. It is also the most critical, since all the thinking and planning and money and time spent will be largely wasted if you don't follow through with your plans.

The key to successful implementation of your business plan is the use of the following principles as a guideline during the development of your plan:

1. Make an emotional as well as an intellectual commitment to creating the plan. You have to really want the plan, not just think you need it.

2. Make sure that your goals are realistic, doable, and not so far out of reach that frustration will easily overcome your desire to follow through on specified projects.

3. Make sure that your goals are not somebody else's. It is very difficult to do something for someone else's reasons, especially if times become tough.

4. Make sure that your goals, strategies, and action plans are in writing and are not just ideas floating around in your head. Reaccess them periodically to make sure you stay on time and schedule or know why you must change time frames.

5. Make sure that your goals suit your purpose in life as well as your mission in business. Your post-planning activities must fit your self-image so that you feel comfortable about really committing to each project.

6. Make sure that you are not afraid to succeed. Visualize yourself being successful and where you always wanted to be in business.

7. Work smarter, not necessarily harder. To this end use your resources wisely, follow through, and do it right the first time.

With these principles in mind during the planning process, your original plan will be developed in such a way that implementation will be natural and logical.

As the planned projects start to come together on time, there is a certain reaffirmation that helps other planned activities develop on time. If an opportunity not originally planned becomes a consideration, then review the original plan and either explore the new option and change the plan, or stay on the original track.

The more closely you stay on plan and/or review it for possible change, the more efficient you will become as a business person. And that means serving more people more effectively and being more profitable. That is why implementing the plan is the most exciting part of the planning process. Don't plan just to plan. Plan to implement.

The completed business plan is a means of communicating your ideas to others, and it provides a means of measuring your success at the end of the year.''

—AIVARS ZIEDINS, M.S.F.S., CFP, CLU, GRI, ChFC

Aivars Ziedins, CFP, CLU, GRI, ChFC, M.S.F.S., is owner and President of Ziedins & Co., Ltd., a financial planning firm in Denver, Colorado. He received a bachelor of science degree in business from the University of Colorado and a master of science in financial services from the American College in 1985. Mr. Ziedins is a Registered Principal of FSC Securities Corp., Atlanta, Georgia, and is a licensed real estate broker in the state of Colorado, where he is a managing general partner of over 100 real estate properties.

Developing a Business Plan for Your Practice

Mr. Ziedins has presented numerous seminars and workshops locally and nationally on financial planning to professionals and to the general public. He has been an adjunct faculty member of the College for Financial Planning, a board member of the Rocky Mountain chapter of the International Association for Financial Planning, a charter member of the Ambassador Program for the Institute of Certified Financial Planners' Educational Foundation, and an advisor to the Planned Giving Committee for the University of Colorado Foundation. Mr. Ziedins has written numerous articles and hosts a television show called ''Ziedin's Money Trends,'' which airs throughout metropolitan Denver.

What is a business plan? • The Middle English word "bissinesse" means "diligence," and the word "plan" is derived from the Latin word "planus," which means "ground plan" or "map." Therefore, we could define a business plan as "a map for diligence." In order to succeed, your business requires industrious effort applied to a systematic approach toward your objectives.

Should all companies prepare a business plan? • First of all, business plans are generally used for venture capital. In other words, a business develops a business plan on the basis that it will succeed and then goes out and borrows money for the business venture. On the other hand, an ongoing company should develop a business plan in order to see where it is going, where it wants to go, and whether or not it can get there.

There are three major reasons for going to the trouble of creating a *written* business plan. They are

1. For objectivity • The process of putting a business plan together, which includes the thought put into it *before* you would begin to write it, forces you to take an objective, critical and unemotional look at your business project in its entirety.

2. For use as an operating tool • The written business plan is an operating tool which, when properly used, will help you develop the planning process, will help you manage your business and will put the planning into operation towards the success of the business.

3. For communication and measurement • The completed business plan is a means of communicating your ideas to others, and it provides a means of measuring your success at the end of the year. The importance of planning cannot be overemphasized. By taking an objective look at your practice, you can identify areas of strength and areas of weakness, channel in on the directions that otherwise might be overlooked, spot problems before they arise, and measure how you are achieving your practice goals.

As an operating tool and as a means of measurement, your business plan should be written down exactly as you would develop a financial plan for your clients. In a financial plan you set out the goals that your client would like to reach. You look at your client's resources and the time frame that your client is projecting. Then you begin the implementation process for your client, and you measure the success. This is no different from developing a business plan for your practice. Remember, when one sets goals, one will generally reach those goals.

In order for your business plan to be effective, you must do most of the work, if not all of the work, to generate the plan. A plan that is prepared by someone else will not do you any good unless you understand it thoroughly. This understanding comes from actually sitting down and writing the plan yourself, looking at all your options and the resources available to you.

Like the financial plan that you have developed for your client, no business plan will be worthwhile unless it is implemented. Just like your clients, it may be difficult for you actually to do the implementation, but it is very important to do it, nevertheless. Remember, most businesses will fail in the first five years of being in business. Statistics indicate that four out of five businesses that start today will not be in business in five years, and the main reasons are a lack of financial resources and a lack of good executive planning. Your business plan should be able to overcome these obstacles by realistically determining your resources and your abilities in order to implement the business plan.

Let's dive right in and go through a quick process of developing a business plan:

First, ask yourself, "What business am I in?" Think about that. It sounds like a silly question. But do you realize that most business people do not understand the business they are in? Write down, in 25 words or less, a description of your business. For example, you might say, "I am in the business of financial consulting through a professional firm that provides customized, written financial plans and financial services to affluent individuals in the areas of investing, tax planning, risk management, retirement and estate planning, and most importantly, the implementation of the recommendations in the financial plan."

Next, define your mission statement. This is the statement that all employees of your firm need to know. Exactly what is their purpose at this job? For example, "To help create wealth for the client by decreasing taxes and accumulating and managing investments." In addition, what about you, the owner of the firm? What is your mission statement? Your statement might be that this is the primary source of income for you to accumulate wealth for yourself as you do for your clients by the utilization of the same services and investments that you would recommend to your clients.

What are your long-range goals for business growth and profitability? Where are you today? Where do you want to be five years from now? That is the key question. Do you want to stay as a sole practitioner? Do you want to merge with other individuals and form a partnership? Or would you like only to share office space with another planner? Would you like to develop and create a professional firm of many associates? You need to answer these questions, because they will determine what you do this year, next year, and the following years.

Do you want to be a manager? Or do you want to be a financial planner and work directly with the individual clients? Do you want to specialize in one area of financial planning, or do you want to be an overall generalist and coordinate financial planning for your clients? These are the questions that you need to ask yourself as you develop your five-year plan. It is important to know where you are going between now and five years from now. If you don't, you will never get there. So sit down and take a little time to look to the future and see where you want to be.

Two other important questions to ask are What are my strengths? What are my weaknesses? This is a good way to determine what you want to delegate in your business. Concentrate on your strengths, and if you like to work in those areas, then go ahead and do so. You can delegate work to other people who are proficient in those areas where you are weakest.

It is important to develop your long-range plan. Where do you want to be in five years? If you can answer that, you will more than likely be there in five years.

SHORT-RANGE OBJECTIVES AND ACTION PLAN

The short-range action plan is the one-to-twelve-month plan, or your annual business plan. What are you going to do between now and the end of the year? Break your goals down into monthly and weekly activities. That is the key. It is nice to know what you would like to do by the end of the year, but it is difficult to accomplish your objectives unless you divide the work into monthly, weekly, and daily requirements. Then make sure that you meet those objectives by keeping good records of what your goals are and what you actually accomplish.

COMPENSATION

Your compensation structure, with built-in incentives, can be built upon your goals and what is actually achieved. If you reach your goals, then there is no problem in paying the incentives to your employees who helped to get you there. If you did not reach your goals, then you need to evaluate the whole

My Income Requirements

LAST YEAR'S INCOME	First year commissions		
	Fees	$_____	
	Mutual funds	$_____	
	Limited partnerships	$_____	
	Insurance	$_____	
	Other	$_____	
	Renewals	$_____	
	Income from other sources	$_____	
	Total last year's income		$_____
ESTIMATED FAMILY EXPENSES THIS YEAR	Food	$_____	
	Clothing	$_____	
	Shelter	$_____	
	Home operating expense	$_____	
	Health, life insurance	$_____	
	Investments	$_____	
	Church and charity	$_____	
	Vacations	$_____	
	Personal allowance	$_____	
	Income taxes	$_____	
	Other	$_____	
	Total family expenses		$_____
ESTIMATED BUSINESS EXPENSES THIS YEAR	Auto and travel	$_____	
	Office, materials, & supplies	$_____	
	Entertainment	$_____	
	Other	$_____	
	Total Business expenses		$_____
	Total annual family and business expenses		$_____
INCOME REQUIRED THIS YEAR	Total year's income required		$_____
	Expected renewal income	$_____	
	Expected income other sources	$_____	
	Total expected income (−)		$_____
	Net annual income required from first year commissions		$_____
	Net **monthly** income required from first year commissions		$_____

Figure 1 Income requirements worksheet.

picture. What did you do right? What did you do wrong? Do you have the right employees doing the job that you want them to do?

This brings us to performance standards and controls. By having broken down your annual goals and your business plan to monthly, weekly, and daily expectations, you can now measure these goals and determine the standard that you want and that which is acceptable, thereby having a means of control. If you and your staff are not accomplishing the objectives, then you need to reevaluate your plan to see if your goals are too high and impossible to reach. Consider readjustments to the business plan to make it more realistic. Consider whether or not your staff is lacking in important areas; perhaps they're not doing their job and need training or more guidance—or perhaps someone should be replaced.

As an aid in the development of your performance standards and controls, you need to know your income requirements and needs, breaking them down by month, by week, and by day. In addition, you need to know what services and products you need in order to generate this income goal during a given time period.

Figure 1 through Figure 7 are some forms which will help you determine the goals and objectives found at the top of page 123:

Production and Activity Required To Meet My Income Goal

LAST YEAR'S PRODUCTION	First year commissions from BFPs*	$_____
	Number of BFPs I closed	÷_____
	First year commissions per BFP closed	$_____

		FOR YEAR	EACH MONTH	EACH WEEK
THIS YEAR'S PRODUCTION AND ACTIVITY GOALS	Net income required from first year **commissions**			
	Number of BFPs I must **close** to meet **commissions** goal above			
	BFPs **presentations** I must have to obtain **closes** needed above			
	BFP **questionnaires** I must pick up to obtain **presentations** above			
	BFP **concept** interviews I must have to get **questionnaires** above			
	Telephone calls I must make to obtain **concept** interviews above			
	Prospects I must have to meet **telephone calls** needed above			

*Balanced financial plan.

Figure 2   Production and activity requirement worksheet.

My Results

	Prospects Obtained		Telephone Calls		Concept Interviews		Question- naires Obtained		BFPs Presented		BFPs Closed		First Year Commissions							My Com- missions Goal
	Goals	Results	Goals	Results	Goals	Results	Goals	Results	Goals	Results	Goals	Results	Fees	MFs	L.P.s	Insur- ance	Other	Total Results	
January													$	$	$	$	$	$	$
February													$	$	$	$	$	$	$
March													$	$	$	$	$	$	$
April													$	$	$	$	$	$	$
May													$	$	$	$	$	$	$
June													$	$	$	$	$	$	$
July													$	$	$	$	$	$	$
August													$	$	$	$	$	$	$
September													$	$	$	$	$	$	$
October													$	$	$	$	$	$	$
November													$	$	$	$	$	$	$
December													$	$	$	$	$	$	$
Totals													$	$	$	$	$	$	$

Figure 3 Results.

Your income requirements
Production and activity required to meet your income goal
Results
Financial success charts
Daily to-do lists

As you can see, before you can complete these charts, you must first determine what kind of service and product mix you will have. In other words, how much in fees are you going to charge? What kind of products will you be selling, and how much will you be earning from each type of product? This will determine your service and the type of financial plans you will write. If your fees are low, you may not be able to afford to write a 50- to 100-page financial plan. You may be willing to do only a one- to three-page financial plan. On the other hand, if your fees are high, you will be able to generate a very thorough financial plan. With regard to your product mix, are you selling only one, two, or three types of products? Then you need to realize that your market will be limited. If you are selling many types of products, then your market is unlimited. Define how

Financial Success Charts
My Income Goal and Results

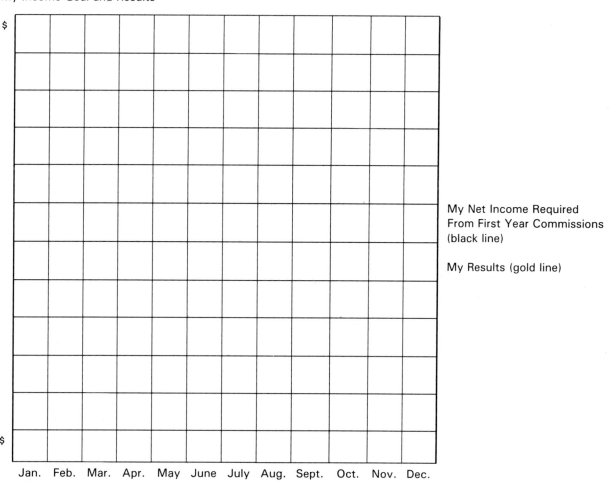

My Net Income Required
From First Year Commissions
(black line)

My Results (gold line)

Figure 4 Financial success chart—income goal and results.

My Production and Activity Goals and Results

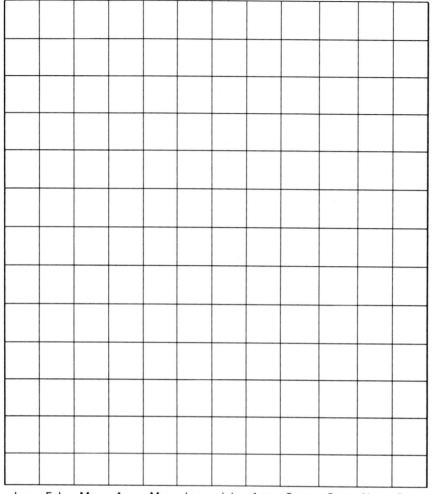

$

$

Number of BFPs I Must
Close to Meet My
Commissions Goal
(black line)

My Results (gold line)

Jan. Feb. Mar. Apr. May June July Aug. Sept. Oct. Nov. Dec.

Figure 5 Financial success chart—production and activity goals and results.

much you are able to earn from each product and how long it would take you to sell that product in order for you to determine how many hours in a day you will have to work.

Let us take the fee for services as an example. The first thing you want to do is describe your client profile. For instance, if you are dealing with teachers, you will have a limited number of products for their retirement plan, since they generally already have a retirement plan. Their income is usually modest, and therefore would not require a complicated plan. On the other hand, if you are dealing with small business owners or doctors, your product mix may be much larger, the financial plan will be much more complicated, and you will be able to charge a larger fee, since their affairs are more complex.

How much should you charge? This is a difficult question, especially for fee-only planners. One way to determine this is to work backwards. Let us make the assumption that you would like to earn $100,000 a year. How many clients do you need to work with in order to earn $100,000? If you feel that you can work with ten clients a year, then a simple solution is to charge $10,000 per client. But can every client pay a fee of $10,000? On the other hand, if you feel you can develop one client a week, then divide 50 weeks (give yourself a two-

Name _____   Day and Date _____

TO DO	CK	TO SEE		CK
FIRST THINGS FIRST	✔	*TIME*	*PERSON/PLACE*	✔
		IMPLEMENTATION		
		AMOUNT	*PRODUCT*	
		TO PHONE		
		NUMBER	*PERSON/ REGARDING*	
TO FOLLOW-UP				

Figure 6   Daily organizer.

Daily Time Log

EMPLOYEE _____   Day & Date _____

Time		Activity	For Whom	Telephone Calls	For Whom	Comments or Interruptions	C/
6	00						
AM	30						
7	00						
	15						
AM	30						
	45						
8	00						
	15						
AM	30						
	45						
9	00						
	15						
AM	30						
	45						
10	00						
	15						
AM	30						
	45						
11	00						
	15						
AM	30						
	45						
12	00						
	15						
PM	30						
	45						
1	00						
	15						
PM	30						
	45						
2	00						
	15						
PM	30						
	45						

Figure 7 Daily time log sample.

Time		Activity	For Whom	Telephone Calls	For Whom	Comments or Interruptions	C/
3 PM	00						
	15						
	30						
	45						
4 PM	00						
	15						
	30						
	45						
5 PM	00						
	15						
	30						
	45						
6 PM	00						
	15						
	30						
	45						
7 PM	00						
	30						
8 PM	00						
	30						

- Please be as specific as possible.
- P = Personal.
- Indicate breaks taken.
- Indicate for which company and/or person the work was performed.
- Keep this form in a notebook (ZCO, ZEP, ZRE, ZPM: initials of pln/mkt)
- C = Chargeable; NC = Not chargeable.

Figure 7 (*continued*)

week vacation) into $100,000, which equals a fee of $2000 per client. Now that is not as large a fee to pay. So, if you want to earn $100,000 a year, you know how many clients you will have to process in one year at $2000 each.

The next question you might ask is how many hours does it take to process each client? You will need to actually run a time schedule to see how long it takes you to prepare a financial plan for a client, meet with that client, and make a presentation of your financial plan to that client. If, on the other hand, you are paid by fee and commission, you can decrease the fee by the amount of commission you may earn on that particular client. If you will be earning $1000 per client in commissions, then you need to charge that client only $1000 in fees to earn the $2000 that you need from that client—not that this is a good idea. Remember, you should be paid separately for the financial plan, the fee for which should carry the cost of producing the plan, and for the implementation, which will require more of your time.

So, in the case of the fee and commission planner, determine how many hours it will take you to work on the financial plan, write the financial plan, make a presentation of the financial plan, *and* do the product implementation.

PROSPECTING

Prospecting is another ball game, as you might say. Since you have to accomplish all of the above in order to earn $100,000, you need to find time for prospecting or marketing. A rule of thumb is that, when you start out in the business of financial planning, you will be successful on a 10 and/or 25 percent ratio. In other words, out of every ten people (or what may be called suspects) you talk to, you will convert one to a prospect, or potential client. Out of every ten prospects, you will find one *qualified* prospect. Out of four qualified prospects, you will be able to convert one to a client.

The process is: suspects—all names that you might have available as contacts; prospects—more targeted or qualified suspects; qualified prospects—individuals with whom you can actually sit down and go through a short questionnaire to provide information such as income, net worth, family, etc.; client—a fee-paying individual who utilizes your services.

If this makes sense, then you should begin working backward and fill out the form, "Production and Activity Required to Meet My Income Goals." As an example, to develop one client, you will need four brief questionnaires—in other words, you need to get some information from four qualified prospects. To get four questionnaires, you will need 40 prospects—out of every ten prospects, you would be able to get one qualified prospect. To get 40 prospects, you will need 400 suspects, or 400 names per week or about 20,000 suspects per year. On the basis of this fact sheet, to earn $2000 per week, you must talk to 20,000 contacts per year, or 1666 contacts per month, or about 400 contacts per week, or 80 contacts per day, or 10 contacts per hour.

Now this is almost impossible. The key is to convert four qualified prospects to one client. What you need to do is to have a suspect list of between 2500 to 5000 names from your target market that you may draw upon to generate prospects. This is the area in which you will want to channel your resources and energies, making your target market aware of you and you of them.

TARGETING YOUR MARKETS

The first thing you want to do is to define what kind of client you are looking for. If it is a teacher, then go after that market. If it is a business person, then go after that market. If it is an executive, go after that market. But first you must define that market. The following list gives you some sample guidelines to help you describe your market:

1. Occupation
2. Industry
3. Geographic location
4. Age
5. Sex
6. Personal income
7. Net worth
8. Liquid assets

Consider these areas and put your criteria beside each item to determine what type of individual (what age group, what income range) you want as a client, and then begin to market that individual. It is difficult. When you start out in this business, you will take anybody and anyone; if they breathe, they can be clients. But remember, it takes as much time and effort to work with a very small client who cannot afford to pay you as it does to work with a client who has substantial assets.

MARKETING STRATEGY

The marketing avenues available to you for reaching your target market are

1. Referrals from CPAs, bankers, attorneys, and clients
2. Seminars
3. Speaking engagements and teaching
4. Newsletters and direct mail
5. Door-to-door soliciting
6. Using the phone; going down lists and making cold calls

Of course, the preferred method is by referrals, which bring you and your business to a level of high professionalism and respect in the community and industry. But all of these methods work. I know. I have used them all and have listed them in order of effectiveness, the top being the best and the bottom being the least effective. But they all will bring in clients if you are willing to go out and work.

OPERATIONS AND STAFFING

Remember, the most important job you have is to work for and communicate with your clients. If you promised to produce a financial plan in four weeks, then the client expects the financial plan in four weeks and *not* in four months. The best way to lose good clients is not to produce and not to communicate with them.

The most important aspect of financial planning is communication with your clients. Communicate with them through your operations: generate a good plan, give quarterly updates, semi-annual updates, or annual updates. Also, have your staff communicate with your clients on a consistent basis—through newsletters, letters of information, etc., and always give good service to your clients.

Be staffed appropriately and be sure that your operation of business is systematic, organized, well-thought-out and able to produce the financial plan. You will find that your clientele will grow, and they will be knocking on your door for financial planning.

By taking all of the items above into consideration in developing your business plan, thinking it through, writing it out, being realistic about your goals, and implementing your business plan, you will find that your business will succeed, whereas the vast majority of businesses do not. Someone once said, ''If you plan your work and work your plan, you will be successful.''

"The practitioner should provide the same service for himself or herself that he or she would provide for a client."

—RAYMOND A. PARKINS, JR., Ph.D., CFP, ChFC, CLU

Building and Managing a Successful Asset Management– Financial Planning Practice

Raymond A. Parkins, Jr., Ph.D., is a graduate of Clemson University with a B.S. in industrial management and holds a M.S. degree in industrial management from the Georgia Institute of Technology. He received his Ph.D. from California Coast University. Dr. Parkins is a Certified Financial Planner, a Chartered Life Underwriter, and a Chartered Financial Consultant. He is the Executive Officer of The Parkins Investment Companies, Inc., Orlando, Florida.

Dr. Parkins is a board member of the Institute for Certified Financial Planners and a member of the International Association for Financial Planning, where he has served as President of the central Florida chapter. Currently, he is a member of the Board of Regents of the College for Financial Planning, Denver, Colorado, and a member of the Board of Directors of the IBCFP. He has written articles in *Newsworthy* and *The Financial Planner* and has spoken to numerous professional groups.

In my opinion, the most important step in building a practice is to recognize the need for sound business planning. A specific written business plan will also be helpful, because it will help the individual practitioner to confront himself with the fact.

A business plan developed by and for the financial planning practice would be similar to the one that he or she would suggest for a client. If the business plan format is worthwhile for the client, it is essential for the financial planning practitioner.

The business plan should include an analysis of the market for asset management–financial planning services in the geographic area the financial planning practitioner intends to serve. In addition, the plan should include an analysis that is realistic with regard to the individual practitioner's capability and access to the various segments of the identified market.

The initial business plan may recognize that various segments of the market are not accessible at the immediate time. However, with proper planning with regard to the acquisition of additional licenses and credentials, which may allow for expansion of services, the additional increments of the market may be available to the practitioner.

In my opinion, the patience to pursue incremental progress and to staff and expand services accordingly is essential to the future success of the individual practitioner. Expansion of staff and services usually calls for additional capital. Careful planning with regard to the financial structure of the firm and the proper revenue, accumulated earnings, and short-term debt will often separate the successful from the unsuccessful practitioner.

Often, the real test of patience in incremental planning is the willingness to pay the price to run a successful practice at the current time in order to build a base of revenues. The next test is to retain a portion of the net revenues for future expansion of staff and services. A lack of patience, in many instances, will result in excessive or premature short-term borrowing, which can become long-term debt under the wrong market conditions, business environment in the local community, or inaccurate projections with regard to future revenues.

As a final thought, regarding the development of a business plan, a practitioner should be sure not to be overly influenced by others who suggest that some areas of interest are ''too difficult,'' ''too highly regulated,'' ''too expensive to administer,'' and the like. In many instances, the accumulation of objections by others may suggest continued consideration of the idea. Sometimes others, with good intentions, may suggest that a practitioner not pursue other areas of interest simply because they have not had the energy, the capital, or the genuine interest to pursue the area and hope that their business friends will take the same approach. Movement into new areas of service may often cause practitioner friends to become uncomfortable because they have previously made different choices. As a result of practitioner's choices, some business friends may begin to question their own prior decisions. The central thought here is simply that the practitioner must remember to think for himself and to make business judgments based upon analysis, which should include a weighing of the opinions of others whose business judgment is respected.

Following the implementation of a successful business plan, the day-to-day management of an asset management–financial planning practice is critical. Scheduling approximately fifteen appointments per week with clients or prospective clients to establish new business relationships, present recommendations, implement recommendations, or provide service is necessary for the development of a new practice and continuity of an existing practice. Effective use of the telephone to maintain contact with existing clients on a regular basis is necessary for maintenance of practice-clientele relationships.

In order to manage the financial aspect of the practice effectively, practitioners should review a cash management report regarding the cash receivables and payables on a weekly basis. In addition, the progress of the firm's management plan, which should be established and measured closely against results each year, is essential. By doing this, the practitioner can measure the results of his efforts and adjust accordingly in the areas that seem to be most and/or least productive.

As a clientele is established, effective use of the telephone will be enhanced by maintaining investment account records for key clients in a notebook near the practitioner's desk. Consequently, when a call is placed to a client or received from a client, sufficient information is on hand to provide current thoughts and recommendations regarding the investment of new funds without delays regarding "a review of the file." Certainly, in some instances, where the questions require a review of financial planning objectives, current circumstances, and the like, recommendations should be deferred until the review is complete. However, in many instances current portfolio information will allow for the client's needs to be met during the telephone conversation without unnecessary delays. The benefits for the client and for the practitioner are obvious—for instance, the receipt and delivery of effective service on a timely basis.

Finally, with regard to financial management and control of the practice, monthly financial statements should be produced in-house or, in the early stages, by an outside accounting firm for review of the practitioner in order to be sure that the revenue, profit, and expense control goals of the firm are being attained. Where deficiencies are obvious, conclusions regarding the underlying reasons should be developed so that adjustments can be made in effort, efficiency, product development, service delivery methodology, and so on.

In summary, the best guide to building and managing a successful practice is to plan carefully, work hard, work smart, and be prudent. In a nutshell, the practitioner should provide the same service for himself or herself that he or she would provide for a client.

"Financial planning is not an end in itself, but a discipline that assists the client in both the accu-mulation and preservation of wealth. Financial planning is not the sale of a product to a client, but the strategic placement of assets for the client's benefit."

—MARTIN J. COHEN, CFP

Building Asset Management Services With a Multiplanner Team

Martin Cohen is an independent financial planning and investment services practitioner in the North Texas area. He has more than a quarter-century of experience in securities and finance.

Mr. Cohen is a graduate of Union College and the Wycoff Institute of Technical Market Analysis. In 1977 he earned his Certified Financial Planner (CFP) designation. He is a Registered Principal of the National Association of Securities Dealers (NASD), a Registered Investment Advisor, and a licensed real estate, insurance, and securities broker in Texas.

Within the financial planning industry, Mr. Cohen is cofounder and former president of the North Texas chapter of the IAFP and has served on the national board of the Institute of Certified Financial Planners. He was also a founder of the Dallas Society of the ICEP, as well as an ambassador to the ICFP educational foundation, representing Texas.

You may recall attending your first IAFP national convention, wandering through the exhibit hall with the dazed eyes of a new student. Confronting you was an array of products and services that bent the mind with confusion as each syndicator, service company, broker-dealer, insurance group, and the like extolled the virtues of his or her particular product or service. You were implored to exchange your calling card for product literature and make time for a special product presentation to be held that evening in a hotel hospitality suite. You attended a number of these events and decided that, at a minimum, it's a lot of fun.

The meetings were over, and you returned home, hauling two bags of product literature, not to mention an additional pile squeezed into your suitcase. How can you sift through this voluminous amount of literature and select high-quality products suitable and timely to offer your clients? That selection may come following a call from a product wholesaler, from a specific broker-dealer-approved list, or you may try to pick your own list of products for presentation. It is, usually, a haphazard decision.

A good many planners utilize this "bottom-up" approach, picking the products and then trying to use them to meet the perceived needs of their clients. The major problem is that this approach does not fit well with a strategic or asset management approach to client service.

Bottom-up product picking is inefficient in both the selection and product tracking process; furthermore, the products and services selected may have been excellent for the prior five-year market cycle but inappropriate for the period ahead.

The total asset management approach is beyond the resources of a typical one- or two-planner office or small offices of national firms, but it must be incorporated into the planning process to achieve client financial goals. We must remember that financial planning is not an end in itself, but a discipline that assists the client in both the *accumulation* and *preservation* of wealth. Financial planning is not the sale of a product to a client, but the strategic placement of assets for the client's benefit.

Why is it critical to take a *strategic* versus a product selection approach to planning and implementation? Because the rapidly changing social, political, financial, and economic environments make certain investment products uneconomical and obsolete unless they are purchased with a view to medium- and long-term trends. This is amply demonstrated by the wrenching change from inflation to deflation between 1983 and 1986, replete with significant losses in tangibles, real estate, and energy-related investments: Not only were many syndicators put out of business by not anticipating this economic transition, but more importantly, clients and their planners were financially and professionally hurt. How, then, are we going to avoid the same catastrophe in the future?

The answer lies in carefully crafted associations of planners under one roof, combining specialized professional skills to leverage time and effort. Together they should bring a higher level of expertise to bear on clients' financial problems. The industry trend has already shifted toward planners who specialize in areas of cash, investment, risk, and tax management. A team of specialists can thus apply their combined talents to the clients' financial and asset management; they can successfully take a more thoughtful and disciplined approach to achieving client objectives.

You are no doubt thinking that you already have these experts available through your national firm or specialists in your city; however, in the rush of everyday business, communication and client service can break down at even short distances. It is essential that the financial team be housed under one roof to benefit from the proximity and interaction of specialists who add value to the planner–client decision-making process. Additionally, there is substantial benefit and efficiency to the planner team in sharing capital resources in a combined operation.

What, then, are the steps necessary to establish a team approach to asset management? How is the process administered and how is implementation controlled? My suggestions are the following:

1. Through industry networking in your community, identify complementary specialists serving clients in your target market. Specialization may include financial planning, case writing, insurance, investments, real estate, financing and banking, estate planning, or other professionals involved in personal financial services.

2. A joint venture, partnership, or corporate structure should be established. A business plan, a mission statement, a target market, a fee schedule, job descriptions, and especially cross-referral incentives or overrides to motivate the team to work together are the important elements of the relationship.

3. The broker-dealer and other product and service entities should be utilized if compatible with the target market of the planning group.

4. Your financial planning delivery system must be defined and integrated with complementary financial services. Are you going to produce an encyclopedia-type plan or simple financial projections with pinpoint solutions to problems? The most cost-effective, efficient planning process is one in which the client is likely to implement his plan. This should occur by defining problems, alternative solutions, and having a specialist available for implementation.

5. Recruit a mentor group in your community that can relate to your organization, guide you in strategy and operational policy, and serve as a source of leads for your financial team. This mentor group should be selected from various sectors of your business community to provide your planning group with intelligence from various sectors of the marketplace.

Quarterly meetings should be held in which each representative provides a brief report on trends in banking, business, finance, insurance, law, taxation, communication, politics, and the like.

Your planning group must also provide a quarterly position paper to the mentor group related to your firm's position toward the financial and investment markets along with a review of services.

A critique and general discussion of the consensus position should be factored into investment allocation models for short-, medium-, and long-term investment decisions.

6. Develop a strategic asset allocation grid for your planning group. Start your investment decision models with assumptions related to the social, economic, political, fiscal, and financial trends projected for the United States and the world. The current status of the United States business cycle, supply-demand forces in the marketplace, federal reserve policy, inflation, and deflation probabilities must be considered. You can address particular investment segments once you define the financial and economic trend. Major categories of investment include the following:

- Money instruments
- Bonds and notes
- Stocks and equities

- Real estate and resources
- Commodities
- Hard assets
- Business ventures

Your allocation of investments among these major categories will relate to the following factors:

1. Short-, medium-, or long-term economic trends (e.g., deflation, low inflation, moderate inflation, or high inflation), with the low-inflation model emphasizing financial assets and the high-inflation model emphasizing tangible assets.
2. Client personal investment philosophy, risk propensity, and liquidity requirements, as well as interest in tax deferral, current income, capital appreciation, and holding period all should be categorized and weighted in the investment grid for specific asset selection.
3. Characteristics of due diligence for products currently available must include such factors as management capability, track record, financial strength, tax implications, securities compliance, client reporting, and timeliness of investment. A full-time in-house specialist will be needed.

   Products can be selected for review by using your strategic view of the economy and financial markets over the next year, three- and five-year horizon to set the order of priority and need. Your product selection and prioritization must relate to a ''macro'' view of the financial and economic markets rather than a random selection process.
4. Select a complementary mix of products and services to be integrated with the investment process (insurance selection, gifting, pension and trust administration, cash management, etc.). All products and services must be carefully selected, high-quality, cost-effective, complementary, and appropriate for your client's financial goals.
5. The financial planner in this asset management process becomes part of a cost-effective team bringing specialization, market sensitivity, and experience to bear on the client's decision-making process. The lone planner cannot be expected to be knowledgeable about all aspects of financial planning or the wide range of product and service alternatives.

I believe financial planning will evolve into a financial or asset management profession. If you agree, you can accelerate the process for yourself by recruiting or becoming part of a financial planning management team. Table 1 outlines such a team.

TABLE 1

Financial Management Team

Specialist	Services & Skills	Benefits to Team	Benefits from Team
Financial Planner	Generalist & client strategist	Coordinator of client financial affairs	Specialized information
Attorney	Legal & counsel	Tax, estate, & general legal counsel	Financial management information
Accountant	Accounting, tax	Control of client records, audit, income tax	Economic, investment, insurance information
Banker	Credit analysis, lending capacity, Cash management	Client credit source	Pertinent client information
Computer expert	Data management	Control of information	Multiple disciplines for data management & realistic information
Due diligence officer	Investment analysis & investigative ability	Evaluation of products & services	Combined judgment of team & industry contact for information
Investment broker	Stock & bond analysis & charting	Sensitivity to markets	Investment ideas; client support
Insurance agent	Risk management & analysis	Evaluation of insurance products, estate & business planning	Complementary products & services
Management consultant	Business analysis & management control	Complement personal client; consultation with business services	Impact of personal planning on business decisions
Asset management specialist	Asset allocation of client's cash & resources	Strategic approach to money management	Related services that complement asset strategies
Employee benefits specialist	Corporate benefit planning & administration	Analysis of corporate benefit plan	Clients' total plan related to employee benefits
Real estate broker	Analysis & marketing of real estate	Sensitivity to local & national real estate markets	Assessment of personal & business decisions related to real estate
Trust officer	Client or family assets in trust	Trust management	Refined premortem & postmortem goals

"It is important to identify constraints and structure the service you can offer clients so that you do not impair your firm's reputation by promising what can not be performed."

—EILEEN M. SHARKEY, CFP

Structuring Your Practice to Serve Your Clients' Needs While Meeting Your Own Goals

Eileen M. Sharkey is President of E.M. Sharkey and Associates, Inc., a Denver-based financial consulting firm. She was born in England and completed her education at London University before arriving in the United States in 1969. She completed an additional bachelor of arts degree at Newman College, Kansas, in 1971 and received her CFP designation in 1978.

Ms. Sharkey was founder and first President of the Rocky Mountain chapter of the International Association for Financial Planning and presently serves as special advisor to that group. She served as a member of the National Board of Directors of the IAFP and chaired the Ethics Committee from 1982 to 1985. Elected to the national Board of Directors of the Institute of Certified Financial Planners in 1981, she currently serves as Treasurer. She was among the first in Colorado to be admitted to the Registry of Financial Planning Practitioners. Ms. Sharkey is an adjunct faculty member of the College for Financial Planning and frequently contributes to major national publications. She is a contributing author to *Your Book of Financial Planning.*

CLIENTS AND SERVICES

Structuring a practice is a very individual thing. The clients you can effectively help and the services you want to provide will depend to a large degree on your own background and aptitude. You will identify quickly the kind of clients you like dealing with and the kinds of problems you enjoy solving.

Your choice of whether to practice as a sole proprietorship, in a multiplanner practice, in partnership or corporate form, or to be a part of a financial product firm selling securities, insurance, or real estate again will follow from your mix of clients and services. If you find great delight in advising people on investments and really have no wish to get involved in the detail work associated with full-scale financial analysis, you probably will not want to structure your office as a financial planning firm. The main complaint from many financial planners is the sheer amount of detail work involved in dealing with financial planning issues for sophisticated clients. If, on the other hand, investment advising is only a small portion of what you like to do, and your real love is generalized problem solving, then a full-scale financial planning office might be appropriate for you. You might not want to become familiar with all the different variations of financial planning expertise and might wish to associate yourself with other planners who can bring added resources in depth in areas such as estate planning or tax law. These additional areas of expertise can be brought into your firm, or separately contracted, with independent consultants.

CONSTRAINTS WITHIN THE PRACTICE

It is very important to decide how much of your time and your staff's time is going to be spent in each area of endeavor. Some financial planning firms, for example, do the actual preparation of tax returns. Obviously that type of work is very intensive during the first quarter of each year, and those practitioners are severely limited in their ability to do other types of work, especially in March and April of each year.

In my own case, since I come from England and wish to return there on a fairly regular basis once or twice a year, the knowledge that I would be out of the country for large periods of time, for up to a month at a time for each visit, precluded me from setting up a practice that would provide for my clients very heavy trading advice (such as investing in the very popular penny stocks). In such investments, minute-to-minute and day-to-day monitoring would be a service I personally could not offer while away from the office on extended trips. You may have similar restraints in terms of your family situations, need for additional financial education, lack of necessary expertise, and so on. It is important to identify such constraints and structure the service you can offer clients so that you do not impair your firm's reputation by promising what can not be well performed.

LOCATION AND SPACE

Your location will also influence the type of clientele with whom you will feel comfortable dealing. Some financial planners, for example, structure their practice to meet the needs of corporate executives. Corporate executives may spend

80 hours a week working for their corporations and basically want the financial planner to act as their "bodyguard," to run interference for them on all the different financial products and services available and make bottom-line recommendations in a very timely and efficient manner. It would be difficult to help such people if your office were located far from the business center of a metropolitan business area.

Other financial planners do not particularly like working with corporate executives with their unique financial demands and may specialize in dealing with sole proprietors, executives of small corporations, or closely held family businesses. These enterpreneurs have an entirely different set of needs and problems and require the financial planner to be a bodyguard but demand somewhat different skills and expertise, such as a background in management consulting. Such clients may not be willing to drive "downtown" to meet with a financial planner, and a more suburban location or office in the commercial rather than the business district might be appropriate.

The space devoted to meeting with clients and space provided for administrative functions within the office needs careful attention to ensure an efficient flow of work and information.

PERSONAL GOALS

So far we are dealing with structuring the practice to meet your personal goals. The bottom line for this, obviously, is to define what these goals are. Your goal may be to become the expert in your community in financial planning or asset management or tax consulting or investment advisory services based on the talent of the people associated with your company. You may want to provide services and products that are meaningful and goal fulfilling for clients to operate with integrity, and to be on the cutting edge of the industry in service and creativeness.

BUSINESS AND MARKETING PLANS

Whatever set of goals you adopt, you will need to follow up the goals very quickly by devising a business plan. The business plan should set out what your goals are for the immediate future. Plan your anticipated income and expenditures, staff requirements, and overhead. With the business plan and your personal goals firmly in place, you can then define what market you would like to attract. In my own case, I deal with many retired people and asset allocation and management services which have been designed specifically for retirees. Developing a market strategy aimed for retirees is not suitable for every planner; sometimes you may be the only visit of the day. They may love to talk or they may strategically forget to turn on their hearing aids at times when they don't want to hear about the risks involved in various strategies! The type of person you are, therefore, will define the kind of practice you want to have, and that in itself will help you select the kinds of people who can benefit most from your particular strengths. For example, if you really enjoy doing tax work, you would not want to deal with people whose marginal bracket is always going to be 15 percent. If, on the other hand, you like doing budget work and debt reduction, then it is unlikely all your clients will be millionaires.

Once you have defined the markets, then you can structure your marketing program to attract those people. Your program may include seminars, public speaking engagements, participation in civic groups, referrals, teaching courses, radio and TV guest appearances, and the like.

STAFF AND EQUIPMENT

When the marketing plan is ready to be implemented, you are ready to make a final determination in terms of staff and equipment needed. If you anticipate that you will have to provide sixteen financial plans between June and December of 1987, it is too late on July 15 to start to hire people to take care of the paraplanning functions. They need to be trained effectively to use the system you have devised by the time your office gets deluged with requests for your financial planning services. You need to decide, therefore, which things in the process you personally want to do within your office, and which things you want to delegate to other financial planners, partners, or employees. Employees can be hired who are expert at writing newsletters, conducting data-gathering interviews, doing general administrative work, unscrambling securities service problems, and so forth. If you can define very clearly what services you wish to provide, then you can structure your staff and your own time to provide those services in a timely manner. The type of equipment, including computer software and hardware, the number and functions of the telephone lines, copiers, and other office equipment, will be dependent on the number of people in the firm and their responsibilities.

OVERHEAD COSTS

Now we must consider the cost to the planning firm of providing service to clients and the willingness of the clients to pay for the services they receive. There is an ongoing debate in the industry between "fees or commission" as a method of compensation, which in my own opinion is irrelevant. The issue is more properly the competence of the planner and the quality and integrity of the advice given. The overhead costs of a financial planning practice must be met; the rent and the other bills must be paid in a timely manner. It is the responsibility of the planner to put the interest of the client first, and there is inevitable conflict of interest if the planner chooses only certain types of product to solve all client financial problems.

This leads to the inescapable conclusion that, in order to keep the advisory functions of a financial planning practice well structured and profitable, it is necessary to devise a method of compensation to meet the overhead costs which is probably not going to be commission-based, or at least not strictly commission-based. Hence the great movement within the financial services industry is toward the charging of professional financial planning fees for professional service rendered. Some fees will be based on percentages of assets, net worth, or other bases. Others will be charged by the hour or by the project. Fees, however, should be sufficient to provide an incentive for the services to be completed appropriately.

CONCLUSION

In reviewing the wide range of financial planning services and products available in today's marketplace, the role of the financial planner as a general practitioner able to diagnose problems and suggest solutions over a wide range of areas is crucial. It is not an easy role, however, and many practitioners feel more comfortable specializing in one or other of the financial services or financial products available.

For this reason, it is necessary from time to time to review and redefine the structure of your firm to ensure that the services offered are indeed still meeting the needs of your clients and your own goals as an advisor.

"To be creative, we must feel creative. Too little sleep and too much stress can contribute to a tired and dull view of everything in our world."

—GLENDA D. KEMPLE, CPA, CFP

Glenda Kemple, CPA, CFP, joined Carter Financial Management in 1982. Ms. Kemple is recognized nationally in the financial services industry. She is currently serving as the President of the North Texas chapter of the IAFP, was recently elected to the ICFP National Board of Directors and has been admitted to the Registry of Financial Planning Practitioners. She received her B.A. from the University of Missouri.

In demand as a speaker and instructor, Ms. Kemple teaches financial planning courses for the American Institute of Certified Public Accountants. In Texas, she has addressed a myriad of groups, conducting seminars for customers of several banks, savings and loans, major corporations, and various civic and professional groups.

Using Your Own Creativity to Build and Nurture Your Practice

Ask five people what creative thinking means and you're likely to get five different responses. As educator Rudolph Flesch put it, "Creative thinking may simply mean the realization that there's no particular virtue in doing things the way they have always been done."

Creativity is the ability to look at situations differently and apply the facts presented to create a solution. To quote Pablo Picasso, "Some painters transform the sun into a yellow spot; others transform a yellow spot into the sun." Developing this ability and then using it to build and continue the ongoing nurturing process of a financial planning practice will be the focus of this section.

A person who is not creative is stuck in a rut. This person does things out of habit, satisfied with the status quo. Creative people are not satisfied with the status quo. The future will always belong to the discontented.

Financial planning as we know it is undergoing a transition. Computers and competitors are but two causes of the change. In order to survive, you must operate at a more efficient and higher level of creativity.

INDIVIDUAL CREATIVITY

To be creative, we must feel creative. Too little sleep and too much stress can contribute to a tired and dull view of everything in our world.

Adopting a plan for consistent exercise can be one of the best steps to turn on your creativity. For example, a personal commitment to run three times a week can be good for both your body and your mind. Many planners generate their most creative ideas for their practice on the tennis courts or running track. For example, you may be wrestling with a tough plan implementation problem. Simply freeing your mind of external disruptions such as the telephone and other people may be the switch to turn on your creative light. Consistent exercise can stimulate your cutting edge.

Consciously avoiding burnout also chases away the dullness. Well-spaced long vacations out of town and long weekends spent in a new place can help you to stay fresh. Upon return from one of these trips, not only should you be rested and ready to charge forward, but you should have many new ideas and prospects for growth in your practice. Many planners find that visits to the mountains or beach are just the ticket. Even a ride on a chair lift up a beautiful, snow-covered slope can clear your mind for new thoughts.

ENVIRONMENTAL CREATIVITY

Where you work and what your office looks like also plays an important role in just how effectively you conduct your business. Your office should be a place where you enjoy spending time. The office layout and furniture should be comfortable and attractive. Taking pains to rid your office of the piles and clutter that this business generates helps. Fresh flowers and plants also contribute to a personal feel to your work environment.

Another idea to consider to stimulate your right-brain activities is to listen to classical music throughout the day. While you may want to turn it down for client meetings and for periods of deep concentration, leaving it on as background music can stimulate creativity.

PROFESSIONAL ENCOUNTERS

Even though information overload is a problem in the financial planning business, continuing education is always an opportunity for creative thinking. Seminars and courses in our field are multiplying. By attending programs, you can sharpen your skills in your weaker areas, learn about new facets of the business, and develop new ideas for your practice.

The writer has found that attending large national meetings provides tremendous opportunities to be creative and to bring home new ideas. To make this work, you must recognize at the outset that every program you attend may not exactly meet your expectations. Keep a pad of paper for daydreaming. When the instructor launches into an area that you're already familiar with or if you simply get bored in a given session, encourage the daydreaming and record your thoughts and ideas. You may find that the time and money spent at a seminar is worthwhile even if you come home with more ideas from your daydreaming pad than from the seminar notebook.

Seminars also provide an opportunity to network with other colleagues. It's amazing the unrestrained idea exchange that can occur among planners when they are from different locales and are not competitors. Use these meetings as an opportunity to learn first hand what's working for another planner, and be willing to share your own ideas freely.

CAPITALIZING ON ADVERSITY

When times are great, we don't have to be creative. When the phone never stops ringing with new clients' calls, are we forced to think of a better way? Of course not, but let adversity strike and things quickly change. Reduced profit margins and changing tax laws are but two examples of adversities we must face.

Accepting that problems usually force us to make changes, perhaps we should view adversity as challenging rather than dreadful. For example, tax acts continue to affect our practice and our clients' investments. Rather than run for cover and leave the business because tax shelters are dead, capitalize on the adversity. Use your creativity to change your business. While one form of investment may be gone, many more are available.

Personal adversity is also an opportunity. We're all familiar with the challenges that Dallas real estate syndicator Craig Hall faced in restructuring his real estate programs. Every major business publication carried stories of his threatened demise. Did he just fold up his tent and run when the going got tough? Of course not. He directed his company to drastically cut costs and then dug in for some very hard work to restructure his many loans to save the partnerships. Today, as a result of this experience and the publicity it engendered, Hall Financial has embarked on a new business venture to help S & Ls stuck with nonperforming real estate portfolios and to assist general partners with deals which need restructuring. Isn't this a classic case of turning lemons into lemonade?

TECHNOLOGICAL CREATIVITY

Today's economic and investment environment encourages confusion. The ability to put together details and reassemble them into a cohesive and unique strategy is required.

Technology has the capability of releasing and harnessing creative approaches beyond our current abilities. For example, where would the new products in life insurance, such as universal life and variable life, be today without the computer? The ability to play "what ifs" with quick responses can be just the ticket needed to spark your creativity. Technical creativity is the ability to come up with interlinked ideas and then to communicate these to the client for implementation.

Computer illiteracy, which many of us suffer from, must be stopped in order for us to practice creatively. Many new software programs allow us to do a better job of analysis, time management, and record keeping. Increasing the efficiency of our practice can help to increase our creativity by relieving us of the stress caused by the unmanageable piles.

BRAINSTORMING SESSIONS

One of the most successful ways to bring out your creative side and to develop new ideas is through a relaxed brainstorming session with a favorite colleague. The rules of the session must be clear from the beginning. First and foremost, there is no "dumb" idea. Each idea deserves an airing before it can be squelched.

You may pick up a slow day when clients are on vacation. Meet a favorite colleague at a swimming pool or similar watering hole to have this meeting. You may want to begin with a subject matter in mind to brainstorm about and then just let your minds run wild. During these sessions, you can develop many concrete, new approaches to the business.

For example, several years ago this writer and a colleague held such a meeting. We were having problems working with our clients' CPAs. We developed the concept of a lunch seminar; we invited a group of our clients' CPAs and other influential people, such as bankers and attorneys, to come to our office for lunch. We provided a box lunch for our guests. During the first half hour, while we all ate, we gave everyone an opportunity to meet one another and network. During the last half of the lunch we described the services of the firm and arranged a subsequent meeting with our clients' CPAs to review the clients' plans. This resulted in greater cooperation with the CPAs and increased referrals.

PERIODICALS

Getting enough information on financial planning is hardly a problem. The stack of mail and periodicals is always immense. Not only do these show us the current trends, but they can spark new ideas. It's a matter of mindset when you begin reading that determines what you'll get out of it. Keep scissors, a highlight marker, and a note pad readily at hand when you read so that you can clip new ideas for your "idea" or source file.

Books and seminars on the topic of creativity can be valuable. Two recommended books are *A Kick in the Seat of the Pants* and *A Whack on the Side of the Head*, (published by Warner Books and Harper & Row) by Roger von Oech. In the first book the author recommends the following for high creative performance:

When you're searching for new information be an explorer.

When you're turning your resources into new ideas, be an artist.

When you're evaluating the merits of an idea, be a judge.

When you're carrying your idea into action, be a warrior.

Your ability to use what's between your ears to spark your own creativity is limited only by you. This constant quest for a better way will result in a profitable and fun practice of financial planning.

"The approach to success is to keep your cost well-defined and well-controlled while you are building your practice through quality performance and intensive effort."

—ANDREW M. RICH, CFP

Cost Control in the Small Financial Planning Practice

Andrew M. Rich, CFP, is President of AMR Planning Services, Inc., a Registered Investment Advisory firm. He holds a bachelor of arts degree in economics from Queens College of the City University of New York and an M.S. in taxation from Long Island University.

Mr. Rich is the author of *How to Survive and Succeed in a Small Financial Planning Practice*, published by Reston Publishing Company, is a contributing author to *The Money Encyclopedia*, published by Harper and Row, and is profiled in *The Financial Planner: A New Professional*, published by Longman Publishing. He has been quoted in numerous financial publications.

Mr. Rich is an Adjunct Assistant Professor of Financial Management at New York University and a member of the Adjunct Faculty of the College for Financial Planning. He is a Registered Representative licensed through USLICO Securities Corporation and a General Agent for the Bankers Security Life Insurance Society. Mr. Rich is currently the Ethics Vice President of the Long Island chapter of the IAFP and is a member of the ICFP.

There is the old adage that it takes money to make money. Although this statement may be quite true for certain types of businesses, especially a capital-intensive business or a service that requires heavy capital outlay such as a medical or dental practice, it is invalid for a small financial planning firm. For it does not take money to make money; it takes effort. In other words, one must spend long, hard hours devoted to securing and servicing a strong client base with the objective of building clients with little, if any, turnover. If you build a client only to lose that client and have to develop another one, the net result is zero. You can say all you want about marketing but in reality it is an outlay of time for which you cannot bill for services. And billing—maximum billing—is the key to a successful practice. Your objective, in my opinion, should be to build clients and then hold those clients to the point of saturation. Of course, in practice, you will not hold every client. The objective is to hold as many compatible clients as you can.

There are those who are advocates of the fancy offices, the super-powered computers, and the gold-laden facade aimed to hold and impress clients. Although these do work initially, I believe that it is you, your performance and the manner in which you service your clients that retain their trust and faith. The myth that a lot of money is necessary to be successful in this business is only in the imagination of the product vendors and the egotists. Again, we are talking about a small practice and not a large, multiplanner firm. That is, without question, a different world with different rules.

I have been in a full-time practice for more than seven years now, and I find it interesting that I spend little more in certain expense areas than I did when I first started. Only salary expense, a variable cost, has had a radical change. And even though my net income has increased manyfold, I still enforce my practice of intensive cost control. Am I cheap? I do not think so. I am just practical. Why spend money for the sake of spending money? Your objective, just as you would advise any client, is to maximize the bottom line. If you were a corporate director, you would have a duty to the shareholders. A financial planner has a responsibility to himself to maximize profits. Accordingly, I value the approach that if it is necessary and adds to the total utility of my business, either long-term or short-term, it gets purchased. If it is unnecessary, it does not. As previously stated, I even take a dim view of advertising, since it costs money and requires an outlay of time that is not billable. Your business should strive to turn each hour that you work into a productive and billable hour. Financial planning is a service-oriented, referral business where the bulk of your referrals should come from the fruits of your hard labor. A steady stream of client referrals does not cost you any down time or expense outlay for marketing. Top-quality professionals do not need to advertise; their clients do it for them.

The approach to success is to keep your costs well-defined and well-controlled while you are building your practice through quality performance and intensive effort. Ironically, what really counts is the net income, not the gross income. If you have to outlay expense after expense just to pay the landlord, the bank, the computer company, the advertising media, and the employees, what have you really accomplished? In my first book, *How to Survive and Succeed in a Small Financial Planning Practice,* I stated that you could operate out of a telephone booth if you had to. This I still hold, in spirit, to be true. The vast majority of your clients will not reject you because you do not wear a $500 suit, drive a Mercedes Benz, or carry a Louis Vuitton briefcase; they do reject you because you do not care about them.

Costs can be classified into two types: fixed and variable. Fixed costs are steady, periodic costs that do not vary with the volume of business such as rent, lease payments, essential salaries, and insurance payments. You would have relatively the same costs whether you earned $1 or $100,000. The heavier the fixed cost, the more you have to earn just to break even. Variable costs, on the other hand, fluctuate, based on business volume and management priorities. Nonessential salaries, publications, advanced education, advertising, travel, and entertainment are examples of variable costs. A practitioner has almost total control of the outlay. The biggest mistake that I have seen many financial planners make is to immediately get strapped with heavy fixed costs.

One of the parameters of the financial planning business is that it is a business subject to sudden change. In fact, of all the businesses that I can think of, the financial planning business would be more subject to change than most. We live our daily lives in a sea of volatility. The tax laws change each time a politician thinks he or she has a better idea; the economy changes on a daily basis, while the stock market is as predictable as a roulette wheel. If you read the *Wall Street Journal*, bond prices plunge on Monday, soar on Tuesday, and oscillate through a myriad of descriptive verbs that only financial writers can create. And then there is regulation, the SEC, the NASD, the IRS, the state regulators, and insurance departments. What will happen next? Whatever it is, only one fact is clear: there will be change—a great deal of change.

A business operating in such an environment will find it difficult to operate if it is tied to heavy fixed costs coupled with antiquated methods. The modern financial planning business, large or small, must be able to move with the times, to shift priorities on a moment's notice. Today you may rely on the majority of your income from commissions and not fees, while tomorrow may dictate the complete opposite. Or vice versa. The small planner must be able to swing through these cyclical periods without always having to recoup dollars outlaid for antiquated equipment and material. Then there is another major factor of change that you will no doubt experience along your career path. Your priorities may change. Suddenly, you may decide that you no longer wish to work the hours or the weekends that you have been working and opt for an easier lifestyle and less stress. A financial planning business locked into heavy fixed cost may cause a problem for a practitioner who changes personal priorities. One must realize that very few financial planners have had the same priority since the day they started.

Let's review some of the costs that a planner encounters in a small financial planning practice:

Your Office

Rent is a fixed cost that varies widely depending on your location. If you are going to rent an office, thoroughly review your space requirements and rent only what you specifically need. If your thoughts are toward expansion, stay with a short-term lease (two to three years), or rent a larger facility only if you can sublease. I like to think of this in a way as a "covered rent option." Many planners may even find sharing space with other planners or other professionals to be the answer. The common sharing of expenses such as secretary and/or receptionist, copiers, computers, professional publications, and the like, can significantly reduce the cost of these items. Today, even the least expensive professional tax service runs several hundred dollars. And do not rule out working from your home. As described in Alvin Toffler's book, *The Third Wave*, the electronic cottage is here to stay.

Computerization

What do you really need? That is what you should buy. It takes time to figure out just what is necessary, so do not let your impatience propel you into a mistake. The key is to select the proper software that will do the job necessary for a successful practice. Selection, of course, is a matter of due diligence and common sense. If you are going to spend $5000 on software and another $1000 or so a year to keep the software updated, make sure that you can derive enough revenue to make the purchase worthwhile. Quite a number of planners have invested tens of thousands of dollars in state-of-the-art integrated packages that serve as nice decorations in their offices. Be careful! Know your needs and make sure that you learn word processing, spread sheet, and data base applications. I also suggest that you buy the most advanced hardware that you can afford. Buying the fastest and the best computer will only enhance its useful life. I suggest only an AT level computer. Do not rule out a portable. Today's portable has been shrunk to the point of real portability. Remember, financial planners do not get paid while waiting for computers to do their thing. Fast computers generally add to productivity.

Publications

Are you going to spend all day reading, or are you going to work on productive, revenue-producing financial planning? In essence, you can not read everything. A good tax service, a good financial planning service, and a few periodicals to keep current can cover 95 percent of your needs. Subscribing to every publication is not only costly, it can be counterproductive, since you might have the tendency to read rather than work. Studying financial planning is wonderful, but there are not enough hours in the day to master it all. Settle for what is essential. That is plenty!

Your Brochure

As you are no doubt aware, the Investment Advisors Act of 1940 requires you to give to your clients a copy of your ADV Part II or a brochure containing material required in the ADV. Since financial planners may, with good reason, change their practice very periodically, I do not suggest sinking significant dollars into glossy brochures that may wind up in the trash can. Every time you make a material change, the Investment Advisors Act requires you to update your brochure. In my practice, I change part of my brochure at least once a year. Accordingly, I resort to a word processor and a photocopier to produce a very adequate brochure. Do not forget: This is the age of desktop publishing, and brochure costs can be kept to a minimum if you use just a little ingenuity.

Other Costs

There are many other costs that you encounter such as employees, office supplies, education and training, advertising, interest expense, telephone, travel and entertainment, automobile, insurance, professional fees, and licensing. To control these costs requires little more than common sense. Is the cost justified? Does it add to current or future productivity? Is it egotistical? How do all these costs measure in the aggregate? If you are doing any type of cash flow planning for your client, you should be doing it for yourself and your practice.

Perhaps the most important aspect of cost control is knowing where you are at any point in time and on a periodic basis. This, of course, translates into balance-sheet and income-statement analysis. You must control your business on a continuous basis. You can not afford to wait until the end of the year to analyze your profit and loss. Accordingly, I strongly advocate the use of your own general ledger program that you update on the first of each new month. I find it sad when financial planners tell me that they wait for their accountants to come in to figure out what they are doing. This is one business where that is inexcusable. The task of a financial planner is to plan for others. You must do it for yourself. All it takes is just an hour or two a month. That's it!

The time to spend freely is when you are making more money than you know what to do with. Even then, the spending may not be justified.

"The satisfied client will add to your bottom line and give you referrals."

—JAMES J. BURKE, CFP

"Flat Fees" Method and the "Relationship-oriented" Practice vs. The "Transaction-oriented" Practice: Which One Is Right For You?

James J. Burke is a Certified Financial Planner and manages a growing financial planning practice on Long Island. Prior to becoming a CFP, Jim earned a bachelor's degree from New York University and enjoyed a successful career in the field of international banking.

Jim is a member of the Institute of Certified Financial Planners and was elected president of the Long Island Society in June of 1985. He has taught Personal Financial Management at New York University and has conducted a number of training seminars for Citibank, the nation's largest bank.

He has appeared in well-known publications such as the *New York Times, Newsday,* and *U.S. News and World Report.* His practice specializes in real estate investments and advice for home-buyers and -sellers.

The vast majority of people in need of your services have never before had any contact with a full-time financial planner. When they call for an appointment, they usually aren't quite sure what they should expect—and they often don't have a firm idea of what they should expect to pay for your services, either.

Attorneys have provided legal advice for centuries, and almost everyone has a good idea what they do—and don't do—and what it costs the client. Likewise, accountants' services are fairly standardized, and the person hiring an accountant for the first time will probably have realistic expectations about the services and costs.

However, the financial planning profession is so young, and the array of services offered is so broad, that a random sample of a dozen practitioners might uncover a dozen different *modi operandi* and fee schedules. It should not be surprising, then, that the potential new client enters your office for the first time with a high degree of bewilderment and apprehension.

In the early stages of building my client base, I found that it was very helpful to raise the potential client's comfort level by letting him or her know right away that there would be a "cap" on my fee. After all, most consumers would be justifiably suspicious of someone who was proposing to bill them on an unlimited per-hour basis, especially when that person had not yet had time to build a level of trust and confidence.

This policy of capped fees became an immediate success, as I quickly found that new clients were willing to pay even more for a complete financial plan than I had previously been charging as long as they knew *exactly* what the cost would be. It fit well with my business style, because I set out to build a "relationship-oriented" practice rather than a "transaction-oriented" practice.

A transaction-oriented practice weighs the relative merits of doing business with a particular client based on how profitable the contemplated transaction will be. No other factors are as important as the bottom line.

The decision to take on each new client depends on the degree of instant gratification that is expected. Under this methodology, one might use low-cost advice as a loss leader to gain other business. Your practice will probably be very profitable in its early years if you master the skills needed to be transaction-oriented. Obviously, one's method of compensation must be "fee plus commission" in order to be transaction-oriented.

The relationship-oriented practice, on the other hand, emphasizes building strong bonds over long periods of time. You may accept new clients with whom your relationship does not initially have much impact on your bottom line but who can be expected to blossom into profitable clients in the long run.

At the conclusion of the first interview with a potential client, an experienced planner will usually be able to make a reasonably accurate estimation of the number of hours of work involved. That number, plus a certain margin for errors, multiplied by the planner's hourly rate results in the flat fee needed to make the case worth taking. This has worked well for me, because I am almost always fairly compensated for the time I spend on a plan. Planners who use low-cost fees to attract clients that *may* bring in large investment or insurance sales may be disappointed if the client takes his or her low-cost plan and implements with someone else.

Andy Rich has often spoken of the merits of building your practice slowly and steadily with a strong emphasis on providing a high level of personalized service and establishing yourself as a trusted advisor over a period of time. Without ever mentioning the phrase ''relationship-oriented practice,'' he has embraced the concept and urged others to do so.

How well would the flat-fee method fit in with your practice? Your own comfort level regarding this approach may depend on whether your prior business experience was transaction-oriented or relationship-oriented. Planners who come from a background in the brokerage, insurance, or syndication areas tend to be transaction-oriented, whereas those who are attorneys, accountants, or bankers will probably be more relationship-oriented.

These two orientations are not mutually exclusive, however. In fact, they can work quite well together. The seasoned planner will no doubt possess the skills and experience to be able to build strong bonds with clients and go after the really big sales, too. After all, satisfied clients will add to your bottom line and give you referrals regardless of which method resulted in their becoming satisfied clients.

"Planners must recognize that the value of their advice and service is significant. It cannot be depreciated by the providers of the service, or it will be regarded similarly by the recipient."

—JERRY L. FRECHETTE

Converting Free Clients to Fee Clients

Jerry Frechette is a principal and Senior Vice President of Financial Planning Consultants, Inc. of Middletown, Ohio. His responsibilities include marketing of comprehensive financial planning services to corporate executives and individuals, coordinating the financial planning process with internal planners and professional advisers, supervising the implementation, monitoring follow-through with clients, and serving as the internal compliance officer for the firm. Prior to joining FPC in January, 1980, he spent twenty years in banking and served as an instructor at Miami University, teaching management of financial institutions, commercial, mortgage, and installment lending. He has served on various boards, including the Cincinnati chapter of the American Institute of Banking. Frechette is also a principal instructor in the training sessions of Confidential Planning Services, Inc., an international network of financial planning firms.

Many persons make the transition from product sales to fee-based financial planning. There are two problems encountered on this journey: how to convert old clients to fee-paying clients and how to receive an adequate fee.

There seems to be a sense of guilt towards these older clients—as if providing free service in the past placed the salesperson in debt to them. Logic might say that the situation should be reversed. Many of these customers have received service and support for a long time without paying any fee.

However, as illogical as it may be, the salesperson turned financial planner has a sense of guilt towards these old clients. That is a regrettable attitude as well as an unprofitable one. Fortunately, it is an attitude which can be corrected.

This attitude commenced with the orientation of the young sales trainee by the product manufacturer. To put it another way, it is a guilt trip put on the agent by the insurance company. The young salesperson is conditioned to believe that service should be free, and that free service would then lead to a purchase of products by the recipient.

When one stands apart from this, it is easy to understand why the insurance company or securities firm might encourage free service. They are not the ones giving the free service. Over the last century the life insurance industry has groomed a sales force conditioned to the philosophy, "Free service earns the sale."

The Agent's Job

It was perhaps appropriate to provide free service when the principal sales training involved policy programming and simplistic analysis. When there were only a few types of policies and rate books changed every two or three years, the sales representative had it much easier. Today, the following elements complicate the process of selling a "simple life insurance policy."

- Variable policies are also securities, which require additional licensing, education, disclosure, and more administration after the sale.
- Many purchasers need and acquire very low-cost term insurance. The lower commission percentage and the much lower initial premium can reduce the net commission by as much as 80 percent. There is not a sufficient compensation for free service.
- Many universal life policies are illustrated showing *three* interest rates: guaranteed, current rate, and a slightly lower rate. This increases the multiplicity of ways to illustrate the same product and greatly complicates the communication process. The computers and training required to illustrate the universal life flexibility must also be considered.
- State-regulated disclosure procedures require more paper and more time to be spent with the client.
- The income tax treatment of policies has been further complicated, and tax considerations now weigh more heavily in the consumer's and agent's decision process.
- Many more organizations are selling insurance: direct marketing, credit unions, banks, savings institutions, educational institutions, professional associations, securities firms, and, of course, financial planners.

To give the client added value in the way of financial advice has likewise been complicated by new regulation, legislation, deregulation, ever-changing tax codes, and more people giving the consumer free and frequently conflicting advice.

With "60 Minutes," "The McNeill-Lehrer Report," and Lifetime and Financial News Cable networks, the consumer can be financially redirected at least 20 times per week.

Part of the agent's and planner's job must now be to keep people from attempting to become credit card millionaires or supreme distributors in some pyramid scheme. Couple this with the effect of the so-called financial planners who are not really qualified and the "replacement artists" of well-known infamy. It is almost a full-time job keeping clients from harm's way!

The Planner's Job

The financial planner embraces a much wider scope of responsibility than the person acting only as an agent. The planner must probe more deeply into goals and objectives as well as all financial facts. It is not that this knowledge would have been inappropriate for the agent. Much of it was merely not necessary.

The planner must be familiar with each form of investment that the client owns as well as those the client does not own. After all, if what the client owns is not accomplishing the objective, what must it be shifted toward?

Financial planning has rightly been described as a process, rather than a product. The essential elements include:

- Gathering all the client information and documents.
- Determining the client's goals and attitudes toward investment risk, career path, and social purposes, and toward other family members.
- Confirming all of the above with the client so as to be focused on target when moving to the next steps.
- Analyzing the client's problems. This includes not only quantifying but determining the timing of the increasing or declining liabilities and assets. A far more involved cash-flow analysis is required than merely determining if the client can continue the monthly insurance premium.
- Developing recommendations for consideration by the client. Since very few clients can immediately accomplish all their objectives, this means developing priorities and alternatives. It is critical to the client and the planner that no problem go unaddressed.
- Communicating these problems and recommendations to the client. A major burden, this requires verbal and psychological skills as well as a financially literate background. All this would be ineffective if there were also not a great capacity for empathy.
- Presenting implementation schedules and checklists for approval by the client. If the client were taken only to the point of analysis and recommendation, then nothing would have been accomplished. Unfortunately, many poorly trained planners view implementation as merely selling some of their product, be it securities, real estate, hard assets, or insurance.

Procrastination is the greatest reason that most Americans fail to achieve financial independence. People always intend to save more money, intend to invest it wisely, intend to arrange their affairs so as to reduce taxes, and intend to protect their assets against foreseeable perils. A critical responsibility of the financial planner is to monitor the progress of the clients towards the accomplishment of their goals.

Overcoming the Free Service Guilt

Agents and planners must recognize that the value of their advice and service is significant. It cannot be depreciated by the providers of the service, or it will be regarded similarly by the recipient.

If an agent-planner says, ''I have been taking some courses on financial subjects,'' it will not seem very important. But if the agent had prefaced his discussion with the following, it would be perceived much differently:

> For the past four years I have been engaged in a professional education program through the —— institution. This has included courses on investments, income taxes, estate planning, risk management, asset allocation, and economics. These were culminated by a series of exams and the professional designation of ——.
>
> In addition to this, I have attended a number of lengthy conferences and educational retreats to refine the techniques learned in the courses.
>
> My firm has also made a major investment in computer equipment, sophisticated software, and an extensive library. We have retained several highly regarded specialists.
>
> We are fully prepared to offer you the most professional financial advice and service available anywhere. Furthermore, I have the advantage of having known you for —— years and having already become familiar with your insurance-related needs. Now we are qualified to address your other financial areas.

If the planner does not make light of his preparation, qualifications and commitment, neither will the client.

Evaluating the Benefits of Planning

If a planner is to be compensated only on his or her hourly involvement, then the hourly rate must be large enough to include staff, capital, continuing education, and all overhead expenses. This will produce a fairly high hourly rate, which many planners find difficult to quote at the outset of their careers.

Other new planners, having read consumer magazines, think of planning fees in the range of $100 to $300. If that is their starting point, then it is a major leap for them to contemplate a $750 fee.

This low-fee concept has been supported by research conducted by LIMRA, the Life Insurance Marketing Research Association, and by several other published studies. LIMRA's customers are the insurance companies. In these studies, consumers were asked what they felt was reasonable to pay for a financial plan. Surprise! Most consumers who replied felt that $250 was a good fee.

Now let us suppose you were approached by a car salesman. He says to you, ''Outside your house, sitting at the curb, I have a car I would like you to purchase. You have agreed that you need a way to get to work and to social activities. How much would you like to pay?''

Quite naturally, you might say, ''Yes, I need a car, but what type is it? How many doors and what year? Does it have power steering and air conditioning? Is it new? Does it have a warranty? Until I know more about the benefits, I cannot possibly tell you the amount I would be willing to pay.''

Now suppose the car salesman said, ''Actually, I have three cars. One costs $250, one costs $1000, and the other is a real bargain at $4000. Now, which do you want?''

Again, you have to respond, "I don't know! Does the $250 model run? Is it safe? How many miles are there on the $1000 model? What are the accessories on the $4000 model, and why might I want it at four times the cost?"

This is precisely analogous to asking a consumer the following question: "What amount would you consider it appropriate to pay for a financial plan? $150? $250? $500? $1000? $4000?"

Without any knowledge of benefits, the consumer cannot make a buying decision. No one likes to pay insurance premiums. But when customers perceive the benefits, then they will buy, and not until then.

But do financial planners convey the benefits effectively? For the most part, the answer is a resounding "No!" Many experienced planners do not prospect at all. They are totally dependent upon the calls they receive from the friends and family of their satisfied customers.

This does not mean that financial planners do not possess good communication skills. In fact, most financial planners have exceptional communication skills. But since their primary role is no longer that of a salesperson, they do not "sell" financial planning.

To persuade the customer to agree to financial planning requires the same essential points that selling a life insurance policy or any tangible product does, such as:

- Arouse interest
- Establish the need
- Create desire
- Convey a solution
- Ask for the order

Selling the financial planning engagement is distinct from selling a financial product. What the customer is buying is the belief that the subsequent service will convey benefits that are well in excess of costs.

While most planners have a sales background, the tendency is to put all the sales training behind when one is securing the financial engagement. This is a serious mistake. The planner should go through the five steps of the sales cycle listed above. There are several guidelines:

1. Be prepared. The planner will need brochures, a sample financial plan and a fee chart or fee guidelines. These should be attractively packaged, but need not be elaborate.
2. Have a track to run on. My suggestion is to have two copies of an agenda for the meeting, one for the prospect and one for the planner. By following the agenda the planner will proceed to the conclusion.
3. Use motivational tools. While these could be verbal, most planners will benefit from using slides, overheads, flip charts, or audiovisuals.
4. Have a sample financial plan that illustrates a client in the approximate age and income range as the prospect.
5. Have a technique for conveying the prospect's expected cost-benefit ratio. Perhaps illustrate the cost-benefit ratio of the sample financial plan.
6. Have an engagement letter or agreement ready for execution. How else could you ask for the order?

Let's return to our original problem—how to turn old free clients into fee clients. First, we have prepared our discourse on the preparations made for financial planning. We have written it down and rehearsed it. We are believable, and we believe we can deliver superb, valuable service. Second, we have prepared all the materials and props needed for the interview. We are prepared to demonstrate how planning has benefited others and that the prospect can expect significant value. In preparing the sample plan, we have rekindled our conviction that financial planning is a truly valuable service.

To Conclude the Transaction

The prospect has been aroused to the benefits of planning, has acknowledged the personal need, and has indicated a desire to plan for retirement, education, estate distribution, and the like. The prospect has reviewed a sample plan and understands that his problems and the solutions will vary, but that significant improvement can be expected. The prospect understands the commitment he or she is making in terms of data collection and interviews.

Now we are ready to ask for the order:

"John, you have seen the benefits that we were able to produce for the persons in the sample plan. The cost of their service was only $3000, and yet the benefits were over $50,000. That represented a cost-to-benefit ratio of 1 to 25. For every dollar they paid, we generated $17 of benefits.

"Our firm believes that for the financial planning engagement to be successful, for you as well as for us, the cost/benefit ratio must be at least 1 to 5. We are looking for a long-term relationship with our clients, and that is what we feel is the *minimum*.

"Based on what you have told us about your goals, and what I know about you because I have handled your (insurance), the fee to provide our service would be $3000. That will include all the steps we discussed, plus assistance in implementing your plan.

(Optional) "However, since I am already very familiar with your insurance program, we would extend a 20 percent discount. Your fee would be only $2400.

"You will have our service until the end of the year. After that, you can renew our services at a reduced rate if you would like.

"Now, based on our 1 to 5 cost/benefit ratio, that means your benefits would be at least $15,000. If we are figuring this plan based on the future value of those benefits in ten years, the benefit would be $30,000. In other words, we would expect to improve your net worth by at least $30,000 over the next ten years. Do you feel that $30,000 warrants an investment of your $2400 plus the time to sit down with us?

"If you would like to go ahead, we can complete the engagement letter now—or you can send a copy back to us with your check."

What if the prospect says, "But you've always handled my insurance matters for free?" That appears to be an objection, a question seeking a response, but it is much like the purchaser of a Cadillac asking about the gas mileage. He asks, but really doesn't care—he's going to buy a $25,000 car or not, and gas mileage just doesn't matter. The response might be:

"Yes, I have handled your insurance with no fee. You had some big insurance problems, and you purchased insurance from me in the past. But now, we are looking at many more problems: education, retirement, investment diversification. You wouldn't want to try to solve those problems with more insurance, would you? Wouldn't you want me to be objective and to recommend everything that might help you achieve greater financial success?''

For the prospect who is not absolutely sure, you might take the pressure off a bit with a second close, as follows:

''John, you have been a client and friend for over 15 years. I don't want you to feel pressured in any way. You know what we're trying to accomplish—to help you get from where you are today to where you would like to be financially. You know the cost, and you know the minimum benefit.

''Take this folder and the engagement letter home. Think about this. If you want to proceed, sign one copy and drop it in the mail with your check for the first half of the fee.''

If you are still a bit uncomfortable, you might offer a guarantee:

''John, when we've finished your planning, if you are not 100 percent satisfied that we have accomplished what we set out to do, then I will refund your fee. You can't ask for anything better than that, can you?''

Personally, I feel the guarantee is unnecessary and a bit unprofessional. Other professionals do not offer to refund their fee. But a planner will do much better to offer a guarantee for a sufficient fee than to discount the fee or charge too little.

Try these techniques. They will work for you as they have for many other planners.

"Fee-based service planning is the foundation of planner-client relations, and fee for service will be the revenue source for the firm's future survival."

—WILLIAM C. HEATH, CFP

Understanding the Service Side of the Financial Planning Business

William C. Heath, CFP, has a bachelor of science degree from the University of Southern California and an MBA from the University of Houston. He played eleven years of baseball behind the plate for the Houston Astros, the Detroit Tigers, and the Chicago Cubs. Off season, he spent three years as an auditor for Haskins & Sells, Certified Public Accountants; after hanging up his mitt in 1970, he became a member of the professional audit staff of Price Waterhouse & Company.

In 1972, Mr. Heath founded William C. Heath & Associates, which in 1983 became the Center for Financial Planning. He has lectured to many educational, civic, and business organizations on a variety of topics and has written several professional articles.

Mr. Heath is an adjunct faculty member of the College for Financial Planning, president of the Houston society of the Institute of Certified Financial Planners, a member of the International Association for Financial Planning, and a registered representative and member of the Advisory Board of Southmark Financial Services. He was nominated for CFP of the Year in 1985.

Service—always a promise, seldom a reality. Yet, for the financial planner seeking to establish himself with other financial professionals, service is the one uncompromising essential. Without service, the financial planner is little more than a peddler. Webster defines service as "complying with the commands or demands of the client." The planner's work should be to help clients through solving their problems or needs. Problem solving is generally accomplished by either products or services, or a combination of both. Herein lies the difference in financial planners. Providers of products pay commissions, and services pay fees for time as the means of compensation to the planner. Therefore, the form of compensation often defines the expectation of financial planning methodology utilized in client problem solving.

Financial planning was founded by product problem solvers. They saw the need to integrate the insurance and securities product approaches to solutions with the fee for (time) service of the attorney, accountant, banker, actuary, etc. That coordinator became the financial planner.

Over the past fifteen years, financial planning has come to depend on the fee for (time) services of a planner to document the comprehensive integration of the services of these other specialized-service professionals. Planners have become professional coordinators, choosing not to be specialists, but rather catalysts that cause solutions to be found for the client's problems. Although financial planners are not specialists professionally, many have areas of specialization which compliment their practice of financial planning.

The definition of the fee-for-service financial planner must be *a catalytic coordinator of problem solutions*. These planners prefer to document the fact-finding and conclusions in a written plan that serves as the resource for guiding the implementation of products or additional services.

The commission planner is marketing-oriented and tends not to like the detail necessary to write comprehensive plans. The fee-for-service planner is analytically oriented and tends not to like the marketing of products. The hybrid fee-and-commission planner has a little of both. Since fee-based plans are less profitable to the planner than commission products, the fee-and-commission planners can provide extensive fee services because of the commissions earned from the products implemented. Also, fees are kept about one-third lower due to commissions earned.

There are far more commission-only planners than fee-only planners. As the public becomes more willing to pay fees for their financial planning, we have seen a proliferation of fee-only or fee-and-commission planners. Additionally, the decline in product commission payments has caused many of the commission-only planners to begin to charge fees for their services. I have always believed that you get what you pay for and that if we, as professional planners, expect our services to have value, then we must stop giving them away. The issue is not that your commissions compensate you for your services in the long run. The point is how the receiver of your service values it. To see how valuable your client perceives your commission-only service to be, ask the client to pay you a fee for your work. The answer should not surprise you.

If fee-based service is so important to our profession, then why is it so rare? The answer is quite simple. Fee-based service is expensive. The expense lies in the cost of support people who have a high level of technical expertise. Also, it requires considerable time to provide quality service. Most financial planning firms are relatively small, one- or two-planner firms. Often, the principal of the firm is the only person capable of rendering the level of service required. When the principal's time is consumed with providing service, the cost of doing business increases significantly, and the marketing, which the proprietor must do, generally comes to a halt, thereby affecting future revenues and profitability.

Fee-based service planning is the foundation of planner-client relations and fee for service will be the revenue source for the firm's future survival. The recent trend is reduced commission payouts to the selling group members for both insurance and securities. These reductions have come about partially through the pressures of tax legislation which emphasizes economic performance. Although economic benefits for clients have always been the professional planner's primary concern, we are experiencing a great deal of public attention to economic return because of the media exposure and the fact that the investor cannot use tax dollars any more to replace economic dollars in calculating the return on investment. The squeeze is causing product manufacturers to reduce their front-end loads and also to make the commission payouts to the product marketing people smaller.

When commission dollars are reduced, financial planners will look to other revenue sources, and fees will begin to gain popularity with the commission-only financial planner. As the commission-based planner enters the fee-for-service side of our profession, he will be faced with new and very demanding methods of delivering his services.

Because return on the service investment is long-term rather than immediate, there is a tendency to give it a great deal of lip service but very little actual delivery to the client. At the bottom line, we really see marketing (the product mentality) versus production (the service mentality).

In order for financial planners to provide quality fee-based service at affordable prices, it may be necessary to focus introspectively on the delivery of service in the practice. Quality service at affordable prices can be achieved and, further, it *must* be done.

Financial planners are facing a crossroad in the development of their practices into the profession we would like to see gain recognition and respect from the "establishment" of financial professionals. Planners today who have been trained as product-salespeople endeavoring to provide financial planning to the public must recognize and change their old habits if they sincerely wish to become fee-charging financial planning professionals. To avoid being perceived as product peddlers with self-serving commissions as the only objective, they must begin the metamorphosis and join the change into the increasingly respected fee-based comprehensive financial planner. Be warned that not only is the transition expensive, but it is a long-term commitment as well.

As you know, the personal financial planning process consists of three phases:

1. The plan **design** phase
2. The plan **implementation** phase
3. The plan **review** phase

Phases 1 and 3 are fee-for-service functions, while Phase 2 may be both fees and commissions.

Comprehensive financial planning identifies problems and then seeks to determine the appropriate strategy that will remedy the client's malady. The solution may take the form of additional services and/or products.

A products-only approach to problem solving for clients is naive, especially if the product sellers promote themselves as total financial planners. Some distinction is needed so that the client can tell how the financial planner achieves the client's objectives. The public deserves to know in advance of doing business with *any* financial planner exactly which camp the financial planner ascribes to—products or services—as the primary source of problem solutions.

The public's confusion has developed as the first financial planners struggled to make respectable livings commensurate with their level of skills. During the early years of the financial planner's profession, it was very difficult to convince clients to pay professional service fees for designing their financial plans. Many financial planners had to give the design phase of financial planning away in order to prove to clients that a comprehensive written financial plan does provide benefits in excess of the fee paid by the client. This cost versus benefits relationship is vital to the process of educating the general public that comprehensive financial plan writing does provide real dollar benefits. If it did not, why would we, as planners, believe that anyone would be foolish enough to continue paying the necessary fees to the service-based, plan-writing financial planner?

We might be asked, "Where do these cash dollar benefits come from each year of the financial planning process?" Primarily, they are derived from three areas during the financial plan design phase:

- Improved cash flows
- Reduced income and estate taxes
- Better return on investments

A financial planner should be able to improve the client's cash flow by providing better information as to where the client is now directing the cash outflows. Typically, 40 percent of the client's cash inflows are used to pay variable consumption expenses. Further, approximately 10 to 20 percent of these variable cash outflows are impulse-type expenditures. Correcting this misuse of cash saves the client four to eight percent of the total cash inflows. Rather than asking the client to change these habits, it is better to create an annual "spending plan," which provides for the first dollar of cash outflow to be designated for wealth accumulation.

The tax savings benefits range from sheltered income to estate taxes saved. In the past, planners generated most of the dollar benefits for clients from taxes saved. With the Tax Reform Act of 1986, most of these benefits will be gone. Nevertheless, there will still be work to do for our clients.

As service-oriented professionals, we have an obligation to report each year to our clients the performance of our investment recommendations, thereby helping to validate the objectivity for our recommendation, especially for the fee-and-commission-earning planner. The financial planner should be able to add at least a two percent real return to that which the client is achieving without the planner's help.

Clients need and deserve financial professionals who will assist them in maximizing their resources to achieve their objectives. This will require many hours of data gathering, analyzing data, communicating recommendations to clients, and follow-up procedures. Comprehensive financial planning cannot be done in a one-hour interview, with a computer report culminating in a product sale. This time investment by the planning firm for the client is service. The fee-for-service time *must* satisfy the client's needs by solving his problems.

The first step in providing quality service for a fee is the commitment of the principal to the concept that service is essential. Once the principals have made this commitment, they must come to the realization that not all service has to be provided by the principal. There is no misconception more limiting to the growth of the business than the attitude "If you want something done right, you have to do it yourself.'' With that attitude, the business can never grow beyond what the principals can handle themselves.

Accepting the concept of delegation of authority is much more difficult than the general commitment to service. Delegation of authority is the most efficient means of reducing the cost of service. Once committed to the concept that service is essential and that service can be delegated, then we can proceed with three key elements in providing quality service:

1. Accessibility
2. Technical competence
3. Planned approach

ACCESSIBILITY

The senior planner cannot always be available to handle all requests for service. A critical breach in the service promise occurs when the client is not able to reach a competent authority when he has a problem. Many clients are lost for this reason. Additionally, not all service problems require the attention of the principal. As a qualified substitute, it is better to have an employee of the firm with whom the client feels comfortable and whose judgment the principal can trust. The time a principal spends in training a competent service representative will repay the firm many times as the principal is relieved of the routine servicing needs.

The selection and training of the service representative is not the place to cut corners or costs. This person *is you* in the eyes of your client, so choose carefully. We suggest you look for the following qualities.

1. *Intelligence.* You can teach whatever has to be learned if you start with an individual with an ability to grasp ideas and concepts quickly.
2. *Communication skills.* It is irrelevant how knowledgeable the individual may be technically if he or she is unable to communicate with other individuals—especially your clients!
3. *Professional appearance.* Since this individual is your personal representative, he or she must look as professional as yourself.
4. *Technical expertise.* This is a plus if you can find it. However, since the industry is so new, a fully trained individual is difficult to locate. Nevertheless, the person selected should be willing to enroll in a course of study in order to develop the technical skills required of the comprehensive financial planner. The team approach needs individuals with strengths in different areas, for example, taxes, insurance, and the like.

TECHNICAL COMPETENCE

Once the service representative has been selected, training becomes the top priority.

The paraplanner program offered by the College for Financial Planning is a good beginning but is limited to teaching basic financial planning concepts. We feel that the service representative must become certified and must develop comprehensive planning skills. There can be no substitute for the principal's personal time spent in training. The service representative must be taught every facet of plan development. He or she must know *why* as well as *how*. Allow this individual to sit in on client interviews and attend seminars. Keep this individual informed of new concepts, laws, and techniques relevant to the business.

As the training progresses, client contact can be initiated gradually. It is important that the principal relate the trust and confidence he or she has in this individual to the client. If the principal trusts him or her, so will the client. In the event of a subordinate's error, deal with the error in whatever manner deemed appropriate, but never in front of the client.

PLANNED APPROACH

Fortunately, the client's financial situation is dynamic. Therefore, the principal must realize that no matter how carefully the plan has been developed, it should be periodically reviewed during the year. By recognizing the need for future annual maintenance, the principal can estimate the costs and add them to the annual fee structure.

Obviously, not every client will require the same degree of service. How much service time is built into the plan should be based upon experience and an assessment of the client's needs and personality. There will be clients who require assistance with the slightest decision, while others avoid calling when they should. By allotting each client a specific number of meetings per year, service-prone clients have a tendency to wait until their scheduled meeting, and the more reserved client will not get lost in the crowd. The net result is a reduction in service requests but, more important, better client communication.

The written plan becomes the blueprint for future fee and/or commission service. The plan must be specific to the last-known detail, yet remain flexible and responsive to the client's changing needs, resources, and goals. The plan will list in detail when actions are to be completed. By scheduling regular meetings, the principal will be able to ensure that the plan has been fully implemented and necessary interim changes accomplished.

The service representative will arrange the meetings. At the time the appointment is scheduled, the service representative will determine any specific areas that need to be addressed other than those listed in the plan. With this advance knowledge, the service representative can conduct the necessary research, secure proposals, and prepare documents for the meeting. The principal should meet with the client but need not be present for the entire meeting. The routine signing of documents and so forth can be completed by the service representative, who is properly licensed, as needed.

Making the transition from a product-oriented practice to the fee-for-time, service-oriented professional is difficult. The answer may be in not attempting to do everything yourself. For the planner lacking experience, technical knowledge, computer systems, and support personnel, there is a viable alternative. By attending professional meetings, it will become obvious which financial planning firm is producing the kind of plans and fee-paid service you desire. It may be possible to negotiate an agreement whereby you can contract for the services of the more experienced, established professional firm in the preparation of your plans, thus leaving you free to provide marketing and the client services necessary. Such an arrangement could save you time and many overhead dollars by eliminating the need to purchase sophisticated computer systems, could reduce personnel costs, and could result in a more comprehensive, thorough, professionally written plan. The small planning firm thereby can convert fixed overhead expenses to variable overhead expenses, thus helping to ensure profitability. Also, this alternative should result in savings from economies of scale and the ability to network with other sophisticated, service-oriented, plan-writing financial planners.

By following the planned approach, maximizing the skills of a service representative and utilization of other professionals, the principal will be able to achieve the objective of providing quality fee-paid service at an affordable price. What are the returns on the service investment?—a satisfied client who is eager to refer you to his friends and an increase in your prestige as a financial professional to the "establishment" of financial professionals.

"Pricing of services is an issue that hits all fee-only and fee-plus-commission financial planners. There is no one answer to how financial planners should price their services."

—JEFFREY L. SEGLIN

Alternative Methods of Compensation: Creative Pricing Methods

Jeffrey L. Seglin is a Boston-based writer and editor. His most recent book is *America's New Breed of Entrepreneurs: Their Marketing Strategies, Techniques, and Successes.* He holds a B.A. in English from Bethany College in West Virginia and a master's degree in theology and literature from Harvard.

Seglin has written for *Inc., Boston, Financial Planning, Venture, Personal Investing, Banker & Tradesman, USA Today,* among others. He is a contributing writer for *Boston* magazine and a contributing editor and writer of a monthly selling and marketing column for *Financial Planning.* He is also coauthor of *Personal Financial Planning in Banks* and *Job Descriptions in Banking,* and is the author of *Bank Letter Writing Handbook.*

Seglin was the content editor and consultant for the PBS 13-week national television series *On the Money.* In addition, he speaks frequently to professionals and students about writing, entrepreneurship, banking, and personal finance. He lives in Boston, where he is president of Seglin Associates.

Late one summer, a certified financial planner from Austin, Texas, was visiting Boston. As most visitors to Boston are wont to do, she picked up a copy of *Boston*, the city's magazine, to get an idea what was going on in town. In the issue, she happened upon an interview with the president of the Greater Boston Chapter of the International Association of Financial Planning (IAFP).

The Austin-based planner is a fee-only planner in a city that has been hit with the same economic malaise that has hit many Texas cities. In addition to her work as a financial planner, she was an enrolled agent who could practice tax preparation before the IRS. The income from that work helped to keep cash flow coming into the firm, which has one other employee—a paraplanner—and services somewhere between 40 and 50 clients. Earlier in the year, she had also raised her hourly rate from $60 to $75, which helped increase cash flow.

But when she read the interview with the Framingham, Massachusetts-based planner, she discovered another pricing strategy that would help cash flow. In the interview, the Framingham-based planner, a fee-plus-commission planner whose income is 90 percent derived from fees, when asked what her initial fee was, answered that while some planners charge nothing for the first hour of planning, she charged for the first hour of financial planning at a discounted rate.

"I had originally been offering a free first hour," the Austin planner said. "I was realizing that some people were just coming in looking for a few hours. When I read the article in *Boston* magazine about that woman who was discounting the first hour, I decided to try it."

The Austin planner's regular hourly fee is $75. She offered the initial hour for a fee of $50. "Charging the initial fee worked very well," she says. "The number of people coming in hasn't stopped at all. [Considering that] Austin is quite depressed at the moment, we're holding up remarkably well."

Pricing of services is an issue that hits all fee-only and fee-plus-commission financial planners. How can I price my services to make sure that my business is profitable?

"The way I work is when somebody calls, I do a quick interview on the phone," explains the Framingham-based planner. If the person decides he needs financial planning, "we set a date. We send out a personal financial survey, which he completes and mails in or brings with him. At the first meeting we go over the survey and identify concerns and financial issues which need to be addressed.

"For that first meeting, I charge a reduced hourly rate of $55 for the first hour as opposed to a normal hourly rate of $85. I tell them the rate up front."

The Framingham planner explains that the reason she doesn't give the client the first hour for free is that she found that she "was frequently giving financial planning advice right from the beginning. Occasionally, I even ran into a client for whom 1.5 hours would take care of his problem."

If that's the case, why charge a discounted rate?

"The reason for the reduced rate is that a large portion of our first meeting is dedicated to just getting to know each other. As a result, they are not getting 100 percent of my brain power, my financial expertise."

There is no one answer to how financial planners should price their services. Some planners will offer the first hour of planning for free; others will charge. Still others, like the Austin and Framingham planners, will offer the first hour at a reduced rate.

When asked how she arrived at the $55 reduced rate for the first hour, the Framingham planner responded: "There was no scientific method; it just sounded good."

To establish the $85 hourly ticket price, she had "shopped" around in her area to find out what other professionals were charging, asked herself what she felt comfortable charging, and placed herself within that range.

Dr. Robert Pritchard, professor of finance at Glassboro State College in New Jersey and one of the authors of *Strategic Marketing: A Handbook for Managers, Business Owners, and Entrepreneurs* (Addison-Wesley), likes the reduced first-hour approach. "I think there's a lot to be said for the adage that if a person's not willing to pay for something, they don't really want it," he says. "I'm inclined to say if they want it, they've got to expect to pay for it."

But Pritchard sees that with competition heating up from the behemoth financial services firms for the same financial planning customers, times ahead will be tough for the smaller financial planning shop. "I think the smaller outfit is going to have to depend very heavily on referrals, maybe even provide some incentive for referrals," he observes. "Let's say you do financial planning for me and you charge me for the plan. Maybe we can make a deal that if I can refer a couple of people to you, the three-year checkup I would normally pay for is going to be done at a discount or for free."

"We've played with the reduced rate idea, but a few clients reacted negatively," says one of the principals in a financial planning operation in Boston. "It didn't sit right with them."

His firm, which has 67 full-time employees who handle 350 ongoing clients, charges solely on a retainer basis for its financial planning services. At the end of 1986, it began to evaluate how it charged for services.

"One way is just to bill by the hour," he says, "but we rejected it. It's a system we never used. We felt we should tell a client when he comes in that this is what it's going to cost to do the job."

But pricing still was an issue with this Boston-based planner and his partners, because, while the first year of the retainer was turning out to be very profitable, he observes: "We think maybe the second or third year is not as profitable because it's open-ended."

This planner and others at the firm used old statistics to figure out how much revenue each client brought in. "We found out we were doing a lot for clients that we were not charging for," he says. "So how do you price the retainer? We have to price it so we don't lose money.

"We're trying to find out how to make the second-year retainer profitable. We're doing research to find out what our people do." Once the firm has established exactly how much time its professionals put into the planning process, they are going to offer clients a "full-service" retainer, priced accordingly.

"We're going to say if you want full-service retainer, this is what it's going to cost," he says. "Maybe we'll offer a lesser service retainer as well, but we'll lay it all out and tell them."

Laying it all out for the client is critical. While pricing decisions may be difficult for the planner, it's even more difficult for the prospective client if the planner isn't clear about his fee.

"Maybe financial planners should be more like medical doctors and list their prices on the wall," suggests Pritchard. Some planners do just that.

One fee-only financial planner in Charleston, South Carolina, gives each prospective client of his firm a "standard fee schedule." The fee schedule is based on a client's gross income, taxes for the previous year, and gross assets. Within each of these categories a client assigns himself a certain number of points and multiplies the total by $125 to come up with the price of his financial plan.

The point-based fee schedule looks like Table 1.

For some planners, the resulting price of a financial plan based on this point chart may seem inappropriate. By adapting the $125 fee or lowering the various point levels, a more appropriate price range can be derived. Like all pricing methods, this point system must fit the needs and comfort level of the planner using it.

In *Strategic Marketing*, Pritchard and his coauthors, Bruce Bradway and Mary Anne Frenzel, write that in service industries, such as financial planning, the "job jacket" approach to pricing—where each person working on a particular case bills out to that case—may be one of the most efficient methods of pricing, but it is not without problems. They point out that no employee is 100 percent productive during the workday, so the unbillable time must be charged to overhead. They argue that productivity improves when each employee "keeps a record of time spent in ten- or fifteen-minute segments." They also suggest that setting standards, such as "85 percent of working time must be billed to jobs," increases productivity.

The authors also suggest that while traditionally many service businesses have billed out their time on a basis of three times the hourly rate, because of inflation and rising costs of fringe benefits and computerization, the "formula during the coming decade for service businesses will be more like four times the hourly rate per employee."

Pritchard reminds us, "85 percent is a target." With a glut of lawyers in the marketplace, for instance, he suggests, "Probably if most [lawyers] are at 50 percent they're doing pretty well. Many lawyers work long hours to get the number of billable hours at a reasonable level."

The Austin financial planner follows the three-to-one formula for billing out her paraplanner's time. "With the paraplanner I can charge probably three times her overall hourly rate for her time," she says. "She makes an hourly rate plus a percentage of everything on the computer. It should work out to three to one."

TABLE 1

Standard Fee Schedule

Gross Income		Taxes		Gross Assets	
Income	Points	Taxes	Points	Assets	Points
$25,000	4	$5,000	0	$50,000	6
$35,000	5	$5,000	6	$100,000	7
$40,000	6	$10,000	7	$200,000	8
$50,000	7	$15,000	8	$300,000	9
$65,000	8	$20,000	9	$400,000	10
$80,000	9	$28,000	10	$500,000	11
$100,000	12	$40,000	11	$750,000	12
$125,000	13	$54,000	12	$1,000,000	13
$155,000	14	$70,000	13	$1,500,000	14
$190,000	15	$88,000	14	$2,000,000	15
$230,000	16			$2,500,000	16
$275,000	17			$3,000,000	17
$750,000	18				
$1,000,000	19				
$1,250,000	20				
Total personal points = ____		Total tax points = ____		Total asset points = ____	

Grand total of points = _____ × $125 = _____ (Total fee)

Only seven or eight hours of her paraplanner's time are billable to clients, the Austin planner says. The remainder of the time she puts in (around 22 or 23 hours) during the week are billed to overhead. To meet the costs of overhead, the Austin planner tries to have 20 billable hours a week.

The Framingham planner shoots for a similar goal. "My goal is for 20 hours a week of billable hours, but no more," she says. "That's maxed out. It's actually closer to 18 hours. When I can hit 18 hours a week, I can hit the income stream that I want."

Unlike the Austin planner, however, the Framingham planner bills out her paraplanner's time at the same rate she herself charges. She contracts with clients for how many hours she will bill them for estimated "desk time" (actually working on the plan), and puts a cap on that rate. "Meeting time is additional," she explains. "Desk time is the only time I can control."

Pricing for the financial planner may vary from planner to planner, based on the factors each planner uses to make pricing decisions. Fortunately there are some standards in the decision-making process that the planner can use.

In their textbook, *Marketing: Basic Concepts and Decisions, 4th edition* (Houghton Mifflin), William Pride and O. C. Ferrell list eight stages for establishing prices. While they point out that these stages are not "inevitable," they do serve as guidelines to logically analyzing and establishing a pricing strategy.

- Stage 1 is to select your price objective, which may include concerns such as profits, return on investment, market share, and cash flow.
- Stage 2 is to assess your target market's evaluation of price and its ability to purchase your services.
- Stage 3 is to determine the demand for your services.
- Stage 4 is to analyze the relationship between demand, costs, and profit. To stay in business, you have to be able to cover your costs, so you must evaluate if the price you can charge based on demand is enough to cover those costs, plus give you some profit.
- Stage 5 is to evaluate your competitor's prices.
- Stage 6 is to select a pricing policy.
- Stage 7 is to develop a pricing method.
- Stage 8 is to determine a specific price.

When all is said and done and a pricing structure has been established, it's up to the planner or the firm's management to decide if that structure is appropriate. The fee-only planner in Charleston, South Carolina, for one, thinks his price-by-point pricing system is just fine. "It's working pretty well," he says, declining specifics. "Yes sir, it's working pretty well."

"Your main objective when developing a color scheme is to provide colors that are as rich and comfortable to you as they are to your clients."

—DEBORAH DANIELSON, CFP

Dressing Your Office For Success

Deborah L. Danielson is a Certified Financial Planner practicing in Las Vegas, Nevada. She holds an NASD Series 7 license and is a Registered Principal and Branch Manager of Private Ledger Financial Services, Inc. She is also a registered investment advisor. Ms. Danielson has attended the University of Nevada Investment Training Institute, where she has since taught numerous continuing education courses.

Ms. Danielson is a member of the Institute of Certified Financial Planners and has served as President and Chairman of the board for the International Association for Financial Planning, Las Vegas chapter. She has had articles published in the *Las Vegas Living Magazine* and the *Las Vegas Sun* and has appeared on local television. Currently, she has her own financial planning firm.

So you are in business now. Where will the new office be? How will it be decorated? What type of image are you trying to project? Do these questions really matter? Absolutely, they do.

Potential clients will often feel some sort of uneasiness in meeting with a financial planner, especially the first time. What you need to do for them is to create as much comfort as you can, so that they feel as though they fit in and belong there. It's the same feeling as going to the doctor and taking off all of one's clothes, except that they are baring their fiscal souls. This can be equally, if not more, uncomfortable for them. We all want to feel as if we are at home and feel comfortable in our surroundings.

Look at your practice, or the one you are trying to build, and design your office to create the image that is appropriate for you and your type of clientele. Many variables go into the decor of an office. Critical care should be given to even the smallest of details, not only where your office is located but where you are located within the building. Color and furnishings also play a big part in the image that you are trying to create within your profession and within the community.

Color has long been a topic of conversation as to its mood-creating abilities. Is this color a hot or cool color? Does it feel tranquil? Is it too busy or too boring? The psychological aspects of color can be used to benefit or hinder your operations, so it would behoove you to acknowledge its presence and work with it instead of trying to fight it. For example, blue is cooling, soothing, and sedative, but it cannot be overused or it will produce melancholia. Greens, depending upon the shade, can be rich, cooling, and sedative. Yellow is cheery and stimulating, but it can also demand attention and caution one to danger. Red is exciting and stimulates the brain. Reds are thought to stimulate either ideas or tempers and add warmth and amour to a room. Orange is a very stimulating color for an office, but people will become ill at ease in a short period of time and use every excuse to leave. Brown is restful and warming but, unless used in combination with other colors, can be depressing. Violet is thought to be a regal and dignified color. Pink is soft, calm, tender, and sweet but can also be effeminate. White is pure, innocent, and spiritual, but it can also be thought of as sterile. Black is thought to be a strong and powerful color, but possibly intimidating. Some colors are fashionable, and others are old standards. For years we have grown up with some fairly familiar corporate colors, the navy and powder blues and the grays and burgundies. Does this mean that if you deal with corporate executives, your office must be in these colors? Absolutely not, but you might not want to decorate in pink and purple flowers. You have the flexibility to decorate not only to please yourself but your coworkers and your clientele as well. Your main objective when developing a color scheme is to provide colors that are as rich and comfortable to you as they are to your clients. Color should be harmonious, not distracting.

Let's begin at the beginning and explore your options from the bottom up in selecting an office. First, where is the office going to be located? Will your office be in a major office building in the financial district, in a low-rise garden-style office complex, in a remodeled home, or in a shopping center complex? The type of clientele you are trying to attract will have a bearing on your choice. Next, where will your office be located within your building? You can choose the ground floor, the penthouse suite, or any floor in between. Are you in the front of the building or the rear? Should you choose the corner office or the one with the window? Think of the psychological impact and impression each would have on your practice and your clients. Will this location be convenient, impressive, or overbearing? If you are dealing with corporate or high-net-worth clients, the penthouse suite may fit your needs. If you are dealing with medium-to lower-net-worth clients, it may be quite intimidating for them, and they may wonder if you can really help ''them.'' Clients feel most comfortable in surroundings that are similar to or better than those to which they are accustomed.

The type of furniture you select is also an integral part of your office. Will it be chrome and glass, art deco, traditional woods of walnut, mahogany, and oak, or formica? These choices will have a bearing upon the image created. If you are dealing with clients in the music or entertainment business, an office with chrome and glass or art deco and trendy colors will be appropriate. The same decor, however, may not work for Mr. Corporate Executive. He may feel that your ideas are equally flamboyant. Ms. Entertainer may feel that you are too stuffy in your pinstriped grey and burgundy with the traditional black leather sofa and walnut furnishings. Gear your image toward those you want to feel most comfortable. Furniture should be bought to be comfortable and functional. Your desk should look good and also be efficient. You will need adequate storage in the office for all the ''paper''—enough to make it easy to keep organized. Think of the number of hours you and your staff spend in the office in any given year. Shouldn't you feel good in those surroundings? If you do, your work performance will reflect this.

To create a comfortable but homelike environment, you may want to shop at a regular furniture store rather than an office furniture store. Usually the prices will be better, and the selection could be greater. Choose furniture that creates a pleasant and homelike atmosphere. Furniture should lend itself to the mood of the decor as well as being functional. A good, but not trendy, interior decorator can be invaluable in helping you achieve your goal.

Time should be spent in research, thought, and soul searching before you spend the capital. Office decor is one of your major expenses, and it does not get used up and replaced. Choosing wisely the first time around can be critical to your future success. What are your goals? Areas that need to be considered are storage space, filing space, adequate desk space, conference rooms, reception areas, computer work areas, and where to put the coffee pot and copier.

An office is not complete with just a desk and a file cabinet. What type of accessories should be used to complete the picture of success? Carpet, oriental rugs, drapery, blinds, wallpaper, mirrors, paneling, plants, trees, flowers, original oil paintings, prints, sculpture, clocks, ash trays, coasters, mugs, glasses, and novelty items are an integral part of your decision. How will your certificates, licenses, and degrees be matted or framed? What colors will you use; which frame and what glass will enhance your chosen decor? Do you want to serve clients beverages and/or food? Do you want to use styrofoam cups or china cups and saucers with a silver coffee service? Everything creates a statement, as well as possible problems. Who washes and dries those dishes? Is it an efficient use of the staff's time for them to do so?

To create the professional image, research says your office should be large and in the corner of the building or should contain a large window with a view. Your desk should be large with a closed front, and a small conference area is an asset. Remember, in this business you do not need to sit on the other side of the desk and intimidate. Your job is not to oppose your clients but to be on their side and assist them in their decision making. The higher the status image you are trying to create, the less you will want to use family pictures, business charts, and chalk boards. Plants are always appropriate.

To create a more artistic image, you may want to have a curved or rounded office with a nonsymmetrical floor plan. Vertical louvers on the windows, a hardwood floor, and exposed beams or duct work may help you to create this type of look. Your office could be warmed with shades of mauve, teal, or even pink. Your desk could be small with an open front, possibly curved or even round. You may want to accent with souvenirs, mementos, photos and advertisements, maps, or charts.

Image is very important! It sells you long before you have the opportunity to sell yourself. Time spent in careful consideration of your options will pay off handsomely. Your office should always provide a win-win environment. You feel good, your staff feels good, and your clients feel good. If all this is true, you should have no problem building a successful, rewarding practice.

"In a business as unregulated as financial planning, it is easy for someone with no credentials and a smooth sales pitch to call himself a financial planner. . . . A professional image will put you far ahead of a smooth talker, no matter how 'professional' he at first seems to be."

—ROBERT J. OBERST, SR.,
Ph.D., CFP

Fourteen Keys to Projecting a Professional Image

Robert J. Oberst, Sr., Ph.D., CFP, founded Robert J. Oberst, Sr. & Associates in 1969. The first firm established to do financial planning in New Jersey, it is one of the oldest financial planning firms in the United States.

Oberst is the first recipient of the Certified Financial Planner of the Year Award given by the ICFP. He is considered one of the central figures in the establishment of financial planning as a profession and is a former chairman of the board of regents of the College for Financial Planning. He is admitted to the Registry of Financial Planning Practitioners and currently serves on the national board of directors of the IAFP. Additionally, he is former chairman of the board of the Central New Jersey IAFP and ICFP chapters.

Oberst has been quoted by publications such as *Money, Sylvia Porter's Personal Finance, New York Times, Best's Review, National Business, Christian Science Monitor,* and the *Digest of Financial Planning Ideas.* He is the host of New Jersey's Cable TV Network's "Financial Planning Today."

In a business as unregulated as financial planning, it is easy for someone with no credentials and a smooth sales pitch to call himself a financial planner. You may have the degrees and certification he lacks, but how can you be sure clients recognize your expertise? A professional image will put you far ahead of a smooth talker, no matter how "professional" he at first seems to be.

Projecting a professional image is important for three reasons:

- It will help you attract and keep the kind of clients you need to build up a successful practice.
- It will put you on an equal level with your client's other advisors (for example, his accountant and attorney) so that you can effectively coordinate their activities on behalf of your client.
- It will help establish you in the media and your community as a reliable source of information on financial topics.

But how do you communicate to clients that you are a professional? First, you have to understand what a professional is—and what he is not. By definition, a professional is someone who has acquired specialized knowledge after long and intensive academic preparation. Lawyers and doctors are professionals. Their rigorous degrees and licenses tell us so.

A professional sells services—time, effort, and expertise—not products. He is interested in a long-term relationship with clients, not a quick sale, and he tries to give the best and most objective advice he can to his clients.

Building a professional image takes time, but is not as difficult as you may at first think. Here are fourteen ideas that will help establish you as a professional in your community, with prospective clients, and with clients you already serve. If you follow even a few of these recommendations, you are certain to build respect as a dedicated professional.

ACTION PLAN

In Your Community

The first thing you need to do is make up your mind that you are a professional and communicate that to others in everything you do. Start with the town where you live and work. Remember, when you are building an image, not every expenditure of time and money will result in a client. It is the sum total of your efforts that will enhance your practice.

1. Get involved in your community • Volunteer your time to service organizations in your area such as the Red Cross, your local hospital, senior citizens' centers and area colleges. This will establish your name and face among the prominent members of your community, and others will begin to know who you are and what you do for a living.

2. Join local professional business associations • An organization that has helped me tremendously is the Estate Planning Council. Through the council, I have established relationships with lawyers, accountants, trust officers, and insurance people that have lasted twenty years. It takes time to win the trust of other pros. Do not come across as too eager, or you will appear hungry. Other professionals do not want to do business with someone less secure than they are.

3. Be available for the media • Keep alert for opportunities to be interviewed by local newspapers, radio, and television. Write a couple of speeches on the topic of financial planning, so that you can be ready to deliver them on short notice. Give lectures and seminars through your local college. All of these efforts will serve to establish you as an authority on financial planning.

4. Use the proper professional designations after your name • ''John Jones, B.S., M.S.,'' or ''Mary Smith, RIA,'' are not professional designations. They are initials designed to fill up a page. College degrees are important, but they do not belong on your business cards or letterhead unless they serve to communicate your expertise (e.g., M.B.A., Ph.D.). And anyone with a few dollars can become a registered investment advisor. I would rather see one legitimate professional designation, such as CFP or ChFC, than a host of meaningless initials.

5. Consider consulting a professional public relations firm • When you have built a solid base in your community, you might consider the services of a PR firm. Be cautious about spending PR money too soon, however. To start, a professional PR firm can help you design a brochure that will communicate your expertise and credentials. The firm can also send press releases to local newspapers and television stations that will explain an idea and get you noticed quickly.

With Prospective Clients

From the moment prospective clients make contact with your office, they have put their trust in your ability to offer competent advice and service. In a sense, you are their financial ''doctor,'' and your manner should reflect the same responsible attitude as any other professional's.

6. Make your appearance work for you • Our first impressions of people are always the strongest. Make yours a good one. Men should wear a conservative suit and tie. Women should wear a tailored dress or suit. Dressing well lets your clients know that they are important. Professionals dress as if they mean business.

7. Let your office convey your status • When clients walk through your door, they should see quality furniture, attractive art work, and credentials identifying your professional attainments, interests, and activities. These credentials might include:

- Your CPA, LLB, MBA, ChFC, CFP or other certificates attesting that you have passed a professional course of study
- Undergraduate and graduate college degrees
- Membership in professional associations, such as the IAFP or ICFP, that indicate your area of expertise
- Local service or business group awards or membership certificates showing community involvement
- One or more leather scrapbooks containing your monthly newsletter,

information about client procedures and your business philosophy, or articles about you in community papers

Remember over the course of a year how many clients pass through your doors. Do not fail to use every means to educate your clients through what they see in your office.

8. Develop a polite, professional staff • Take the time to train your staff to be friendly and helpful. Provide clear instructions on how you want them to greet clients on the telephone and in person. Reward instances of high-quality client service with compliments, and continuously reemphasize the importance of prompt, careful, and caring attention to client needs.

9. Make your first consultation free • An initial free consultation has been a successful strategy for my firm. When prospects sense that they are under no pressure, they are much more at ease. In fact, almost all prospective clients who come in for a free consultation do end up retaining my firm—if not immediately, then at some future date. Most important, this strategy reinforces a professional, service-based stance—rather than a sales approach. When clients are relaxed, they are more receptive to your firm's ideas.

10. Don't discuss fees over the telephone • One of the reasons I give a free initial consultation is so that I do not need to discuss fees over the telephone—a practice that I believe reduces the effectiveness of our professional image. It is easier by far to discuss fees and commissions face to face after clients see your practice's high standards and know what they are paying for.

11. Listen first • When a patient comes to a doctor with a complaint, the doctor's first job is to examine that patient. He does not rush to prescribe a pill before he knows what is wrong. The same applies to a financial planner. I use questions like these to get clients to talk:

• Why do you feel you need financial planning?
• What are your goals?
• What kinds of experiences have you had with prior investments?

This works best when the client and I are seated informally at a conference table instead of with my desk between us. I listen to the client's needs, take notes, and then explain how our firm can best serve him or her.

With Your Own Clients

Maintaining a professional image is all the more important once clients have selected you to do their financial planning. More than one client has been lost through inadequate and sloppy follow-through. A thorough, consistent, and dedicated approach to your clients' needs will assure them that you are committed to giving them top-notch service.

12. Give clients a letter of engagement • Once clients have selected our firm to do their financial planning, I send them a letter (Figure 1) that outlines

• The services the firm provides
• The services the firm is not authorized to provide (e.g., legal or accounting services)

ROBERT J. OBERST, SR. & ASSOCIATES

Personal Financial Planners

218 BROAD STREET   RED BANK, NEW JERSEY 07701   TELEPHONE (201) 842-2300

Robert J. Oberst, Sr., Ph.D., CFP

Robert E. Freedman, CFP

Nancy M. Kegelman, CPA

This letter sets forth the agreement under which Robert J. Oberst, Sr. and Associates will perform financial planning services for you.

Our practice consists of total conceptual financial planning, and we are compensated on a fee basis (set forth below) for those services. A proper financial plan will analyze and make recommendations in the following areas:

1. Money Management

2. Investment Management

3. Risk Management

4. Tax Management

5. Estate Management

We are not authorized to practice law, or accounting, and will not do so. All recommendations relating to legal and accounting matters must be reviewed and implemented by an attorney or an accountant as appropriate.

We will analyze your present financial situation and will make certain recommendations, which in our opinion will allow you to improve your overall financial position. We will work with your other professional advisors when authorized to do so by you.

Your responsibility to this firm will be to complete your Confidential Financial Planning Guide in its entirety and return it to our office along with all requested and relevant documents for review. The planning phase of our work shall be considered complete upon the presentation of a written report.

In consideration of the above service, you will compensate this firm at the rate of $ per hour. This fee does not include the initial consultation meeting, which is provided at no cost to you. Whenever possible, and upon request, we will provide an estimate of the approximate cost of the Financial Plan. A check in the amount of $_____ is due upon the signing of this Letter of Engagement and will be credited against all charges due and payable upon presentation of the report. Additional or continuing work will be at the same hourly rate.

Implementation of your Financial Plan may involve the purchase of financial products. You are under no obligation to purchase said products through us; however, should you elect, we will research the market and arrange for placement by our licensed employees. This may involve additional compensation to our firm in the form of commissions. Your only obligation is for the fee outlined above. You may terminate this arrangement at any time, and your obligation will be for time actually expended by us on your behalf as reflected in our time-keeping records.

Your signature below indicates your acceptance of the terms outlined above, and receipt of SEC form ADV, and your engagement of this firm to provide Financial Planning services.

_____

Robert J. Oberst, Sr. and Associates

_____

Signature

_____

Address

_____

Telephone   Date

Figure 1   Sample letter of engagement.

- The client's responsibility to complete in full a personal financial statement and to provide relevant documents
- The firm's hourly billing rate and required retainer fee
- An explanation of the firm's commission policies

Charging a retainer fee commits clients to follow through with the plan once they have chosen your firm. It reinforces the fact that your time is valuable and that they have engaged the services of a professional.

13. Keep your letterhead simple • Rainbow-variety stationery and brochures and business cards with fancy logos may catch someone's attention, but they do not necessarily convey a professional image. Model your firm's materials after those used by law practices. My business letterhead simply states the name of my firm and my name and credentials—Robert J. Oberst, Sr., certified financial planner—across the top of the page with the address directly below and my associates' names and professional designations down the side.

14. Be firm about your procedures and thorough in follow-up visits • I have had clients walk into my office with half-completed personal financial statements, and I have sent them right back home. I stress to them that, as professionals, we simply will not make a diagnosis based on half the data. This is something they come to appreciate.

This also applies to later visits with your clients. I do not commit my clients to a mandatory number of meetings each year, but I do monitor their progress, and I encourage them to phone me if they have any questions. I do not charge for phone time, which I believe helps reinforce my contact with clients. It is not enough to simply service a client and say goodbye at the door. A professional maintains a long-standing relationship with clients.

Summary

Projecting and maintaining a professional image is a lifetime endeavor. But no effort, no matter how small, is wasted when you are building your reputation. Your professional image combined with your hard-earned credentials are the most valuable part of your practice. No one can compete against that winning combination simply by hanging a shingle from the door.

Figure 2 will be a helpful measure of your professional image building.

Quiz—Am I Building a Professional Image?

A highly professional image doesn't happen overnight—you build it slowly over the years with a series of well-thought-out actions. You can use this quiz to assess how actively you're working to enhance your professional image. And, if you answer no to a question, there's space to jot down one step you or someone on your staff can take to improve things—and to set a date for getting it done.

	Yes	No	If ''no'', action to be taken and date
• Has my name appeared in the local (or other) media in the past three months?	☐	☐	_____
• Have I added one new name to my network of professionals in the past month?	☐	☐	_____
• Have I received at least one referral from a professional I met through my association memberships?	☐	☐	_____
• Have I looked closely at my promotional materials in the past three months? Do they accurately describe the full range of my services?	☐	☐	_____
• Do my office, staff, stationery, cards and brochures convey the image I want to project?	☐	☐	_____
• Am I giving clients information about my fees in the most effective way?	☐	☐	_____
• Am I getting enough information from clients? In an easy-to-work-with form?	☐	☐	_____
• Have I reviewed my letter of engagement and other standard forms recently? Are they up-to-date—or do we modify them each time we use them?	☐	☐	_____
• Are my yearly (quarterly/semiannual) meetings with clients on schedule?	☐	☐	_____
• Have I done a client information mailing within the past three months?	☐	☐	_____
• Do I know where my clients stand right now? Am I keeping up with the paperwork?	☐	☐	_____

Figure 2 Professional image quiz.

''Fourteen Keys to Projecting a Professional Image'' is reprinted here by permission of Robert J. Oberst, Senior, Ph.D.

"When considering a potential firm affiliation, your personal needs and preferences must be clearly defined in advance."

—CAROL A SANDSTROM, CFP

Choosing
a Broker-Dealer

Carol A. Sandstrom, CFP, is Founder and President of Fast Start, Inc., a consulting and referral firm servicing NASD Registered Representatives and broker-dealers. Her clients include securities professionals and organizations in both the domestic and international markets. She is former president and compliance officer with the broker-dealer arm of Pioneer Western Corporation as well as Vice President/Sales Manager for FSC Securities prior to starting her own company. She is a board member of the Tampa Bay chapters of IAFP and ICFP and is a member of the Florida Securities Dealers Association.

In a financial planning practice, some brokers may have to kiss a lot of frogs trying to find their prince—of a broker-dealer, that is! There are over 6000 firms registered as members of the NASD. But, as representatives will discover, all broker-dealers are not alike. Many planners are apt to spend a great deal of effort attempting to find the "best" firm only by seeking the opinions of their peers and associates. This is not an effective method of choosing a broker-dealer. Why? Let's compare it to asking your associate for the best place to dine. One person may prefer a fast-food restaurant, even though it requires that you serve yourself because it's inexpensive. You may desire a "serve yourself" broker-dealer with high payout and very few services. On the other hand, another choice of a restaurant could be one that serves only ethnic food, and there are representatives who seek a broker-dealer based only on its product menu in one particular area. Then, of course, there are those who would prefer a four-star restaurant with a gourmet menu and extra services in spite of very high prices. In comparison, there are planners who need a firm with a gourmet selection of products and additional support services, and they feel it is worth the price in terms of lower commission payout.

Choosing a broker-dealer is a major decision and can have a dramatic effect on your practice. Being affiliated with the right firm, one that is structured to *your* needs and preferences, is critical to success; therefore careful evaluation of possible choices must be made. Let us now examine some areas you might look into when doing your own due diligence on a broker/dealer. Your individual requirements based on your business plan determine which things you should consider in a broker/dealer and which you might ignore.

THE FIRM

First, the basics: is the home office located conveniently, and/or are there provisions for any difference in time zones, mail delivery, and meetings? Does the firm have a good reputation in your area and among other financial planners? Is it well capitalized, either itself or through a parent/affiliate company? What is the ratio of representatives to home office employees? Has the number of representatives been growing or decreasing recently? Is the firm's management style akin to your own, and is the chemistry right between you and the staff? Is the firm very large or very small? (As a general rule, the smaller firms are able to be more flexible and can adapt to the special needs that an individual might have.)

TRADING

If you do equity business, does the firm self-clear or use the clearing services of another company? Is the commission schedule competitive regarding discounts, minimum ticket charges, and execution time? Are the people on the trading desk order takers or order generators? To what extent and in what time frame are research, quotes, and reports on executions available?

MUTUAL FUNDS

Are you able to place wire trades and secure the current day's price, or must these orders be mailed in? Must you deal direct with fund companies for sales help, service problems, and literature requests, or is the home office staffed to take care of these needs? Are fund confirmations provided promptly, in hard copy form or via computer modem?

LIMITED PARTNERSHIPS

The firm's due diligence processes must be explored in depth if much partnership business is anticipated. Does the firm extend only the minimum effort to be covered legally, or do they go the extra mile? Are previously approved programs monitored on a regular basis? How many programs were reviewed, and how many were accepted? Can a big producer "railroad" in a favorite product regardless of merit, and are the load fees on approved products better for the client or the firm? Do the due diligence officers have tenure with the company? Are the due diligence fees passed on to the representative, or kept by the firm?

REGULATORY

The regulatory and compliance attitude of a broker-dealer is paramount in making your choice. A broker-dealer firm has a legal obligation to supervise its registered representatives and must assume the responsibility of taking steps to detect and prevent violations in securities laws. While a nit-picking atmosphere is not conducive to the sales effort, it is for your protection to affiliate with a firm that has a strong commitment to compliance. Here again, we are looking for a firm that will say *no* to a top producer. Failure to maintain adequate supervision can result in sanctions to a broker-dealer as well as the offending salesperson, and negative publicity about your broker-dealer affiliation can affect your image even if you had no knowledge or part in the problem. Look for a firm that will answer your regulatory questions with a focus not on *"if* you can do it" but on *"how* you can do it" within regulatory guidelines. Check how the firm fared on their NASD and state audits. Were there any disciplinary actions taken on representatives under their supervision, and are there any pending lawsuits? The lawsuit question is of particular importance if the firm is thinly capitalized, since an adverse decision could affect the net capital of the firm. Ask to see a statement of financial condition. All advertising and correspondence must be reviewed and approved by a registered principal. What is the firm's procedure and time frame for such approvals?

INVESTMENT ADVISORY

If the firm is also a Registered Investment Advisor, you may not have to qualify, depending on your activities. But will the firm allow you to become an RIA individually if you choose to? Are there people on staff qualified in plan writing and/or qualified to answer any technical questions in tax planning or estate planning, or will you need to find these resources outside the firm?

OPERATIONS

A frequent area of frustration is the operations department. The old stand-by phrase "garbage in–garbage out" does apply here in that the initial responsibility lies with the representative to deliver required checks and documents with clear instructions and within the procedures outlined by the home office. However, excessive problems can interfere with your practice if the operations department does not use its own initiative and good judgment in processing your orders. For instance, will the instructions you submit be taken in the most literal sense, or will you be asked to clarify a questionable or unlikely request? Will the home office pick up the phone to call and ask you for an answer to an obvious oversight, or will they mail paperwork back to you as incomplete? In short, do you get the feeling that the clerks care about you and your clients, or is it just a job? Communications between you and the home office are of importance also. Can you get due diligence information, client information, commission data, and/or research materials via a computer, or is it sent in hard copy form? If so, how often?

TRAINING AND EDUCATION

A broker-dealer's attention to this function may be a blessing or an aggravation, depending on the scope of your needs. Some firms will hold meetings at locations requiring you to leave your office for one or more days. These meetings may take on several different focuses: product(s), motivation, sales skill-building, networking and public relations, practice management, and recognition (such as award conferences). Other firms may keep you current on the latest industry changes via telephone conference calls, mail, cassettes, or visits by a home office employee. Still others may do nothing, and you will need to finance your own further education by attending one of many industry meetings put on by organizations such as IAFP, ICFP, American College, College for Financial Planning, and the like. Any registered representative with a professional designation will need to be concerned with the amount of continuing education units (CEUs) required each year for validation.

SALES/MARKETING/PRACTICE MANAGEMENT

Increasing business and doing it profitably is the name of the game. Is there a special person or department who will help you close a sale if needed? Can you take clients to your home office and have them speak to management on occasion? Are sales materials such as mailers, newsletters, and/or company brochures available?

Most planners can sell, but do they possess the skills needed to run a successful practice? Being a broker-dealer *is* a business, and therefore its management should have in-depth expertise in the practice management field. Can you call upon them for answers and help in writing your business plan, defining staffing needs, or office layout? Is there assistance available to help you in making the transition to the new firm and in orienting you and your staff with home office procedures?

PAYOUT

Last but certainly not least is the question of payout. Commission schedules will vary not only in the base amount but in additional bonuses, perks, or charges against commissions. Therefore, it is important to evaluate the entire package and translate it into bottom-line numbers. Consider the following:

- Rates and bonuses may differ for different product lines, such as general securities, unit trusts, mutual funds, limited partnerships, proprietary products, and insurance.
- Rates can scale upward with production or length of service. Is a retroactive amount paid upon reaching a new level? Do you start over again each calendar year?
- Can you override another representative? Can you determine the override percentage?
- Do the commission statements provided with your check give enough detail to determine if you have been paid correctly?
- Is equity participation in the firm itself available?
- Check for insurance benefits and reimbursements for continuing education classes and seminars.
- Can you get a draw against commissions or a commission advance with or without interest charges?
- What is the payout frequency and number of days between submitting business and payday? If your commission goes astray, do you get paid by special check, or must you wait until the next pay period? Does the firm pay you when the trade hits the blotter, or do you have to wait until they are paid by the appropriate company?
- What fees are charged against commissions:
    Monthly service fees
    Licensing/renewal fees
    Bonding fees
    Production quota assessments
    Postal charges
    Supplies charges
    Computer charges

CONCLUSION

You are now aware of some of the many variations of products and services a broker-dealer may offer. Recognize that there is a correlation between services offered and the payout, since each service is an expense to the firm and is considered in the compensation arrangement. There is no need to "pay" indirectly for services you do not want. The initiate will require more assistance in several areas and should be willing to give up more commission dollars for this help. On the other hand, the sophisticated representative may not need any ancillary services, only a vehicle for processing securities transactions legally. In this case, a higher-payout firm may be the logical choice. When you are considering a potential firm affiliation, your personal needs and preferences must be clearly defined in advance, much like data gathering in the financial planning process. Select the firm that can meet the needs for your experience level and type of practice, avoiding the broker-dealers that offer extensive support in areas where you have no interest.

There will be a time when you might wonder if you should be your own broker-dealer. The answer lies in whether you can duplicate the services you need for less money than you are now leaving on the table. In general, the narrower the focus, the sooner your production numbers will allow this possibility to make sense.

Selecting the right broker-dealer is important. Aligning with the wrong choice can spell disappointment and frustration, but the right association can enhance your practice immensely and make the running of your own planning firm a fulfilling and rewarding experience.

"When you choose a company to work for, or a broker-dealer to represent, look beyond the payout to get an overview of the total package."

—LEO R. BURNS, CFP

Broker-Dealer Support and Compensation Beyond Payout

Leo R. Burns, CFP, is a financial planner with IDS Financial Services, Inc. He practices in Leominster, Massachusetts, and was one of the eleven original charter members of the IDS "Gold Team." He has been providing full-service, comprehensive financial planning counseling to middle-and upper-income businesspersons, professionals, and individuals for thirteen years.

Mr. Burns teaches College for Financial Planning curriculum for Northeastern University in Boston. He is treasurer of the Greater Boston Society of the Institute of Certified Financial Planners, a member of the board of directors of the Boston chapter of the International Association for Financial Planning, and former president of the Montachusett Estate Planning Council. Mr. Burns is a U.S. Navy veteran who flies his own airplane to see clients and attend professional conferences.

To most people, the word "compensation" converts subconsciously into dollars. This commentary will attempt to put the finishing touches on a conversation begun in a hotel lounge in Philadelphia in September of 1986 between myself and Andrew M. Rich, the author of this book, and will point out additional elements that I consider to be compensation.

There are over 80 colleges and universities in the United States that have become affiliated with the College for Financial Planning in Denver and that are teaching the CFP curriculum. As an adjunct faculty member of the college, I have had the opportunity to observe the phenomenal increase in the number of enrollments. As I observe, the questions arise. Where will these future planners work? With what potential clients? Who will supervise them? Regulate them? Help them to do the kind of job with their clients that they have given me the impression they want to do?

There are other questions, too—such as professionalism, liability, products, due diligence, S.E.C. compliance, and the like. Above all is the question of earning a living. For whom will they work? Should they become employees of large companies or independent contractors, or should they start their own broker-dealerships? Ultimately, the decision could turn on such tacky pivots as the compensation that the financial planner will earn.

In the final analysis, the financial planning process depends on the benefits derived by the client. The planner must earn a living, and the vendor of the products that the planner uses to implement plans must make a profit. These three entities form a triumvirate, each one of whom is attempting to improve his or her own circumstances while either providing a service to or paying a fee for services to each of the others. None of the three is much good without the others, and in the words of a veteran financial planner who taught me a lot of the fine points, "A three-legged stool won't stand if one leg is missing." This short essay will attempt to address some of the points of interest to that leg of the stool represented by the financial planner.

Let's consider some of the items that we think of as compensation. The first, of course, is cash income. In most cases that comes as financial planning fees and commissions from the products that we use when implementing the financial plans our clients pay us to develop for them. Fees compensate us for the time and expense to develop our clients' individual financial plans. Commissions are paid to us by the companies whose products we use to implement the clients' plans. The fees and commissions are used by us to offset the expense of maintaining the appropriate skill levels and awareness of the changes in the techniques, tax laws, and diversity of products available to fill various needs. In addition, we are confronted with the expense of maintaining a staff and providing service on an ongoing basis to clients who utilize the products and services that generated the income in the first place. Finally, we are responsible to our own families and must earn a fair amount of money that we can use to cover their needs.

With all of those things to bear in mind, it is no wonder that a fair amount of planners are concerned with their fees and commissions on a perpetual basis. We are all at least fairly familiar with the variety of compensation plans that have been designed to attract us, and the opportunities that we are provided with. There are commissions, bonuses, conventions, trips to exotic places, deferred compensation, pension and profit-sharing plans, and so on.

I will not attempt to pass judgment on the "best" compensation package available. If you thought that by reading this article you would learn where the most attractive employment opportunity lay, then I am sorry to disappoint you.

On the other hand, if you think that you will learn a few ideas to help you in your financial planning practice, read on.

In my opinion, we are compensated when we do not have to spend money to perform due diligence. When I am able to recommend a product to a client that I am fairly confident will achieve its stated objective, then I am compensated. If I do not have to spend time before my client making excuses for poor performance, or explaining why a particular general partner has had to file for bankruptcy, or why a check wasn't mailed on time, then I am compensated. Bear in mind, I'm not referring to the occasional clerical error. I'm talking here about the outright poor performance and the loss of large amounts of client money that is often the direct responsibility of the broker/dealer and or general partner/sponsor.

A financial planner is not relieved of the burden of due diligence by his or her broker-dealer. While the broker-dealer has to perform due diligence on the product, the planner is held accountable for the contents of the prospectus and for seeing to it that it is an appropriate investment for the client. There are countless planners in the United States who will be happy to tell you war stories about their experiences with investments gone bad. It should be noted here that some of these planners were just plain greedy. Had they been more diligent, and less concerned with the size of their commission, they might very well be spending less time defending themselves and therefore might be more profitable today. I am aware that these are harsh words, but they may save you a lot of grief if they are taken seriously.

Another area of compensation that is invaluable is in the area of service. Regular financial statements to a client by a broker-dealer that are readable can save valuable time and effort. Conveniences, such as 800 telephone numbers, where service is available to clients for such things as transfers and redemptions, both by wire and by mail, are client pacifiers. Happy and agreeable voices on the end of a telephone line can tame the most ferocious of beasts.

Accessibility to home office types who are ready and willing to be of assistance makes life easy. Large case proposals, underwriting, actuarial and qualified plan maintenance, to say nothing about accounting and law, are areas in which most financial planners lack expertise. While these kinds of services are made available to financial planners by broker-dealers so that the products become easier to use in client plans, it should be remembered by the planners that they are generally less expensive by far (if any direct expense at all) than they would be if we were to have to pay for them out of our net income. To be sure, this kind of ''home office overhead'' is a determining factor in establishing commission structure. But in my opinion, there is just so much that an individual planner can pay attention to. These kinds of services, provided in a professional way, pay for themselves by helping us do the best possible job for our clients. If in the process they keep us out of trouble, then their worth is beyond measure.

Another area of compensation is in advertising and marketing. For the new planner, these can be invaluable. Most people who start a new business have to concern themselves with this consideration. Attracting and keeping new clients can be an overwhelmingly expensive proposition. It is far easier to hold yourself out as a representative of a firm that has instant name recognition and an image created by advertising that is positive and identifiable.

Recently, I attended a convention at which there were over three hundred financial planners. It was an educational event, and one of the objectives was the sharing of information. It was amazing to me to hear the stories about client investments that had not performed as represented by the sponsors and/or the broker-dealers. Some of the planners in attendance were spending time in court to defend themselves against claims made by their clients. It would seem to me, therefore, that planners will have to take it upon themselves to require better disclosure of information from those broker-dealers whom they represent. The obvious conclusion is that the planners who have not had to endure these kinds of experiences are being compensated fairly as well as adequately.

An item that should be considered very carefully is the people you will be associated with. We are all products of our collective experience. Many times, our associates will affect our attitude and professionalism. Choose well the people you spend time learning from and working with. Their skills and abilities could some day be yours.

When you choose a company to work for, or a broker-dealer to represent, look beyond the payout to get an overview of the total package. In addition to the questions already raised, get an idea of how the possible B-D is thought of in the industry by other financial planners and B-Ds. More important, perhaps, is how the B-D sees itself. What are its corporate values? Does it have a mission objective? Is it compatible with your own? Will you be proud to have your name associated with it? Look at its advertising. Is it honest and straightforward, or is it misleading?

It is to be hoped that some B-Ds will read this and begin to accept the idea that there is a new breed of financial planner on the front line today. They're honest, hard-working, sincere planners who want their own reputations to be above reproach and untarnished by the errors of others. But most of all, they want what is best for their clients. They have true grit.

Chapter IV

Regulation and Liability

Andrew M. Rich, CFP
Ronald R. Riva
Wendy J. Heifetz
Jacqueline H. Hallihan
Edwin P. Morrow, CLU, ChFC,
CFP
Henry I. Montgomery, CFP
Stuart A. Ober
Paul J. Lockray, J.D.

"An investment advisor is a fiduciary who has a duty of undivided loyalty to his investment advisory clients and must deal fairly and honestly with them."

—ANDREW M. RICH, CFP

Investment Advisor Registration and Compliance

Andrew M. Rich, CFP, is President of AMR Planning Services, Inc., a Registered Investment Advisory firm. He holds a bachelor of arts degree in economics from Queens College of the City University of New York and an M.S. in taxation from Long Island University.

Mr. Rich is the author of *How to Survive and Succeed in a Small Financial Planning Practice*, published by Reston Publishing Company, is a contributing author to *The Money Encyclopedia*, published by Harper and Row, and is profiled in *The Financial Planner: A New Professional*, published by Longman Publishing. He has been quoted in numerous financial publications.

Mr. Rich is an Adjunct Assistant Professor of Financial Management at New York University and a member of the Adjunct Faculty of the College for Financial Planning. He is a Registered Representative licensed through USLICO Securities Corporation and a General Agent for the Bankers Security Life Insurance Society. Mr. Rich is currently the Ethics Vice President of the Long Island chapter of the IAFP and is a member of the ICFP.

Under the Investment Advisors Act of 1940, persons or entities who are in the business of providing investment advice to others must register with the Securities and Exchange Commission. Nevertheless, there are exceptions.

The general rule is that any person who holds himself or herself out to be a financial planner and charges a fee to the client must be registered with the SEC. This applies whether you provide investment advice on specific securities or just investment advice in general. The point to remember is that if you charge a fee for your advice, you must be a Registered Investment Advisor. Furthermore, if you hold yourself out to be a financial planner and receive the compensation (other than fees), in all likelihood you would be required to register under the Act. Any questionable situation should be checked thoroughly with an attorney who handles SEC matters.

Fee planners are required to register regardless of the number of clients they have. There is no minimum number of clients. The rule is clear that if you hold yourself out to be a financial planner, you must be a Registered Investment Advisor. Yes, that means that even if you have only one client, you must register. The only exception to the rule is if you have fewer than 15 clients and you do not hold yourself out to the general public to be an investment advisor or financial planner. In other words, the investment advice must be incidental to your principal function, such as attorney or accountant. Commission-only planners may be relieved from registration if they qualify under the broker-dealer exclusion or if their broker-dealer firm is registered under the act and they are properly supervised. Any licensed registered representative should obtain counsel regarding his or her responsibility for registration. Under many circumstances, the broker-dealer exclusion does not apply.

Financial planners who are not Registered Investment Advisors, but should be, have a threefold problem. First, they are conducting business in violation of the Investment Advisors Act of 1940. Second, clients can sue for refund of their investments, and, in some cases, for punitive damages. Third, states can take further action for failure to comply with state security laws. All of these problems, together or separate, spell disaster.

Planners who fail to register as required may face the SEC, which has the right to seek an injunctive action. In other words, the SEC files suit in the U.S. District Court asking the court to direct the planner to cease rendering investment advice without being registered. Should the court enter a judgment for the SEC and should the planner continue to practice without regard to the court order, the SEC may ask the court to find the planner in criminal contempt.

The application for registration for investment advisor begins on Form ADV, a thick booklet. There are many questions that require careful thought, such as who will be the investment advisor—an individual? A corporation? A partnership? The business form of SEC registration, the positives and the negatives, are beyond the scope of this article.

Nevertheless, no matter what form you choose, most planners find registration to be a struggle. I strongly advise any registrant to talk to as many registered financial planners as possible, to his or her attorney, and perhaps to the SEC staff itself. There are even services that assist planners in registering as investment advisors. Although there are many reasons why investment advisor applications get rejected, many are rejected because original signatures and not mechanical reproductions must be on all copies of the execution page.

The whole process of registration should take less than 45 days. In fact, the SEC legally has only 45 days to act on an application, or it must show cause for rejection. The time clock begins from the date on which the SEC determines that all information is in the application period. A financial planner may request that the application for registration be expedited by submitting a cover letter with the application.

Don't forget the $150 check, which is a one-time, nonrefundable filing fee.

Once registered, you are under the jurisdiction of your regional office of the SEC.

What is an investment advisor? Every financial planner must know the answer to this question. The term "investment advisor" is defined in Section 202 (a)(11) of the Investment Advisors Act of 1940:

> Any person who, for compensation, engages, in the business of advising others, either directly or through publications or writings, as to the value of securities, or who, for compensation and as part of a regular business, issues or promulgates analysis or reports concerning securities.

In other words, an investment advisor is a fiduciary who has a duty of undivided loyalty to his investment advisory clients and must deal fairly and honestly with them. In both theory and practice, financial planners owe their allegiance to their clients and not to anyone else.

THE BROCHURE RULE

SEC Rule 204-3 requires the financial planner to deliver to the prospective client one of the following documents: either (1) a current copy of part two of advisors Form ADV or (2) a brochure containing information similar to Form ADV Part II. The advisor must deliver or offer to deliver each year to the client a copy of the brochure or Form ADV Part II.

In regard to a new client, the investment advisor must deliver the brochure at least 48 hours before entering into an advisory contract; or the advisor can deliver the brochure, as long as the contract provides that the client has five days to terminate the contract and provides full or partial refunds, as mandated in the law.

I believe that planners should opt for the brochure rather than Form ADV Part II. Unfortunately, Form ADV Part II appears to be the kind of document that would be delivered by a process server and not a financial planner. It is official-looking, and it is laden with technical questions and procedures. Most importantly, it is boring for the client to read. On the other hand, a well-written brochure not only complies with SEC regulations but also increases planner marketability.

DISCLOSURE OF COMMISSIONS

Since the investment advisor is a fiduciary to the client, commissions and compensation received as a result of investment recommendations must be disclosed to the client. More importantly, the disclosure of commissions or any form of back-end compensation helps to build a strong trust relationship with your client. How disclosure should be made, whether written or oral or simply just an offer to disclose, is a matter that should be discussed between a planner and legal adviser.

ANNUAL REPORTING

The investment advisor is required to file an annual report with the SEC on Form ADV-S. The purpose of this report is primarily to let the SEC know that you are still in business. Actually, you could be out of business for years and the SEC would never know it, since the average SEC audit is about every six years or so.

Form ADV-S is a very simple reporting form and should not take more than a few minutes to complete. It is required to be filed within 90 days after the end of the adviser's fiscal year, and failure to file is a violation of Rule 204-1 (c) under the Investment Advisors Act of 1940, which could result in action by the Commission to revoke your registration.

Certain advisors are required to file an annual balance sheet with the SEC. Any adviser who takes custody of client funds or charges fees more than six months in advance must submit a balance sheet with Form ADV-S.

BOOKS AND RECORDS

Any person or entity registered as an investment advisor should become familiar with Rule 204-2. This rule specifies what books and records the advisor must keep and for how long.

In respect to the financial planner, this rule requires that the planner keep every piece of paper relating to the client. This includes written financial plans and recommendations, all contracts and agreements, written disclosure of commissions, communication concerning receipt of the brochure and/or annual offer for a brochure, and all financial records. In effect, you are required to keep just about everything except your carbon paper and used typewriter ribbons.

EXAMINATIONS

About every six years, give or take a few years, you can expect a visit from a representative of the SEC examination staff. The intent of an SEC examination is to see whether you are complying with all the rules and regulations. The examination has a twofold purpose: (1) to detect fraud and (2) to correct human mistakes. The vast majority of deficiencies are human mistakes and usually are corrected on the spot. Many of the mistakes involve improper paperwork procedures on the part of the advisor. Nonetheless, all the deficiencies are analyzed for three specific areas:

1. Does it involve fraud?
2. Is the integrity impaired by deficiency?
3. Is the deficiency an error of omission or commission?

The advisor will then receive a deficiency letter, which is really a directive to resolve the matter. It is likely that only in the case of repeated violations will the SEC take formal action.

SEC ACTION

The only way that an action can be commenced is by a formal vote of the Securities and Exchange Commission. A formal investigation cannot be commenced without the approval of the Commission. The Commission consists of five members, each having a five-year term with one member's term expiring each year. Each member must be appointed by the President with the approval of the Senate, and no more than three of the Commission members can be members of the President's political party. The purpose of an SEC action is to restore the parties involved to equality and to prohibit violations. The SEC, in itself, does not punish and cannot sue for punitive damages. Only in a state court can a client sue an investment advisor for punitive damages.

You are urged to learn everything that you can about SEC compliance. But most important—for your sake and the sake of your client—comply!

Much of the preceding information has been taken from Andrew Rich's *How to Survive and Succeed in a Small Financial Planning Practice*, ©1984. Prentice-Hall, Inc., Englewood Cliffs, New Jersey.

"The RIA should view an initial informal investigation as an excellent opportunity to confirm compliance under the various requirements established by the Act. An SEC inspector can be tremendously helpful."

—RONALD R. RIVA

Ronald R. Riva is Vice President of Investment Adviser Client Services for National Regulatory Services, Inc., a Lakeville, Connecticut-based consulting firm for broker-dealers and registered investment advisers. Mr. Riva has written for other industry publications and has lectured to private audiences and public seminars. He is a graduate of Hotchkiss School and received his B.A. from the University of Connecticut, where he majored in economics.

Regulatory Inspections: Audit-Proofing for the Registered Investment Adviser

All investment advisers, subject to registration by Section 203 of the Investment Adviser Act of 1940 (the Act), shall be bound to inspection by the Securities and Exchange Commission (SEC) and, in most cases, by state securities authorities. To become a registered investment adviser (RIA), the SEC registration materials must be filed (in triplicate) with the SEC in Washington, D.C. Copies are then disseminated to the applicable SEC regional office, and notification will also be sent to governing state securities offices. The RIA will be subject to, at least, inspection by the SEC and by those states that have established regulations (and filing requirements) for RIAs. There are currently 38 states which have enacted investment adviser laws, and additional states have proposed amendments specifically including the term "financial planner." The regulatory superstructure under which RIAs must conduct business is, in comparison to the broker-dealer, much less restrictive. A broker-dealer becomes the subject of regulations by at least three entities and, in some instances, by as many as five additional entities.

With this in mind, RIAs should find their regulatory web much less intimidating. The RIA should not, however, entertain the idea that he or she will somehow escape detection. It is certain that at some time the investment adviser will be the subject of inspection by a regulatory body. The number of RIAs conducting a public business is increasing greatly (present registration numbers reveal some 12,000 RIAs, with incoming application volumes nearly doubling those of previous years). The pressure of these increasing numbers will eventually result in enlarged enforcement staffs, while "bad publicity" and eroding public confidence will also add to the building demands for augmented controls.

Authorization to conduct inspections by the SEC is promulgated under Section 209 of the Act. Section 209(b) provides that for the

> purpose of any investigation, or any proceeding under this title, any member of the commission, or any officer thereof designated by it, is empowered to administer oaths and affirmations, subpoena witnesses, compel their attendance, take evidence, and require the production of any books, papers, correspondence, memoranda, contracts, or other records which are relevant or material to the inquiry.

However, in connection with the above, Section 213(a) of the Act includes the provision that

> any person or party aggrieved by an order issued by the Commission . . . may obtain a review of such order in the United States Court of Appeals . . . by filing in such court, within sixty days after the entry of such order, a written petition praying that the order of the Commission be modified or set aside in whole or in part. No objection to the order of the Commission shall be considered by the court unless such objection shall have been urged before the Commission, or unless there were reasonable grounds for failure to do so.

During most routine inspections, however, invoking Section 213 of the Act would be considered highly unusual. In general, an inspection will either be initiated as an informal investigation, or the much less favorable "formal" investigation.

A routine inspection may occur anytime after registration. If state registration is also applicable, inspection by state authorities may also occur. The RIA should view an initial informal investigation as an excellent opportunity to confirm compliance under the various requirements established by the Act. An SEC inspector can be tremendously helpful. It is important to recognize the fact that the Commission's initial purpose in inspecting a RIA is to uncover potential violations, "nipping them in the bud" before serious problems arise. It is not an SEC inspector's desire to escalate any compliance problems.

A formal investigation, however, is an entirely different matter. This type of investigation can be triggered by a client complaint, complaints from other practitioners, a public advertisement not in compliance, or, actually, whenever the SEC believes there is cause to undertake such an investigation. It is imperative to have legal counsel present during any formal investigation.

Inspections which are not "for cause" routinely begin with an interview by the inspector(s), asking the RIA to describe the nature and type of business conducted, the names and identities of any new personnel, and any recent changes that may have occurred. The adviser may be asked to describe any special problem or asked whether the firm utilizes any computerized equipment to assist in generating advice or maintaining required records.

A formal investigation, on the other hand, will begin by written notification of the "for cause inspection," disclosing the rights of the RIA. The SEC will begin with direct inspection of books and records, including client files. Due to the serious nature of the examinations, the examiners come well prepared and may already have an excellent idea of exactly where the problems occurred and how best to detect them. It is important for the RIA to keep in mind that access to records may not be denied. In *SEC v. Olsen d/b/a Fitch Investors Service* (September 2, 1965), denial to reproduce records, on the ground that production would have violated the constitutional privilege against self-incrimination and the prohibition against unreasonable searches and seizures, resulted in a temporary injunction. Failure to comply with an injunction may result in additional civil proceedings.

Due to a limited number of enforcement personnel, the nature of an examination will depend upon the type of business conducted. In general, the RIA will be categorized by "risk," with the Commission and state authorities will base the urgency of an inspection on the type of business presently being conducted. High on the priority list are investment advisers having custody (as defined) of client funds or securities or investment advisers with an associated person (as defined) having custody of client funds or securities. Other high-risk categories include discretionary asset management accounts, corporate structures which include broker-dealers registered as investment advisers, an RIA who has a parent company which is a broker/dealer, or an affiliate of the RIA. These types of RIAs can expect earlier and more frequent inspections by regulatory bodies.

While "less-risk" categories are associated with a less-frequent inspection rate, the fact remains that an inspection will occur sooner or later. This category of investment adviser may simply receive a letter or phone call from an SEC district office, or from a state inspector, inquiring as to any problems or difficulties the investment adviser may be experiencing, and the communication may include an invitation to meet with an officer of the commission (or from the state, should it be a state inspection). The types of services offered by an investment adviser considered "less risk" include: nondiscretionary asset management accounts, financial planning (excluding any of the above services), newsletters, nondiscretionary timing services, or general consultation services. During the course of an inspection, the RIA will be requested to provide the examiner(s) with a number of different items. (It is, unfortunately, impossible to even briefly touch upon all the areas which an examiner may possibly explore.)

If an investment adviser can demonstrate that proper books and records and a proper filing system are all in place, then a major hurdle of the inspection process will be successfully cleared. Ascertaining that maintenance of proper books and records has been adequately undertaken is of paramount importance during the inspection process. The following list includes those major items requested during an inspection. (This list is intended to be only a summary, and every RIA should, as a minimum, carefully review all the books and records that must be maintained and design proper compliance procedures.)

1. A list of all officers, directors, partners, employees, and stockholders, including their addresses, social security numbers, percentage of ownership, titles (for officers), annual salaries, and bonuses (if any).

2. A list of any branch offices, including applicable information as itemized in Item 1.

3. A list of all personal securities transactions, as required by Rule 204-2a (12) or (13).

4. A list of any prior, current, or potential litigation.

5. Total number of clients receiving the following services and the value of their accounts:
   a. investment supervisory services
   b. managed accounts
   c. discretionary accounts
   d. consultation
   e. advisory services to investment companies
   f. subscription-based publication account

6. A sample of each contract, subscription agreement, custodian agreement, power of attorney, and any other agreement entered into between the RIA and its clients and all fee schedules.

7. A list of all broker/dealers used by the firm (or by any associated persons) and the sum total of commissions paid each during the past year.

8. Name and address of current auditor or accountant.

9. Name and address of legal counsel.

10. A statement as to the adviser's sources of information used in formulating investment advisory recommendations.

11. If the adviser has custody or possession or access to any funds or securities, then the adviser must provide:
    a. The number of clients receiving this type of service and the value of the account.
    b. Copy of custody or possession agreement.
    c. Location of securities held in safekeeping.
    d. A list of all custodians and depositories used for clients' funds and securities.

12. Copies of adviser's latest balance sheet, trial balance, and income statement.

13. A copy of each advertisement, radio or television script, newspaper advertisement, or any general solicitation letters.

14. A copy of the written disclosure statement that the adviser is currently using to comply with Rule 204-3 and a recent copy of each publication or any other information distributed to any present or potential client or any other person describing any aspect of the adviser's activities.

15. A list of loans, including those from clients and any other sources.

Indicate terms, amounts, dates of liens, and current balances (also indicate collateral, if any).

16. A list of all clients who are related, directly or indirectly, to the adviser or any of its associated persons.

17. Copies of all amendments to the most current ADV and all annual reports required under the Act (ADV-S). (It is of major importance to maintain an accurate Form ADV on file with the SEC and the states in which the RIA services clients.)

The details of an inspection will concentrate on three main areas: (a) books and records, (b) administration and procedures, and (c) advisory services. An inspector will review in detail the financial strength of the RIA by examining all financially related books and records, including fees charged to clients (substantiating that fees charged are consistent with the fee schedule and advisory contracts). Inspectors look specifically for evidence of churning, scalping, suitability, deceptive advertising, improper record keeping, and best execution. Registration materials will be reviewed for current accuracy.

Compliance with proper disclosure is a major concern. An RIA must be able to submit evidence of disclosure delivery for every client, and, in subsequent years, that an offer to deliver a current brochure has also been made. Conflicts of interest are carefully reviewed to ensure that honest and full disclosure is provided to every client. Do recommendations match client objectives? Are accounts churned or scalped? Are any rules with respect to prohibited soft-dollar arrangements being violated? Contracts will be reviewed to confirm compliance with Sections 205 (1), (2), and (3) and to check for any objectional hedge clauses within the contract. An examiner will also look for evidence that an RIA may be acting contrary to contractual arrangements. All aspects of client transactions will also be closely reviewed.

After the initial inspection, a written report will be reviewed at the inspector's main office; within approximately 90 days after a visit by an SEC field inspector, the RIA can expect a letter itemizing any deficiencies. The RIA should carefully review all areas of concern and seek immediate clarification of any questions which may exist. It is standard SEC procedure to request a written explanation of any unclear areas noted in the deficiency letter. All deficiency letters should be responded to in a timely and efficient manner. Remember, a RIA is a fiduciary and, as such, the burden to prove compliance is placed solely on the RIA.

Follow-up inspections may be conducted to ensure that all deficiencies have been properly corrected and that procedures have been adopted to prevent future occurrences.

In the case of serious offenses, an RIA may be temporarily enjoined while further investigations are conducted. Repeated violations to SEC requests can result in a permanent injunction against the adviser (*SEC* v. *Blauin ED Michigan*, 1983). The SEC may limit the activities of a RIA, or bar the firm and any of its employees on a temporary or permanent basis. Therefore, RIA compliance should be taken seriously. While many RIAs anticipate the inspection process with a bit of trepidation, the SEC's role is to supervise and maintain public confidence in the investment industry, and the inspection program is an effective method to ensure and maintain compliance. In other words, the examiners are merely doing their jobs.

What follows are some suggestions to help an RIA ''survive'' an inspection.

Initially, after preliminary introductions have been dispensed with, ask what triggered the inspection. If the suspected problem does not exist, provide the examiner with supporting documentation. If, however, it is a formal investigation, call counsel immediately.

Make a strong effort to provide the examiner with a private room and easy access to a phone, and identify a specific individual as his or her liaison. If the private room is an individual's office, remove all materials. If the examiners ask for specific information, provide it promptly, even if in doing so a disturbance is likely to be created. If information is requested which will take a substantial amount of time to generate, an RIA may request that the information be provided in a more convenient form. However, always provide the examiner with everything requested. If an examiner asks to interview anyone in the firm, have a principal or your attorney present during the interview. Resist, gently, private interviews with employees. If possible, review or make copies of all materials delivered to an examiner.

In summary, the RIA is bound by the rules and regulations promulgated under the Investment Adviser Act of 1940. Section 209 of the Act empowers the SEC to inspect any investment adviser, at any time. It is in the RIA's best interests to establish sound compliance procedures during the start-up period. Always remember: there is a great deal more to a successful compliance program than merely filing with the SEC and paying $150.00.

Hand in hand with the paperwork involved in the registration process, an RIA should prepare for a mock inspection by reviewing and establishing compliance standards to ensure that the appropriate standards have been developed right from the start. It's a great deal easier to keep up than it is to catch up. It's also less time-consuming, more cost-efficient, and offers much more peace of mind, to be in compliance from day one!

The author acknowledges, with appreciation, the assistance of Jacqueline H. Hallihan, President of National Regulatory Services, Inc., and Marianne Czernin, Assistant Manager, Broker-Dealer Client Services.

"As a financial planner, holding the proper licenses needed to receive commissions will enable you to earn a greater income."

—WENDY J. HEIFETZ

Securities Licensing for Financial Planners

Wendy Heifetz entered the securities industry nearly a decade ago with degrees in finance and business management and an in-depth knowledge of the psychology of the teacher-student relationship. As training director for a Wall Street training school, she initiated and trial-tested innovative learning techniques designed to eliminate the humdrum and to keep student interest high. Now, as president of the fastest growing training corporation in America, she personally supervises all instructors and still personally teaches classes to test the materials developed for her programs. "Getting ahead was easy," says Ms. Heifetz. "Staying ahead is the challenge!"

WHY THE NEED FOR NASD LICENSING?

The need for a well-informed financial planner is becoming more and more important as the tax laws change and two-wage-earner families have more discretionary income. Financial planners need to keep current, as their clientele are becoming more informed.

As a financial planner you play a multifaceted role. You may give:

1. Financial advice for a fixed fee.
2. Financial advice for a fixed fee with the ability to execute trades based upon your portfolio recommendations to generate commissions.
3. Financial advice with a fee based upon a percentage of the net worth.
4. Financial advice with a fee based upon a percentage of the assets in the portfolio.
5. Financial advice with a fee based upon commissions only.

So far, there are no licensing requirements to be fulfilled in order to call yourself a financial planner. (This will most likely change shortly.) Your knowledge concerning investments and portfolio strategy is obtained from your own research and experience. If you charge a fixed fee and do not receive commissions on your recommendations, your income will be limited. Your advice will enable an already licensed NASD (National Association of Securities Dealers, Inc.) financial planner to obtain commissions on your suggestions.

As a financial planner, holding the proper licenses needed to receive commissions will enable you to earn a greater income. To explore what a financial planner must do to obtain these licenses and to provide information regarding the licenses you might need are the purpose of this article.

THE EXAMINATIONS

In order to obtain your NASD license, you must successfully complete a licensing examination. There are different licenses available, depending on the products you wish to sell. I will list a few.

Series 6—investment company products/variable contracts limited representative qualification examination • If you wish to sell mutual funds and variable annuity products exclusively, you will need to sit for the NASD Series 6 examination. This is referred to as a limited registration, since you are limited to sell a limited number of products.

The Series 6 exam is a 135-minute, 100-question, multiple-choice exam. A passing grade of 70 percent is required. This exam will cover subject matter such as:

General Area	Percentage of Questions
Investment securities, exchange markets, investment risks, and types of portfolio investment objectives	20%
Open-end investment companies, use of a prospectus, customer accounts, and services	40%
Variable annuities and retirement plans	20%
Securities industry regulations	20%

This exam is administered on a computer by the Plato System. Results are transmitted within a few minutes.

Series 22—direct participation programs limited representative qualification examination • If you wish to sell direct participation programs exclusively, you will need to sit for the Series 22 examination. This is also referred to as a limited registration, for you can only sell a limited number of products.

The Series 22 is a two-hour, 100-question, multiple-choice exam also administered on the Plato system. A passing grade of 70 percent is required. The subject matter covered on this exam includes:

General Area	Percentage of Questions
Direct participation program offerings	25%
Types of direct participation programs	24%
Taxation	35%
Regulation of direct participation programs	16%

Series 7—general securities registered representative • This is by far the most comprehensive and useful license to obtain. This one exam covers the products included in the Series 6 (variable annuities and mutual funds) and the Series 22 (direct participation programs) and also includes equity securities, such as common and preferred stock; debt securities, such as corporate, municipal and United States Government bonds; as well as options (equity, debt, and foreign currency). By qualifying for this exam you will be able to eliminate all the limited registration exams.

The Series 7 is a six-hour, 250-question, multiple-choice exam administered the third Saturday of every month. It is a paper-and-pencil test, and results will be obtained in less than one week.

The subject matter covered on this exam includes:

General Area	Percentage of Questions
Advertising, qualifying customers, industry regulations	12%
Securities instruments	33%
Handling customer accounts, taxation, and margin	14%
Securities markets, order handling, confirmations	14%
Economics, securities analysis, sources of financial information	12%
Portfolio analysis, investment strategies, retirement plans	15%

Series 24—general securities principal qualification exam • The Series 24 General Securities Principal examination is required for individuals who will be managing salespersons selling all types of securities. A manager of an office containing Series 7 registered representatives is required to sit for this examination.

The Series 24 is a three-hour, 125-question, multiple-choice examination. This exam is administered on the Plato system. A passing grade of 70 percent is required.

The subject matter covered on this exam includes:

General Area	Percentage of Questions
Supervision of investment banking activities	24%
Supervision of trading and market making activities	12%
Supervision of brokerage office operations	24%
Sales supervision, general supervision of employees, regulatory framework of NASD	24%
Compliance with financial responsibility rules	16%

HOW TO OBTAIN YOUR LICENSE

In order to qualify to sit for an exam, you must have an admission ticket. This ticket is obtained by completing a U-4 application. The source for this application is a brokerage firm, insurance company, or bank with a broker-dealer license with the NASD. These firms are referred to as *sponsors*. You must have a sponsor in order to sit for the exam.

HOW TO PREPARE FOR THE EXAMS

Most individuals preparing for the securities examinations attend a preparatory course.

The Series 6 and Series 22 examinations usually require a three-day course. Students attend the lecture series and sit for the exam approximately one week after the class.

The Series 7 General Securities examination usually requires a six-day course. Schools offer these courses either over a four-week period of time or a cram course held over a one-week period.

Students must allow sufficient time for a prestudy prior to class.

"It's fine to take one of the numerous exam crash courses, but make certain you really learn and don't merely cram to pass the test."

—JACQUELINE H. HALLIHAN

Registering as a Broker-Dealer

Jacqueline H. Hallihan is President and Chief Executive Officer of National Regulatory Services, Inc., a corporation she founded five years ago which specializes in registration and compliance areas of concern to investment advisers and broker-dealers.

Ms. Hallihan frequently prepares articles for various industry publications including, among others, *Financial Services Times, Financial Product News, Financial Planning Magazine,* and the *IAFP Broker Dealer Digest.* In addition, she writes and publishes her firm's *Regulator Register,* a monthly compliance newsletter.

Ms. Hallihan has spoken at conferences sponsored by the ICFP, the CLU, several IAFP chapters, and the IABDF, among others, including many privately sponsored symposiums. Additionally, under her direction, National Regulatory Services, Inc. has hosted six national broker-dealer conferences, each bringing together influential and well-respected members of the financial services industry to address topics of concern to industry professionals. Most recently, Ms. Hallihan has been involved in the creation of a new company, Regulated Systems.

The entrepreneurial drive to control one's own destiny will always prevail, in good and bad markets, good and bad economies, and in ever-changing regulatory environments. As history indicates, amidst talk of new "SROs" (self-regulatory organizations) for investment advisers, new government dealer regulation requirements, ongoing battles between banks and the Securities Industry Association (SIA), and insider scandals, entrepreneurs continue venturing off in record numbers to sit at the helm of a newly formed broker-dealer.

What makes them do it? What kind of experiences do they encounter along the way? How do they prepare for the process? What specific issues do they face?

Certainly, the majority should not attempt this process alone. This is not to say it can't be done; surely there are successful broker-dealers who poured over the regulations, sifted through the maze of papers, and wrestled with federal and state agencies. It's definitely not a recommended course of action, however—there are too many pitfalls, too many interrelated regulations, too many opportunities for the unknowing to find themselves unwittingly immersed in serious trouble with federal and state law violations.

The task of registering as a broker-dealer breaks down into two components: (1) the registration process itself and (2) the educational element—that is, *understanding* the underlying issues in order to be prepared to act lawfully once you have become a registered broker-dealer.

Let's look at the first component.

THE REGISTRATION PROCESS

SEC Registration

The registration and regulation of broker-dealers are governed by the Securities and Exchange Act of 1934. Section 15(a)(1) of the Act requires all broker-dealers to register as such, unless their business is exclusively intrastate and they do not make use of a national securities exchange. A *broker* is defined as a person engaged in the business of effecting transactions in securities for the accounts of others. (Banks are excluded from this definition.) A *dealer* is defined as a person engaged in the business of buying and selling securities for *his or her own account,* through a broker or otherwise. (Again, the term *dealer* does not include a bank, nor does it apply to a person who does not engage in these activities as part of a regular business.) Under the provisions of the Act, a prospective broker-dealer files a BD application with the Securities and Exchange Commission (SEC). Every broker-dealer who registers with the SEC (*unless* an exchange member effecting transactions exclusively in securities listed on the exchange with which he or she is a member) must join a registered securities association. The National Association of Securities Dealers, Inc. is currently the only registered securities association.

Rule 15b9-1 provides a further exemption from joining the NASD if the broker-dealer (1) is an exchange member; (2) does not carry customer accounts; and, (3) has an annual gross income from nonexchange securities transactions of $1000 or less.

Section 15(b) of the Exchange Act requires a broker-dealer registration application to be filed on Form BD, in triplicate, each originally signed and notarized. Form BD is a five-page form, with five schedules (A–E).

Schedule A is used for applicants which are corporations, Schedule B is for partnerships, Schedule C is for those applicants other than corporations or partnerships, Schedule D is for responding in detail to affirmative responses on Form BD, and Schedule E is for reporting branch office information.

No fee is required to be submitted to the SEC. However, a statement of financial condition must accompany the application (two original copies), as required by Rule 15b1-2.

Rule 15b1-2 requires that the statement of financial condition be as of a date within 30 days of submission of an application (and later, if necessary, to reflect any material changes). The statement must (1) disclose the nature and amount of assets and liabilities and net worth and (2) contain a computation of net capital and aggregate indebtedness pursuant to the net capital rule (Rule 15c3-1). Any securities holdings are to be listed on a separate schedule and, if bound separately, will be deemed confidential.

Additionally, a statement is required, in duplicate original, which makes representations as to the capital, financing, and facilities required to carry on the proposed business, together with an oath affirming that the statements are true.

Specifically, the statement must:

1. Represent that the capital has already been contributed and will continue to be devoted to the business as a broker-dealer, and describe the nature and source of the capital.

2. Represent that adequate arrangements have been made to establish and maintain facilities, and undertake to continue to maintain facilities and financing adequate for the business. This representation should be detailed, including a discussion of personnel, physical facilities, maintenance and preservation of books and records (Rules 17a3 and 17a4), and methods and procedures to be employed for supervision.

3. Describe the arrangements for obtaining funds for the operation of the broker-dealer for the first year, and the uses of the funds, including the expenses to be incurred during the first year. A statement is also required detailing how additional funds will be obtained, if necessary.

The SEC also requires a notice (in triplicate), designating the name and address of the person who will be the recipient for service of notice of any proceeding before the Commission.

The SEC also requires the submission of Page 2 of Form U-4 for any individuals appearing on Schedule A of Form BD who will not be processing a complete Form U-4 with the NASD. (Form U-4 is the uniform application for securities industry registration or transfer.)

Thus, in summary, the SEC application includes:

1. Three originally signed and notarized Form BDs.
2. Two statements of financial condition, within 30 days, each with an oath.
3. Two detailed statements with respect to capital, financing, and facilities (pursuant to SEC Rule 15b1-2), with an oath of certification.
4. Three Consents to Service of Process.
5. Three Page 2s of Form U-4 for individuals appearing on Schedule A of Form BD who will not be processing a complete Form U-4 through the NASD.

Once the SEC accepts an application for filing, it will either grant registration within 45 days or initiate proceedings to deny registration. A written request may be made for the Commission to accelerate the process.

The applicant, once registered, is required to update the Form BD as necessary, by filing amendments at both the federal and state level.

The broker-dealer also must file a statement with the SEC and NASD (principal and regional offices) annually, indicating that it has entered into an agreement with an independent public accountant to conduct the broker-dealer's annual audit during the following year. This statement is due by December 1. Alternatively, if the broker-dealer indicates, on initial filing, that this designation is of a continual nature (providing for successive annual audits), the broker-dealer is not required to file the statement annually. However, if this relationship changes at any time, the broker-dealer is required to notify the SEC pursuant to Rule 17a-5.

All broker-dealers registered with the SEC must join the Securities Investor Protection Corporation (SIPC), unless the broker-dealer meets one of the following exemptions: Their business is exclusively in

1. the distribution of registered open-end investment companies on unit investment trusts,
2. sale of variable annuities,
3. the business of insurance, or
4. investment advisory services to one or more registered investment companies or insurance company separate accounts.

Once the firm is registered with the SEC, the SEC will automatically notify SIPC, which will in turn mail an informational packet to the member, including a request of payment of a $100 fee. The broker-dealer will need to evidence ''proof'' of payment.

NASD Registration

Prior to incorporating a prospective broker dealer firm, the prospective applicant should submit three name selections to the NASD. This will save time and expense further down the road, as the NASD will not register an applicant with a name identical or similar to that of an already existing member. The name reservation request must be in writing and, if granted, the reservation will remain in effect for a period of 30 days. Additional 30-day extensions may be requested in writing.

For a $20.00 fee, the NASD provides a membership kit, including a booklet, ''How to Become a Member of the NASD.'' (Write to NASD, Book Order Department, 1735 K Street, NW, Washington, DC 20006). Also available is their ''Guide for CRD Form Filings,'' a useful tool for processing forms with the NASD's Central Registration Depository (CRD) once the firm is effectively registered.

As a prerequisite to NASD membership, the broker must be effectively registered with the SEC and ready for approval within its home state.

NASD applications include:

1. Originally signed and notarized Form BD (including Page 2 of Form U-4 for individuals appearing on Schedules A, B, or C who will not have a Form U-4 filed with the CRD).
2. Form U-4s, originally signed, for all personnel to be registered.

3. Fingerprint cards.
4. Statement of financial condition.
5. Appropriate fees, as follows:
   $500 member firm
   $ 50 per principal representative
   $ 50 per exam request
   $ 50 per branch office
   $ 14 per fingerprint card

If an applicant wishes to apply for a waiver from the two-registered-principals requirement, this request must be included in the application. Similarly, a request for a waiver from the financial-and-operations-principal requirement must also be submitted in writing. The NASD central office processes the application, and upon completion of its review, forwards it to the specific district office responsible for the applicant's region. The district office will require additional documentation, such as:

1. A current net capital computation, trial balance, and supporting schedules (such as a bank statement) for the most recent month end.
2. Books and records (such as general ledger).
3. For general securities broker dealers:
   a. A copy of the clearing agreement.
   b. Evidence of registration with the Securities Information Center (SIC) and direct inquirer agreement.
4. A copy of the fidelity bond.
5. A copy of the 15b1-2 statement filed with the SEC.
6. Description of the firm's securities business mix.
7. Copy of written supervisory procedures.
8. Proof of MSRB membership and designation of registered municipal principal (if applicable).
9. Copies of SEC and home state notice of registration.
10. Copy of the designation of accountant agreement.
11. Copies of account information forms.
12. Evidence of exam qualifications.
13. A statement indicating that the applicant has been inactive prior to effectiveness.
14. Subordination agreements (if any).
15. Evidence of membership with a registered exchange (if applicable).

Premembership Interview

Once the responsible district office has received all the required documentation and information from the NASD in Washington, and once all the applicant's principals have successfully completed the required principal qualification examinations, certain management personnel of the prospective broker-dealer will be required to attend a premembership interview (PMI) at the district office. Generally, the principals who must attend the PMI are those responsible for supervising the firm's activities, as well as any principals responsible for preparation of the firm's financial statements.

The PMI allows the NASD to judge whether an applicant firm can reasonably be expected to comply with all applicable rules and regulations once membership is granted. As outlined in the NASD kit, the district office reviews all pertinent material submitted by the firm in its membership application prior to the PMI for (1) the nature and scope of the firm's intended operations; (2) the business history and experience of all key registered principals; (3) the particulars involved in any criminal conviction of a prospective principal by any state or federal judicial authority; and (4) the details surrounding any disciplinary action against any person who is to become associated with the firm (whether in a registered or nonregistered capacity) by any securities regulatory body, as well as any past or present association with a broker-dealer for whom a SIPC trustee had been appointed.

At the close of a PMI, the NASD issues a ''restriction letter,'' to be executed by the applicant, outlining the operational restrictions and activities under which the applicant will be authorized to operate.

Following the PMI, and upon receipt of the executed restriction letter by the district office, the application will be referred to the NASD District Committee for membership approval. If membership is denied, an appeals procedure is available to the applicant. Once members have been approved, they must notify the NASD in writing if they wish to expand their business activities beyond that included in the restriction letter, demonstrating that they are qualified to engage in the areas into which they wish to expand.

State Registrations

A firm must also register as a broker-dealer in its home state, as well as in any other state in which it plans to do business. Registration applications are available directly from the states, and requirements vary from state to state.

Personnel Registration

The broker-dealer, once effective, submits a Form U-4, a fingerprint card, and exam qualifications, with the appropriate fee, to the CRD to register its principals and registered representatives with the NASD and appropriate states. (It is important that all checks include the member's name and CRD number.)

All branch offices are registered as such on Schedule E of Form BD. Fees are $50 per branch office.

EDUCATIONAL ELEMENT

With the firm's registration process now behind us, let's look at the second element—the educational perspective.

As you have read, the registration phase is a detailed process and involves a number of steps that must be carefully followed. It is, however, only a beginning phase.

Equally important, if not more so, is the continuing necessity of all involved principals and personnel comprehending, on an ongoing basis, the underlying compliance requirements in order to conform to federal and state requirements. This can be accomplished in a number of manners.

First, the personnel can pay particular attention throughout the examination qualification; it's fine to take one of the numerous exam crash courses, but make certain you really learn and don't merely cram to pass the test. It's vital to maintain the information beyond the day of the test. Second, read the written supervisory procedures carefully, and review them periodically. Take advantage of the compliance newsletters and conferences available, and consider an independent compliance audit from time to time. Train your personnel carefully and diligently.

It cannot be stressed strongly enough that adequate and proper procedures and systems be established from the onset; it's always easier to keep up than to catch up. From a compliance point of view, the catch-up game can be a great deal more costly than an investment of effort and time today.

"The financial planner should develop internal procedures to be used by himself, or by a fellow practitioner, to review the completeness of the work."

—EDWIN P. MORROW, CLU, ChFC, CFP

Techniques for Reducing Planner Liability

Edwin P. Morrow, CLU, ChFC, CFP, is Chairman of the Board of Confidential Planning Services, Inc., a network of independent planning firms throughout the United States and the United Kingdom, headquartered in Middletown, Ohio. He is the host of a weekly radio show and author of a weekly column, both entitled "Money Talks." He has taught as an adjunct instructor at several universities and is the author of *How to Select a Microcomputer*. Mr. Morrow has been admitted to the Registry of Financial Planning Practitioners and is affiliated with numerous professional organizations including the American Society of CLU's, the Institute of Certified Financial Planners, and the Ohio Association of Life Underwriters. He is a frequent speaker at professional conferences and has authored many articles.

As litigation against professionals became more popular, the initial concern of the practitioner was the escalation of liability insurance premiums. Today that is only a small part of the iceberg which threatens all professional persons. As the newest recognized profession, financial planning is now a fresh target for these suits. There is not just one liability threat; there are many:

- Escalation of liability insurance premiums
- Reduction in coverage limits
- Reduction in the scope of coverage
- Cancellation of coverage entirely
- Threats of simultaneous regulatory proceedings
- Threats of criminal (fraud) proceedings
- Professional society disciplinary response
- Litigation expenses
- Business interruption expense
- Loss of professional reputation and esteem
- Unfavorable media coverage
- Attachment of business assets
- Possible requirement to notify customers of pending claims
- Attachment of personal assets
- Loss of professional staff
- Extreme personal stress

The great majority of financial planners, and those who are making the transition to financial planning, can be characterized as having:

- both business and personal integrity
- strong desire to do nothing which is illegal or immoral
- empathetic and verbal communication skills
- a sincere desire to help others
- a very solid work ethic
- a spirit of independence

LIABILITY INSURANCE IS NOT ENOUGH

Even if adequate coverage for malpractice, errors and omissions, and financial bonding can be obtained, it is still wise for the financial planner to take loss control measures that can reduce the likelihood of a claim or lawsuit in the first place. A financial planner emerging victorious from a lawsuit still loses.

- Tremendous amounts of time will have been spent in court appearances, conferences, depositions, gathering files, and preparing memoranda. This will be nonbillable time for the planner and will be very disruptive on the work schedule.
- The frustration with the legal process will be incredible. This will have an effect on the planner's mental attitude and marketing activities.
- The planner's professional reputation will have been damaged, since

many persons will not be aware of the lawsuit's outcome or may believe, "where there's smoke, there's fire." The planner may have legal expenses for personal counsel in addition to those covered by the malpractice insurer, since there is always the possibility that the insurer may be of the opinion that the event in question is not covered under the provisions of the policy. This is a very real issue when there is a question of whether or not an act is one of planning advice or security sales and whether or not the insured may have been in violation of regulations or law.

DOCUMENT DISCLOSURE

Registered Investment Advisers (RIAs) are familiar with the disclosure requirements, but many financial planners have not registered with the Securities and Exchange Commission because they feel (however accurately or inaccurately) that they are not required to be a RIA. If a lawsuit should arise, it will not be within a few months. It may be several years after the initial discussions with the client. A recollection by the planner that he or she did disclose certain aspects of the client-planner-vendor relationship will have little weight in front of a judge or jury. The planner will appear to be self-serving. Likewise, a series of notes or memoranda developed years or months after the event are regarded with skepticism.

Records of disclosure and advice to the client should be:

- Executed contemporaneously with the event, such as notes or checklists completed during the planner-client interview.
- Prepared in an unequivocably clear fashion, as opposed to doodlings on a yellow legal pad or scribbling in the margin of a data form.
- Delivered to the client for review and agreement or acquiescence.
- Documented that the client did, in fact, receive them, such as a signature on a confirming copy or a return by the client with acceptance.

This documentation should be a regular part of a planner's operations and should be done in a similar fashion for all clients. Imagine yourself on the witness stand: The domineering attorney for the plaintiff glares at you with a "knowing smirk" to the jury and challenges:

My client has no record of your ever having mentioned (your fee, limit of services, securities relationships, etc.) to him. But here you have furnished us with your materials, four years later, that you'd have us believe you delivered to my client and kept in your file! My client says he was never advised of. . . . How can you expect us to believe those papers? Were they developed last week just for the trial?

If you have no papers, you are in bad shape. But wouldn't it be nice for you to be able to respond as follows?

I'm glad you asked that question. Our firm has a standard client disclosure process that consists of those elements which we follow with every client. Here is a copy of our checklists for Mr. Client which indicate the dates of each of the over one hundred clients of our firm. We always make full disclosures, and we always keep a record of it, for our benefit and for the benefit of our manysatisfied clients.

RECORD KEEPING

If the client is not engaging services for a comprehensive plan, but merely is getting some advice on a specific holding or proposed product, the planner who does provide comprehensive planning services should confirm the limit of the engagement. This is important to do even if there is no fee. Otherwise, a suit-prone client might say that he believed he was getting the comprehensive advice referred to in a brochure picked up in the planner's office. The planner should:

- Confirm all engagements in writing.
- Take detailed interview notes.
- Have a record that the client received all critical materials.
- Use a communications and disclosure record system (Appendix A).
- Staple or clip critical items to the client file.
- Keep reference copies of documents loose in the file.
- Insert key items into the client's plan.
- Insert key items into the planner's copy of the plan and all copies reproduced for other advisors.

If challenged by a court of law, arbitrator, regulatory agency, or a professional body to substantiate proper business practice, how can the planner respond, except with copies of contemporaneous records?

PLANNING AGREEMENT

The engagement letter, or planning agreement, defines the business relationship and mutual responsibilities of the client and planner. This document is the bedrock of the client-planner relationship. It must match the scope of services and expertise of the planning firm. Planners should strongly consider an arbitration clause to avoid litigation and its attendant publicity and expense.

POST-ACQUISITION

Following the introduction (engagement) interview with the client, the record keeping should commence. The client should receive frequent communication with notes and confirmations of information, attitudes, and actions. Frequent correspondence is reassuring to the client, encourages referrals, and keeps the planning objectives uppermost in the client's mind.

Most of this correspondence should be standard text. Each item may be customized in two ways:

- The planner indicates changes to the secretary/word processor operator, and they are typed into the letter.
- The planner makes a penned personal footnote on the standard letter. This works well for short items. If the comments become too lengthy, the planner merely writes ''Retype'' at the top and gives it to the secretary.

Frequent use of standard letters will improve client communications and save time (Appendix B).

INTERVIEW AGENDAS

Planners need to plan their meetings as well as they plan their clients' financial affairs. While each client's circumstances vary, the planning process does not. For that reason we suggest that the planner develop standard agendas for commonly held meetings. These may be easily personalized with the client's name and the meeting date. An organized meeting will be more efficient, and the client or prospect will be impressed by the use of agendas (see Appendix C).

TAKING INTERVIEW NOTES

Few clients are comfortable with tape-recorded interviews. Furthermore, the tapes merely have to be transcribed later. If the planner tries to write up the notes later, they will frequently be incomplete—or never finished. The interruptions which follow the client meeting will dim the planner's memory.

If the planner takes notes during the meeting, it will interrupt the flow of conversation and the concentration of the planner and the client. Usually the planner becomes exasperated with this and ceases taking effective notes.

The best solution is for a second person to take notes. This can be a secretary, planning intern, paraplanner, or fellow planner. This is excellent training and will produce fine notes promptly.

Interview notes should be prepared in very brief, numbered paragraphs on a word processor. The primary counselor then reviews and edits the notes before their mailing to the client. It is a good idea to include a copy in the client's plan so that it will be reproduced when copied for other advisors.

CONFIRMATIONS

The planner should make it a regular practice to confirm critical items with the client before making final recommendations:

- *Planning assumptions.* Those required by the planning software and those which the client has offered.
- *Planning objectives.* What the client wishes to accomplish. This might also include the client's attitudes toward risk tolerance and estate distribution.
- *Financial data.* The schedules of assets, income, and expenses should be confirmed before the plan is prepared. When faced with the entire plan and the desire to take action, the client may not notice critical omissions.

INTERNAL REVIEW CHECKLISTS

Many professions are now recognizing the need for internal review of their work before it is offered to the client. Major accounting and law firms have used this method of liability reduction for some time. The financial planner should develop internal procedures to be used by himself, or by a fellow practitioner, to review the completeness of the work:

- Analysis of the problems
- Review of the recommendation
- Final plan review

MASTER PLANNING CHECKLIST

It is easy for the planner to omit some aspect of the client's circumstances, which may later emerge as a significant liability. Airline pilots do not try to take off, even if it is their two-thousandth flight, without using a preflight checklist. A master checklist will need to cover many areas of potential client concern. Most items will not apply to a specific client, but all will be important to some clients.

A planner may start the construction of such a checklist by reviewing the most recent plans. It will help to break them down into areas, such as employee benefits, government benefits, retirement, estate planning, general insurance, and the like. The first draft of the checklist may have over one hundred items, and it will lengthen gradually as more plans are finished. This checklist may also be used to assemble a summary for the client (Appendix D).

PLANNER'S LEGAL RESPONSIBILITIES

The laws of agency and the legal relationships among a life insurance agent, the underwriting company, and the client are fairly well defined. There is also a large body of case law as well as company practice which delineates the agent's role, authority, and liability.

However, the legal position of the financial planner is not nearly so well-known. First, most financial planners wear several hats:

Employee (of a financial planning firm)

Agent (selling insurance products)

Registered Representative (securities)

Principal (of a securities firm)

Agent (of the financial planning firm—authorized to take certain actions on its behalf)

Employer (supervising other planners and staff)

Registered Investment Adviser (state and federal)

Clearly, we are into the realm of legal and regulatory issues that can have critical importance to the planner. Under certain circumstances, the entire personal wealth of the planner is at stake.

A recent *Wall Street Journal* article estimated that as many as 200,000 persons currently may be holding themselves out to the public as financial planners, with new entrants joining the ranks every day. Presumably, the reader is, or plans to be, a part of that veritable army of new financial professionals who have begun providing specialized financial planning services.

Even the most astute professional cannot be an expert in every field and would be foolish to try. Imagine how much more difficult the task must seem for the inexperienced or beginning planner seeking the most basic information necessary just to manage his or her practice. Still, survival as a financial professional is dependent in large part on learning as much as possible as quickly as possible and on knowing the law that applies to this type of practice.

There are a variety of reasons why today's financial planner needs a more thorough grounding in the legal aspects of practice, and especially a working knowledge of the applicable federal and state securities laws. For one thing, regardless of a planner's educational background or prior experience in tax planning, accounting, insurance, or real estate, his or her knowledge of law, and securities law in particular, is likely to be minimal. Yet he or she has entered what may well be the most highly regulated and legally circumscribed of all areas of professional activity, with ramifications that can be highly significant.

A recent issue of the *Ohio Underwriter* commented, ''There are over 100,000 more practicing attorneys than are needed at this time. Many are hungry. . . .'' This has encouraged the filing of many lawsuits—many of which are unfounded or are for amounts far out of proportion to the alleged loss.

It is possible, however, that you may someday be at fault. This might be through your personal act of commission or omission, or through that of an associate or employee. What can be done to protect all you have, and will someday accumulate, from a lawsuit?

The Financial Planner's Legal Guide by Eli P. Bernzweig, Esq. was published in 1986 and deals very effectively with these issues. Every planner and would-be planner should read this volume. In a very recent conversation, Bernzweig commented, ''Nothing in this book has been outdated as of June 1987. No significant legislation has been adopted, nor have there been any national regulations.'' That is not to say that some state may not have promulgated some local regulations or administrative procedures.

Bernzweig, a former practicing attorney specializing in liability issues, chose financial planning as a second career, and he found,

A good part of that process has involved just trying to keep abreast of all the legal requirements imposed on financial planners by statute, regulation, and securities industry pronouncements. Even as a lawyer, I was amazed to learn how all-embracing was the regulatory environment I had entered. To say it was intimidating would be an understatement—threatening comes closer to the mark.

He observed,

Words and phrases with great legal significance were bandied about by colleagues who admittedly had only the vaguest idea what they meant or how they applied. I kept hearing words like due diligence, fiduciary, RIA compliance, Reg D, OSJ, suitability rule, SROs, full disclosure, brochure rule, exempt offering, jurisdictional means, securities principal, private placements, public programs, selling away, off-book transactions, 10b-5 actions and many others that I knew were significant, but did not fully understand.

A quick search of legal literature reveals that practically no information is available which discusses the financial planner's common law liabilities to his or her clients, let alone any practical advice for coping with the customary legal issues faced by all planners.

The purpose of *The Financial Planner's Legal Guide* was to fill that perceived deficit. It reflects the realization that there must be many financial planners practicing today who have no legal background or training and who more than likely have not the foggiest notion what their legal responsibilities really are or how to live up to them.

1. Authoritative legal information and the knowledge gained therefrom is a prerequisite to meaningful action.
2. The financial planner who knows and understands the legal consequences of his or her professional activities is more likely to act in a manner that will assure compliance with all statutory and regulatory requirements.

3. Knowledge and sound procedures will greatly minimize the chances of being sued for malpractice.

Bernzweig's book was written primarily for persons who are either practicing financial planners or students in the process of becoming financial planners. It is intended to be a resource tool and practical guide for all who work in the financial services field, to help them meet their legal responsibilities to their clients, to their employers, and to themselves.

It sets forth in understandable language an overview of the relevant legal problems and issues facing today's financial planner: regulatory agency disciplinary proceedings and malpractice suits.

Most competent financial planners understand the need to establish and maintain good rapport with their clients in order to succeed in practice. However, they are probably unaware of the fact that certain types of individuals pose a greater than average litigation threat to them, as well as to all the professionals to whom they turn for help. These individuals seldom exhibit any *obvious* signs that they are unusually inclined to file lawsuits against professionals with whom they have real or imagined grievances. Their underlying *attitudes* give important clues to their litigative tendencies. Studies conducted by researchers in other fields have shown that these litigation-prone individuals have certain common psychological traits that may be described in general as follows:

1. Unreasonable expectations about what professionals can and cannot accomplish. They have a strong determination to hold professionals responsible when results do not match their (often unrealistic) expectations.

2. Unreasonable attitudes toward paying (or not paying) for services rendered by professionals unless completely satisfactory results are obtained.

3. Excessive suspicion and widespread distrust of all professionals, notwithstanding their almost childlike dependence on the professionals they turn to for help.

4. Generally uncooperative attitudes, evidenced by foot-dragging and an unwillingness to follow instructions.

5. A pronounced reluctance to assume personal responsibility for their own decisions and conduct.

In short, the client with malpractice-suit tendencies is one who is psychologically immature, unreasonable, uncooperative, dependent, and suspicious. This person is unusually quick to blame others when things do not go his or her way. Bernzweig has also developed a *Client Psychological Profile* which makes it possible to detect at the very outset of the relationship those clients *most likely* to bring a professional liability claim when they suffer investment losses or experience other disappointments in the planning process.

The planner who is forewarned in this manner should either *handle these individuals with exceptional care* or, if possible, avoid accepting them as clients in the first place.

Financial planners have a distinct edge over most other professionals in being able to spot the individual who is most likely to sue them. That edge comes about because the typical planner already employs some sort of detailed questionnaire to elicit not just financial, but *personal* information about each prospective client. Planners wishing to develop a more in-depth procedure to identify the suit-prone client may obtain a 20-question Client Psychological Profile for only $10 from Eli Bernzweig, 4180 Donald Drive, Palo Alto, CA 94306.

It is highly unlikely that the questionnaire you are presently using asks the types of questions designed to ferret out persons with malpractice-suit tendencies. However, by merely incorporating in your present questionnaire the appropriate questions, you will be better able to detect the suit-prone client by simple analysis of the answers given.

If the client *should* display undue concern or suspicion and decline to answer these questions, you already have the first important clue to a suit-prone personality.

A LITTLE FEAR

If the reader has been frightened by the possibility of a lawsuit's arising from his or her financial planning practice, that is a good thing! A little fear may motivate immediate action to tighten practice procedures. Every item referred to in this article can be accomplished with little effort and negligible cost. Clients will be better informed and better served. The efficiencies achieved by good communication prior to plan development will more than pay for the administrative steps that have been recommended. Happy clients will offer more referrals.

It is not bad to sleep a little better at night, knowing that you have taken the important steps towards professional loss control.

REFERENCE

ELI BERNZWEIG, *The Financial Planner's Legal Guide.* Englewood Cliffs, N.J.: Prentice Hall, 1986.

APPENDIX A: DISCLOSURES AND COMMUNICATIONS RECORD

Disclosures and Communications Record

Date	Person	Communication Action	Item	Planner Comment
————	————	Introduction meeting AG.03	LT.01	————
————	————	Engagement letter (agreement)	LT.03	————
————	————	Firm disclosure materials	LT.29	————
————	————	Printed marketing brochure		————
————	————	Engagement confirmation	LT.05	————
————	————	Information interview AG.05	LT.07	————
————	————	Information interview notes	LT.09	————
————	————	Notes revision, if any		————
————	————	Objectives confirmation	LT.11	————
————	————	Assumptions confirmation	LT.13	————
————	————	Objectives, assumptions rec'd		————
————	————	Data confirmation sent	LT.15	————
————	————	Data confirmation intv. AG.07	LT.17	————

Disclosure and Communications Record (*cont.*)

Date	Person	Communication Action	Item	Planner Comment
_____	_____	Data Confirmation intv. notes	LT.19	_____
_____	_____	Plan internal review AG.09,11,13		_____
_____	_____	Financial plan delivery AG.15	LT.21	_____
_____	_____	Delivery interview notes	LT.23	_____
_____	_____	Plan notes revisions, if any		_____
_____	_____	Risk review memorandum	LT.25	_____
_____	_____	Plan acceptance letter	LT.27	_____
_____	_____	Implementation checklist	LT.02	_____
_____	_____	Implementation intv. AG.17	LT.04	_____
_____	_____	Implementation invt. notes	LT.06	_____
_____	_____	Implem. Request form MI.219	LT.08	_____
_____	_____	Add'l implem. intv. notes	LT.06	_____
_____	_____	Attorney plan review AG.19	LT.08	_____
_____	_____	Advisor plan review AG.21	LT.08	_____
_____	_____	Implementation acceptance	LT.10	_____
_____	_____	Commission disclosure letter		_____
_____	_____	Cont./periodic service LT.12	LT.14	_____
_____	_____	Periodic review mtg. AG.23	LT.16	_____
_____	_____	Annual review prep. letter	LT.18	_____
_____	_____	Annual review delivery AG.25	LT.20	_____
_____	_____	Annual review meeting notes	LT.22	_____
_____	_____	Request for referrals (form)	LT.24	_____
_____	_____	Information to referrals	LT.26	

APPENDIX B: LETTERS

LT.01 Introduction interview reminder

LT.02 Implementation checklist revision

LT.03 Engagement letter (agreement)

LT.04 Implementation interview reminder

LT.05 Engagement confirmation

LT.06 Implementation interview notes

LT.07 Information interview reminder

LT.08 Adviser contact (w/request form)

LT.09 Information interview notes

LT.10 Implementation acceptance signed

(Appendix B: Letters, *con't.*)

LT.11 Objectives confirmation	LT.12 Continued service reminder
LT.13 Assumptions confirmation	LT.14 Periodic review invitation
LT.15 Data confirmation	LT.16 Periodic review reminder
LT.17 Data confirmation mtg. reminder	LT.18 Annual review preparation (form)
LT.19 Data confirmation notes	LT.20 Annual review reminder
LT.21 Plan delivery reminder	LT.22 Annual review notes
LT.23 Plan delivery interview notes	LT.24 Request for referrals (form)
LT.25 Risk management memo	LT.26 Information to referral
LT.27 Plan acceptance (sign-off)	LT.28 Corporate prospect introduction
LT.29 Disclosure material (brochure)	LT.30 General prospect introduction
LT.101 Custom (LT.101)	LT.103 Custom (LT.103)
LT.102 Custom (LT.102)	LT.104 Custom (LT.104)

APPENDIX C: AGENDAS

AG.01 Disclosure record form	AG.02 Introduction—corporation
AG.03 Introduction—individual	AG.04 Corporate presentation
AG.05 Information gathering	AG.06 Introduction—association
AG.07 Data confirmation	AG.08 Association presentation
AG.09 Internal problem analysis	AG.10 Introduction—closed corporation
AG.11 Internal recommendations	AG.12 Participant group meeting
AG.13 Internal plan review	AG.14 Public relations speech
AG.15 Financial plan delivery	AG.16 Bank presentation
AG.17 Implementation session	AG.18 Adviser presentation
AG.19 Attorney plan review	AG.20 Two-day workshop
AG.21 Adviser plan review	AG.22 Three-session workshop
AG.23 Periodic planning review	AG.24 Six-session workshop
AG.25 Annual review	AG.26 Preretirement workshop
AG.101 Custom (AG.101)	AG.105 Custom (AG.105)
AG.102 Custom (AG.102)	AG.106 Custom (AG.106)
AG.103 Custom (AG.103)	AG.107 Custom (AG.107)
AG.104 Custom (AG.104)	AG.108 Custom (AG.108)

APPENDIX D: IMPLEMENTATION

Implementation Item Checklist

Do?	By Whom?	Done	Employee Benefits
[　]	[　]	[　]	Assign group life ins. to irrevocable trust—client.
[　]	[　]	[　]	Increase deductible 401K contribution.
[　]	[　]	[　]	Consider exercising some of present stock options.
[　]	[　]	[　]	Reconsider pension reduction with survivor benefit.

Do?	By Whom?	Done	Government Benefits
[　]	[　]	[　]	Audit Social Security accounts to verify records.
[　]	[　]	[　]	Audit Social Security account for quarters coverage.
[　]	[　]	[　]	File for juvenile Social Security account.

Do?	By Whom?	Done	Income Tax
[　]	[　]	[　]	Use Yearly Tax Organizer to assemble data for returns.
[　]	[　]	[　]	Amend employee exemption Form W-4 to reduce withholding.
[　]	[　]	[　]	Consider gift of professional library upon retirement.
[　]	[　]	[　]	Consider a gift and leaseback business transaction.
[　]	[　]	[　]	Charitable contributions using appreciated property.

Do?	By Whom?	Done	Cash Management
[　]	[　]	[　]	Establish personal cash flow management system.
[　]	[　]	[　]	Establish credit union account.
[　]	[　]	[　]	Maintain three months of income in liquid assets.

Do?	By Whom?	Done	Investment
[　]	[　]	[　]	Consider self-directed IRA for investment flexibility.
[　]	[　]	[　]	Consider refinancing your home mortgage.
[　]	[　]	[　]	Discontinue commodity futures investment.
[　]	[　]	[　]	Consider sale of vacation home property.
[　]	[　]	[　]	Convert Series EE bonds to Series HH for income.

Do?	By Whom?	Done	Education
[　]	[　]	[　]	Consider a minor's (2503) accumulation trust.
[　]	[　]	[　]	Make regular gifts to prefund education.
[　]	[　]	[　]	Consider Series EE bonds for children currently taxed.
[　]	[　]	[　]	Consider student internships for college credit.

Do?	By Whom?	Done	Retirement
[　]	[　]	[　]	Prepension survivor option should be elected.
[　]	[　]	[　]	Consider IRA rollover for retirement plan funds.
[　]	[　]	[　]	Establish qualified TSA plan for spouse.
[　]	[　]	[　]	Make TSA contributions for previous years of service.

Implementation Item Checklist (*cont.*)

Do?	By Whom?	Done	Estate and Legal
[ ]	[ ]	[ ]	Consider an exemption unified-credit trust.
[ ]	[ ]	[ ]	Have client's present will revised.
[ ]	[ ]	[ ]	Consider having bank serve as successor executor.
[ ]	[ ]	[ ]	Consider clause for guardian's financial relief.
[ ]	[ ]	[ ]	Include sprinkling provision in trust(s).
[ ]	[ ]	[ ]	Include invasion (Crummey) provision in trust(s).
[ ]	[ ]	[ ]	Use qualified terminal interest property trust (Q-TIP).

Do?	By Whom?	Done	Life Insurance
[ ]	[ ]	[ ]	Discontinue juvenile policies, reallocate resources.
[ ]	[ ]	[ ]	Consider a universal life policy.
[ ]	[ ]	[ ]	Change ownership of life insurance—client.
[ ]	[ ]	[ ]	Withdraw accumulated dividends and reinvest funds.
[ ]	[ ]	[ ]	Add family coverage rider on life insurance.
[ ]	[ ]	[ ]	Remove assignments of insurance contracts.

Do?	By Whom?	Done	Health Insurance
[ ]	[ ]	[ ]	Extend disability coverage benefit period.
[ ]	[ ]	[ ]	Extend disability waiting period.
[ ]	[ ]	[ ]	Consider adding residual disability coverage.
[ ]	[ ]	[ ]	Consider excess major medical coverage.

Do?	By Whom?	Done	General Insurance
[ ]	[ ]	[ ]	Increase casualty "umbrella" liability coverage.
[ ]	[ ]	[ ]	Add replacement cost coverage for contents.
[ ]	[ ]	[ ]	Obtain personal director's liability insurance.
[ ]	[ ]	[ ]	Photo or videotape contents and personal articles.

Do?	By Whom?	Done	Career and Lifestyle
[ ]	[ ]	[ ]	Consider having an employment contract.
[ ]	[ ]	[ ]	Consider a career change for spouse.

Do?	By Whom?	Done	Business Interest
[ ]	[ ]	[ ]	Install split dollar insurance plan.
[ ]	[ ]	[ ]	Key person disability insurance to reimburse company.
[ ]	[ ]	[ ]	Consider gift and leaseback arrangement.
[ ]	[ ]	[ ]	Add group dental expense coverage.

Do?	By Whom?	Done	Miscellaneous
[ ]	[ ]	[ ]	Use financial documents portfolio for records.
[ ]	[ ]	[ ]	Place items in your safe deposit box.
[ ]	[ ]	[ ]	Deliver copy of report to attorney.
[ ]	[ ]	[ ]	Consider methods of reducing residential energy use.
[ ]	[ ]	[ ]	_____
[ ]	[ ]	[ ]	_____
[ ]	[ ]	[ ]	_____
[ ]	[ ]	[ ]	_____

"Treat the due diligence process like a trial. You be the judge and make the promoter or wholesaler prove beyond a shadow of a doubt that their products are worthy of your clients."

—HENRY I. MONTGOMERY, CFP

The Spirit of Due Diligence

Henry I. Montgomery, CEP, is a fee-and-commission financial planner. He is President, financial principal, and compliance officer of Planners Financial Services, Inc., an NASD broker-dealer firm.

Mr. Montgomery is a graduate of Tulane University, where he received his B.B.A. in 1951. He has also graduated from the Revac Institute for Investment Real Estate Analysis and Syndication. Currently, he lectures on financial planning, mutual fund portfolio construction, and investment real estate to both the public and financial professionals.

Mr. Montgomery's professional affiliations are abundant. He served six terms on the Board of Directors of the International Association for Financial Planning. He served six years on the Board of Directors, was the President of the Institute of Certified Financial Planners in 1981, and in 1982, served as Chairman. Currently, Mr. Montgomery serves as Chairman of The Financial Products Standards Board, an autonomous organization funded as a public service, established by the ICFP. In 1984, he was named "CFP of the Year" by the 19,000-member institute. He is included in the Marquis 24th and 25th editions of *Who's Who in Finance and Industry,* the Marquis edition of *Who's Who in the Midwest,* and the Marquis edition of *Who's Who in the World.*

Financial planning begins with integrity, the very heart and soul of our profession. It requires hard work, deep commitment, and no short cuts.

> The planner who shortcuts is not long for this profession. Your relationship with your clients is everything. If you think you are a product salesman with the greatest delivery system of anyone in the financial services, I think you better go back to hardware or pumping gas because that's not what financial planning is all about. Financial planning is a commitment to the client. It is a client service. If you happen to make money out of it, that's fine. But if you start out with the thought of making big money quickly, you're going to only hurt yourself. Unfortunately, there are many people today who can see nothing but the dollar sign. If you service the clients, the dollars will follow. But if you are looking for the dollars first, the clients won't follow.*

Just remember, when investors suffer, planners die.

To understand financial planning, you must understand due diligence. They go hand in hand. The lack of due diligence is the deathbed of the financial planner.

Everyone desires to have a successful financial planning practice. There are certain steps that you must take to ensure success. Let's review a few of the basic requirements that planners must keep in mind:

1. The role of the financial planner during the due diligence process is that of a probing questioner. It is critical to ask the wholesaler and product sponsors lots and lots of questions. Don't forget to take copious notes. Be alert when you ask question "A," that you do not get answer "F." Listen carefully and make sure that they did not just talk around you. Did they really answer the question you asked? Or did their lips move and their enthusiasm ignite, and did you get led down another trail? Keep in mind that when you feel safe and have a spirit of confidence, it could just be the beginning of the end. Be very much aware of overly zealous wholesalers and promoters who burn to instill in you trust, confidence, and excitement about their products. Oh, yes, when the wholesaler tells you, "It's just like a bond," walk toward the door. The safety exists only in the wholesaler's mind.

2. The financial planner must learn how to use a telephone and call references as well as other planners nationwide. There is no substitute for experience and track record. We are by no means in a position to know everything about every product or even every industry that we come across. There are many times that we are in the dark. There is no substitute for good communication with your peers. If another planner can keep you out of trouble by giving you the inside scoop on a bad or marginal product, it's a plus for the whole industry. Maybe one day you can return the favor.

3. As a financial planner, you must learn how to have an analytical, inquiring, and disbelieving mind. You are the barrier between the client and a bad or marginal product. You are the only line of defense. To be skeptical is to be professional. Remember four simple rules:

*As quoted in *How to Survive and Succeed in a Small Financial Planning Practice*, by Andrew M. Rich (Reston, Virginia: Reston Publishing Company, 1984), p. 9.

- **Rule 1.** Keep in mind that all wholesalers do not tell the truth.
- **Rule 2.** Most wholesalers tell most of the truth, but not always the entire story.
- **Rule 3.** Not too many wholesalers know the whole story, even though they think they do. They often tell all that they know, but they are not told it all. What they do know, they are very good at telling.
- **Rule 4.** If you ever want to know the whole story, ask the wholesaler after he has gotten his next job. Then it will all come out, the seamy underside.

4. Financial planners must realize that for a wholesaler to be good, he must be a true believer. True believers make dynamite storytellers and salespersons. You can not allow this type of person to be you. You must separate the salesperson from the product. How many financial planners have bought the salesperson and not the product? Don't be influenced by personality, zeal, or a good pitch. The better salesperson you are, the easier you are to sell.

5. If the product sounds too good to be true, it probably is! Simple and sweet, there is risk to everything. In fact, if the product were that good, the promoters wouldn't need to be selling it. They would be buying their own product.

6. The biggest farce alive is the so-called "due-diligence trip." Need I go further? However, it need not be so. Look for the malcontent on the trip who has been selling the product. Seek out the disbeliever. Read the annual report. Note how directly questions are handled. Take notes. Stay removed from the crowd mentality and try to see through all the self-serving information. Be a skeptic. You can learn much. Always remember the movie *The Sting.*

Perhaps the biggest danger that a client faces is from the naivete, inexperience, and ego of the financial planner. We are all human; our resources are based on our life experience and, to an extent, common sense. It may require the misfortune of being burned one or many times before a planner eventually matures to the cold, wide world of products. Some never do. Trust is an asset that a financial planner must possess to be successful. But trust must be restricted to the client. View products skeptically and distrustfully. Treat the due diligence process like a trial. You be the judge and make promoters or wholesalers prove beyond a shadow of a doubt that their products are worthy for your clients. Don't let inexperience be your teacher. Never, under any circumstances, become closed-minded and stop thinking.

Like everything else, due diligence has a historical cycle. In the past, the problem products have been in energy; the present points to real estate; the future, in my opinion, will be in the mutual funds. I am not saying that mutual funds or real estate or energy are bad products. I am saying that exceptional due diligence to select the quality products is always necessary.

Unfortunately, we have come to the point where many financial planners place far too much reliance on their broker/dealers because they do not understand the process of product selection. The SEC staff has repeatedly stated that the financial planner has equal liability with the broker/dealer and is not entitled to rely on the broker/dealer. Planners who believe that they can rely on the broker/dealer are seriously mistaken. Nor is it prudent to brush work off on anyone else to make your load easier.

Never forget that many of you are independent contractors. This is a much more vulnerable position legally than that of an employee. Even more serious a concern is your clientele. How many times can you start over? Think of the work and time it takes. One bad product is all it takes to wipe you out. Clients seldom forgive.

Stop being a believer. There are no magic answers. Only you can ask the right questions. In retail the old saying for success is ''Well bought is half sold.'' In financial planning, it is ''Good financial products can create a successful planner.''

"The purpose of due diligence is not merely to create a 'liability shield' for underwriters. It is also to protect the best interests of investors."

—STUART A. OBER

Analyzing Tax Advantaged Investments: Ten "Do's" of Due Diligence

Stuart A. Ober is a Registered Investment Advisor and President of Securities Investigations, Inc., a firm that specializes in conducting due diligence investigations and providing investment evaluations on tax-advantaged investments. He has worked for Wall Street brokerage firms for over ten years, where he has managed tax shelter departments and has structured tax-sheltered investments.

Mr. Ober graduated from Wesleyan University (bachelor of arts) and from the Sorbonne (license). Currently, he is a member of the Financial Product Standards Board established by the Institute for Certified Financial Planners. He is the author of *Everybody's Guide to Tax Shelters,* editor of *The Ober Income Letter,* and the publisher of the *Investment and Tax Shelter Blue Book.* He has also contributed numerous articles on tax shelters to leading industry publications. Mr. Ober frequently lectures at tax-shelter seminars and has appeared on talk shows throughout the country.

Exercising due diligence on potential investments is a necessity for a financial advisor to help clients make decisions about how to position substantial assets. The term "due diligence" first came into common usage as a result of the Securities Act of 1933. This act held that underwriters must conduct due diligence on all securities sold to determine if any part of the registration statement submitted to the SEC was untrue or misleading or omitted material facts. If the underwriter could not demonstrate that it had conducted due diligence, investors could sue everyone involved with the sale of the securities, including every participating underwriter.

Today, however, the term "due diligence" has a much broader application. It is part of the ethics of being a financial professional. The purpose of due diligence is not merely to create a "liability shield" for underwriters. It is also to protect the best interests of investors. In considering any potential investment for clients, whether a private placement or a public offering, the ethical and responsible financial professional will be absolutely certain that proper due diligence has been exercised. In some cases—for example, a private-placement real estate offering in your own area—you may be able to conduct the due diligence yourself, provided that you have the time and the expertise. In most cases, however, you will probably have to rely upon the opinions of others. In any case, you will want a thorough familiarity with all the basic elements of proper due diligence. On the basis of many years' experience of conducting due diligence both for broker-dealers and for sponsors, I have come up with what I believe are the ten essentials for proper due diligence. You should note that while this list is basic to my due diligence, it is by no means complete, and in itself would not relieve a financial advisor from the exercise of additional reasonable investigations and care that may be prudent for his or her particular needs.

Only by giving careful consideration and thorough investigation of each of these ten points will you be able to answer the two key questions imperative in any due diligence investigation. Question one is whether or not the offering materials of an investment provide complete disclosure of every material fact that might affect an investment decision. Question two is whether or not information is provided in a manner that makes it possible to evaluate thoroughly both the economic and the tax merits of an offering. Being able to answer Question one affirmatively means that the offering materials are in compliance with the regulations of the SEC. Being able to answer Question two affirmatively means that you have adequate information to make a realistic recommendation to a client. With these goals in mind, the following are the "Ten Dos" of effective due diligence:

1. *Do thoroughly investigate the business experience, integrity, and track record of the principals or general partners of an offering.* An investment is not an abstract thing. It is real, live, ongoing business with mundane, day-to-day problems that must be solved. An investment is only as good as the people who are in charge of it. Ideally, the principals of a business investment or limited partnership will have a great deal of pertinent experience. They will have been through many of the day-to-day problems that beset any enterprise. They will have a track record of success in programs similar to the one you are considering. Most important, they will be people of unquestioned integrity, with the firm respect of their peers. These are the kind of people who will stay with a deal through good times and bad. In all likelihood, some of their own money will be invested along with that of the limited partners. The principals will be good communicators, with a sensitivity to investor needs and concerns. A thorough investigation of

the principals may involve talking with their attorneys, accountants, bankers, their employees, competitors, past investors, or others.

2. *Do look carefully at the economic merits of the enterprise.* It is not enough that an offering has reputable sponsors. The whole project must make economic sense. You must take a broad perspective of the entire enterprise. No matter how good the track record of the sponsors, you might question the investment if they propose developing an apartment complex in a city with a declining population and a growing vacancy rate.

You must have more than a rudimentary knowledge about the business of the enterprise. For example, a developmental drilling partnership may have drilling contracts on a turnkey basis. This sounds good, and it is not an uncommon practice. However, the purpose of a turnkey contract is to lay off risk on the driller. Developmental wells in an known area are generally the least risky kind of drilling. Turnkey contracts always cost a substantial premium over ''cost-plus'' contracts, because the driller in his bid has to cover every eventuality. It may sound good to investors to know that they cannot pay more than a certain amount for their drilling. But if upon examination of the drilling prospects you determine that all the wells in the area are being successfully drilled without complication, you might question the economic reasonableness of a turnkey contract. Investors may be paying a substantial premium beyond the level of the risk involved.

3. *Do look at the physical property.* Whether a real estate investment, a drilling program, a research and development program, or equipment leasing, physical examination of the material assets is a must. This examination must go beyond merely ''kicking the tires.'' As an example, in a real estate venture, it makes good sense to talk with local bankers and realtors about the general conditions of real estate in that area. If it's a shopping-center product, you should talk with the shoppers. Ask them where else they shop, and what their most common shopping problems are. In an apartment building venture, it is a good idea to speak with tenants, and ask them what they think of the building and of the current management.

4. *Do look at the organizational expenses, management fees, and commissions.* Since the sponsors have created the offering, you can assume that any fees and expenses involved are fair to them. The real question is are these fees fair to the investors? This does not mean that the best partnerships are those in which the organizers receive the least compensation. Naturally, those people who have the breadth of experience and a good track record in the business will expect a good compensation for lending their expertise to an enterprise. However, any such management fees, organizational expenses, and commissions should be compared with similar programs to determine whether or not an inordinate amount of investor dollars are being eaten up in this way. The more that goes into organizational costs and management fees, the less available to generate economic return.

One must watch out not only for clearly stated ''organizational'' costs but for hidden ones as well. As an example, an offering may state that only $50,000 will come out of investor contributions to pay organizational costs. However, careful scrutiny may reveal that another $150,000 will come out of initial cash flow to pay deferred organizational expenses. In such a situation, technically only the $50,000 counts as ''front-end fees,'' although the total actual cost to investors is $200,000.

5. *Do look carefully at the sharing arrangement between the general partner and the limited partners.* An investment program in which the sponsors have confidence and concern for the investor's money will generally direct cash toward a repayment of original investment before the general partner starts substantially participating in income. A partnership in which the general partner starts sharing substantially in income before the investors have been repaid is subject to question.

6. *Do look at the validity of the tax position.* After you have thoroughly examined the written opinion of the lawyers or accounting firm, it is time to confer with them personally and go through a list of questions you have developed. You want to develop an impression of how risky they feel their tax position is and also develop an impression of their competence as tax specialists.

7. *Do look at the financial viability of the sponsor.* The sponsors of a program should have substantial assets so that the livelihood of their business is not dependent on any one program. They should have pockets deep enough to turn around an investment that might begin to go sour. Sponsors with limited financial resources and limited credit, no matter how well qualified they may otherwise be, are a risk.

8. *Do examine conflicts of interest.* This means not only checking to see if any subcontractors or suppliers happen to be cousins or in-laws. It means a thorough examination of all the business interests of the sponsor. As an example, an investigation may disclose that a general partner owns drilling rights on properties adjacent to the prospect site. Examination of the acreage may reveal that no exploratory drilling has been done in that area. The general partner could be laying off the risk of exploratory drilling on the limited partners. If the exploratory well is not successful, none of the general partner's money has been spent. If it is successful, then the general partner's drilling rights on adjacent acreage have skyrocketed in value at no cost to the general partner.

Take a shopping center project, for example. Close examination should be made of all the other real estate owned by the general partner or connected corporations or individuals. There is always the possibility that friendly interests may have purchased land surrounding a shopping center project on a speculative basis. The limited partners are then brought in to put up a tremendous amount of capital to build a shopping center. The values of adjacent land will consequently rise spectacularly, without any investment cost.

You should also search for conflicts of interest in the compensation structure of the sponsor companies. Compensation incentives in the actual offering partnership may be perfectly reasonable, but one also must look out for marketing overrides or completion bonuses that may be in the compensation structure of the general partner corporation.

Truly successful sponsors will have conflicts of interest. They will have other programs to attend to, other investments which may draw upon their resources or their time. No truly first-rate investment prospect will be without some conflicts of interest. But these should be clearly identified and should be mitigated wherever possible. One should be able to see where the particular partnership under consideration fits into the overall financial interests of the general partner.

9. *Do look at all pertinent reports.* Thorough due diligence requires not only looking at offering materials, but also examination of any ancillary reports. These may be engineering reports in drilling programs, or appraisals of real estate property. Outside research regarding the state of the art may be pertinent in terms of research and development partnerships. In addition to thoroughly versing yourself in any of these ancillary reports, you should talk, if at all possible, with their authors. Interview the appraiser. Determine whether the appraisal is based upon a current or prior situation of a property or whether it is based upon projected cash flow and rates of return after the property has been sold to the investment partnership. Talk with the consulting engineers, who may have written an engineering report, and determine how they feel the particular prospects under consideration compare with other prospects which they have reviewed. In other words, do not only thoroughly examine all ancillary reports, but examine their sources as well.

10. *Do call in professional help if you can't touch all the bases yourself.* Proper due diligence is very time-consuming, and calls upon an extraordinarily broad range of experience and expertise. There are professionals who can help with all or part of the due diligence process. Frequently, sponsors will absorb the costs of professional due diligence because a thorough and objective due diligence examination will lend credence to their offering. To help ensure the objectivity of sponsor-paid due diligence examinations, the agreed-upon fee is put in escrow, so that the due diligence firm is not influenced to create a favorable report in order to collect its fees.

Broker-dealers will also pay for due diligence reports on partnerships which they are interested in selling. Paying an outside professional to conduct a due diligence examination can help ensure its objectivity (broker-dealers will often have other relationships with the sponsors which have little to do with the particular partnership, such as selling the sponsors' stocks or bonds), and it will also relieve the broker-dealer of the considerable time which can be involved.

The cost of a complete due diligence examination of an investment program can range from $8000 to $20,000 or more, depending on the complexity of issues involved. It is also possible to have a partial due diligence examination done. For instance, analysis of an offering memorandum or prospectus alone might run from $1500 to $3000. A background check on individuals can be conducted usually for $1000 or less. A thorough property or prospect inspection might run $1500 to $3000.

Responsible and ethical due diligence is obviously much more than attending a luncheon and watching the president of a company throw a few slides on a screen. Although these ''dog and pony show'' luncheons are frequently referred to as ''due diligence'' meetings, they are, in most cases, no more than a marketing device. It is incumbent upon the responsible financial professional to have a good understanding of what real due diligence is. Whether you do this kind of investigation yourself, or whether you rely on others to do it for you, you must understand all the elements involved. Only then can you be certain that you are doing everything you can to protect the best interests of your clients. It still takes extra time and extra effort to make sure that all the right questions have been answered. In the long term, however, you will find that usually only the best deals come your way because you have developed a reputation as someone who seeks proper due diligence. More importantly, your clients will have learned to rely on your persistence and integrity to protect their investments.

"In many states, the unauthorized practice of law is a criminal offense; most often, it is considered a criminal misdemeanor."

—PAUL J. LOCHRAY, J.D.

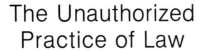

The Unauthorized Practice of Law

Paul J. Lochray is an Academic Associate with the College for Financial Planning and is coordinator of the estate planning division. He received his bachelor's and master's degrees in English from Creighton University, Omaha, Nebraska. He received his J.D. degree from Creighton University School of Law in 1979. After graduation from law school, he clerked for Chief Justice Charles Donaldson of the Idaho Supreme Court from 1979 to 1980. From 1980 to 1983 he was Director of the Legal Assistance Program at Iowa Lakes Community College, Estherville, Iowa. He has been employed at the College for Financial Planning since 1983. He is currently a member of the Iowa Bar, the International Association for Financial Planning (IAFP), and the Financial Planning Advisory Council for Financial Planning and Management, Inc., Boulder, Colorado. He is currently a member of the adjunct faculty of the University of Denver School of Law, where he teaches courses in estates and trusts. He is the author of numerous articles in the area of estate planning and is the author of *The Financial Planner's Guide to Estate Planning*, published by Prentice Hall.

INTRODUCTION

Financial planning practitioners are justifiably concerned when they hear the phrase "unauthorized practice of law" in connection with the behavior of a particular financial planner. This concern stems from the fact that many financial planners do not really know what the phrase means; or, if they are familiar with the phrase, they are uncertain as to whether it applies to behavior in which they have engaged.

Because many financial planners are uncomfortable in dispensing information that could lead to accusations of the unauthorized practice of law, these planners refer a case in its entirety to an attorney and refrain from providing assistance to the client for a particular portion of the financial plan, e.g., the estate planning portion of the client's plan. Unfortunately, many financial planners are unaware that they can provide invaluable assistance to their clients in situations that do not constitute the unauthorized practice of law. These financial planners are presently turning away valuable clients as a result.

To facilitate a better understanding of what is meant by the term "the unauthorized practice of law," this chapter has three purposes:

1. To educate the financial planner by defining the term "unauthorized practice of law" so that prohibited conduct can be avoided by the financial planner.
2. To assist the financial planner in becoming aware of the legal, financial, and economic implications that can occur in the event the financial planner has engaged in the unauthorized practice of law.
3. To alert the financial planner to precautionary steps that can be taken to reduce the risk of engaging in the unauthorized practice of law.

Each of these purposes is analyzed in greater detail throughout the rest of this chapter.

UNAUTHORIZED PRACTICE OF THE LAW DEFINED

Unfortunately, there is no all-inclusive definition of behavior that constitutes the unauthorized practice of law. Because the qualifications for being admitted to practice law before each state are controlled by its state supreme court, state bar association, and by legislation limiting those who can practice law within the jurisdiction, there are varying definitions as to what constitutes the unauthorized practice of law.

As a general rule, certification of an individual is required before that individual may practice law in a particular state. This rule requires an examination of two tests directly related to the issue of what constitutes the unauthorized practice of law. These tests are (1) Who is entitled to make application in order to be licensed? (2) What activities constitute the authorized practice of law? By examining both, and by determining who is eligible to practice and what activities constitute the practice of law, it can be said that all other individuals who do not meet this two-prong test are engaged in the unauthorized practice of law.

As a general rule, the identity of those *who* can practice law is limited to a group of individuals who can establish that they meet all certification requirements. These requirements generally necessitate completion of a formal course of legal training at a law school, successful completion of a state bar examination, a residency requirement (though this may be optional in some states if the applicant can establish an intent to reside permanently in the state to which application is being made), and sufficient proof of sound moral character and a "fitness" to practice law. If all of these requirements are met, the applicant will be considered for admission to practice law in the state to which application is being made.

The second prong of this test—*what* activities constitute the practice of law—is generally more difficult to answer. Oklahoma defines the practice of law as "the rendition of services requiring the knowledge and the application of legal principles and technique to serve the interests of another with his consent."[1] Rhode Island goes a step further by describing the practice as "not limited to appearing in court, or advising and assisting in the conduct of litigation, but embracing the preparation of pleadings, and other papers incident to actions and special proceedings. . . . It embraces all advice to clients and all actions taken for them in matters connected with the law."[2] Kansas defines it as "maintaining an office where he is held out to be an attorney, using a letterhead describing himself as an attorney, counseling clients in legal matters, negotiating with opposing counsel about pending litigation, and fixing and collecting fees for services rendered by his associate."[3] Conceivably, by using these differing definitions, a financial planner could be engaging in the unauthorized practice of law if participating in any conduct that meets these definitions.

At a minimum, most courts have determined that the following types of behavior constitute the practice of law; thus, if anyone who is not licensed within the state attempts to engage in any of these activities, he or she is engaging in the unauthorized practice of law.[4] These activities include:

1. The drafting of legal documents, such as wills, trust agreements, and contracts.

2. The rendering of legal opinions on matters where the opinion requires complex judgment, legal research, or other applied legal research skills to successfully respond to the matter.

3. The interpretation of a statute, court decision, or administrative regulation where the interpretation does not have a universally understood meaning and requires legal analysis and application of law to a specific set of facts.

4. The recommendation of a given course of conduct by a client based upon a legal interpretation of a statute, court decision, or administrative regulation or ruling.

5. The interpretation of a clause, paragraph, or any other portion of a legal document, where such interpretation forms the basis of a client's

---

[1] *R. J. Edwards, Inc.* v. *R. L. Hert*, 504 P. 2d 407, 416 (Okla. 1972), a case in which the Oklahoma Supreme Court held that defendant municipal bond marketers and their agents were not engaged in the unauthorized practice of law when the marketers and their agents merely reproduced forms previously prepared by the Attorney General, furnished them to school districts, and filled them out according to directions set out in the Attorney General's handbook.

[2] *Rhode Island Bar Association* v. *Lesser*, 68 R.I. 14, 26 A 2d 6, 7 (1942), where the operator of a fire loss appraisal bureau was held to be engaging in the unauthorized practice of law.

[3] *State* v. *Schumacher*, 214 Kan. 1, 519 P. 2d 1116, 1127 (Kansas 1974), a case in which a suspended attorney attempted to continue practice in all areas except for making court appearances.

[4] For further explanation and clarification of specific behavior that constitutes the unauthorized practice of law, the financial planner should consult the following articles: "The Role of the Financial Planner in Estate Planning and the Unauthorized Practice of Law," College for Financial Planning's Estate Planning Curriculum: Part VI, pages 1-5 and 1-6, August, 1986; Lochray, "The Role of the Financial Planner in Estate Planning," *Financial Strategies and Concepts*, Summer 1985.

behavior; for example, the client's use of a certain type of trust as a result of relying on the financial planner's interpretation of a will provision.

6. The rendering of an opinion as to whether a particular document, e.g., a will, is in compliance with specific legislation.

These six behaviors should be carefully avoided by the financial planner when working with a client on any portion of a financial plan because of the possibility that any one of these activities could result in the unauthorized practice of law.

On the other hand, there are certain activities that can be engaged in by the financial planner where such activities are not generally regarded as unauthorized. These activities include:

1. Compiling data for financial statements, including the extent and form in which title is held on property interests, and determining whether the client has a will.

2. Determining the nature, identity, and status of those individuals who would be the client's heirs if the client were to die—this would include personal information, such as the identity and location of children born of previous and present marriages, children who have been adopted, or who have already received inheritances in the form of advancements, and other such related information.

3. Identifying and prioritizing the client's retirement planning and estate planning objectives, or any other objectives that require the application of legal principles in order to attain the stated objective successfully.

4. Performing various calculations as part of a projected financial plan to show the client the income, estate, or gift tax savings between one projected plan and another projected plan.

5. Informing the client of various options available where the adoption of any of the options could achieve the client's objectives; at the same time, informing the client of the advantages and disadvantages of each option so that the client can make an informed decision as to which option is most appropriate for the client's needs.

6. Making *suggested* recommendations as to options that might be suitable for the client, but informing the client that the advice of an attorney or accountant should be obtained on any matters of law or accountancy.

Thus, a financial planner could do a projected calculation showing the estate tax savings in Plan B over Plan A, and this would not constitute the unauthorized practice of law; however, drafting a trust agreement or analyzing the language of a client's will to suggest how a particular clause could be rephrased in order to take advantage of the unlimited marital deduction would be an instance of the unauthorized practice of law if either were performed by the financial planner.

When a financial planner is in doubt as to whether specific conduct is the unauthorized practice of law, the financial planner should consult with the local bar association, or a trusted attorney with whom the financial planner has worked in the past prior to engaging in the act in question. Since there are few reported cases on the subject, a review of state supreme court cases on the subject of unauthorized practice of law is likely to reveal few identifiable guidelines upon which the financial planner can rely.

REPERCUSSIONS OF UNAUTHORIZED PRACTICE OF LAW

In the event the financial planner does engage in any of the activities previously described that constitute the unauthorized practice of law, the implications for the financial planner can be both far-reaching and permanent. They include:

1. The possibility that the financial planner has committed a crime. In many states, the unauthorized practice of law is a criminal offense; most often, it is considered a criminal misdemeanor.[5] In addition to the payment of fines,[6] court costs, and legally related expenses, the financial planner must now also bear the stigma of being a convicted criminal. This stigma is likely to drive clients away, including those who previously had a good working relationship with their financial planner.

2. The likelihood that the financial planner will have his ability to engage in financial planning temporarily suspended or even revoked. Depending on the gravity of the offense, it is possible that the financial planner will face suspension or revocation or other disciplinary proceedings. In the event the financial planner pleads guilty or is found guilty of engaging in the unauthorized practice of law, the financial planner could be temporarily or permanently deprived of the right to use designated trademarks that have attracted clients to the financial planner in the past.[7] A revocation of this nature could have a serious financial impact on the ability of the financial planner to earn a living as a certified financial planner.

[5]For example, Iowa Code Section 727.9 describes any unauthorized act as follows:

> Unless another penalty is specifically provided, any person who without a license carries on or transacts any business or occupation for which a license is required by any law of this state, commits a simple misdemeanor.

In Colorado, such an individual is guilty of contempt, pursuant to C.R.S. Section 12-5-112. The statutes of each state define the nature and severity of the unauthorized practice of law, and a financial planner should become aware of the instances where his or her activity might constitute the unauthorized practice of law. Consultation with an attorney is strongly recommended.

[6]If found guilty of the unauthorized practice of law, which is a simple misdemeanor, the maximum sentence would be imprisonment not to exceed thirty days, or a fine not to exceed one hundred dollars. Iowa Code Section 903.1(1)(a). Other states have statutes similar in nature, and a financial planner should consult with an attorney to determine what the criminal sanctions are in his or her state.

[7]For individuals who hold the designation of CFP or Certified Financial Planner, such an individual is subject to disciplinary action by the Board of Ethics and Standards of the IBCFP (International Board of Standards and Practices for Certified Financial Planners). If grounds for disciplinary action have been established and it is the finding of the Board of Ethics and Standards that the Certified Financial Planner has engaged in any act or omission that violates the IBCFP's Code of Ethics, the Board of Ethics and Standards may impose any of the following sanctions: a private letter of admonition which may be issued without a hearing, a private censure (an unpublished written reproach), suspension of the right to use the marks CFP or Certified Financial Planner for a specified period of time not to exceed three years, or a permanent revocation of the right to use the marks. Revocation of the professional designation of CFP could result in serious economic harm to the financial planner's practice as a Certified Financial Planner as well as a loss of professional credibility within the financial planning profession.

The grounds for suspension or revocation of the CFP or Certified Financial Planner marks include the following according to the IBCFP's Disciplinary Procedures Brochure:

> any act or omission which violates the provisions of the IBCFP's Code of Ethics and Standards of Practice; any act or omission which violates the criminal laws of any state or the United States; any act which is the proper basis for professional suspension; any act or omission which violates the IBCFP's Disciplinary Procedures; failure to respond to a request by the Board of Ethics and Standards without good cause; or obstruction of the Board of Ethics and Standard's performance of its duties.

3. The possibility that the financial planner would bear the burden of any economic loss resulting from the unauthorized practice of law. Even if the financial planner had adequate professional liability coverage, if a client were to suffer harm because of the activities of the financial planner *where those activities constituted the unauthorized practice of law,* the financial planner's professional liability coverage would not protect the financial planner against those losses. The only protected losses are those resulting from activities engaged in *as a financial planner.* Since the unauthorized practice of law constitutes unauthorized activity and is not included as a covered activity under the terms of most professional liability policies, there would be no coverage for any harms resulting from this prohibited activity. If the client chose to sue the financial planner, and the damages sought were substantial, recovery against the financial planner could economically destroy the financial planner, or cause the financial planner to file for bankruptcy.

These examples should serve as a vivid reminder of why the financial planner should refrain from engaging in activities considered to be the unauthorized practice of law.

HOW A FINANCIAL PLANNER CAN AVOID THE RISK OF ENGAGING IN THE UNAUTHORIZED PRACTICE OF LAW

A financial planner can avoid the risk of engaging in the unauthorized practice of law by using a number of guidelines in his or her financial planning practice:

1. The financial planner can adopt the philosophy of working with a licensed attorney or accountant as a member of the financial planning "team." By using a "team" philosophy approach, the financial planner can use the attorney and the accountant as a part of the team and can refer the client to the attorney or accountant when specific questions of law or accountancy arise. By referring the client to another team member, the financial planner has greater assurance in the abilities of another known member of the team rather than referring the client to an outsider. In addition, the likelihood of the financial planner's attempting to engage in any activities meeting the definition of the unauthorized practice of law is severely curtailed.

2. The financial planner can educate the client on the alternatives available to the client so that the client can make an intelligent, informed decision. Rather than *recommending* a particular solution to a client's problem, the financial planner might find it more advantageous to *suggest* options from which the client can make a choice. Educating the client on the advantages and disadvantages of each option allows the client to make an informed, intelligent decision as to which option is most appropriate for the client. The financial planner is not making a recommendation *per se;* rather, the financial planner is illustrating the options available and suggesting that the client make an appropriate decision based on the information provided. Such an approach avoids the risk of appearing to make *one specific* recommendation, especially where that recommendation may only be appropriate after consulting with an attorney or accountant.

3. The financial planner can use cautionary language and disclaimers in documents that urge the client to seek the advice of an attorney for interpretations of the law or opinions as to how the law may affect the client's plan. For example, one practicing Certified Financial Planner,[8] whose firm's work has been reviewed and approved by the Indiana State Bar Association, uses the following disclaimers in all plans, calculations, data gathering forms, and suggested plan options:

> All references to tax laws and legal questions based on the law are included solely to demonstrate the compelling need of putting your affairs in order.

On all financial statements, client data forms, and related documents used by the financial planner, the following disclaimer also appears:

> The benefits of confidential analysis are dependent on the services of your attorney for approval, including legal and tax opinions, and the implementing and drafting of documents which will implement your plan. YOU MUST RELY ENTIRELY ON YOUR ATTORNEY AND ACCOUNTANT WITH RESPECT TO LEGAL AND TAX MATTERS.

This disclaimer should make it clear that the client should not rely upon the opinions or interpretations of a financial planner when implementing any portion of the plan that requires the skill and expertise of an attorney or accountant. This Certified Financial Planner reports that the use of such disclaimers carefully conveys to his clients the obligation of the *client* to seek legal advice on those portions of the plan that require the interpretation and analysis of an attorney.

4. To minimize the possibility of unauthorized practice of law or accountancy, the financial planner should compile a list of specific activities; these activities should be reduced to writing and inserted in visible, plain language into the client's file. This list should be reviewed with the client during the initial conference, or at some time during a follow-up conference, and the list should be signed by the client with an understanding that the client acknowledges the terms of the list and the accuracy of the information provided by the client to the financial planner.

Among the statements included in the list should be the following:

1. A statement that the financial planner does not review wills, trusts, contracts, or other legal documents.
2. A statement that the financial planner does not perform legal research or render legal opinions on matters that require the expertise and knowledge of an attorney.
3. A statement that the financial planner does not make estate planning or other legal recommendations that require both knowledge and application of relevant law.
4. A statement that the financial planner does not draft legal documents and that any such documents that appear in the client's file are merely specimen documents and are designated as such.
5. A statement that the client has accurately and knowingly provided financial, economic, and personal data to the financial planner and that the dissemination of this confidential information does not constitute

---

[8]Special thanks and consideration are extended to Mr. Brent Emerick, CFP, of Comprehensive Financial Planning Services Corporation, Indianapolis, Indiana, for data, sample forms, and procedural information provided.

an attorney-client relationship between the financial planner and the client.

6. A statement that the financial planner may examine various options available for consideration by the client, but that the examination of the tax consequences, and the advantages or disadvantages of each option are designed to educate the client to permit the client to make an objective, educated choice, and are not intended to serve as the rendering of legal advice; further, that the client should consult with his or her attorney if the client has questions regarding the interpretation, implementation, or design of any particular part of the plan requiring a legal opinion.

In conclusion, if financial planners are aware of those situations in which they could be engaged in the unauthorized practice of law, and carefully avoid such situations, the financial planner will be able to render better service to his or her client while also avoiding the financial and legal pitfalls encountered in the unauthorized practice of law.

Chapter V

Computerization

Donald R. Woodwell
Robert T. LeClair, Ph.D.
David M. Stitt
Judd Kessler, CFP
David C. Huxford, CLU, CFP

"Replacing a typewriter with computerized word processing software can pay early dividends to a planning practice by increasing a secretary's productivity and improving the quality of work. At the same time, it gives valuable experience in operating a small computer system."

—DONALD R. WOODWELL

Computer Requirements for Financial Planners

Donald R. Woodwell is President of D & D Royalties, Inc. Previously, he achieved 25 years experience in the computer field at IBM and the United States Air Force. As an Adjunct Professor at the City College of New York, Mr. Woodwell also teaches computer science.

Mr. Woodwell received his B.S. in industrial engineering from Pennsylvania State University and his M.S. in systems management from the University of Southern California. His publications include *Automating Your Financial Portfolio, Managing Personal Computer Workstations, Using and Applying the Dow Jones Information System,* and *How to Get the Most from Your Home Computer.*

The most difficult task when one is considering computers for a financial planning practice is deciding what role they are to play in the practice. You should ask yourself, "What do we want the computer to do for our practice?" The success of any computer installation, whether in a small financial practice or a corporate data processing center, is largely dependent on the answer to this question, which comes from clearly defining computer requirements in your practice. This chapter explains how to define those requirements.

FOUR BASIC AREAS

The four basic areas in which a computer can benefit you are the following: record keeping, computations, data display, and word processing (Figure 1). Computer record keeping is analogous to an office filing cabinet with electronically encoded information on computer media instead of typed data on paper. The second area, computation, includes all those number-related activities such as calculating after-tax return and yield on an investment portfolio or balancing your monthly accounting entries. Data display involves transforming business and client-related data into graphics or other pictorial representations so as to communicate best the quantitative recommendations to your clients. Last, word processing includes letter and proposal writing, mailing list maintenance, and periodic distribution of important information to clients.

These basic areas of information processing can be done manually without computer assistance. For example, paraplanners compute all sorts of client planning data on desktop calculators, while secretaries handle the correspondence and mailings and file records in metal cabinets. Client proposals usually are

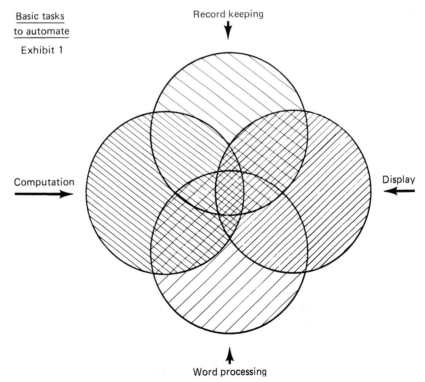

Basic tasks
to automate

Exhibit 1

Record keeping

Computation

Display

Word processing

Figure 1-1 Basic tasks to automate.

prepared with a typewriter as the only mechanical assistant. A financial planning practice may continue successfully in this fashion for a long time if it maintains a fairly stable client base. But as the practice grows, a greater number of clients means more handling of information, preparing of letters and proposals, and tracking of performance of client portfolios. Thus, when a financial planning practice's volume of business increases, a computer becomes necessary to the future success of the business.

It is essential that you keep the four basic computing areas in mind as you plan for computing. In this way you can segment your plans according to the area in which your computing needs are greatest or in which you can achieve the greatest returns from automating.

DEFINING REQUIREMENTS

Financial planners who have not previously dealt with computers may find it particularly difficult to evaluate their needs due to the unique characteristics of their practice, and the variety of possible alternatives to computerization. Successfully selecting computers also requires that you consider staff issues such as: Who can be trained to use a computer system? How much time is required to learn the software? What outside help is available to get me started? Last, the financial elements must be thoroughly understood. For example, how much will it cost, what benefits are quantifiable, and when will we get a return on our computer investment?

The answers are not often readily discernible. They can be, however, determined if a good set of requirements is clearly stated. The needs of the practice must be defined in both qualitative and quantitative terms. In this way, you may identify and prioritize your automation objectives and define the steps necessary to achieve your goals.

For example, you may find that the amount of repetitive typing done by your secretaries on client proposals is excessive. This results in considerable slowness in proposal preparation. Although they had tried to copy repetitive sections (often called ''proposal inserts''), the copies just didn't look good in the proposal body, so they returned to typing them individually each time.

The resulting slowdown in proposal preparation time was from one to two days. In busy times such as the spring tax season, the preparation delay often extended to a week. Fortunately, your secretary had operated a word processing machine in a previous job and suggested that all the repetitive proposal work could be stored in the word processor. Whenever it was needed, another copy could be printed. The proposal inserts would look attractive while saving a large part of the secretaries' time. Thus, two typical requirements are the reduction of secretarial time, and more timely preparation of proposals. Replacing a typewriter with computerized word processing software can pay early dividends to a planning practice by increasing a secretary's productivity and improving the quality of work. At the same time, it gives valuable experience in operating a small computer system.

On the other hand, if you are experiencing difficulty tracking the performance of your client's portfolio, then record keeping may be the area where computer support is indicated. Similarly, requirements can be defined in the areas of computation and data display.

It should not take long for you to define your requirements. Sit down with your staff and list those operational elements that are the least efficient, tedious, slow, and cumbersome, as well as those that affect client relations or inhibit cash flow. Categorize them within the four key computer functional areas, and you will have a much better idea as to where your computer emphasis should lie. Finally, prioritize your requirements and rank them from high to low. This will set your schedule for implementing the necessary computer solutions. Several typical criteria for setting a priority sequence can be the following: easy versus hard to implement, the magnitude of the dollar benefit, impact on your clients, and cost. These are by no means the only criteria, but are key considerations.

SOFTWARE SELECTION

When financial planners undertake to select software packages without knowing what is needed by their practice, they may buy the wrong one. A list of required job functions that solve the operational problems which you identified must be written down. The ability of the different computer programs to meet these requirements will be the primary determinant as to whether or not they are suited for the practice. But in addition to unique job needs there are the human needs for ease of learning and use.

This brings us to the four basic questions which should be asked whenever a planner is considering a computer system to automate his or her practice:

- Does the software have the general capabilities that we need?
- Does it meet our job requirements?
- Can my staff be trained to use it effectively?
- Can we afford it?

The key to successful information management with personal computers is to provide quality software that meets the needs of a financial planning practice. Selecting the right software for a specific set of needs is both an art and a science.

SELECTION CRITERIA

Developing a list of selection criteria from a set of job requirements is not difficult. What is important is gathering the needs from your staff so that they actively participate in the planning. Such participation involves them in automation planning and helps resolve differing opinions as to how the job should be mechanized. In this way, job procedures can be streamlined, and this will pay significant future dividends.

If there is more than one criterion by which software will be selected, then each criterion will have a different value to the using department. For instance, suppose that there are three general categories of criteria for computational software: flexible capabilities, ease of learning, and reasonable cost. Each of these are probably not equal in their relative value to your practice. For example, the first criterion may be the most important, accounting for 50 percent of the total value. Ease of learning may account for 40 percent of the decision, and cost may be only 10 percent.

Each selection criterion has a value that represents its priority. In this way, any single program feature can be weighted in terms of its usefulness to the evaluating department. These priorities are multiplied by the rating given to a particular software feature. This rating is generally subjective and is the result of software demonstrations or recommendations. Comparison among different program alternatives can be quantified by this method, and it helps to remove much of the personal bias from the software decision.

TABLE 1

Financial Planning Program Selection Chart

Program Functions	Relative Importance	Product A Rank	Product A Points	Product B Rank	Product B Points
Calculations	3	5	15	4	12
Cash flow analysis	3	3	9	4	12
Cost	2	2	4	3	6
Ease of learning and use	2	3	6	3	6
Education	2	2	4	4	8
Financial plans	2	1	2	3	6
Instruction manual	2	3	6	4	8
Investment analysis	1	3	3	2	2
Life insurance needs	3	4	12	4	12
Net worth—					
Assets	3	3	9	4	12
Liabilities	3	3	9	4	12
Reports	3	3	9	3	12
Personal records	1	3	3	4	4
Retirement planning	3	4	12	4	12
Tax planning					
Annual plan	2	2	4	4	8
Estate	1	2	2	1	1
Est. federal	2	2	4	4	8
Shelters	1	1	1	1	1
Year-end	2	2	2	4	8
Tutorial	1	3	3	2	2
Total Points			119		152
Overall Ratings			②		①

Relative importance: 1 = low; 3 = high
Rank: 1 = low; 5 = high

TABLE 2

Portfolio Management Program Selection Chart

Program Functions	Relative Importance	Product A Rank	Product A Points	Product B Rank	Product B Points
Data entry & editing					
Repricing					
Manual					
Automatic					
Number of portfolios per disk					
Number of records per portfolio					
Security types					
Type of reports					
Time critical alert					
Commission accounting					
Partial sales					
Short sales					
Dividend adjustment					
Instructional manual					
Tutorial					
Ease of learning and use					
Cost					
Total Points					
Overall Ratings					

Tables 1 through 3 show software selection criteria for financial planning (computation, data display), portfolio management (record keeping), and tax preparation (computation and data display) software. The criteria were derived from a requirements study of a typical financial planning practice. You may find that your requirements are similar. If they are different, you can substitute selection criteria for the ones shown. Finally, you can set up similar charts for word processing, client tracking, or other financial planning applications in your own practice.

TABLE 3

Tax Shelter/Investment Planning

Selection Criteria	Relative Importance	Product A Rank	Product A Points	Product B Rank	Product B Points
Tax shelter projection in years					
Investment planner projection in years					
Side-by-side comparison features					
Tax benefits/costs					
Cumulative benefits/ costs					
Net proceeds on sale					
Affect on net worth					
Affect on cash flow					
After-tax analysis					
NPV					
NFV					
IRR					
Adj. return					
Income averaging					
AMT					
Limitations for					
50% charitable contributions					
Medical expenses					
Casualty & theft losses					
Capital losses					
Post-9/10/75 investment expense					
General Business Credit					
Capital gain deduction					
Indexing > 1985					
AMT BEP					
Zero bracket amount					
Integrated tax/investment worksheets					
Partial investment units					
Optimization procedure					
Annual updates					
Other updates					
Documentation					
Tutorial					
Costs					
Total Points =					
Ranking =					

"Successful planners in the future will be those who can use computers effectively to improve the productivity of their business, and at the same time free themselves to carry out the important human role that can never be automated."

—ROBERT T. LECLAIR, Ph.D.

Computer Applications in Financial Planning

Robert T. LeClair, Ph.D., is an Associate Professor of Finance at Villanova University, Villanova, Pennsylvania. He is a graduate of the Wharton School of the University of Pennsylvania and of Northwestern University's Graduate School of Management. Prior to joining the faculty at Villanova, Dr. LeClair served on the faculties of the American College and the University of Illinois.

Dr. LeClair is a frequent speaker for business groups and professional organizations in the areas of finance, investment, retirement planning, taxation, and personal financial planning. He has also been a consultant for numerous banks, thrift institutions, insurance companies, and professional associations. Among his publications are *Money and Retirement, A Consumer's Guide to Personal Investing, Financial Planning Software Tool Kit,* and *The Tools and Techniques of Financial Planning.* He has also coauthored, with Stephen Leimberg, two financial planning computer software packages, "The Financial and Estate Planner's Numbercruncher," and "Financial Planning Toolkit."

INTRODUCTION

Consider the dream: a large and growing client base, a wide range of quality products and services, the opportunity to meet client needs by bringing these two together, and the opportunity to be rewarded with a considerable income. Now, the hard part. How to accomplish all of this in an efficient way with limited resources?

Successful financial planners recognize that they will need to have more clients, make more presentations, retain more information, prepare more reports, and communicate more effectively than at any time in the past. In trying to accomplish these goals, planners have grasped the personal computer as an essential ally. The purpose of this chapter is to survey three essential applications of personal computers to financial planning:

1. word processing,
2. data management, and
3. graphics.

WORD PROCESSING

No function of personal computers has been looked to so expectantly as word processing. *InfoWorld* magazine reports that approximately sixty percent of all new personal computer buyers initially buy a word processing program with their computer. For business users that figure is probably even higher. The variety of these programs is extraordinary, with literally hundreds of features available in dozens of different packages. Choosing among them forces us back to three fundamental questions:

1. What do we want to do?
2. Is there software available to do it?
3. What hardware is needed to accommodate the software?

The first step in this process is analyzing what *you* mean by word processing. Do you write an occasional business letter to a large number of clients or potential clients? Or are you interested in preparing comprehensive financial plans that may run to fifty or more pages of repetitive text, numerical data, and graphs? The software that may be perfectly adequate for the first of these assignments may fail miserably at the second.

If you are shopping for word processing software, begin by writing out a list of functions or operations you expect the program to perform. Prioritize your list so that you concentrate on the features that are most important to you, not the ones that are easiest for the salesperson to demonstrate. In the financial services field the ability to mail-merge names and addresses, search a compatible database for particular characteristics, and integrate specific data with boilerplate sentences and paragraphs are essential features for a word-processing package.

Speed of operation is also important, but needs to be carefully defined in terms of professional productivity. Some word processors lend themselves to easy creation of text and are particularly suited to writers, editors, and others who function in that type of environment. This is *not* the world of financial services, however, which might better be characterized as a production-oriented environment. Improved efficiency means producing the same output, or very similar output, faster, and for a larger number of clients. Rather than writing speed, productivity here is better measured in terms of formatting flexibility, ease of interaction with other software, such as a database of client files, or the ability to network with other computers in the same office.

Once you've determined your particular needs, you're liable to find that there are several software packages that seem to fit them. Which one to choose? Here, if not sooner, is a good place to involve your office manager, secretary, or whoever is actually going to be doing the work of word processing. They may have personal preferences that will be just as important to your office's overall productivity as the software itself. And being involved in the decision will make them a lot happier about this change in the office routine than if you simply walk in one day with a computer under one arm and a word processor under the other.

Another important factor in selecting word processing software is the hardware configuration you already have, or the one that may be needed in order to get the most out of a particular package. This is also related to whether you're producing that occasional two-page letter or the comprehensive 50-page report.

The more sophisticated the word-processing package, the more likely it is to require an advanced hardware system. A hard disk may be essential as well as additional random access memory (RAM) in the computer itself. In fact, the cost of some software may be a fraction of what you'll need to spend in order to get it up and operating efficiently. It may be better to select a program with fewer features that still meets your needs and that will work with your existing system.

Other hardware-related questions involve the type of printer you may already have or need. Buying a fancy word-processing package with every available print function may be a waste of money if your printer cannot carry them out. Ask for a demonstration of the package using your printer or a similar one. One important item to note here is the desirability of a "buffer" for your printer. This device allows you to send output to your printer while continuing to use the computer at the same time. This may be more important to improving your speed and productivity than any feature of the word-processing software.

A final hardware consideration is the type of monitor you use to display your work. Word processing typically requires more time in front of a display screen than any other computer function, and your software should be capable of producing the best image your monitor can display.

In summary, word processing has great potential for improving the productivity of all financial service professionals. Through its adaptation to personal computers, this function is as readily available today to individuals as it has been to those working in a corporate environment. Making effective use of word processing can improve your ability to service a larger number of clients, to meet their individual needs more easily, and to provide a greater degree of satisfaction and compensation in carrying out your professional responsibilities.

DATA MANAGEMENT

In today's business environment sales professionals who don't have full knowledge of their clients' situations won't be around very long. Increasing competition, new products, changing regulations, and individual changes make client data management one of the most important functions for the financial planner.

Fortunately, the personal computer offers some real help in this area, if it is used effectively. We all know that the computer can *store* large amounts of detailed information. More importantly, from the point of view of client management, it can *retrieve* that data quickly, and *process* it in a short time. It is this ability to sift through hundreds of records, to sort out those meeting certain requirements, and to present them in a meaningful way that makes today's personal computers so valuable to the financial planner.

A good filing system, or *database management program*, as they are often called, is among the most important software available to the financial services professional. These programs allow the user to design customized electronic files, or databases, and to fill them with a wide variety of information on clients, products, and other important data. However, simply having the information isn't very valuable unless you use it and manage it effectively. Client management should be interpreted in a positive way, implying that you are making use of your information system to provide the best possible service in an efficient and profitable manner.

The first step in designing an efficient client information system involves thinking about what use you want to make of the information you have available. This can range from the simple, such as printing mailing labels for all of your clients, to the complex, such as a search for clients who are age 55 or older, married, with children, earning more than $75,000, who have a particular type of life insurance policy. The design of your file will limit or enhance your ability to store, search, and retrieve information effectively.

In general, the more detailed your file design, the more useful it will be in refining your searches for clients who have particular needs or meet specific characteristics. It will also be more effective when tied in with a word-processing function to produce individualized letters and reports. One cost of this refinement, however, is additional time and effort that must be devoted to data gathering and to entering the information into the computer system. A complex design may enable you to pick the proverbial needle out of a haystack, but may also be unnecessarily cumbersome for your day-to-day use.

One helpful note here is that you don't need to fill in every data item for every client all at once. If you're like most of us, you'll start with certain essential items and then add new information as you go along. Make sure that the software you select allows you to reshape and redesign your files by adding, deleting, and moving items from one part of the file to another. In some cases, redesigning a file means that some or all of the information must be reentered.

A good place to start in designing a client database is with any fact finder or data gathering forms you currently use in your practice. You may not want to reproduce the entire set of forms on your computer, but they certainly can provide you with a good list of data items to consider. Also, some items may not lend themselves to use on a computer. For example, personal attitudes toward risk are difficult to quantify, yet assigning a ''score'' from one to ten, or high or low, can be useful as a sorting characteristic.

The following is a list of major areas of information that should be included in every client database:

1. Personal data: name, age, marital status
2. Sources of income: salary, dividends, interest
3. Expense categories
4. Business interests
5. Liquid assets
6. Investments: stocks, bonds, tax shelters
7. Personal property: home, autos

8. Major liabilities
9. Insurance coverage: life, health, liability
10. Employee benefits

The nature of your own work and the type of clients that you deal with will determine the specific items that go into your database system.

Once it has been established, you will need to continually update the system by adding new information on existing clients and establishing files for new prospects. One effective way of maintaining accurate client information is to send them a copy of their personal file on a regular basis. You can request that they review the data, make any necessary changes, and return it to you. Or you might want to schedule an appointment so that you can review it with them.

In either case, clients are likely to be impressed by the fact that you have an effective information system and are interested in working with them to keep their files up to date. The process of maintaining the system will give you regular opportunities to meet with your clients, discuss their particular situation and needs, and, not unimportantly, present ideas for sales.

GRAPHICS

The person who said, "A picture is worth a thousand words," probably was not an insurance agent or a financial planner, but those professions should take these words to heart. The use of personal computers in financial services has focused primarily on functions like word processing and electronic spreadsheets. Software products in these areas have been used to create customized letters, reports, and proposals along with projections and other forms of financial analysis.

An often overlooked and underutilized capacity of these machines is their ability to take a great deal of numerical information and convert it into effective charts and graphs. A variety of software is available for most models of personal computers that can produce line, bar, and pie charts in many different configurations. Data may be entered manually through the keyboard or "read in" from other sources, such as a spreadsheet or database file.

In addition to the graphics software itself, you may need some additional equipment for your computer system. This will depend on the volume of graphs you intend to produce and the level of sophistication you desire. At a minimum you will need a dot-matrix printer with graphics capacity. So-called "letter-quality" printers are fine for producing text but do not have the capability of printing graphs. Color printers are beginning to appear on the market, and you may want to consider a plotter capable of producing sophisticated graphs in as many as six colors.

Why charts? Simply because, for most of your clients, they are a more effective means of communication than words alone—one that gets your ideas across more concisely and with a greater likelihood of being acted upon. Nothing is more frustrating for the financial professional than to spend a lot of time and effort in preparing and presenting a proposal, and then to have the client reject it or take no action. In both cases lack of client understanding may be the most probable cause.

The very nature of financial planning leads to complexity and a lot of details. A great deal of information must be collected, analyzed, evaluated, and presented to clients in a meaningful way. Introducing projections and other "what if" scenarios only adds to the potential for confusion and inaction. The growing use of personal computers has even compounded the difficulty by churning out voluminous paperwork that often seems to do more harm than good in motivating and impressing clients.

The effective use of graphics in your reports and presentations should make them more attractive visually, more likely to be read and studied, and more likely to get results in terms of action and sales. Another benefit of using graphs is an increase in your own understanding of the factors involved in a decision and their relationships with one another. Reviewing data, selecting the most appropriate type of graph, and merging it into your overall report will make you more effective in discussing proposals with your clients.

Graphs can be very useful in compressing pages of printouts, tables, and text into a single, action-oriented illustration. For example, an investor may have a portfolio consisting of a number of stocks and bonds. As a financial adviser you may want to provide your client with a report on the performance of the portfolio during the past six months. Think about how much text or the number of spreadsheets you would need to describe the portfolio's ups and downs over that period.

While a single graph may not convey all of the information clients would like to have about their investments, an effective chart tells a lot about the makeup of the portfolio and its performance during the past six months. It would enhance a letter or report from you reviewing the client's holdings, describing current market conditions, or suggesting future investment opportunities.

Using graphs will make your reports and presentations more effective and more likely to get the results you want. With some additional equipment, or through the use of a professional service, they can also be made into overhead transparencies or color slides. Clients will appreciate seeing their financial information in graphics form and will be more likely to act on your specific recommendations.

CONCLUSION

To a large degree the financial planning industry is as much a product of technology as a user of it. Without the communications and data processing industries, many of the products and services offered by planners could not exist. For example, universal life insurance is often cited as a product that could not be offered without large-scale computer support.

Similarly, the planning function is dependent on being able to collect, store, manipulate, and update information. Communicating that data to clients and other advisers is also an important part of the financial planning process. In all of these activities the personal computer is playing an increasingly important role. Successful planners in the future will be those who can use computers effectively to improve the productivity of their business, and at the same time free themselves to carry out the important human role that can never be automated.

"There is no one system that is perfect for everyone. In making your purchase decision, there are going to be tradeoffs."

—DAVID M. STITT

The Essentials of Purchasing Hardware for Financial Planners

David M. Stitt is employed by GEM Financial Corporation in Dayton, Ohio. He is a graduate of Miami University in Oxford, Ohio, with a degree in finance and holds the designations of Chartered Financial Consultant and Chartered Life Underwriter. He is a candidate for the Master of Financial Services degree and the Certified Financial Planner designation.

Mr. Stitt has spoken before many groups nationwide about computerization of a financial planning practice as well as about the financial planning process itself. In addition, he was a guest host of the weekly radio talk show, "Money Talks." He is a member of the Daytona Chapter of the International Association for Financial Planning, the Institute of Certified Financial Planners, and the American Society of Chartered Life Underwriters.

Assumptions and disclaimers are an important part of a financial plan; this article is no different. My assumptions are outlined below. The disclaimer: The opinions offered are those of the author and do not constitute an endorsement of any specific product or manufacturer. Products mentioned are those with which I am familiar.

Assumptions • (1) You have studied your business plan and determined that a computer will help you reach your goals. (2) You have made that all-important decision on what software will perform the task(s) required. Software is the most important part of any system, because it is the key that unlocks the power of the computer. It tells the computer what to do. Hardware is the machinery that performs the task.

This article will address the IBM and compatible machines. In my opinion, this is the computer to consider for a financial planning business. The Apple Macintosh is making headway in the business environment, but the IBM and compatibles are still the best bet. There is more business software available for the IBM and compatibles than for any other choice. The newest Apple MacII is supposed to be IBM-compatible, but I have not seen one as of this writing. If it is, it should be a real competitor, since the user interface of the Apple is more friendly.

Making a decision about a new computer calls for a multiplicity of considerations. This is true whether it is your first computer or an addition to an existing system. And the decisions are getting tougher! There are some 250 different models to choose from. With new standards emerging and the variety of options available, this is a most confusing time to be buying a computer.

Computers don't have tires to kick. And if you try to "look under the hood," it won't help much. We could compare the decisions to purchasing a car. What body style do you like? What type and size of engine do you need? Do you want the turbo-charged model? How about diesel or gas-powered? Do you want clear or tinted windows? Do you want cruise control? And on and on. So how do you know if you're making the right decision?

There is no one system that is perfect for everyone. In making your purchase decision, there are going to be tradeoffs. We are in a transitional time, with new systems being announced regularly. It's like a game of leapfrog. One company announces its latest and greatest, and another comes along with a new and improved version. Over the last ten years or so there has hardly been a six-month period without some new technological advance or promise made. You should be aware that **not all promises are kept!**

It may seem like the thing to do is to wait for the "best" system to come out. That day will never come, because there will always be something new on the horizon. Who said, "He who hesitates is lost"? Charles E. "Tremendous" Jones says, "Don't spend all your time trying to make the right decision. Make a decision and then spend time making it right." It takes about 18 months for new technology to have good useful software programs. The sooner you buy a system, the sooner you'll reap the benefits, and they'll be much greater than any possible price reductions. People who are interested in looking for the newest technological breakthroughs are interested in machines, not solutions. In other words, they don't know what they want. You didn't buy your last car because it had digital displays. You bought it so you could get where you wanted to go. Buying a computer is the same thing. If you are solution-driven, focus on the way the machine will meet your needs and forget the bells and whistles.

Ask yourself questions such as these: Can it grow with me? Is there a clear migration path? Is it possible to add workstations? Is it upgradable to add more data storage? How about main memory (RAM)? Can you use different kinds of printers? After using a high-speed draft printer, can you switch to a letter-quality printer? You may pay more initially to be sure that this growth is available, but you'll save in the long run.

Let's look at the main components and consider what is necessary and desirable—there is a difference!

CENTRAL PROCESSING UNIT (CPU)

The brain of the computer, where all calculations and logical decision activity take place. It is the electronic circuitry that receives instructions and performs the task(s). The CPU executes the programs and controls the operations of all components of the computer.

There are two considerations, **speed** and **capacity**. All computers have an internal clock that controls the speed of all operations. The older PC- and XT-type machines run at 4 MHz (megahertz). The newer systems, like the AT and hopped-up compatibles, run at 8 MHz or faster. The faster clock speed is not a necessity. You will probably become aware of the system's operational speed only after using it for a while. It is the perception of speed that will cause you to want to speed up your system. As with a new law, most don't worry about it until it affects them. When you realize that there can be true productivity gains from increased speed, then you can justify the expense. The addition of a speed-up chip at any time will improve the performance of the system.

Most financial planning software is file- or disk-intensive. This is the case with all database-type programs. These programs are dependent upon disk input/output speed. For most financial planning purposes, the 8087 math co-processor will not noticeably affect calculations. If you are going to be using a lot of complex spreadsheets and/or insurance illustrations, the chip would be a good investment.

There are accelerator boards that replace the system's standard processor. A problem could occur if a program uses the computer's hardware directly. Some memory resident programs do use the hardware directly. A memory resident program gets loaded into memory and waits to be called upon to operate. An example would be Borland's Sidekick, which includes a pop-up calculator, note pad, calendar, and other desk-top utilities. An accelerator board may be too fast for the hard disk and therefore may not take advantage of the full capability of the board. It is important to match the timing of all the components so that the full benefit of accelerators may be achieved.

There are software programs such as Lightning, from Personal Computer Support Group, that do speed up the disk access. These act as intermediate directory storage for the most-used files. This speeds up finding a file on the disk when the program searches for it. Like chips and accelerator boards, these programs can greatly increase the speed of operation. But both hardware and software speed-up approaches can cause real compatibility problems. They can cause your application software programs to do strange things. Sometimes the system may even refuse to do anything at all. A word of warning: **Test** any such product *before* committing to a purchase. Be sure that you test the exact combination of software and hardware you plan to use.

Software programs such as Disk Optimizer from SoftLogic Solutions can offer some speed increases by reorganizing the stored information so that it doesn't take as long to load the files into the CPU. After a while the files can become fragmented on the disk, because the system stores information wherever it finds space, not necessarily sequentially or together on the disk.

INTERNAL STORAGE

There are two types of main memory:

ROM (Read Only Memory)

Contains preprogrammed functions which cannot be changed or erased. It is also known as Firmware and is usually part of total memory, so the more ROM used for permanent operations, the less RAM there is available. This static memory is retained when the machine is turned off and is faster than RAM.

RAM (Random Access Memory)

This is important to you because it determines how large a program you can run. More sophisticated software uses more RAM. Most small business computers have a main memory capacity of at least 64,000 or 64K bytes. Each character represents 8 bits, 1 byte; 1024 bytes is abbreviated as 1K. 1K of data is about $1\frac{1}{2}$ pages of double-spaced text.

You can set up a portion of memory to simulate a disk drive, RAM disk. This is approximately 50 times faster than a floppy disk and is helpful in improving throughput. Of course, this reduces the amount of memory available for programs.

The *practical minimum* amount of RAM to have is 256K. Give serious consideration to 512K or 640K. The extra RAM can be used for the RAM disk and memory resident programs such as Sidekick, or some other pop-up type of calculator, disk speed-up program, note pad, and the like. The price of RAM chips is coming down, so the cost to increase (upgrade) RAM is very low.

EXTERNAL STORAGE

This is usually done on disks, and there are several choices:

Floppy Disk

This looks like a flexible phonograph record. It is a magnetic oxide-coated mylar disk enclosed in a protective envelope. They are inexpensive and are easily damaged. The read/write head sits on the disk surface and can cause the surface to wear out. The capacity of these range from 360Kb (about 360,000 bytes) to 1.2Mb (about 1,200,000 bytes). The sizes vary from $3\frac{1}{2}$ to 8 in., but the most common is $5\frac{1}{4}$ in.; it normally has a capacity of 360Kb.

It is necessary to have at least one floppy disk drive to transfer information and programs onto, or off of, the system. The 360Kb floppy is the most popular. Consider as a nice extra either a second 360Kb floppy or preferably a high-density floppy drive.

The new $3\frac{1}{2}$-in. floppy disks are safer because of the heavier jacket in which they are enclosed. They also can hold more data than their larger counterparts. Not many are in use yet, so this would not be suggested if you need to exchange any data with other computers. The software available is also limited at this time.

Hard Disk

This type is more expensive but offers many advantages: The storage capacity ranges from 10Mb to over 100Mb. The hard disk has become virtually a standard for business use.

Speed is critical to a hard disk. The measure used is "average access time," the time between a request for data and the time the data is received. This is almost as important as CPU speed. Hard disks of most personal computers respond in between 20 and 80 milliseconds. It is essential that the speeds of the CPU and the hard disk be compatible to take full advantage of the potential speed. It is a waste of money to buy a fast hard disk if the processor doesn't operate fast enough to take advantage of the potential speed. Generally speaking, the higher the capacity of the drive, the faster the disk. The fastest hard disks at the time of this writing were in the 17-Ms range.

One or more disks (platters) are sealed in a special container, and the surface of the drives is safe from the contamination that can ruin their counterparts. The read/write head never comes into contact with the surface of the disk, thereby eliminating any surface abrasion. These round metal platters are covered with a thin layer of ferromagnetic material.

There is an advantage to having external storage as a separate unit. If something happens to the hard disk, the disk can be taken in for repair without losing the use of the system in the meantime. Of course, you would need to rely on another type of external storage in the meantime, such as the floppy disk.

Take a close look at the Bernoulli Box by Iomega. This system gives you the best of both worlds, the flexibility of floppies and the capacity of hard disks. This is because the system uses cartridges that are handled like floppies and can hold up to ten megabytes on a single disk.

The *practical minimum* external storage capacity is a 10Mb hard disk. Some manufacturers are discontinuing this size in favor of the higher-capacity models. I suggest you consider buying as large a hard disk as you can afford. The convenience is well worth the price. All of your application programs would be stored on the hard disk. It is possible for programs to require 60 percent or more of a 10Mb hard disk. There is one financial planning package that takes 8Mb just for its program. And that does not include any other software. Once you allow for space for the applications programs, all the rest can be used for data storage. This means that you effectively triple or quadruple data storage when you increase the disk capacity from 10 to 20 megabytes, because all the additional capacity may be used for data. The cost for each additional 10 Mb is small in the overall picture, sometimes as low as $300.

Other hard disk considerations

- Automatic head parking.   This feature returns the read/write head to a "neutral zone" to prevent destruction of any data.
- Transfer rate.   This is the amount of data moved in and out of memory per second. The range is from 5Mb to 10Mb.
- Mean time before failure.   This is the number of hours before a failure can be expected. The industry standard is at least 20,000 hours. That is over two years if the system runs continuously.

Price should be the *last thing* you consider when buying a hard disk. It makes sense to err on the high side rather than the low side. Remember your first motorcycle? How soon after you drove it off the lot were you convinced that you needed a larger bike? If you are anything like me, it only took a few successful rides to "need" a more powerful bike. The same will be true of a hard disk. **Big is better.**

- Hard disk cards. These are an interesting new technology that allow you to add storage capacity in an expansion slot of the system's mother board. An additional benefit, in addition to the small space they take up, is the fact that they require less power than a complete disk drive.

TERMINAL

The terminal is your control panel and allows you to communicate with the computer. There are *two main parts*, the **monitor** (screen) and the **keyboard.**

Monitor

This is commonly called the CRT, for *cathode ray tube.* There are two types: monochrome and color. Monochrome is best for text operations. Clarity of information on the screen is affected by the color used to display the characters and the resolution (the number of dots in the matrix used to form the character). The monochrome comes in several "color" options and in varying degrees of resolution. The combination is strictly a personal preference. Green characters on black seems to be the most popular. Amber on black is popular in Europe and gaining popularity here. The higher the resolution—the number of dots in the matrix—the more crisp the character appears on the screen.

Color monitors are more expensive than monochrome. If you are developing games or instructional programs, color is helpful. It is also helpful when generating graphics. If you think you will need color, get it initially. They are much more expensive if you add one later, because you have to add a separate video board at the same time. If you do add color, you will want an enhanced graphics board for the best results. Color comes in two types, composite and RGB. RGB is the only type acceptable for a business environment. A color display will, however, be more tiring on your eyes during long sitting. Color initially may add as little as $400 to the cost. When added later the cost can approach $1000.

You should have at least 24 horizontal lines and 80 vertical columns. Other features to look for include: a nonglare screen, swivel base, tilt capability, and ergonometric considerations, such as footprint (space it takes up on a desk) and shape.

Choice of a monitor is a decision not to be taken lightly. You will be spending a lot of time looking at the screen.

Keyboard

Your preference for keyboards will be determined by your feel and prior experience. The software you will be using may play an important role in the best layout. Some software takes advantage of special-function keys.

It may, however, be more important to match the layout of a new keyboard with existing ones if several people will use it. This will make the operation more efficient, because people will not have to get used to several layouts.

A separate numeric keypad with a separate ENTER key facilitates input of numbers. Separate cursor control keys are great for programs like Lotus 1-2-3. LED lights that indicate the status of the special keys NUM LOCK and CAPS LOCK are a nice convenience.

PRINTERS

Printers are generally not dependent upon a system and are interchangeable. The important question about printer selection is "Will the software I am using 'drive' the printer and will it utilize any of the special features?" Additionally, there are five considerations when one is selecting a printer.

- What type of output is desired? Text only? Or will you need to be able to print graphic characters? Is color desirable?
- What quality is desired? Do you demand true letter quality such a typewriter gives? Or is near letter quality acceptable?

The type of output desired may force part of the decision for you. Letter quality printers (LQP) can produce only very limited graphic characters. So if graphics is a requirement, you will not be able to even consider a LQP unless you get two printers.

- What quantity of output is expected? Will there be large amounts of printing done? Will the printer be in constant use?
- What environment will the printer be placed in? Is it a quiet private office? Is it an isolated spot where noise is not a factor? How much space is available? How far away will the printer be from the computer?

Information is sent from the computer along a cable. There are two ways in which the signal can travel, parallel (eight bits at a time) or serial (one bit at a time). A parallel printer cannot be more than 10 or 12 feet from the computer. If you intend to have the printer very far away from the computer, you will need to be sure to get a serial printer. Most printers can be configured either way, but you have to order it as you want it.

Letter-Quality Printers

These are the standard for quality output. Documents printed on a LQP look as if they were individually typed. These account for only 25 percent of the printer market today. Characters are fully formed by a daisy wheel or thimble printhead. They are slow and noisy. The print speed, measured in characters per second (CPS), ranges from 12 to 55. Since the fastest typist in the world was clocked at 15 cps, this may seem fast, but it really isn't. Generally they are less than half as fast as other choices. As in most purchases, the more you pay, the faster and more durable machine you can expect. The cost of these can be anywhere from under $300 to over $3000.

Letter-quality printers do some things perfectly (such as legal documents), some adequately, and some not at all (such as graphics).

The noise has been measured in the 55- to 65-decibel range. Acoustical hoods can be purchased for these or for dot matrix printers (which also can be noisy) for $100 to $400. A hood would be a wise investment if the printer will be located within "earshot" of either workers or clients who are visiting.

Dot Matrix Printers

These printers form characters by printing a series of dots in a matrix, rectangular box. The less expensive printers have a column of nine pins that hit a ribbon to print dots. The newer and more expensive printers now have 18 or 24 pins. Of course, the more dots printed, the more closely a fully-formed character may be represented. Some of these printers make more than one pass to increase the density (number of dots) and produce "near letter quality" print. Some are very good and quite acceptable for most purposes. None, however, can produce true letter-quality print. They also have varying degrees of graphics capabilities.

Dot matrix printers are much faster than LQPs. The CPS ranges from 160 to over 600. That equates to as many as 6 pages of text a minute. A feature the dot matrix has that gives it much more flexibility than the LQP is the ability to print different styles of letters in addition to graphics characters. Generally the higher-speed printers are more durable and more expensive than the slower models. The cost ranges from $150 to over $4000.

The dot matrix printer is preferred for most uses because of its versatility and price. These advantages have helped them corner 67 percent of the printer market. Some applications programs take advantage of many of the special features of these printers. The ability to alternate between 10 characters per horizontal inch and 17 or more is just one example. There are also memory resident programs that will work with application programs that can do all manner of fancy printing.

Ink Jet Printers

These are a new type of dot matrix printer. It forms dots by squirting small streams of ink on the paper. The quality of those I have seen is excellent, and they are very quiet. These can be an excellent alternative to a LQP. They are generally faster (150 to 220 CPS) and quieter than the LQP. They are also quieter than the dot matrix printers, but they are not as fast. The cost of these can run between $500 and over $2000.

A cartridge of ink will last about 5 to 6 million characters, or 200 pages of text. The print head itself will last about 10 billion characters or 4 million pages.

Laser Printers

These are similar to copiers. A laser beam writes characters onto a drum, then transfers the image to paper. The quality of output is excellent as long as the machine is kept clean. They are very fast, printing 5 to 20 pages per minute. As with dot matrix printers, several different fonts are available. These are probably the most expensive printers currently, because of the newness of the technology. They take more space than most other printers, but they are very quiet. They cost between $2000 and $10,000. That is a lot of money to give your clients "copies" of the output. But they are extremely fast, quiet, and produce excellent copy. They make up five percent of the market.

Thermal Printers

These burn a hole on specially treated paper. I would not consider these, because the print quality is not acceptable for client presentations and the special paper required is expensive. They are inexpensive initially, however, costing between $100 and $700.

Electronic Typewriters

Some manufacturers sell their typewriters with "interfaces" to computers. I would not try to let a typewriter do double duty as a printer. None are built to take the constant use that a computer demands. Remember the statistics on the typist earlier? Well, a computer is much faster and doesn't have to take coffee breaks. If you want the ability to type, buy a utility program that turns your computer into an expensive typewriter, or better yet, buy a typewriter.

Regardless of the printer selected, a wide carriage will be necessary only if you need to print out wide reports, such as accounting spreadsheets. Normally an 80-column printer is adequate and less expensive. I would suggest that whatever printer you select, you get a tractor to allow for continuous feed paper. A sheet-feeder is nice, but expensive. I would suggest it only if you do a lot of letters on special stationery. It is possible to get stationery mounted on continuous forms or special laser perforation paper that uses a tractor feed.

Additional Printer Considerations

Bidirectional printing • The printing is accomplished on both passes of the print head. The result is 35 percent increase in speed.

Logic-seeking head • Skips all blank spaces and goes directly to the next space to print.

Buffer • Temporarily stores information while the printer is printing until the printer catches up with the computer. The computer will send information to be printed as fast as 960 characters a second. Very few printers are capable of keeping up with that. A buffer will allow you to go on to other work while the printer works on the print assignment.

Ribbons • While spools will last longer, the cartridges are much easier to use. The best quality of print for a ribbon comes from a film ribbon that can be used only once. These are generally only used on LQPs, because the movement of dot matrix print creates heat that will melt the filament. Cloth ribbons may be used over and over. When you have exhausted the ribbon, you can get it reinked; reinking is cheaper than buying a new one.

PLOTTERS

Plotters are necessary for quality graphics. There are enough considerations in the purchase of one of these to merit a separate article.

BACKUP

Backup is a security procedure in which files are duplicated as a precaution against something going wrong. You have two choices of how you handle this insurance.

Floppy Disk

The floppy disk is probably the most common because of the initial cost of the alternative. It is a relatively simple procedure and can be done as files are altered. After there is a lot of information on the hard disk, one begins to look for an easier way to ensure the integrity of all that work.

Magnetic Tape Cartridge

The cartridge is a popular device because of its very dense storage capacity (up to 10 million or more characters). To copy the same data onto a floppy would require more than 25 standard, double-sided, $5\frac{1}{4}$-in. disks, representing potentially an hour or more of operator time. A complete tape backup procedure requires a single command, takes only a few minutes, and doesn't need to be monitored. Because the tape is enclosed in a hard plastic case, your important system and data files are stored in something more reliable than floppies encased in paper. Tallgrass Technologies has a nice unit.

MODEM

A modem is a device which enables your computer to talk to other computers over phone lines. This will enable you to move information from large databases such as stock quotes from Dow Jones News/Retrieval. Some computers require an external modem, while others have space inside for the modem. You would also need communications software.

The cost of a modem is directly related to the speed with which it transmits/receives data. The speed at which data is transferred is measured in bits per second, known as *baud rate*. You can convert this baud rate to characters per second by dividing the baud by 10. Each character requires a start bit and a stop bit added to the 8 bits per character. Although a 300 baud (30 characters per second) is a choice, it is very slow. Most databases now support 1200 baud, and some support 2400 baud units. The best choice would be a modem that can both answer and originate calls. Modem prices range from $150 to over $700.

SURGE PROTECTORS AND UNINTERRUPTABLE POWER SUPPLIES

These should be considered wherever a constant range of power is not available. They are relatively inexpensive, in the range of $35 to $200.

Large motors in offices draw a lot of current when they start up. A fluctuation in power can occur during and after each occurrence. A spike lasts only a short while, microseconds, and can increase the voltage to 9000 v. That is enough to fry anything. A surge, on the other hand, is longer lasting and is a much lower voltage. Either situation can create a problem. ''Noise'' on an electrical line should be filtered. Look for a surge protector that also handles this.

In situations where a brownout may occur, an uninterruptable power supply is a wise investment. These cost much more than surge protectors, because there is more to maintaining a power supply for a period of time than merely intercepting variations. They store energy while the line is up and provide energy when the line is down. They can cost anywhere from $600 to over $15,000.

SERVICE AND PRICE

As Milton Freidman says, ''There is no free lunch!'' As it is in life with most things, you normally get what you pay for.

If this is your first computer, then the issue of service is more important. Once you have had a computer for a while, you will be more comfortable with performing some of the service yourself. Most problems today require only replacing a plug-in part. A word of warning: if you are a first-time buyer, **don't be a pioneer!** Stay with standards. Remember, pioneers are the people alongside the road with arrows in their backs.

Most of the makers of generic clones will offer a one-year warranty. Ask if the computer can be repaired at the store, or if it will have to be sent back to the factory (who knows where) for repairs.

Would you drive a car without insurance? That is what a service contract is. The main reason to have it is to ensure peace of mind.

The company you buy your computer from can be as important as the computer you choose to buy.

Be aware that some add-ons can invalidate a warranty, so ask before you buy.

Lower prices are not necessarily a reason to wait to buy, especially if you are buying the system for business purposes. The use and production you can get from the system could outweigh the few dollars you may save by waiting.

Author John Ruskin once said, "It is unwise to pay too much, but it is worse to pay too little. When you pay too much, you lose a little . . . that is all. When you pay too little, you sometimes lose everything because the thing you bought was incapable of doing what it was bought to do." You can't go wrong with IBM, but it will cost you more money, and you may lose some of the performance that a compatible system would give you.

The advertised price is not always what you will pay. Be careful when comparing prices that you are comparing apples with apples, not oranges. Some dealers advertise a low price for the basic equipment and make it up on the accessories.

COMPATIBILITY

To be 100 percent compatible a system must not only be able to run the same software, out of the box with no changes, but must accept the many add-on boards that have been developed. Most systems today are compatible in the first area, but check before you buy. A test used by many is the machine's ability to run Microsoft's Flight Simulator for the IBM. Not as many are compatible in the second area. It pays to check this out as well.

Compaq was the first and is consistently the most successful compatible model. It is the fastest-growing company in American history.

Name brand clones include ITT, AT&T, and Sperry. They are less expensive than IBM, but more expensive than generic clones.

Generic clones are similar to generic drugs. Give serious consideration to these systems. They have come a long way and offer some significant performance bonuses while costing less. Just be sure you understand what you are doing. In some cases, you can get two or three clones for the same price as the name brands.

ONE FINAL NOTE OF WARNING

There are dealers out there who are less than scrupulous. A lot of software is being **pirated!** Guarantee that you have a legitimate copy of any software installed by the dealer. This is done by being sure you receive the original user manual, a registration card, and the distribution disk with the manufacturer's label on it.

Good luck and good computing.

"Instead of believing the advertising, believe the successful planners who are using the software in which you are interested."

—JUDD KESSLER, CFP

Choosing User-Friendly Financial Planning Software

Judd S. Kessler, CFP, has helped over one thousand financial planners computerize their financial planning practices. He is the founder and president of Abacus Data Systems, Inc., of Del Mar, California. Mr. Kessler has over fourteen years of experience in asset management and investment consulting and is licensed in securities, insurance, real estate, mortgage, and business brokerage. He is a practicing financial planner and president of Kessler Financial Group. Mr. Kessler earned a degree in economics and computer science from the University of California and is a frequent speaker at IAFP and ICFP events nationally.

You can tell almost immediately if software is user friendly or not. Just sit down and enter a sample case. As simple and obvious as this sounds, almost nobody will spend an hour actually using a program that the vendor claims will do everything. Instead, many planners will resort to spending tens of hours gathering information on all of the competing programs, comparing the reports, talking with the salespeople, and agonizing over which one to buy, or hiring a computer consultant to do it for them.

Like financial planners, consultants gather data, analyze the client's situation, know the alternatives available, select the best alternative for the given situation, and assist the client in understanding and implementing the recommendations. It takes many hours for a consultant to do a proper job. He must first understand the intricacies of your particular financial planning practice. (He needs to know how to do your kind of financial planning before he can select and properly test software that will meet your needs. Essentially, he needs to be a financial planner.) Then, he must research all of the available software products, narrow the field to those that claim to do what you need, and finally spend the time to actually test the programs selected to see if they fulfill the claims and expectations. If the cost of hiring a consultant to do a proper job seems nominal to you, beware. Sometimes the consultant will be taking a hidden commission or markup, or getting a duplicate copy for sale to another client, or will make a recommendation that will ensure that you'll be paying him or her for more consulting/training after you purchase the recommended software.

How can you best protect yourself and avoid this frustration and agony? There are two simple precautions: First, try before you buy; second, ask a planner who's already doing what you want to do.

Prepare a sample case for inputting in the selected software. Many of the software vendors at the IAFP or ICFP events would be happy to assist you and allow you the time to test their product. If you find that it takes you longer than one hour to input a sample case and print meaningful reports, pass. It's not user friendly, period. Gone are the days when you had to spend a week at a training class or a month on your own learning how to use the software before you could become productive. Certainly, there are still some programs in the market like that. They claim to do everything for you that a computer could possibly do in a financial planning practice, and they probably can. But there is a very high price you will pay for those seldom-used features.

Don't be seduced by the demo disk or the money-back guarantee. Your time is too valuable. A money-back guarantee will refund to you the cost of the software, but how can you recover the many hours spent trying to educate yourself about a program that doesn't do what you want it to?

Don't be seduced by full-page, four-color ads and 800 telephone numbers. Just because a firm has fabulous advertising doesn't mean the program is best for you. Instead of believing the advertising, believe the successful planners who are using the software in which you are interested. Most reputable software vendors would be happy to arrange for you to speak with planners who are successfully using their software. If you talk with a number of computerized planners who operate in the way you would like to, it makes sense to use the same tools that they use in their successful practice. Why reinvent the wheel?

If you spend your time as a computer operator instead of financial planner, you'll starve as a financial planner. If your financial planning software is not user friendly enough that your secretary can use it, you're on your way to losing the battle. And, given the fact of life of staff turnover, if a replacement person can't use your system within an hour or so, you'll be held hostage by your software and/or your secretary forever! Who will do the planning you should be doing?

It's ironic how some financial planners, trained to examine investments, often fail to consider the total investment in their software. Instead, they look only at the initial cost of software. Indeed, the initial investment to acquire the software is small compared to the investment in hours spent learning and using the system. If you use your computer an average of three hours a day, in five years you'll have over 3000 hours invested. If a more user-friendly system could save you only half an hour per day, that's over $25,000 saved at $50 per hour. The initial price of the software is small compared to the continuing cost of using it.

If you avoid upgrading your computer system simply because of the initial price of the software or hardware, you're making a serious and costly mistake. You see, the new financial planner who is just starting his practice is buying faster and more powerful hardware and software than you are now using. And that new planner will be offering service that you simply do not have the time to offer. The new planner will get the new clients, and as your clients move away or die, your practice is destined to shrink.

A very wise and experienced financial planner once said, "Hands that shape the client's mind should never touch the computer." Does this mean that you shouldn't bother to become computer literate or know how to use the tools you've acquired? Of course not. It does, however, mean that your time is much too valuable to spend it as a computer data input operator. Hire that work done. You say staff turnover makes that impossible? By the time you train one, he or she is gone and you find yourself back at the computer doing it yourself, because it's easier than training a new one. That's because you have the wrong software. Truly user-friendly software can be learned by a staff person in less than a day, independently using the tutorial or operator's manual that comes with the software. If your software cannot be learned and used that way, get rid of it. It's costing you too much money!

One of the most important features of user-friendly software is the ability to print quarterly updated reports for all clients without having to input each client name or account number. This type of batch processing allows you to input the reports desired and the range of client account numbers for whom reports are to be printed, and walk away from the computer until the job is finished. Without this feature, you could spend all day in front of the computer selecting reports and account numbers one at a time.

Other important features include the capability of updating all prices, cash flows, or taxable incomes for every client with just one input, the capability of having the reinvestment of dividends and capital gains automatically updated in each account, and the capability of automatically allocating suspended passive losses to each passive asset.

In conclusion, nonuser-friendly software, which is any software that does not free up more of your time so you can spend it more productively in front of clients, continues to cost you money long after you pay the initial purchase price.

"No two planners are alike, which means that they have different needs for software support."

—DAVID C. HUXFORD, CLU, CFP

Should You Buy Integrated Financial Planning Software or Should You Develop Your Own?

David Huxford started in the insurance business as an agent for Northwestern Mutual Life in 1967 and throughout his career has developed an extensive knowledge of computer systems. In 1983, he founded the Advanced Planners Users Group (APUG).

Mr. Huxford holds a bachelor of arts degree from Auburn University and a Certified Financial Planner designation from the College for Financial Planning, Denver, Colorado, and a Chartered Life Underwriter designation from the American College. He has written numerous professional articles on the topic of computerization for *Life Insurance Selling, Life Association News, Stanger Register,* and *Financial Services Times.* He is also a popular speaker to professional groups.

There is integrated financial planning software that requires large investments in time and money to make it work properly. Some planners should take the plunge and pick a package in this price range, while others should look for alternatives. The purpose of this article is to offer ideas for the reader's consideration in determining if a higher-priced integrated package should be selected or if the planner should look for alternatives.

Note: There are many different shades of grey between black and white. But the categories and assumptions made in this article are treated as black and white for ease of conceptualization. The reader will have to decide which category fits best. Note also that the term "integrated" is used to mean a package that automatically changes calculations and recommendations upon change of underlying assets and assumptions in the client database.

CATEGORIES OF PLANNERS

No two planners are alike, which means they have different needs for software support. This article arbitrarily divides planners into three different categories.

Category one • In the first group is the person who is just getting started in the business and has a great deal to learn about preparing a plan and the calculations that support it.

Category two • In the second group is the person who is very knowledgeable about preparing a plan, including the calculations that support it, but who does a low volume of plans, about two or less a month.

Category three • In the last group is the person who is very knowledgeable about preparing a plan and who does a considerable volume of plans each month.

INTEGRATED SOFTWARE PACKAGES

Two factors for consideration by the beginning planner looking at sophisticated integrated software is its relatively high price and the difficulty of knowing what happens when data is entered.

Learning the Package

Beginning planners are unlikely to anticipate the effects of plan calculations when items of data are changed. Why did income taxes go up when a large tax shelter asset was added to the database? Could it have been because of the alternative minimum income tax calculation? A beginning planner might ask, "What is alternative minimum income tax?"

Another problem is knowing where in the software to enter what types of data. Each software package has its own set of codes that tell the software how to handle client data. Learning the codes and what they mean can be very confusing. Not only must beginning planners know how to do the calculations by hand, but they must also know how the software will treat client data. Even very knowledgeable planners have a difficult time learning this phase of using an integrated package.

No planner should attempt to use integrated financial planning software until every facet of a plan can be manually calculated and prepared with ease. This ability can only come from actually preparing a lot of plans by hand.

Integrated planning software can produce a plan with specific recommendations that are correct for the data entered but entirely wrong for the client. This can happen because the planner codes data incorrectly. The planner could be sued and would probably lose.

The Cost

There are two types of costs associated with advanced integrated packages. The first is the one we all think about—dollars out of pocket. But equally important is the cost of planner's time in making the package work.

As a rule, advanced integrated software packages begin at the $4000 price range and go up from there. Additionally, there is usually a maintenance charge of $600 or more annually.

The time required for a planner to get an integrated package up and running effectively can be very extensive. A month of effort before a planner becomes comfortable with a package is not unlikely.

The combined dollar and loss of time cost for integrated packages should cause a low-volume planner to move cautiously.

Who Should Buy An Integrated Package?

There is little question that a knowledgeable high-volume planner needs an advanced integrated package. A knowledgeable, low-volume, category two planner can also cost-justify the integrated package if he or she spends enough time with it to become proficient at getting an accurate plan. The beginning planner should not buy integrated software.

ALTERNATIVES TO INTEGRATED SOFTWARE PACKAGES

Data management and calculations are two functions that must be handled by the planner. Of the two, data management is the most time-consuming and difficult to accomplish. Therefore, the critical path is to solve the data management problem properly. Once listings of assets, liabilities, and cash flows with subtotals by the owner can be obtained, calculations are much easier to make. Estate and income taxes can be done with a spreadsheet or stand-alone tax utility packages.

Therefore, an alternative to the integrated package is a good database management system, a spreadsheet like Lotus 1-2-3, and relatively inexpensive estate and income tax calculation packages.

Client Asset Management System (CAMS)

The planner can buy a database utility package like dBASE III PLUS and personally develop a set of files and programs to keep track of client data. This is easy to do in its simplest form such as keeping track of client, spouse, and children names, addresses, phone numbers, and dates of birth. It even makes sense for a planner to track client assets and liabilities. But developing systems beyond this simple listing process gets considerably more complicated and takes far too much of the planner's time.

In most cases, the planner should buy a very good client asset management system (CAMS) package that keeps track of assets, liabilities, and cash flows. This type of software package is considerably less expensive than an integrated package. Some user groups have this type of software for as low as fifty dollars.

Financial Reports

This package should produce financial and cash flow statements for the client, client and spouse, and for the family.

A set of financial reports generated by CAMS could be used by the planner to make recommendations. After repositioning assets, the planner could use CAMS to produce a second set of reports which, when combined with the first set, would provide supporting detail for the written plan.

Asset Management

The CAMS package should provide automatic update of client assets when market values for traded assets change. This allows the planner to change the value of a stock in one place and have the value of all client portfolios containing the stock change accordingly.

Planners may want to take an active role in asset management for their clients. If so, the CAMS system should provide for portfolio management and client billing. It should allow the planner to track transactions that underlie assets, such as the transactions that take place in a client's mutual fund or stock portfolio.

TODO System

The CAMS package should provide a TODO (suspense) system designed to produce a daily list of tasks for each person in the planner's office. This should be done by the CAMS package because most items that have to be done are associated with a client and are generated when dealing with client data. The task lists should identify not only the task and client but also pull the client's phone number and the like from the client's file. The TODO system should be accessible with a single key from any client screen. The planner will find a properly designed TODO system one of the most valuable administrative support tools used.

Database Design

The first criterion is to begin with a database utility package that is powerful enough to do all that the planner will ever want to do. Some simpler packages may get a planner started but ultimately prevent the planner from developing a more advanced application. For example, the planner will probably need a multiuser version of the software to run on a local area network as the planner's practice expands. Don't select a utility package that does not have multiuser capacity.

Multiple files • Powerful database packages like dBASE III PLUS allow multiple files to integrate and appear as one file. Consider a file as a yellow pad list of clients' names and addresses. A file is a collection of records. Consider a record as a row on the yellow pad of information about one client. A record is a collection of fields of information. Consider the name on the yellow pad as one field and the street address as a second field. There would be fields for city, state, and zip codes. Visualize the fields as being the information down a column on the yellow pad, like the name column.

Good design requires multiple files to contain client information. For example, children would be kept in a children file, assets in an asset file, and insurance in an insurance file. This allows any number of children, assets, or insurance policies to be added to each "yellow pad."

Poor design would be to have one file with a given number of spaces for each item. In this case, there might be four spaces for four children's names, thirty spaces for assets, and ten spaces for insurance. The same amount of storage space on the disk would be used for the client who has only three policies as for the one with ten. And, of course, if the client has more items than spaces, they cannot be entered.

Field selection • The computer will become a bottleneck to the planner's operation. The number of keystrokes and amount of printer time will increase as the planning practice grows until it can't be handled by one computer. Therefore, it is very important to limit fields as much as possible, which will reduce keystrokes and printer time.

There are two rules for determining if a field of information should go in the database. A field should not go in the database if it does not satisfy one of these two rules.

Rule 1. The field must aid in production of a list of names for marketing activity.

Rule 2. The field must facilitate the reduction of an administrative overhead function.

Examples of fields that qualify under Rule 1 are client income, worth, tax bracket, date of birth, and whether the client has an IRA or not. These fields would allow the computer to produce a list of all clients born before 1940 with incomes greater than $50,000 who don't have IRAs. Examples of fields that would not qualify under Rule 1 are insurance policies' cash values and beneficiary names.

Examples of fields that qualify under Rule 2 are name, address, phone number, and type of calendar. These fields would allow the computer to handle the administrative task of addressing one letter or label to all clients who get a small desk calendar and another to all who get a large wall calendar. An example of a field that would not qualify under Rule 2 is a memo field in which random notes and memos can be entered about the client. The memo-type field would actually increase administrative overhead.

The basic rule is that the computer is not a substitute for the file cabinet and file folder. It does not make sense to make notes on paper about a client, have the secretary enter them in the computer, and then have the computer print them on paper. Just put the original paper in the file folder and cut the computer out of the loop. It may seem reasonable to enter notes in the computer initially, but eventually most planners will find it more efficient to use a file folder.

A cash value and beneficiary name excluded under Rule 1 may qualify under Rule 2 if the planner intends to provide a written report to the client containing this information.

Too much information in the computer usually makes the system slow to operate, requires large amounts of disk storage, and becomes out of date because it is just too time-consuming to keep it up to date. The planner should not attempt to have the most complete database but rather a lean and effective one. Additional fields can always be added later.

A Client Asset Management System Example

The end of this article contains a file and field structure of the CAMS system. The planner should feel free to use this example as a basis for designing a database.

Calculations

Playing "what if" for a client is a necessity to the planning process and practical with the right type of calculation software. The two types of software packages that support repetitive calculations are spreadsheets and specific function utility software such as an estate tax calculation package. These types of packages allow the entering of client data once and saving it to a disk file. Calculations for new assumptions and recommendations can be made as fast as items of data can be changed.

The disadvantage of using these types of packages is that data must be entered twice—once in the database and once again in the calculation software. Integrated packages usually require data to be entered only once.

Spreadsheets

All planners should have a spreadsheet even if they have advanced integrated financial planning software, and someone in the planner's office should have a working knowledge of how to use it. In most cases, it should be the planner as well as others responsible for making calculations. A whole new way of looking at planning will occur once the planner knows how to use a spreadsheet.

Visualize a spreadsheet as a series of rows and columns which intersect to make grids. Each grid can contain data or a formula. Each grid can be identified by row number and column letter and can be used by formulas in other grids. Therefore, changing a number in grid A1 would cause all other grids referencing A1 to automatically recalculate based on the new number in grid A1.

The most popular spreadsheet in the financial industry is Lotus 1-2-3. It can do any calculation the planner will ever want to do. It can automatically look up a rate in a tax table and use it in a tax calculation. Templates can be established which provide reports formatted in any way that the planner desires. Once a template is developed and stored on disk, it can be used over and over again for different clients.

A planner or planner's staff should never do calculations manually when the calculations will have to be done more than once. Use of a spreadsheet may initially be slower until the planner becomes proficient, but it will ultimately become much more efficient.

One of the advantages of a spreadsheet is the ability to eliminate typing by printing reports to either the printer or a disk file. A report printed to a disk file can later be merged into the word processing document for the written plan.

An advantage of a spreadsheet is that the planner can get exactly what is needed based on the planner's style and methods and on the specific client's case. Existing templates can be changed if they don't exactly fit the current client.

Planners should consider a spreadsheet by Paperback Software called VP Planner. It is a Lotus 1-2-3 clone, costs less than $100, and will read and write dBASE III PLUS files. This means that a template could make calculations based on data contained in a dBASE CAMS file.

Specific-function Utility Packages

Good income and estate tax calculation packages are much more cost effective for the planner than trying to duplicate their functions in a spreadsheet. Some tax packages deal with each asset and income item, whereas others use only totals of assets and income in specific categories. Those dealing with each item have the advantage of being able to show more detail about the calculations and distribution. On the other hand, those dealing with totals are faster to use.

Four major calculations needed by the planner are family budget projections, capital needed for survivors at client's death, estate tax calculations, and income tax calculations. There are several others such as mortgage amortization, college cost analysis, business valuation, and retirement and disability income analysis, just to mention a few.

An advantage of specific function software packages is that they are generally easier to understand and use than massive integrated software packages. If a better income tax package is found, it can be used without disrupting other packages, such as the estate tax package. Finally, a vendor can afford to develop a much better package than can a planner working alone with a spreadsheet, because the vendor is spreading the development cost over many users.

The Pitfalls of "Rolling Your Own"

The major problem of building software is the opportunity costs. The time spent building worksheets and databases could be spent generating new business. It is generally better for the planner to buy the major specific-function utility software, such as CAMS, income and estate tax programs, than try to develop them. Let the vendor worry about updating the software every time the tax laws change.

Computer Can be Addictive

Working with the computer can be addictive for some planners. It can take enormous amounts of the planner's time away from the business of planning and from the planner's family. In many cases, the planner does not realize the progressive addiction until major problems occur like loss of significant income or family concern.

It all begins with learning how easy it is to develop a template that will instantly calculate an internal rate on an investment's cash flow with a spreadsheet. Now the planner realizes that all reports and calculations needed can be done on a spreadsheet with just a "little programming effort." This offers freedom from software vendors and has no direct dollar cost.

For some planners, there is a great satisfaction in being able to prepare calculations and reports "their way." After many hours of getting the basic templates done, the planner has become a very accomplished spreadsheet user and knows how a template should be done. The planner looks back at the first template and realizes it could be greatly improved. So the planner starts over with the first template and "fixes" it. The cycle never ends.

Errors Increase Liability

The probability of catching errors in programming and formulas is much greater when a vendor develops a program, because the vendor has professional programmers and multiple users. Ten users might miss an error, but the eleventh user will find and report it.

Errors offer additional chances for the planner to be sued for incorrect advice. The planner might look at the cost of vendor software as the price of insurance.

Design Limited to One's Experience

The planner can get exactly what is desired when building a template. That can be both a major advantage and disadvantage. It will be an advantage and the template will be appropriate if the planner is capable, knowledgeable, and accurate.

If the planner is ignorant of a major factor in preparing a template, then there is no way a planner can know a mistake has been made. The ignorance can occur in how the spreadsheet works, such as the order of calculations in a formula of multiply, divide, add, and subtract. And the ignorance can occur in things like tax law or how to calculate rates of return.

The Advantages of a User's Group

There are two types of computer users' groups available to the planner. Most large cities have a hardware-specific computer users' group. For instance, there may be groups for Apple, Osborne, and IBM owners. Within these groups there may be special interest groups (SIGs) that specialize in a particular area of use such as word processing, accounting, and spreadsheets. There might even be an investment club SIG that would be of particular interest to a planner. Information about hardware-specific user groups can be obtained from most computer stores.

The second type of computer-user group is an industry-specific user group. Financial institutions such as insurance companies provide their representatives support specifically designed to help them do their jobs. There are also national and independent users' groups supporting the financial industries.

There is no substitute for experience. If a planner with a problem can call a user who has already been faced with the same problem and get concise how-to-do-it information, then the planner's participation in the users' group will be well worth the effort.

The planner might consider forming a local user group to support all planners' operations. Such a group could provide training for member planners' staffs. This is the most cost-effective method of helping planners and their staffs become computer literate.

CLIENT ASSET MANAGEMENT SYSTEM FILE STRUCTURE

TABLE 1

NAME: Structure for: FNA.DBF

	Field	Type	W	D
1	CLTNO	Char	11	
2	FNAMEMI	Char	15	
3	LNAME	Char	20	
4	CORRNAME	Char	40	
5	ADD1	Char	30	
6	ADD2	Char	30	
7	CITY	Char	18	
8	STATE	Char	2	
9	ZIP	Char	10	
10	HOMEADD	Char	1	
11	PHOFF	Char	12	
12	PHHOME	Char	12	
13	SALUTE	Char	25	
14	DNEXTCONT	Date	8	
15	DTEMP	Date	8	
16	DLASTCONT	Date	8	
17	DREVIEW	Date	8	
18	PORTFOLIO	Char	1	
19	DOBC	Date	8	
20	SMOKER	Char	1	
21	SEX	Char	1	
22	KEY	Char	48	
23	CATEGORY	Char	1	
24	NOTEDATA	Char	1	
25	NOTES	Memo	10	
26	FLAG	Char	1	
27	STATUS	Char	2	
28	AGTNO	Char	5	
Total			338	

TABLE 2

CLIENT: Structure for: FCL.DBF

	Field	Type	W	D
1	CLTNO	Char	11	
2	ALTADD1	Char	30	
3	ALTADD2	Char	30	
4	ALTCITY	Char	18	
5	ALTSTATE	Char	2	
6	ALTZIP	Char	10	
7	MAILCAT	Char	11	
8	BDAYCARD	Char	1	
9	IRA	Char	1	
10	PLANPOTEN	Char	22	
11	POSCODE	Char	2	
12	TAXCAT	Char	1	
13	TAXBKT	Num	2	
14	INC	Num	3	0
15	WORTH	Num	4	0
16	NOEES	Num	3	0
17	SPNAME	Char	12	
18	DOBS	Date	8	
19	SSOCNO	Char	11	
20	SSMOKER	Char	1	
Total			184	

TABLE 3

SPOUSE: Structure for: FSP.DBF

	Field	Type	W	D
1	CLTNO	Char	11	
2	LNAME	Char	15	
3	FIRM	Char	30	
4	PHOFF	Char	12	
5	INC	Num	3	0
6	WORTH	Num	4	0
7	POSCODE	Char	2	
8	NOEES	Num	3	0
9	KEY	Char	22	
Total			103	

TABLE 4

OTHER: Structure for: FOT.DBF

	Field	Type	W	D
1	CLTNO	Char	11	
2	NAME	Char	30	
3	DOBOT	Date	8	
4	SOCNO	Char	11	
5	WORTH	Num	4	
6	KEY	Char	22	
Total			87	

TABLE 5

BUSINESS: Structure for: FBU.DBF

	Field	Type	W	D
1	CLTNO	Char	11	
2	FIRM	Char	30	
3	SIC	Char	4	
4	FEDIDNO	Char	12	
5	NOEES	Num	4	0
6	PLANPOTEN	Char	22	
7	GPCARR	Char	25	
8	DGPREVIEW	Date	8	
9	DFISCALYR	Date	8	
10	PRESIDENT	Char	25	
11	SECRETARY	Char	15	
12	TAXCAT	Char	1	
13	SALES	Num	4	0
14	WORTH	Num	4	0
15	KEY	Char	22	
Total			196	

TABLE 6

APPLICATION: Structure for: FAP.DBF

	Field	Type	W	D
1	PLANNO	Char	20	
2	DNEXTCONT	Date	8	
3	DTEMP	Date	8	
4	DAPP	Date	8	
5	DMAILHO	Date	8	
6	DPOLRECVD	Date	8	
7	DPLACED	Date	8	
8	PRMDEPOSIT	Num	10	2
9	DMEDORD	Date	8	
10	DMEDRCV	Date	8	
11	DAPSORD	Date	8	
12	DAPSRCV	Date	8	
13	DINSPORD	Date	8	
14	DINSPRCV	Date	8	
15	DEKGORD	Date	8	
16	DEKGRCV	Date	8	
17	DHOSORD	Date	8	
18	DHOSRCV	Date	8	
19	OTHER1	Char	8	
20	DOTH1ORD	Date	8	
21	DOTH1RCV	Date	8	
22	NOTEDATA	Char	1	
23	NOTES	Memo	10	
24	KEY	Char	22	
Total			216	

TABLE 7

INSURANCE: Structure for: FIN.DBF

	Field	Type	W	D
1	CLTNO	Char	11	
2	PRMREG	Num	10	2
3	PRMFREQ	Num	2	0
4	COMMANT	Num	10	2
5	DCOMMCHG	Date	8	
6	MONTHCOMM	Char	28	
7	FANNCOMM	Num	10	2
8	DPLAN	Date	8	
9	PLANTYPE	Char	8	
10	HONAME	Char	15	
11	PLANNO	Char	20	
12	PLANNAME	Char	20	
13	DIVOPT	Char	2	
14	KEY	Char	22	
15	PLANAMT	Num	8	0
16	CURRCV	Num	8	0
17	LOAN	Num	8	0
18	RATING	Num	3	0
19	DLAPSED	Date	8	
20	ISSAGE	Num	2	
21	INSURED	Char	20	
22	INSCODE	Char	2	
23	OWNER	Char	20	
24	OWNCODE	Char	2	
25	BENE	Char	20	
26	BENECODE	Char	2	

TABLE 7 (cont.)

	Field	Type	W	D
27	AGTNO	Char	5	
28	AGTPCT	Num	5	3
29	FLAG	Char	1	
30	REPO	Char	1	
Total			290	

TABLE 8

ASSET: Structure for: FAS.DBF

	Field	Type	W	D
1	CLTNO	Char	11	
2	ACCTCODE	Char	25	
3	MKTCODE	Char	10	
4	NOUNITS	Num	11	3
5	NAME	Char	30	
6	TYPE	Char	2	
7	CATEGORY	Char	2	
8	LIQUID	Char	1	
9	DBUY	Date	8	
10	DSELL	Date	8	
11	DMATURE	Date	8	
12	COST	Num	10	2
13	MKTVALUE	Num	10	2
14	DEFFECT	Date	8	
15	GROWRATE	Num	5	3
16	OWNER	Char	11	
17	OWNCAT	Char	4	
18	OWNNAME	Char	20	
19	OWNCODE	Char	2	
20	TAXINC	Num	8	0
21	NONTAXINC	Num	8	0
22	INCCAT	Char	2	
23	ITC	Num	8	0
24	WRITEOFF	Num	8	0
25	LOAN	Num	8	0
26	AGTPCT	Num	5	3
27	AGTNO	Char	5	
28	COMMAMT	Num	10	2
29	KEY	Char	22	
30	REPO	Char	1	
Total			272	

TABLE 9

TRANSACTIONS: Structure for: FAT.DBF

	Field	Type	W	D
1	ACCTCODE	Char	25	
2	MKTCODE	Char	10	
3	TRAN	Char	5	0
4	DTRAN	Date	8	
5	TRANAMT	Num	10	2
6	UNITCOST	Num	8	2
7	NOUNITS	Num	11	3
8	BALANCE	Num	11	3
9	FLAG	Char	1	
Total			90	

TABLE 10

MARKET NAME: Structure for: FMN.DBF

	Field	Type	W	D
1	MKTCODE	Char	10	
2	NAME	Char	30	
3	TYPE	Char	2	
4	CATEGORY	Char	2	
5	LIQUID	Char	1	
6	INCCAT	Char	2	
7	TAXINC	Num	10	2
8	NONTAXINC	Num	10	2
9	GROWRATE	Num	5	3
10	ITC	Num	10	2
11	WRITEOFF	Num	10	2
12	HIALERT	Num	10	2
13	LOALERT	Num	10	2
Total			113	

TABLE 11

MARKET VALUE: Structure for: FMV.DBF

	Field	Type	W	D
1	MKTCODE	Char	10	
2	MKTVALUE	Num	10	2
3	FLAG	Char	1	
4	DEFFECT	Date	8	
Total			30	

TABLE 12

COMMISSION: Structure for: FCM.DBF

	Field	Type	W	D
1	PLANNO	Char	20	
2	DATE	Date	8	
3	AMOUNT	Num	10	2
4	AGTNO	Char	5	
Total			44	

TABLE 13

TODO: Structure for: FTODO.DBF

	Field	Type	W	D
1	PERSON	Char	1	
2	PRI	Num	2	
3	CLTNO	Char	11	
4	TASK	Char	55	
5	DSTART	Date	8	
6	DDUE	Date	8	
7	COMPLETED	Log'l	1	
8	NOTEDATA	Char	1	
9	NOTES	Memo	10	
Total			98	

TABLE 14

TODO AUTOMATIC: Structure for: FTODOA.DBF

	Field	Type	W	D
1	CATEGORY	Char	3	
2	PERSON	Char	1	
3	PRI	Num	2	
4	CLTNO	Char	11	
5	TASK	Char	55	
6	DSTART	Date	8	
7	DDUE	Date	8	
8	DUEDAYS	Num	3	
9	COMPLETED	Log'l	1	
10	NOTEDATA	Char	1	
11	NOTES	Memo	10	
Total			104	

TABLE 15

MAIL MERGE: Structure for: FMM.DBF

	Field	Type	W	D
1	LTRCODE	Char	10	
2	LINE1	Char	65	
3	LINE2	Char	65	
4	LINE3	Char	65	

Enter 59 LINEX fields-one for each line of the letter.

	Field	Type	W	D
59	LINE58	Char	65	
60	LINE59	Char	65	
Total			3846	

TABLE 16

COMMENTS: Structure for: FCOMMENT.DBF

	Field	Type	W	D
1	KEY	Char	8	
2	LINE1	Char	78	
3	LINE2	Char	78	
4	LINE3	Char	78	
5	LINE4	Char	78	
6	LINE5	Char	78	
7	LINE6	Char	78	
8	LINE7	Char	78	
9	LINE8	Char	78	
10	LINE9	Char	78	
Total			711	

Chapter VI

Working in the Diverse World of Clients

Karen P. Schaeffer, CFP

Lawrence A. Krause, CFP

Claire S. Longden, CFP

Michael R. Dohan, Ph.D.

Lori Reisman Sackler, CPA, M.S.

Judith Headington McGee, CFP

P. Kemp Fain, Jr., Ph.D., CFP

Gale Lindquist, CFP

Jerry L. Suver, CLU, CFP

Jocelyn R. Kaplan, CFP

"One of the best-kept secrets in the planning industry is the evidence that planners can make over $100,000 net per year working with middle-income clients."

—KAREN P. SCHAEFFER, CFP

Making Money With and For Middle-Income Clients

Karen P. Schaeffer, CFP, is President and Co-founder of Schaeffer Financial, a Registered Investment Adviser. Also affiliated with Hibbard Brown & Co., Inc., a registered broker-dealer, she has been advising clients for over seven years and has developed a diverse client base including professional women, foreign service officers, and physicians.

Ms. Schaeffer is a popular lecturer and seminar leader. She has conducted programs on a wide variety of topics from minimizing income taxes to developing investment strategies to planning for retirement.

Her professional affiliations include membership in the International Association for Financial Planning and the Institute of Certified Financial Planners. She received her bachelor's degree from Grand Valley State College in Michigan and is an Adjunct Faculty member at the College for Financial Planning and George Washington University.

Schaeffer's publishing credits include articles in *Business Review, Best's Review,* and the *Financial Planning Encyclopedia.* She has been quoted in the *Wall Street Journal* and the *New York Times* and has appeared on the *"Wall Street Journal* Review," a syndicated television program.

Let's tackle one myth pervading the financial services industries: A financial planner's success is measured by a wealthy clientele. The wealthy have an allure; they are the decision-makers, lead glamorous lives, and hold powerful positions. Why, then, bother with the client who lacks the money to retire comfortably?

Not only do I believe that planners should bother with the less-than-upscale clients, I believe in the profitability of the middle-income market. The need for financial planning among the middle income is overwhelming, and competition is threadbare. To date, computer-generated plans lack specific advice and professionals trying to leapfrog into the high-income client market leave the field untended. Middle-income clients offer more than a mere training ground. By attending to special considerations, financial planners will find the middle-income market is a rewarding place to maintain a practice.

WHO IS THE MIDDLE-INCOME CLIENT?

Middle income is not defined by specific income levels. In Washington, D.C., middle income can include those with an annual income of $125,000, while in Traverse City, Michigan, the same planning considerations hold for a client with a $30,000 annual income. Middle-income folks either plan for college education expenses or use loans—cash flow isn't enough. Without planning, middle-income clients are forced to reduce their standard of living at retirement, and the odds of inheriting substantial sums of money are slim.

RUNNING AN EFFICIENT PRACTICE

Efficient business practices are the key to middle-income market profitability. These four steps will point you in the right direction.

1. Keep Your Fixed Overhead Low

The concepts are simple, yet easily overlooked. Purchasing rule number one: If it's not essential, don't buy it. Purchasing rule number two: If it is essential, share costs. The easy-to-share overhead items include office space, receptionist, file clerk, computer hard- and software, photocopy equipment, and periodicals. Don't limit your search for office-mates to other planners. Any professional, well-equipped office space is worthy of consideration. Subleasing space from a law firm has the immediate advantage of increasing your library resources and the potential advantage of referrals.

Along these cost-conscious lines, keep in mind that part-time employees can go a long, long way. The part-time student who provides a few hours of clerical relief is nothing new, but don't overlook part-time professional help found among mothers with young children at home, and career changers entering financial planning. Students enrolled in the CFP program also are ideal candidates. The exchange of training and modest pay for the experience of financial planning is a fair deal. Tasks for part-time employees include case writing, holding the fort for the out-of-town planner, computer program development, newsletter writing, and maintaining product information files.

Organized instruction is critical for the cost-effective use of part-time employees. A notebook or instructional cassette tape for each delegated task is a basic. Developing these instructions may appear burdensome, but the benefits quickly fall into place as the baton is handed to a $10-per-hour associate.

Start with the straightforward, like the method for filing client information, and work up to more complicated instructions, such as matching retirement options with various portfolio configurations and assumptions. The benefits derived from simply organizing your practice well enough to teach it to a part-time employee mirror the benefits to your clients during the early planning stages. Just as you tell your clients, "Once organized, occasionally updated."

2. Challenge Your Services

Before automatically including or excluding a service, challenge the idea with a two-pronged test: Do my clients want this? How much will it cost to deliver? Without disregarding the six-step financial planning process, it is bad business practice to assume blanket services for all clients and shortsighted to ignore the delivery costs.

Determining client needs requires more than a simple question. Often clients don't know what they need. It is the planner's job to suggest the necessary process or procedure, then communicate the recommendation's value. Client questions that may require nonbillable research time present a choice: Walk away from the opportunity, refer the query, or research the answer.

Options offer fertile ground for tailored services. Consider the clients who arrive at a planner's doorstep motivated by rapidly approaching college expenses for their three teenagers. The clients need to know how to handle the inevitable expenses. Before jumping into action, delivering brilliant advice and/or quoting fees, the first determination is where the client needs help. Is it (a) investment alternatives for eventual tuition money; (b) advice on loan, grant, or scholarships sources; (c) advice on strategies for titling funds, trusts, or gifting programs; (d) cost projections for alternatives; (e) bookkeeping advice to meet semiannual tuition payments; (f) recommendations on debt structure; (g) a second opinion on the type of school they can afford; or (h) some combination thereof?

While some of these topics are second nature for a planner, keeping one's finger on the pulse of available scholarship/grant money is a highly specialized activity. A better use of a planner's time is to identify a specialist in the scholarship/grant search world and refer that exercise out. Similarly, bookkeeping assistance with family finances is time-consuming, in some cases necessitating counseling on attitudes toward money. Be sure to stipulate whether or not these services should be expected from you.

After listening to the college-concerned clients, you might respond, "If I advise you on which assets to use and why, where to invest in the interim, and the pros and cons of home equity versus first and second mortgage arrangements, do you feel you have enough information to make your decisions?" In this way you have defined what you will do on this topic, received client approval, and left the door open for an additional fee if implementation requires unanticipated effort.

3. Prepare for Volume

Beyond delegating to the well-trained part-time employee, routine office procedures enable a planner to service a large number of clients. Right from the beginning (what to mail when a caller requests information) keep it simple; if it works, repeat it. End the hunt for current phone numbers with a central notebook or computer file that contains a fact page for each client. Collect changes and up-date weekly. Keep the notebook or terminal at your desk and eliminate wrestling with a file that has years of stale information. The fact page should include everything necessary to complete an investment new account form, ideally in a format that can print directly onto the new account form when needed.

Use or develop software that does routine number crunching and allows tremendous flexibility with assumptions and format. At the very least, streamline the calculations for tax, cash flow analysis, retirement and college education projections, estate needs and taxes, internal rates of return, and mortgage variations. Avoid getting locked into a package that accepts limited modifications. Once the numbers start to point to a conclusion, focus the plan with text, beginning with text stored in a word-processing library. By reducing the calculations to a fill-in-the-blank exercise and keeping the original writing to a minimum, maximum effort can be put into developing a plan to truly reflect the client's needs and concerns.

Track work in progress on a computer or a bulletin board. Each task is entered and dated. In the case of a plan, the task may move through the stages of client inquiry, interview, case writing, presentation, and implementation before it is removed from this things-to-do list. By actually moving index cards across a board labeled with those categories, one can tell at a glance when to call the part-time case writer. Nonplan tasks can travel along a shorter but equally obvious production line. By including a category titled ''deep hold'' to file those tasks that are waiting for information, the problem of dropping the ball is reduced.

Develop a rhythm for your schedule to enhance your strengths. Hold calls for a few hours each day and concentrate on research or writing. Divide days between ''client days'' and ''work days'' to establish uninterrupted blocks of time. Allow sufficient time between client appointments to write—or dictate—a summary of the meeting. The meeting summary then begets tasks for the work-in-progress board or becomes a note to the file. Use the same format each time: date, purpose of meeting, attendees, topics covered, questions raised, questions still unanswered, and the person who has the responsibility to answer them.

Look for opportunities to parlay the answer developed for one client into a marketing tool to attract new clients. Weighing the pros and cons of various employee benefit options or retirement alternatives are naturals for these strategies. Translating new benefit decisions into an easy-to-read flow chart may even be marketable at the employer level.

4. Charge Fees for Service

Only after the client agrees to the value of your services should you quote a fee. Having examined the situation, you then are able to determine a fee based on time and costs. Whether you actually track your hours or stick with a cost estimate is not the critical decision. The fact is, the middle-income client cannot afford surprises and may shy away from any unexpected fee.

Let's not get fees confused with commissions. View commission income, if any, as compensation for researching, implementing, and servicing products. This will avoid the temptation to expand overhead beyond a continued ability to meet it while taking home a good income. Planner ranks will undoubtedly thin as practices based on tax-shelter commissions go by the wayside in the wake of Tax Reform Act of 1986. Separating fee-income services from commission-income services avoids the inequity of servicing fairly inactive clients at the expense of those clients with the means to invest regularly.

Don't immediately assume that the middle-income client will pay for planning advice only once. Planners profiting with middle-income clients invariably have ongoing fee income. Annual reviews and updates, tax preparation advice, modest retainer fees for reasonable telephone access are all examples of fee income beyond the initial plan fee. Once the two-pronged test (do my clients want it/can I afford to deliver it?) is applied, the key to successful fee scheduling is effective communication with your clients. Make it clear to your clients just how much you have saved them by avoiding mistakes, how much they have profited by good investment advice, how much peace of mind they have gained by updating insurance concerns, how much time you have saved them by researching and presenting alternatives. No matter what the fee, they are reaping a bargain.

Be clear about your fee and identify the time frame for providing the service. Both you and the client should be able to anticipate when it is time to charge an additional fee. Typically, length of service is spelled out in the contract, but it may be necessary to focus your client's attention on this point at the beginning of your working relationship to set the tone for future services.

Clearly, some clients are financially limited, regardless of the bargain an efficient practice offers. However, this does not have to be a drain on your income. Before turning away the client with little discretionary income, determine if he or she could benefit from a short course in do-it-yourself financial planning. Provide a one-hour tutorial on how to avoid mistakes, bill something for your time, and give the responsibility of implementation to the client.

Keep in mind that your services can be offered in degrees of intensity. Some clients are willing and able to pay you to read their mail. However, if a client is paying only a few hundred dollars, you can't afford to check the file each week to determine if now is the time to refinance. Nonetheless, you can afford to answer a client's phone call and steer him or her in the right direction when a question is asked. And, if the only way to determine the answer is to run the numbers under various assumptions, you can outline the issue for free and, if the client sees the value in the exercise, provide the analysis for an additional fee.

Planning questions raised by middle-income clients are generally less complicated than those raised by wealthy clients. The need to retain expensive outside counsel is, therefore, kept to a minimum. Fortunately, less complicated doesn't immediately translate into boring, considering the wide variety of clients who fall into the middle-income definition.

DISPELLING MYTHS

Assumptions about a middle-income clientele are inaccurate. I have found the classic comments untrue:

The planner is tied to a treadmill • While the potential for the hamster-in-a-cage syndrome exists, the problem lies with the practice, not the client. Undoubtedly it will take more middle-income clients than high-income clients to generate each $10,000 of income. However, it does not need to take more hours, nor the same fixed overhead costs.

All work and no reward • One of the best-kept secrets in the planning industry is the evidence that planners can make over $100,000 net per year working with middle-income clients. These planners are obscured by the proliferation of financial service start-ups. Beginners may find the going rough because of a dearth of clients, or lack of business acumen, or both.

Middle-income clients won't pay fees • There is nothing in our definition of middle-income clients that makes them automatically allergic to paying fees. That perception stems, in part, from the fact that they won't pay fees for services they don't need. They don't need a beautiful leather binder and 10 years of tax projections any more than they need a computer printout with one-size-fits-all general advice. Moreover, they don't need to pay to hear a product sales pitch. Middle-income clients may not be used to paying fees, and they probably aren't in a position to have their corporations deduct the fee as an expense. Nonetheless, the planners charging and collecting substantial fee income from this market are doing so because they tailor their services to client requests.

A very successful planner who has always found his niche among the middle-income clients returned from an ICFP conference slightly cynical about the conference's favored topic—wealthy, sophisticated clients. "I don't have any millionnaire clients," Fritz Fries of Newport News, Virginia, admitted, "but I'm making a few." I like the sound of that—just one more reason to maintain a practice of middle-income clients.

"You had better appear successful if you intend to seek and work with affluent clients."

—LAWRENCE A. KRAUSE, CFP

The Special Requirements for Working With Affluent Clients

Lawrence A. Krause, CFP, is Chairman of Lawrence A. Krause & Associates, a San Francisco-based financial planning firm. Mr. Krause has been a financial planner for over fifteen years and is a former President and Chairman of the Board of the San Francisco chapter of the IAFP. He was voted the San Francisco Financial Planner of the Year by his peers in 1982–1983. In addition to being admitted to the Registry of Financial Planning Practitioners, he serves on advisory and faculty committees for three separate universities.

Mr. Krause is the author of *The Money-Go-Round, Sleep-Tight Money,* and coauthor of *Marketing Your Financial Planning Practice.* He is a frequent lecturer at many professional conferences and seminars and has appeared on both radio and television. Mr. Krause is often quoted in financial publications, including the *Wall Street Journal, USA Today,* the *Los Angeles Times,* the *San Francisco Chronicle, Forbes, Money,* and numerous others.

You've all heard the adage, "Make big mistakes with small amounts of money and small mistakes with big amounts of money." But when working with the affluent, you will discover a small loss still amounts to a large amount of money. Yes, rich clients *are* different from those who are less affluent; the wealthy will invest more dollars. The sheer magnitude of the amount of money involved will therefore magnify a small percentage loss to appear as a voluminous loss. Now add to the formula a client who is ambitious and hard-driving, or one with a large ego, or both, and it can spell *big* problems for you, the planner.

Not all who have wealth are difficult to work with. As a matter of fact, I have found that some sort of ratio probably exists between money and time and pleasantness. The longer the amount of time the wealth has been in existence, and the more amount of money a person possesses, the easier people seem to be to work with. They have less to prove to the world, and their investment expectations are often more realistic. They readily understand that your role is to preserve their capital, not to increase their wealth by some magnificent percentage. Nevertheless, certain common traits often exist for those with affluence. I believe the most common trait is that financially successful people want to deal with others whom they deem to be successful also. So you had better appear successful if you intend to seek and work with affluent clients.

Since financial planners have no established image, your community reputation, community activities, all the way down to the club(s) you belong to, the size and location of your house, and the type of car(s) you drive can all be important image factors which reveal perceived success. This is particularly true in the smaller community, where more of your personal life can be observed. But wherever you practice financial planning, I believe your office and its location are enormously important factors necessary to support a positive image. Your office should be situated in a highly regarded location and should be located in a quality building, and your physical office needs to be tastefully decorated. You must also be attentive to the clothes you wear, to your demeanor, and to the way you speak, for these too are perceived as signs of success. By surrounding yourself with people who maintain many of those same standards, you will further demonstrate that you are a successful professional.

Though I have yet to encounter a wealthy client who considers his or her personal financial situation to be complicated, affluent people often do have a large number of complex issues that must be dealt with. Whether he or she is a possible new client or one with whom you have a long relationship, that person wants to know that you have quality in-house expertise. Therefore, everyone in your firm should have a high level of competence or technical knowledge. If it is unavailable internally, your client or potential client needs to know that you have the ability to obtain it elsewhere. At the very least, you should have an established network of professional, capable resource people. This network can serve the dual purpose of providing answers when you are unable to and enhancing your image. If your network is composed of well-known people in their respective fields, and if you have permission to use their names, promoting their availability can be an effective and inexpensive way to add and maintain prestige. As a matter of fact, boards of directors will often seek to add "important" names for much the same purpose. As a financial planning firm, you might even wish to consider creating an outside formal board of advisors (rather than directors) comprised of respected professionals. Additionally, if your prospective client is wealthy, you might prepare a separate reference list which includes names of existing clients (after receiving permission, of course) who are generally in the same social and economic circumstances as your possible new client. Better yet, attempt to include existing client names who are wealthier.

Beyond technical support, problem solving must also include your understanding a host of other psychological factors which are relatively unique to the affluent client. This is where a number of financial planners err. In order to best serve your clients, you must first understand their attitudes toward their wealth. The way in which they view their money is exactly the way *you* must also view their assets. If your client comprehends his or her financial status, yet does not feel wealthy, then you should treat that person in the same manner as you would a less wealthy client. There are those who will have a multimillion-dollar balance sheet, due perhaps to an inheritance, with a $35,000-a-year mentality. You need to be especially sensitive to that kind of problem; all financial planning must reflect that sensitivity. For example, though your conclusions might call for the need to make several sizable investments, your client might be unable to proceed due to inexperience. Alternatively, you could recommend that your client write several smaller checks in order to first gain a comfort level.

If your client has an enormous net worth and behaves accordingly, you need to be responsive to that person's money attitudes in a different manner. Writing a sizable check won't be the problem, but perhaps data gathering might be. For example, if your client is a ''big picture'' type of person, and his or her net worth will either increase or decrease by a substantial dollar amount at any given moment, you must avoid becoming overzealous when data gathering. To attempt to pinpoint precise dollar-and-cents values on some of the more mundane assets, such as silverware, may only serve to irritate your client.

Then there is the achiever earning more than $1 million a year, with only $600 in the bank. Sometimes that person wishes to be directed as would a child. That is, he or she wants to be told what to do, and admonished if he or she misbehaves. But it can be dangerous to your wealth to assume this paternal role unless you are quite clear that is the only direction you can take, and you also understand the responsibility you are accepting. Unfortunately, such clients have little tolerance for losses, and lawsuits are common. Alternatively, informing your client that he or she is but one step removed from becoming a financial disaster—that financial failure lies ahead—is also a poor course of action. Normally, if a person is earning a great deal of money, that individual considers himself or herself to be financially successful. If your approach is purely analytical, you will often create an adversarial relationship, for your client is unwilling to admit failure. Instead, if you seek to understand the underlying reason(s) as to why this person needs to spend money—for example, social pressure—and take an understanding position, you will gain the client's confidence and willingness to redirect that cash flow for a more positive result.

Still another special requirement when you are working with the affluent, especially affluent entrepreneurial clients, is your ability to be flexible. If you prepare formal plans but are restricted to a limited number of variances, you may be totally out of step with your client. For example, wealthy entrepreneurial clients often have a number of balls in the air (are ''moving targets''). A standard formal financial plan is usually rendered ineffective by the dynamics of constant change. Your demonstrating flexibility by serving only as an advisor—that is, just rendering financial advice—will not only best fulfill the special needs of your special client, but will also enable you to maintain a lasting relationship.

Another situation where your sensitivity must be especially acute is when you are working with the aforementioned inheritor. Inherited wealth, particularly major inherited wealth, often presents very real psychological problems for those on the receiving end. Indeed, private studies have shown that more than four out of five people (especially youngsters) have serious difficulty learning to cope with the problems that accompany major inherited wealth. As an advisor you will sometimes have to deal with a client's guilt ("Why me?") or self-doubt ("Would I be liked if I weren't rich?"); other times inheritors will develop a tremendous sense of responsibility and will either possess a social consciousness when investing, or a need to maintain the assets for their heirs.

In each of the above instances, you as a financial planner and advisor must demonstrate an inordinate understanding of the problems of the affluent. If you can also include an attitude of flexibility when solving the problems of the wealthy, your own reward can be very substantial indeed.

"Clients do not want to be faced with a boilerplate plan two inches thick—they hired you to tell them what to do; the results will be self-evident."

—CLAIRE S. LONGDEN, CFP

Working With High-net-worth Clients

Claire S. Longden, CFP, is First Vice President of Butcher & Singer, Inc. Since 1979, she has also been an independent financial planner working with high-net-worth individuals, corporate executives, and small business owners. Ms. Longden has been quoted in *The New York Times, USA Today, Inc. Magazine, Money Magazine, American Banker,* and *The Christian Science Monitor.* She has appeared on the Channel 2 News, CNN Financial News Network, Moneymakers II, and hosts "Moneyworks" weekly on WHVW 95 AM.

Ms. Longden's professional affiliations include membership in the Institute of Certified Financial Planners, where she serves on the National Board as the Northeast Regional director. In addition, Ms. Longden is the Founder and Chairman of the ICFP's New York Society. She was also former Director and Vice President of the International Association for Financial Planning's NY Metro chapter and former President of the Women's Bond Club of New York. As an Adjunct Professor, Ms. Longden has taught courses in financial planning at New York University's School of Continuing Education.

"You won't believe this, but I don't know a thing about handling money." With a sheepish grin, these are the first words that the high-net-worth client will mutter as the fact-finding interview gets underway.

The high-net-worth (minimum $1,000,000 and more in certain metropolitan areas) client is a fast-track corporate executive, business owner, legatee, or divorcee. The former two are busy knowing their own business, and the latter are bewildered by emotional trauma and the complexities and responsibilities suddenly forced upon them.

These clients do not arrive in chauffeur-driven limousines. More often than not, there is no outward exhibition of wealth. They do not wish to be wined or dined; in fact, the more unobtrusive you are, the more they like it. Confidentiality is the key. There must never be a hint of an outsider's knowing more about them than they wish to project. And never ask to use them as referrals—it is not professional, and they might fear their trust has been broken.

Where to find the high-net-worth client? Not necessarily on the golf course. These people rarely respond to advertising and don't attend seminars for the sake of it. They use the advice of their friends and peers to seek out the professionals they need.

It is essential that you decide that this is your target market. Establish a high minimum fee and don't deviate. When a prospect calls or is referred whose net worth doesn't warrant paying your high minimum fee (you'll turn down four out of five), recommend another planner whom you trust. Establish your name through controlled advertising, press quotes, and television interviews; present seminars when asked to by a specific group as a community service. The contacts you make under this scenario are the people who will provide your initial contacts into the high-net-worth client market.

Once you have established your reputation and ability, the business will come to you. It is essential, however, that you know what you are doing, particularly in the areas of taxes, estate planning, and investments. You will need to be able to work smoothly with lawyers, accountants, and brokers. These clients expect you to take care of the details, but also recognize the value of paying for good services. Their cases take time, and it is most likely that they will retain other professionals, so don't look to make up for low fees through commissions—they are cautious about any possible conflict of interest.

This kind of client looks for ability above all, but sincerity and honesty make up a large part of the rest.

Once you have qualified your prospect, a free, 30-minute "compatibility" interview is the time to establish the required rapport and the fee. Request that fees be paid "up front," thus establishing the total commitment of the client. An in-depth questionnaire, along with a request for all pertinent papers, is essential for gathering all the quantitative information, leaving the two-hour fact-finding session totally open to the important personal preferences and foibles of the client.

These clients do not want to be faced with a boilerplate plan two inches thick—they have hired you to tell them what to do; the results will be self-evident. Plans should average six pages outlining goals and objectives, current situation, recommendations, and summary and implementation. Back-up addenda should include as much information on present and projected cash flow and tax analysis, net worth, portfolios, and the like as is required to get the point across, but these should be kept to a minimum.

The high-net-worth client will implement knowledgeably and intelligently; the brevity of recommendations allows uncluttered action. Where mutual funds are part of the recommendations, no-loads are preferred; however, when clients are particularly busy and can't spare the time, they have no objection to loads since it is probably cheaper in terms of the cost of their time.

Contrary to common belief, these clients do not particularly care for limited partnerships as a tax shelter; they know the value of money and do not risk it on something that doesn't seem to make economic sense. On the whole, they respond enthusiastically to the logic and common sense of a well-written plan and like the idea that, once purposefully redeployed, assets do not need to be moved around in the market. They are uncommonly conservative.

Since stock and bond holdings (including incentive stock options) are often a part of their holdings, you will need to be knowledgeable in the planning uses of these products. Sometimes clients like to play the stock market, in which case suggest that they take a specific amount which they can afford to totally lose, put it into a broker account, and play games. Once it is gone, no more will follow. You'll soon get the point across.

When working with the small-business owner, check pension and profit-sharing plans. You will often see old standards that are badly out of date and, despite a known name as author, these plans may not be fulfilling the client's needs and objectives. You will need to know the ins and outs of small businesses, and since these vary dramatically, depending on the people concerned, each case will be unique and demanding of your time. Some are interested only in ultimate retirement, others in selling one venture and starting another. Develop a large "stable" of professionals in these areas that you can recommend to the client when required.

When working with legatees or divorcees, be patient. More time will be required in guiding them into the rigors of finance; however, the planning process makes the logical results of your recommendations readily apparent, and their gratitude is without peer.

For corporate executives, you will need to know the tax ramifications of all benefits, particularly stock options, since these are often a substantial part of their total assets.

When working with these clients, you are basically on your own. It is vital that you "walk a mile in their shoes" and thoroughly understand them; your relationship is one-on-one all the way. You will need to immerse yourself in their problems and preferences, and doing so, of course, can severely restrict your time. You must pace activities carefully and not take on more clients than your time will allow. Remember, your future business hangs by the thread of referrals, and too many clients may prove to be counterproductive through the loss of valuable referral sources.

You need to be totally involved, including keying information into your software (a very good way of discovering weaknesses and beginning to formulate future plans). Your recommendations will be implemented without question, so be sure (as they refinance the stately home) that you know what you are doing.

Your practice will not need mailing lists or action tracking, since you will acquire only 25 to 30 clients a year. You will, however, need a good assistant to take care of the details such as record keeping, assets transfers, and portfolio updates.

As the years pass, this type of client becomes a personal friend who can be counted upon to send you referrals, not waste your time, and pay your fees. You may not become a millionaire yourself, but the rewards are many, including the thanks of those who always thought they "didn't know a thing about handling money."

"Many do not need a comprehensive financial plan. Rather, they are looking solely for professional advice."

—MICHAEL R. DOHAN, Ph.D.

Family-centered Financial Consulting

Michael R. Dohan received his B.A. in economics at Haverford College in 1961 and completed his Ph.D. in economics at Massachusetts Institute of Technology in 1969. Currently, he is Associate Professor of economics and Director of the Social Science Laboratory for Research and Teaching at Queens College of the City University of New York, where he teaches consumer finance and research methodology. Author of many articles, he is a member of IAFP, the American Economics Association, and the Royal Economics Society. He is the founder and a principal consultant of Family Financial Consultants, Inc.

The family-centered financial consultant works primarily with families and individuals on a fee-for-service basis to help them to make better financial decisions, to manage their day-to-day finances, assets, and debts better, to help resolve conflicts over money management, and to provide many direct services. Serving such clients successfully requires an approach, techniques, and training different from those used by the traditional financial planner, who has been oriented toward writing complete financial plans and then implementing these plans through the sale of financial products. In order to show the nature of family-centered financial consulting, we describe three different types of consulting services for these clients and some of the basic techniques used.

WHO ARE THE CLIENTS?

Families and individuals seek out a family-centered financial consultant for a variety of reasons. Some have a specific question or problem requiring professional analysis, such as analyzing the financial and tax consequences of a property transaction. Others seek help because they have a feeling of "not having enough money" or a major debt-management problem. Many couples come to a financial professional for help in resolving family conflicts over money. Finally, there is a substantial group who want a variety of direct services, from organizing their records and paying bills to tracking family expenses and preparing tax returns.

All these clients have several characteristics in common. Most are seeking professional advice or services for a specific problem or purpose. Few see themselves in the market for financial products (even though they may need them), and many do not want and may not need a comprehensive financial plan. Rather, they are looking solely for professional advice and financial management and expect to pay directly for such services. The challenge to the professional financial consultant is to attract such clients and to provide professional advice and services effectively and profitably on a fee-for-service basis. What types of services are sought by these clients?

HELPING CLIENTS MAKE FINANCIAL DECISIONS

Individuals and families are faced with increasingly complex financial decisions and therefore require highly specialized financial information and professional analysis. Consider, for example, the following questions: Which is the best equity loan or refinancing option? How does the new tax law affect owning a vacation home? Which pension option, lump sum or annuity, is the best? How should a divorce settlement or insurance proceeds be invested? Is this business plan feasible? Thus, they call a financial consultant.

When a client calls for an appointment, the services offered by the consultant and schedule of fees are explained, and selected forms are sent to help him or her to organize personal financial data. These may include expense analysis and asset-debt schedules, a risk-management checklist, and a list of other needed items, such as tax returns.

THE INITIAL CONSULTING SESSION

The first sessions lasts between one and two hours, depending on the complexity of the problem. Experience shows that there are six distinct stages of a successful session. First, the client is asked to restate the initial problem and what he or she would like to achieve with the financial consultant. If a couple comes together, each person is asked to state his or her purpose, for often they may be coming to you as a couple but for very different reasons. The consultant should try to draw out these differences in an impartial manner so as to be able to address the clients' real concerns. Sometimes, in fact, the desire to resolve these differences will be the real but unspoken purpose for coming to a financial consultant. This is discussed below.

The second stage of the interview is crucial, yet it is the least well defined. The purpose is first to explore the parameters of the problem and then to determine the client's short- and long-term goals, personal values, attitudes toward saving, risk-taking, and work, the family structure (children, ex-spouses, parents, etc.), and the family's method of making financial decisions. Finally, a brief financial history is obtained. Often it is found that the stated reason for calling the financial planner is but one symptom of more serious problems. For example, a question about a home equity loan may arise from a serious debt problem. The consultant would be remiss in not exploring these issues. This second stage, often time-consuming, is important because the advice given must be consistent with the goals, values, and financial and family situation of the client.

Third, the client's relevant financial and personal data are reviewed. Often clients need further help in completing the monthly expense/income spreadsheet. Tax returns should be examined and opportunities for tax-planning noted. Where appropriate, the consultant also points out the strengths and weaknesses in the client's financial position.

Fourth, the consultant examines the data and analyzes the problem—for example, works out the estimated taxes on the property sale. The consultant may find it more effective to work through the problem directly with the client, who in turn often wants to understand the underlying analysis and the assumptions and methods used. In more complex cases the consultant may defer analysis and recommendations/conclusions until a later date because of the work or research required.

Fifth, the results of the analysis are presented to the client, recommendations are made—for example, sell the house and buy the condo—and explained with appropriate qualifications and disclaimers. Where necessary, a plan for implementation is developed. If further consultation with a tax lawyer or other professional is needed, the client is informed.

Sixth, before closing the initial interview, it is important to briefly review with the clients their management of risk (life, medical, disability, homeowners, and liability insurance), and to suggest, where appropriate, a comprehensive financial review. The session is closed with a recapitulation of the questions asked, the recommendations made, the fee for the session, and the next steps to be undertaken by both client and planner, including scheduling of future meetings, if necessary.

HELPING FAMILIES MANAGE THEIR INCOME

Some clients need guidance in managing their day-to-day finances, assets, and debts to achieve their long-run goals. Take, for example, a young executive who calls and says, ''We need some help with handling our money.'' Even though the couple are earning $80,000 to $90,000, they feel that they never have enough money left over after paying their monthly bills, that they are not getting ahead financially, that they have a feeling of what might be called ''financial malaise.'' Where the traditional financial planner would focus on asset management, here the family-centered consultant focuses on income and expense management, of which asset management is but one of many components.

Income and Expense Management for Families

Let us assume that the consultant has already completed the first two stages of the initial session described above and is now in the position to work with the client's concerns.

The first step is to help the clients understand their own current financial position and how they are currently earning and spending their income. This is done through a personal balance sheet of assets and liabilities and by working up a month-by-month income/expense analysis for the previous 12 months. For these purposes the income/expense spreadsheet should group current expenses *by function:* housing and utilities, food and house upkeep, clothing, transportation, recreation, medical, pension contributions, income taxes, etc. and should separate out monthly debt repayments for previous purchases and major capital and other unusual expenditures (refrigerator, fur coat, unusual medical costs). (This functional approach is critical to expense management and differs from the standard ''fixed-discretionary expenses'' approach used currently by many financial planners.) The resulting spreadsheet shows the client month by month, the yearly cycle of income, expenses, and savings or dissavings.

The second step is to help clients identify and agree on their financial priorities. Three time horizons are used: the next 12 months, five years out, and unspecified ''long-term,'' encompassing schooling for the children and retirement. Here the consultant has several tasks. One is to convert general goals, such as ''getting out of debt,'' into concrete objectives, such as ''reducing credit card balances by $5000 in 12 months.'' Another is to be sure that, when working with couples, each person's goals are addressed and actively agreed upon. Finally, the consultant must often work with the clients to adjust their spending, savings, and investment expectations to what is realistic, given the client's income.

The third step is to draw up an income and spending projection (budget) and a related asset-debt management plan for the next 12 months. The starting point is the income/expense analysis for the previous 12 months, which is now adjusted for any known changes in income, taxes, and expenses. Then the consultant and the clients review each functional category for efficient ways to: increase after-tax income, reduce essential expenses, adjust spending patterns to priorities, reduce overall spending, and reduce monthly debt payments. This ''optimization'' of income, expenses, and other goals is based on what economists call ''marginal utility theory'' or the theory of trade-offs, which weighs the additional costs and benefits of each change. For example, the benefits of paying off the high-interest, short-term loans are compared to the risks and costs of refinancing them with lower-interest equity loans. This entire planning process is done most effectively by using a spreadsheet on a microcomputer so the clients can immediately see, for example, the impact on their budget of several seemingly insignificant monthly reductions in spending. By working through several feasible scenarios, not only for the next 12 months but also for several years out, the clients get a clearer view of the opportunities open to them.

The fourth step is for the clients to choose one of the income/spending scenarios (projections) that they like best and to work with the consultant to develop a set of specific tasks for achieving these short-term goals. Sometimes a series of small changes are sufficient, such as establishing a specific budget for "dining out," reinvesting assets at a higher yield, giving up the daily lunch out and a cup of coffee, and locking away the credit cards. Even the process of writing down all expenditures and reviewing them on a monthly basis can lead to a dramatic change in spending habits. Occasionally, however, bringing the income and spending plan into balance will require major decisions, such as moving to a less costly house, the spouse's returning to work, and postponement of major expenditures. The trade-offs involved in these major changes, for example, between the personal costs of working a second job and the benefits of having more income should be carefully considered by the clients with the consultant.

Finally, the consultant and the clients should schedule a series of follow-up sessions to review their progress; otherwise, this work will turn into an exercise in futility.

RESOLVING CONFLICT OVER FINANCES

Occasionally clients come directly to a financial consultant because "money has become an issue in the marriage." Usually, however, the consultant finds out that a couple has major disagreements over finances while working with them on other problems, such as budgeting or debt management. The consultant then faces the task of helping the couple to resolve these conflicts as well. Couple counseling is complex, but a few fundamental concepts should be kept in mind.

Identifying the Causes of Conflict

Management of and control over money can cause conflicts in families for many reasons. For example, chronic financial difficulties, such as constantly fighting off creditors and never having any money to do "special things," can erode even long-standing relationships. Fundamental differences in personal values and beliefs about money management, typified by the ancient fable of the ant and the grasshopper, often cause bitter disputes, for example, over saving and spending. And as social values change, disagreements over the financial decision-making structure in the family become increasingly common, especially where the husband insists on retaining control over the assets and major financial decisions. Other sources of conflict range from the real inability of one partner to manage money and disputes over how to spend discretionary income to a spouse's feeling trapped in a job and unrealistic expectations of sustainable life styles.

The financial consultant should be aware, however, that what appears to be a conflict over finances and irrational financial behavior may have its origins in other areas of a couple's relationship or in fundamental psychological problems. For example, a mother may spend unrealistic amounts on gifts for a couple's retarded child out of guilt, or a husband may buy an expensive car every year to prove that he is successful. Alcoholism, drugs, and gambling have a devastating impact on family finances. When the consultant suspects such problems, the couple should be urged to seek psychological counseling as well.

Approaches to Resolving Conflict

The starting point in each of the above cases is to open up communication by each of the partners, with special care being taken to draw out the less dominant partner and to follow up expressions of disagreement and surprise. Often one or both partners want the consultant to sit in judgment about who was right and who was wrong. For this reason, the consultant must be impartial and non-judgmental throughout the counseling sessions.

Once the consultant has identified the sources of conflict, he or she reviews the couple's financial data, following the techniques described above in "Financial Management." For example, the spreadsheet analysis of past income and expenditures gives a couple a comprehensive and impartial view of their spending habits, while the family balance sheet shows them their actual financial position. At this point the couple is often ready to work out an agreement with the assistance of the consultant. This may be merely to agree to plan and manage their family finances together or to work up a list of mutually agreed-upon spending priorities. It could, however, be a difficult compromise requiring major changes in their lifestyles and habits, such as changing careers.

Follow-up sessions are essential to support and help the couple implement these changes.

IN SUM: THE FAMILY-CENTERED FINANCIAL CONSULTING PRACTICE

The practice of family-centered financial consulting in many ways resembles the practice of a family attorney or family physician, both in the breadth of skills required and in the actual conduct of a fee-for-service practice. Compared with the now-traditional financial planner, the family-centered financial consultant serves clients from a much wider range of income levels and occupations and is called on to provide a wider range of services, from analysis of specific financial problems, counseling of couples, and tax preparation, to direct management of an individual's entire finances, portfolio analysis, and preparation of complete financial plans.

Thus the family-centered consultant needs a somewhat different set of skills and knowledge with greater emphasis on, for example, interviewing techniques, on organizing and presenting data in meaningful ways, and on technical analysis of complex financial problems and less emphasis on, for example, presenting and marketing financial products. The analytical basis of the consultant's work is drawn from the theories of present discounted value, portfolio and risk management, consumer choice, and marginal analysis. An extensive knowledge of finance and financial products, insurance, retirement and estate planning, economics, and the federal and state tax codes forms the factual basis. An extensive reference library, financial calculator, and microcomputer with a variety of financial templates are standard tools of the trade. An able staff of paraprofessionals and secretaries, and a network of fellow professionals, however, form the real foundation of the practice.

For the financial planning professional looking for new vistas, the practice of family-centered financial consulting presents challenging opportunities to serve a large and growing market for professional services.

"Women are currently undergoing major societal, cultural, and economic transitions in our society. . . . These changes indicate a significant need for women to plan for their financial futures and have created a sizable market opportunity for financial planners."

—LORI REISMAN SACKLER, CPA, MS

Planning For Women in a Changing Society

A Certified Public Accountant, Lori R. Sackler, has extensive experience in the financial services industry as a tax advisor, investment counselor, and financial consultant. She was a Senior Vice President of a financial services company headquartered in Dallas, Texas, where she was responsible for financial planning, investments and corporate planning functions. Currently, she is practicing financial planning in the New York/ New Jersey metropolitan area.

She has worked extensively with career women in her own practice and has conducted numerous seminars for women about financial planning and money management. Her most recent seminar sponsored by the Dallas Women's Foundation is currently being considered by AT&T for production and national distribution.

Ms. Sackler has been quoted frequently in major newspapers and is a frequent speaker to professional groups and associations. She was Vice President of Education and member of the Board of Directors of the North Texas chapter of the IAFP and is currently a member of a New Jersey IAFP chapter. With distinction, Ms. Sackler earned her bachelor's degree from the University of Michigan; she received her master's degree in marketing and finance from the University of Texas.

Women represent a distinct market segment in the financial planning industry. A newly recognized and untapped marketplace for financial planners, they offer a tremendous market opportunity for the financial planning profession. In order to discuss how financial planners can effectively tap the market potential, it is important to understand the societal forces that are creating the need for women to address financial planning. Three major trends in concert distinguish women in the marketplace: changes in marital status, entry of women into the work force, and the wage gap.

Like men, many women are delaying marriage and, in fact, may never marry. According to a recent "ABC News Closeup" special, 56 percent of women between the ages of 20 and 24 have not married, compared to only 36 percent of that age in 1970. Predictions further indicate that 15 percent of women born in the 1950s may never marry, up from 9 percent of women born in the 1930s.[1]

Despite these statistics, marriage is still the majority practice. In today's world, it is a more complicated arrangement, involving two-earner couples and children from previous marriages. In 50 percent or more of the cases, these marriages will end in divorce. In 1940, one in every six marriages resulted in divorce—in 1980, one in every two. Demographers are predicting that, in the future, two out of three marriages will result in divorce.[2]

As a result of divorce, women experience tremendous hardship. Approximately 60 percent of divorced women are single parents caring for a family. In 60 percent of these cases, they are handling the responsibility with no assistance from the father at a time when their incomes can be depressed by as much as 70 percent.[3]

These statistics indicate the necessity for women to be more emotionally and financially self-sufficient. Financial planning can aid them in their transition from dependence to independence and can help secure their financial well-being.

The extent to which women are entering the workplace is also a major reason for their increasing need for financial advice. It is a major societal trend that is permanently altering the balance of power between the sexes and dramatically changing the role the woman plays in the American family.

In the late 1950s, women accounted for 31 percent of the work force. In the late 1980s, women make up almost one-half of the total work force, and one-half of the jobs in all professions are now held by women. With this additional socioeconomic power, women have become less dependent on men and have outgrown some of the second-class status which they held earlier.[4] They are now breadwinners for the family, participate in making important financial decisions for the family, and, in many cases, manage family finances. According to a 1984 *Newsweek Research Report*, women now have either the primary responsibility for financial decision-making more often than men (30 percent versus 20 percent) or share the responsibility jointly (49 percent). With respect to the single woman, 86 percent are managing their family financial affairs.[5]

The wage gap is the third trend, which, in combination with the two previ-

---

[1]"After the Sexual Revolution," *ABC News Closeup* (New York: August 1, 1986), p. 15.

[2]Sylvia Ann Hewlett, *A Lesser Life: The Myth of the Women's Liberation in America* (New York: William Morrow & Company, 1986), p. 51.

[3]Ibid., p. 62 and p. 66.

[4]Op. cit., *ABC News Closeup*, p. 1.

[5]"Women Who Work: A National Survey," *Newsweek Research Report* (1984), p. 52.

ously discussed, has created an overwhelming need for women to individually plan for their financial futures.

Although women constitute almost 50 percent of the job market, only 7 percent of the employed women in America work in managerial positions. An estimated 75 percent tend to be employed in "women's jobs"—secretarial, nursing, teaching, and the like—and only 10 percent earn more than $20,000 annually.[6] This economic distinction is further heightened by the fact that, according to the Bureau of Census, women earn only 64 cents to a man's dollar. This is the largest wage gap in the Western industrial world, and one which has not improved significantly since 1939, when women earned 63 cents to a man's dollar.[7]

Because of women's continuing predominance in low-paying and non-managerial jobs, they are often technically and economically ill-equipped to plan for their financial futures. They frequently possess little background in long-term planning, limited knowledge of finances and investments, and virtually no experience in making choices between complicated financial options.

Despite these obstacles, they are eager to improve their ability to tackle the task. According to the same *Newsweek Research Report,* women are interested in obtaining advice needed in order to plan for their futures and select the alternatives most appropriate to their financial needs. As indicated in the report, three-quarters or more of all women have not obtained an advisor to help them plan for retirement, borrow for large purchases, invest in real estate, or invest in general investments other than checking and money market accounts. Moreover, 14 percent of women in the study indicate that they would like to work with a financial planner.[8] This suggests a substantial market potential for the planning professional.

In many instances, women are uninformed about finances, are insecure in making decisions, and are conservative investors who are afraid of losing what they have acquired so far. They are more economically aware, yet they need assistance from qualified and competent professionals who understand their unique needs, and who are prepared to work with them with patience and empathy as educators and counselors.

In order to be successful in this particular marketplace, I have identified five major "action" steps.

1. Identify the Market of Women You Wish to Work With

The market can be divided by:

    a. Income
    b. Age
    c. Marital status
    d. Occupation

Depending on your background, special expertise or access to the market, you may choose to work with either the highly affluent or the middle-market group. Obviously, those who will be interested in working with a financial planner and can afford the services will probably be at least in the middle-income range. On the basis of your age and knowledge of a particular generation, you may also feel more comfortable with a certain age range, the baby-boomers or their par-

---

[6]Hewlett, *A Lesser Life,* p. 71.

[7]Ibid., p. 71 and p. 73.

[8]Op. cit., *Newsweek Research Report,* p. 56.

ents. Marital status also is a factor to consider. Recently widowed or divorced women have special concerns and needs that need to be addressed. They require a thorough sorting-out of finances and an involved counselor to walk with them through the economic and emotional crises they are experiencing. Finally, you need to clarify the occupational group with which you wish to work. You may want to focus on the career/professional market segment, which represents a viable and desired market. The women in this market have disposable income and a strong commitment to taking measures to care for themselves and secure their futures. Or you may want to work with another important occupational class, the mother and housewife, many of whom are taking a more active role in managing their family finances. They have been motivated by an increased awareness that they may, at some point, either as a result of divorce or death, be responsible in full for making family financial decisions.

2. Thoroughly Understand the Market

It is important that you recognize the distinctions in each circumstance or market in which you choose to work. Women are sensitive and perceptive human beings who can sense your level of understanding, sincerity, and commitment to helping them resolve their financial problems. Your success is dependent upon the extent to which you can listen to them and relate to their specific problems and needs.

3. Actively Market Yourself

As a marketplace for new business, women are recognized and accepted by many companies. The major auto makers, financial services, and insurance companies have allocated marketing and advertising dollars directed toward attracting the female to buy their products. You, as a financial planner, must also market your services to attract new clients. The vehicles are really no different than if you were establishing a campaign to further your practice in any particular marketplace.

   a. Seminars
   b. Public speaking
   c. Organization work
   d. Community work
   e. Media ''coverage''

Seminars directed toward women are probably already in existence in your community. Banks, women's organizations, and educational institutions are likely to have programs for local professionals to participate in. Find them, offer your services, and take the time to do a superlative job. If you are unable to break into the network directly, sponsor your own seminar for women. You can invite prospects, friends, and advisors, and offer refreshments as an added ''benefit.'' Regardless of the avenue you pursue, you must deliver relevant and useful information in an organized and entertaining format, or the effort you have extended will not create the clients you desire.

Public speaking is another available route. Professional organizations for women (accounting, legal, etc.) are eager to find intelligent and credible sources for their audience needs. Seek out a list of professional organizations, symposiums, or monthly meetings that you wish to speak to. Polish your public-speaking skills and deliver an interesting talk with targeted subject matter. You will make important contact and, provided you're successful, generate interest and possibly clients.

Organizations for women exist in large numbers in most communities. These include investment clubs, career networking groups, foundations, and educational organizations designed to help women and others. In addition, professional organizations that have a significant representation of women are also in abundance. If you give time, effort, and expertise to an organization, you will receive the benefits, maybe not immediately, but the seeds will be planted for establishing name recognition, trust, and credibility as a professional in the community.

Community work is an important avenue to consider in cultivating women as a marketplace. Your local church, synagogue, or favorite charitable organization probably has an organization that utilizes the resources of predominantly female volunteers, and whose focus is directly toward working with women. Offer your services and get involved. While you are making a valuable contribution to your community, you will be adding value to your business.

If you can, make yourself available to the local media as a spokesperson on specific areas. Once they trust you and view you as a reliable source for their audience, they will quote you and use your comments and point of view in their columns. It will bring immeasurable credibility to you as a professional and will further your professional standing with existing client and advisor relationships.

Although each marketing tool mentioned can be used to reach the specific market or markets you have decided you wish to work with, it will take more than one approach to get results. Find the combination of techniques that best suits your needs and pursue them with energy and commitment.

4. Educate Your Women Clients

As mentioned previously, women in many cases lack the financial education needed to make appropriate decisions for themselves and their families. When you work with them, it is important to approach them not only as a counselor, but as a teacher. They are usually interested in moving at their own pace with at least some understanding of the financial decisions that can affect them. They are eager to learn to care for themselves and, with instruction from you, will become excellent clients.

5. Help Them Evaluate Alternatives

It is important to present the alternatives to women clients, to patiently educate them on the choices, and to help them to carefully evaluate the alternatives. They are ultimately responsible for making the decision and will communicate to you the most appropriate one for their needs; however, they will need your due, professional care in reaching that decisive point.

6. Provide Them Ongoing Service

Women clients are no different from any client; they require ongoing service and attention. They may, in fact, need more service in some cases, depending on their level of confidence and experience in dealing in financial matters. You need to be there for them.

Conclusion

Women are currently undergoing major societal, cultural, and economic transitions in our society. The financial repercussions are tremendous, far beyond the limited scope of our discussion. These changes indicate a significant need for women to plan for their financial futures and have created a sizable market opportunity for financial planners. If you have not done so already, I urge you to create your own marketing plan and cultivate your specifically chosen marketplace. Find the appropriate combination of demographics and marketing techniques that are suitable to your individual background, expertise, and personality. In concert with understanding, as both educator and counselor, you will find personal reward and professional success in working with women.

"Divorce is a psychological process. . . . It is a process as real as the legal process, but no official notice arrives in the mail to mark its completion. Planners who hope effectively to counsel clients in divorce must understand this process."

—JUDITH HEADINGTON McGEE, CFP

Working With Divorced Clients

Judith Headington McGee is a prominent member of the planning community. She is a former member of the Board of Directors of the Institute of Certified Financial Planners. She has chaired the ICFP Public Awareness Committee and is past founding president of the ICFP Educational Foundation. She is a past adjunct faculty member of the College for Financial Planning in Denver, Colorado, and has served as the regional officer of the International Association for Financial Planning in Oregon and in Eastern Washington.

Ms. McGee is the sole proprietor of Associated Investment Advisers, which is based in Spokane, Washington, and serves a professional clientele throughout the Pacific Northwest and Alaska. She is a Certified Financial Planner, a NASD registered principal, and a Registered Investment Adviser with Financial Planners Equity Corporation.

A recognized marketing authority, Ms. McGee is the conceptual creator of Financial Independence Week and has pioneered many of the marketing concepts successfully used in the industry today. She makes frequent radio and television appearances and regularly contributes to publications such as the *Wall Street Journal*, the *American Bar Association Journal*, *USA Today*, and *Money Magazine*. She is currently authoring a book for Prentice Hall and remains active in civic affairs.

Young journalism students once were advised to cover divorce court to learn about "real life."

In the charged atmosphere of the courtroom, husbands and wives played out their deepest emotions. They fought over possessions, obligations, and children, their battles serving as a vent for their feelings. Divorce was a war zone and everyone—even the innocent bystander—was a potential victim.

Fortunately, divorce is changing. Society has isolated the problem, and we're moving to solve it. The divorce court of the past is dead, replaced by a gentler process of dissolution.

We haven't found the final solution, but at least journalism students have to go elsewhere to discover real life.

The new system recognizes divorce as a legitimate process of dissolution. It doesn't try to find fault and issue punishment; instead, it promotes mediation and conciliation. It increasingly is concerned with the long-term welfare of the separating partners.

Equity is now the word of the day—equity in the division of assets, in the establishment of cash flow and tax liability, in the matters of child support, custody, and visitation.

This change has the effect of involving the planner more completely in the divorce process. Planners are adept at creating cash flow models; they understand the tax consequences of financial decisions; they are experienced in the structuring and dissolution of fiscal partnerships; they understand net worth; they know how to evaluate assets; good ones know how to work with people in change.

The concept of equitability implies that fairness is not a temporary state of affairs. While great discrepancies still exist among states and among courtrooms, most judges no longer want to issue rulings that look good today but consign one party to borderline poverty—or worse—six months down the line.

"Judges want the people who come before them to be able to answer the financial questions," mused a former judge who is also a client. "They want to see the spreadsheets of the divorcing parties. They want to see cash flow projections that reflect the future needs of the parties—not just current budgets—so they can make more equitable decisions."

Two legal systems have arisen in response to this new attitude. They, or some modification of them, are in place in every state.

Under the community property laws adopted by eight states, all assets and debts acquired during marriage are shared equally. Five community property states have an "equitable distribution" provision that allows the court to consider future need when assigning the assets. The other three states call for the equal distribution of assets upon divorce without regard to the income potential of either spouse.

In common-law states—there are 41 of them—the person whose name is on the title owns the property. But even the harsh provisions of common law have been softened—all the common-law states mandate some degree of equitable distribution.

The odd state out is Wisconsin, formerly a common-law state with equitable distribution, which has introduced a new standard called the Uniform Marital Property Act (UMPA). In Wisconsin, marital property is viewed as jointly owned, much as it is in a community property state.

In virtually all cases, anything acquired before the marriage remains the property of the original owner. Likewise, neither inheritances or gifts received during the marriage are thrown into the communal pot.

Equitable distribution has changed the criteria of a well-administered divorce: property has replaced alimony in establishing fair distribution, and negotiation is fast replacing litigation in dispute resolution.

As always, the court has the last word. Either it will approve an existing settlement, or it will forge its own. The level of its involvement is dependent on the effectiveness of the work done by those who fashion the original agreement. That process is bringing together the skills of a growing number of professionals. Today's divorce can include lawyers, planners and accountants, actuaries, appraisers, tax-shelter experts, and mediators.

The first step in putting together an equitable settlement is to determine family assets and liabilities, a process which is becoming increasingly complex. All the obvious assets—bank and credit union accounts, investments, life insurance cash values, IRAs, KEOGHs, royalties, income tax refunds, stock options, and other pools of family income—must be accounted for. Illiquid assets like jewelry, cars, boats, vacation time shares, and collectibles go into the pot too.

Pensions and tax shelters present their own special challenges. You may need to call on an actuary to determine the true value of a pension. There are companies like the Liquidity Fund Investment Corp. that will appraise the value of real estate limited partnerships.

On other questions, the courts continually redefine the rules. Late in 1985, the New York Supreme Court awarded a doctor's ex-wife a share of his future earnings. She earned a share of the value of his license, the court said, when she put him through medical school.

Corporate attorneys are working overtime to unscramble the effect that recent rulings will have on a number of deferred compensation tools, including nonvested pensions, profit-sharing accruals, and stock and insurance plans. Programs can vary so widely that courts to date have been reluctant to establish universal guidelines.

Questions like who owns the interest earned on investments brought by one partner into the marriage now are adjudicated on a state-by-state basis.

Once a fair value has been established for all assets, the negotiating can begin. Tax implications must be addressed first. Dividing property 50/50 can minimize the tax hit—if a husband and wife split their jointly-owned stock evenly, neither pays taxes until one spouse or the other sells his or her holdings. At that time, the spouse who sold will be expected to pay capital gains tax.

The so-called Davis Tax, which penalized couples for an unequal division of assets, has been superseded. Now when property changes hands as a condition of settlement, neither party gets a tax bill.

Alimony is doing a disappearing act as many states replace it with spousal maintenance, a device which is intended to subsidize the dependent spouse as he or she makes ready to enter the job market. Whatever it's called—alimony or maintenance—it is deductible to the spouse who pays and it's taxable to the one who receives it as income. However, if monthly payments are part of a property settlement and not formally spousal maintenance or alimony, they are not deductible. Child support is never deductible.

The legal fees generated during divorce are not deductible, but tax advice is.

Under the equitable distribution provisions, ex-wives have been receiving only about one-third of the marital assets. Their plight is better than under the old system, in which they received nothing that didn't have their name on the title, but it's not yet at the 50-50 split the courts seem to be aiming for.

Women's salaries are usually lower than men's, and women tend to get fewer assets in a divorce. Lenore Weitzman, a Stanford University sociologist, reports that on average a woman's standard of living drops 73 percent in the first year after a divorce. Typically, a man's increases by 42 percent.

The role for the financial planner is obvious. By taking the long view, the planner should be able to anticipate those kinds of discrepancies. If you are working with a divorcing woman—or a dependent spouse of either sex—push hard for property in lieu of support, maintenance, or alimony. A settlement structured around large current assets can be fashioned into a working portfolio; banking on future payments is risky. But be aware that possession of the family home has little value to a dependent spouse who can't pay the heating bills.

That advice is especially true when one is working with settlements involving child support, a notoriously problematic area. Economist Philip Robins conducted a study for the Social Security Administration and found that of the 2.3 million divorced women with children, only 36 percent were getting the support to which they were entitled. Only 53 percent were getting anything at all.

A new law, the Child Support Enforcement Act, should help alleviate the support problem. It requires each state to develop and implement a working program of support enforcement. States are given power to withhold wages or state tax returns from a delinquent parent. They also may establish a lien on real estate or personal property, and notify credit bureaus of overdue payments. In bankruptcy and credit proceedings, child-support obligations are now given preference over everything but federal income-tax payments.

Unfortunately, no matter how commonplace divorce may become, it will never be pleasant; in nearly every case, the rancor that was the hallmark of the divorce court undermines the more peaceful intent of the new divorce.

The desire to keep emotions from destroying a good settlement has given rise to divorce mediation, a new industry for which planners with a background in personal counseling are ideal candidates. Kathleen Miller, a Seattle planner who works with Northwest Mediation Services, consults with an attorney and a clinical psychologist on divorce cases. Together, they counsel couples who want to avoid court.

Professional mediators can usually mediate a settlement after five to 10 two-hour sessions. Fees typically range from $50 to $100 an hour. For information on certified mediation services in your area, contact the Family Mediations Association, 9308 Bulls Run Pky., Bethesda, Md. 20817.

When the client refuses other help, counseling chores fall to the planner. This shouldn't be unfamiliar territory, since a good planner must be a good counselor, but the responsibility can be intimidating. Some planners fear that they lack the necessary skills, but most have good listening skills and the ability to build a client's confidence; those are the essentials.

Beware: Empathy may be the key to helping a client through a hard time, but sympathy is the trap. Keep your distance from the problems of clients in divorce. When you become personally involved, you stop thinking clearly about their needs, and yours. The result may be a psychological dependency, which can lead to ineffective planning.

Divorce is a psychological process; counselors refer to the "psychological divorce." It is a process as real as the legal process, but no official notice arrives in the mail to mark its completion. Planners who hope effectively to counsel clients in divorce must understand this process.

The stages of divorce parallel the stages of death as explained by Elizabeth Kubler-Ross. In the first, or denial, stage, people can't come to terms with the reality of the divorce. They feel completely powerless. Depression is common.

Anger follows. The bereaved berates the former partner to all who will listen. The parties make outrageous demands.

Anger gives way to bargaining. One partner will make great concessions in an effort to make the relationship work; the other feels guilty. The client who last week bitterly demanded sun, moon and stars now talks reconciliation. If reconciliation is not effected, the couple now will begin to let go. Hopelessness is a common feeling at this point.

Finally, hopelessness is resolved by acceptance. The need to invest in a dead relationship passes, and the client can begin to put life back together.

While a year generally is enough time to complete the psychological divorce, the process can take up to two-and-a-half years and sometimes longer. All the while, the client may be unable to make future-oriented decisions.

During divorce, people look to their peers for direction; word travels fast within the community of the newly single. If you help a divorced client through a hard time, you could be on your way to building a good trade.

Planners can create seminars for divorced or divorcing clients. They can work with local community colleges which provide services to couples in transition. Women's clubs and professional groups are always looking for interesting and pertinent program material. Church singles groups usually are comprised of a high percentage of divorced and divorcing people. The YMCA and YWCA are good resources, as are insightful psychologists who recognize their clients' needs for financial counseling.

Many agencies and schools offer programs for underskilled ex-housewives who need planning and vocational support. These formal courses enable women in transition to learn money management and financial planning skills in the company of others with similar learning needs and with comparable financial and emotional problems. Here they can feel secure and can more quickly adapt to their new life situation.

Working with divorcing people has its own headaches and rewards. Divorcing people are at a unique juncture—they are redefining themselves and their priorities. Divorce motivates people; suddenly, the future is uncertain and they are shaken into action. They learn new habits and shed old ones. The patterns of behavior they develop during divorce set the stage for coming years.

If you have a client in the midst of divorce, remember that patience is your chief ally. For most people, divorce is a long and painful process. Sometimes it will seem that you are dealing with an unpredictable child. It often may seem that you're not making progress, but when the breakthrough comes, it will be like the spring following winter.

Remember to recognize and acknowledge the importance of the three aspects of divorce—the legal, financial, and emotional. Each is real; none can be ignored or their importance underestimated. Learn to understand the long-range needs of your clients, the tax implications of the decisions they will make, and the laws of the states in which you work.

"Helping them not to spend every penny they earn is one of the best services you can provide."

—P. KEMP FAIN, JR., Ph.D., CFP

Working With Physicians, Dentists, and Other Health Care Professionals

P. Kemp Fain, Jr., CFP, CLU, is the founder and President of Asset Planning Corporation. He earned his bachelor's degree from Georgia Tech in mechanical engineering, his master's degree from the University of Tennessee in management, and his doctorate from California Coast University in business administration.

Mr. Fain has taught business and personal finance courses and currently teaches Personal Money Management at the University of Tennessee. He is a contributing author to *Your Book of Financial Planning* and has authored a booklet, *Money Matters*. Mr. Fain has appeared on Cable News Network, Financial News Network, and local television talk shows and has also been quoted in numerous national publications. He is a Registered Financial Principal with the National Association of Securities Dealers and holds many other professional licenses. He has served as National President and Chairman of the Board of the Institute of Certified Financial Planners and is currently serving as Vice Chairman of the International Board of Standards and Practices for Certified Financial Planners.

Over the years, it has been my pleasure and privilege to work with a number of health care professionals. Included as health care professionals are physicians, dentists, chiropractors, physical therapists, and nurses. All health care professionals share several attributes in common. Among them are a dedication to helping others, above-average intelligence, a high degree of professional training, and willingness to work long hours.

Because of these attributes, a financial planner must consider both *personal* and *professional* aspects of dealing with health care professionals. I have organized my comments into personal and professional areas.

First, let's deal with the *personal* area and discuss how a financial planner might be more successful in dealing with health care professionals and in responding to their needs.

To start, you should be aware of some personal traits you will encounter with health care professionals. They are smart and well organized, and they have good discipline. Because they have mastered a substantial body of professional knowledge, they tend to be egocentric, which is understandable. Unfortunately, this trait leads them to be confident in areas outside their training, which may not be justified. The most important thing you can do is establish *yourself* as a valued professional advisor with capabilities similar to those of the health care professional. How do you do this? The following is a list of things which may help:

1. Respect their time. Set appointments and telephone calls for times when they are likely to be available, such as their days off or afternoons off, and around 12:00 P.M. or 5:00 P.M. on a working day.

2. Be well prepared and organized for each appointment and telephone call. Have a specific objective for the call, and don't beat around the bush getting to it.

3. Always do what you say you will do or let them know why it can't be done. Even routine service work should be given extra emphasis in order to minimize the time lapse before the health care professional hears from you. A disciplined personality expects to get action! A justifiable delay may not be appreciated, but it will be accepted with an explanation.

4. Keep up with the financial developments in the health care field. This is best done by reading publications such as *Medical Economics*. It can also be done by having two or three of your close health care clients screen important articles for you as they see them. Further, you should screen the periodicals you read for applicable articles.

5. Keep your business and social life separate. There is nothing wrong with having a social relationship with health care clients, but let them initiate the relationship.

6. Be sure that the health care professional's spouse is included in all possible meetings, planning sessions, and the like. You will gain a valuable ally, which will help when action is needed.

7. Stand your ground on what you believe. In dealing with strong personalities, it is easy to take the path of least resistance and outwardly agree with them. Stick to your beliefs and be prepared to factually defend them. You will be appreciated!

8. Be prepared to deal with other professionals and competitors. Simply because they are health care professionals, they will be on all the mail-

ing and call lists of various sales and professional people who target them as customers or clients. The best defense against losing a valued health care client is to provide exemplary service.

9. Be reasonable and conservative in your recommendations to health care clients. Too often, planners lead their health care clients into high-risk investments because of their clients' high incomes and tax brackets. Resist this temptation! You will be amazed at how much more your health care clients will appreciate a regular monthly investment check than a tax deduction on a K-1 form.

10. Try to have all or most appointments with health care professionals in your own office. This establishes the proper professional image. It helps if the surroundings are nice, and if you serve refreshments using real china, etc. Even though they can afford it, most health care professionals don't get this type of service every day.

11. Circulate a list of important health care clients to all your office personnel. Be sure that they understand that they are to know who "Dr. Smith" is and are to be extremely courteous and helpful when "Dr. Smith" calls.

12. Use newsletters and articles to keep your name in front of your health care clients.

13. Teach your health care clients the important elements of the financial planning process, that is, balance sheets, cash flow statements, annual reviews, etc. We are as much educators as planners in dealing with our clients.

It is to be hoped that doing the things on this list will help you develop satisfying relationships with your health care clients.

Second, let's discuss the *professional* side of dealing with health care clients. One of the most difficult decisions to be made by a high-income health care professional is whether or not to incorporate. Incorporation has some powerful advantages, such as isolating professional liability, eliminating business liability, and making more fringe benefits tax-deductible than can be accomplished through a partnership or a proprietorship. On the other hand, many health care professionals feel that a corporation is impersonal and that it may compromise their professional relationships with their patients. One thing is certain. Sooner or later, your higher-income health care clients will consider the issue of incorporation. Help them make a rational decision, then put this issue to bed. There is no right or wrong answer. The corporate form of practice can be just as personal and satisfying for the health care professional as any other form, but it may or may not be economical. Often, it is simpler and less expensive to remain a proprietor or in a partnership than it is to incorporate. Let your clients' feelings be your best guide to answering this question.

Next, stress the use of qualified and nonqualified deferred compensation plans as the health care professional's major wealth-building mechanisms. There are many advantages to this strategy:

1. Contributions are statutorily tax deductible for qualified plans and are tax favored for nonqualified plans.

2. Investments can be conservative.

3. Plan arrangements can be such that the health care professional can concentrate on providing services and not on being an investment expert, such as an apartment manager, etc.

4. There is the possibility of favorable tax treatment upon withdrawal of assets from qualified retirement plans.

It is to be hoped that both you and your health care clients will be satisfied with fast-growing, qualified retirement plan trusts.

Next, help your health care clients save and invest a reasonable portion of their income. If they have children, it will take a substantial financial commitment to send those children through college. Helping them *not* to spend every penny they earn is one of the best services you can provide. It is easy for them to fall into a pattern of material acquisition, which uses up money at a frightening clip. While their short-term attitude toward saving may be negative, the long-run result will be appreciation for you and your efforts to help them acquire financial security. This will be a continuing battle for you in dealing with these clients.

Be sure to encourage your health care clients to make adequate estate arrangements. Adequate arrangements for this type of client will usually be far more complex than a simple will. Not only do they need wills, but they frequently need one or more trusts, such as irrevocable insurance trusts and accumulation trusts for education. They also need to consider having living wills and powers of attorney for each spouse. While you can't be the designer or preparer of the legal documents required, you can certainly be the catalyst who makes them consider the important estate alternatives facing them.

Finally, encourage your health care clients to acquire the habit of doing annual reviews just as they encourage their patients to have annual medical examinations. You will need good data processing capabilities and extensive financial planning software to properly perform these reviews.

In summary, I have attempted to point out some things from a *personal* point of view and other things from a *professional* point of view that are especially important in dealing with health care professionals. As health care professionals' incomes go up, it is vitally important for you to provide competent and effective services if you are to keep them as clients. This leads to my last observation. I believe that independent professionals are best served by other independent professionals. I am a strong advocate of the independent, professional financial planner, that is, a planner who is in private practice and who has the Certified Financial Planner (CFP) certification and/or the Chartered Financial Consultant (ChFC) designation. While the planner may have other credentials, these are the most significant training experiences for providing financial planning services to the public. Remember that the health care professionals you serve will belong to professional organizations and will be bound by one or more codes of ethics; so should you. You should belong to professional organizations such as the Institute of Certified Financial Planners and/or the American Society of CLUs and ChFCs. These are professional associations serving their members in much the same way that the American Medical Association serves physicians.

Good luck to you in building a financial planning practice serving health care clients. Remember, you *must* pay attention to details and be better than your competitors if you are to survive in this marketplace!

"At one moment your clients can be at the top, and within minutes (with just the stroke of a pen) they can be unemployed."

—GALE LINDQUIST, CFP

Working With Clients in the Entertainment Industry

Gale Lindquist, CFP, holds a bachelor's degree in accounting and a master's degree in banking and finance from Adelphi University. She has taught as an Adjunct Professor of financial planning at New York University.

Ms. Lindquist is a member of the Board of Directors and Vice-President of Programs for the International Association for Financial Planning, Long Island chapter. In addition, she is a member of the American Management Association, Institute of Certified Financial Planners, International Board of Standards and Practices for Certified Financial Planners, Business Women's Association of Suffolk County, and the International Association of Financial Planning. She also serves on the NASD Advisory Board for Registered Representatives for Design Capital Securities Corp. and has been interviewed and quoted in many major industry publications.

There is probably no industry in the world that fluctuates as quickly or with as much volatility as the entertainment industry. At one moment your clients can be at the top, and within minutes (with just a stroke of a pen) they can be unemployed. Due to this volatility, planning for them can be both very rewarding and nerve wracking. It takes one creative financial planner to hold them at bay when they are the "star," and in the black when unemployed.

Exactly what does one do to plan for their volatile lifestyles? First, you must look at these entertainers as "regular" people. They have goals, dreams, and income requirements just like everyone else, so planning can be approached traditionally to some degree. Second, planning is similar to those "business" clients who are self-employed. At times they too have cash flow fluctuation.

Problems somewhat unique to the entertainment industry are:

1. Entertainers rarely have a head for business. Formal or informal training in financial management has been nearly nonexistent.
2. Very often they have spent years as struggling entertainers before they made it big. Having large sums of money suddenly is a new experience and they want to "show off" their new-found fortunes.
3. Unless they are big headliners (and even that can be temporary), contracts favor the sponsors; therefore, three-year contracts could last only six months.
4. Their unemployed periods could last a year or two, and maybe more.
5. Entertainers often respond in an unprofessional way to the vertigo induced by their tax bills. Investing in risky tax shelters is the most common financial mistake made.
6. Other unique features of these professionals include everything from an unusually low or high self-esteem to a low or high expectation of others; from a relatively high personal aversion to taking risk to continually facing a high liability risk; from problems with spousal communication to difficulties with business transactions.

Clearly, the most sensitive issue for most entertainers is taxation. Say what you will about inflation, the fact remains that inflation has given them a rapid rise (for those employed) to life in the fast lane.

TAX PLANNING

Though a few of us may still be trying to digest the impact of the Tax Reform Act of 1986, the general public is still shell-shocked, trying to figure out what action they should or should not be taking. The tax act contains certain provisions particularly identifiable to actors having more than one employer.

In any tax-planning program designed for entertainers, one must consider their income fluctuations. The plans should capitalize as much as possible on federal and state incentives. All investments must be considered for their economic potential first; their risk level, second; their cash flow, third; and lastly, their tax advantages.

More than once I have witnessed people trying to reduce their tax bills first and to consider the economics of the "deal" last, only to have the same people wonder how their "investment" was doing after April 15 has come and gone.

Although the Tax Reform Act has severely hindered tax-advantaged investments, long-term capital gains, and income-transferring to other family members, there are still some traditional and nontraditional tax-advantaged investments in existence, such as:

1. Treasury bills
2. Municipal bonds
3. IRAs and KEOGH plans
4. Corporate pension or profit-sharing plans
5. Single-payment life insurance
6. All-cash real estate programs
7. Deferred annuities
8. Income-producing oil and gas programs
9. Government-subsidized housing
10. Historic rehabilitation

INCORPORATION

When does it make sense for an entertainer to incorporate? Before one considers whether to incorporate or not, several questions must be addressed:

1. What is the probable length of contract, and what is the entertainer's ability to secure another contract should the present contract be canceled?
2. Have the increased costs of legal and accounting services, Social Security taxes, and the like been examined?
3. Will the incorporation help to keep the entertainer's books and records in a more orderly fashion?
4. Have all forms of business been examined carefully?
5. Since personal and corporate tax rates have changed due to tax reform, have hypothetical tax returns been done to see which will be most advantageous to the client?
6. How are the benefits from SAG or AFTRA effected by the incorporation?
7. Does the entertainer anticipate an income of over $200,000 per year for the next several years?

Some benefits of being a personal service corporation include:

1. Business expenses are paid on a before-tax basis rather than being claimed on the personal tax form, so cash flow is increased.
2. Medical reimbursement plans (the corporation pays the entertainer's medical expenses).
3. Group term insurance.
4. Corporate profit-sharing pension plan, since IRAs and KEOGHs are generally no longer available to them.

INVESTMENTS

The investment planning process for entertainers begins essentially in the same way as it does for all clients. Cash flow statements and balance sheets detailing their current financial position are prepared. Existing assets and liabilities are examined first for their appropriateness in relation to the client's lifestyle and objectives, and then for their investment value.

Clients often have a tendency to stay married to an investment, particularly if it has either made or lost money for them. Sometimes these investments are held to reinforce the client's ego. At other times it may have just been an oversight '' . . . I was meaning to sell that stock (bond, real estate, etc.); I just hadn't gotten around to it yet.'' More times than not it takes a professional advisor to do the weeding out and to replace these investments with more appropriate ones.

Certain factors should be considered by financial planners when they are considering repositioning assets.

1. The earning stability of the entertainer. As stated previously their earnings can be rather volatile.
2. Income necessary to meet expenses should their contracts be terminated.
3. Age, health, family responsibilities, dependents, and other family income needs.
4. To what degree liquidity or marketability should be maintained.
5. Risk tolerances. (Can the client withstand market fluctuations?)
6. Anticipated tax liability and status.
7. How the asset should perform through both inflationary and deflationary cycles.

Entertainers are skilled at their profession. They usually do not have the time nor the desire to learn or perform efficient financial management tasks, so they hire other professionals to manage their affairs. However, where investments are concerned, clients often feel more qualified to make these decisions than they actually are.

ESTATE PLANNING

Often the creation or changing of an outdated will elicits the same response from an entertainer as the inappropriate investment. "I was meaning to take care of that, but I haven't had time." Proper estate planning can literally save thousands of dollars. Yet what should be first is often last.

One important factor to keep in mind when one is doing estate planning for entertainers is that their business is not transferable. However, depending upon their niche and their popularity, residuals and income could continue well beyond their mortal years.

There are basically three effective means of estate tax avoidance: first, through the transferring of asset growth to the next generation; second, by taking advantage of provisions in the tax code that exempt certain assets from taxation; third, by gift giving, transferring assets, and charitable gifts or bequests.

One concern that almost all individuals have regarding estate planning is the transferring of an asset. They do not like passing rights or ownership of property to others in advance of death. So the estate plan technique may be sound, but the reality is that the recommendation is often never implemented.

Many entertainers are either sole proprietors or personal service corporations; therefore, when they die the goodwill dies with them. However, for those clients whose legends outlive them, particular care must be taken to form the business entity that will manage these assets. A corporation theoretically has continuity of life—it operates in perpetuity. That is, the corporation, regardless of its size, continues to operate after death of the individual stockholder. It is important for you as their financial advisor to be aware of the state laws governing the disposition of this stock.

In summary, as we meander through the rest of the 1980s, absorbing the continual changes that the government, the economy, and society have in store for us, the formulation of a personal financial plan is becoming more important than ever, especially for the entertainment industry. The entertainer's success and financial survival is directly related to the management and interrelationship of an appropriate investment portfolio, tax planning, risk management, and the constant watchful eye of a good financial advisor.

"Farmers today find themselves facing many problems. A financial planner who understands the problems farmers face and who can communicate with the farmer will secure the engagement."

—*JERRY L. SUVER, CLU, CFP*

The Farm Owner as a Client

Jerry L. Suver is President of Confidential Planning Services, Inc. (CPS) with primary responsibilities for field service, marketing, and training. He is also one of the founders of CPS and a managing executive with Integrated Resources Equity Corporation. He teaches affiliates from financial planning firms all over the country how to develop workshops and productive seminars. He was named outstanding CPS affiliate in 1980, receiving the Ken Edwards Award.

Suver is a graduate of Morehead State University with a degree in business administration and marketing. He is a member of the faculty for the National Institute of Finance, Inc., an organization offering instructions for preparation of Certified Financial Planning examinations. He is a Chartered Life Underwriter and a Certified Financial Planner.

Most financial planners have determined that the most profitable and challenging client is the owner of a business. The problems are manifold, and the need for outside advice is easily recognized by the client. Moreover, for the planner who sells products, this can be the most profitable category of client.

Business owners are also excellent sources of referrals. They understand that all businesses need new customers and that the most valuable source of new customers is referrals. Because they are not reluctant to ask for and receive referrals, they do not resent being asked in turn for the same information.

The largest single category of business owners in America is that of the farm owner. Frequently, we omit them from consideration by placing them in a separate category, as "farmers." But when one considers the gross income of farmers, there is no doubt that they qualify as fairly substantial businesspeople.

However, many financial planners do not have a personal farm background and tend to assume that this precludes them from offering services to farmers. Nothing could be further from the truth.

For the farmer to agree to financial planning requires the same essential points as selling any tangible product:

- Arouse interest.
- Establish the need.
- Create desire.
- Convey a solution.
- Ask for the order.

Selling the financial planning engagement to the farmer is distinct from selling a financial product. What the farmer is buying is the belief that the subsequent service will convey benefits that are well in excess of costs.

While most planners have a sales background, the tendency is to put all the sales training behind when one is securing the financial engagement. This is a serious mistake. The planner should go through the five steps of the sales cycle listed above. There are several guidelines:

1. Be prepared. The planner will need brochures, a sample financial plan, and a fee chart or fee guidelines. These should be attractively packaged, but need not be elaborate.
2. Have a track to run on. My suggestion is to have two copies of an agenda for the meeting, one for the farmer and one for the planner. By following the agenda the planner will proceed to the conclusion.
3. Use motivational tools. While these could be verbal, most planners will benefit from using slides, overheads, flip charts, or audiovisuals.
4. Have a sample financial plan which illustrates a farm client in the approximate age, income range, and size of estate as the prospect you are talking with.
5. Have a technique for conveying the farmer's expected cost/benefit ratio of the sample financial plan.
6. Have an engagement letter or agreement ready for execution.

When dealing with farmers, you must make sure they know that you understand their business and problems. A story from a few years ago comes to mind. After spending a couple of hours discussing a farmer's situation, he said that he wanted to do business with me and my firm. When we had completed the engagement agreement, the farmer asked if I was interested in knowing why he decided to do business with me instead of the firm he spoke to last week; I answered yes.

The farmer said that last week a financial planner, gathering facts, looked at his tax return. This farmer raises registered hogs and buys and sells breeding stock. As the planner reviewed the tax return, he came upon an item called bush-hog. The planner asked what breed was this. The farmer decided then that the planner did not understand his business; a bush-hog is a piece of equipment used to mow grass, not an animal. You must develop trust and a feeling that the farmer knows you understand his business.

Young farmers with high debt loads are not the only farmers affected by today's stressed agricultural economy. Many retiring farmers are finding the nest eggs they have nurtured over the years are not what they're cracked up to be.

One of the problems is that the depressed farm economy has caused the value of farm real estate to fall. Many farmers plan on generating their retirement income by selling the farm and investing the money. But farm values today are only about half what they were in 1981, and in some communities it is almost impossible to sell a farm. Cash rental rates for land are falling too, so even retired farmers who keep their land are not getting the income they might have expected. Another problem for retired farmers is lower return from money invested in certificates of deposit. Not everybody is pleased with low interest rates.

In planning for a retirement nest egg, farmers should consider diversifying their investments. Many farmers put all their eggs in one basket by investing everything they have in their farms. Instead, farmers should look for other investments.

Retiring farmers should be cautious about cosigning loans or giving direct financial assistance to their children. Those cosignature agreements mean exactly what they say. If those children end up having financial difficulties, retired farmers can lose their own financial security.

The current farm economy has made good estate planning more important than before. In better financial times, you could afford to make mistakes, but now mistakes can absorb the business. Farmers can make arrangements to pass their farms to their children without destroying their own security. In some cases, a financially sound farm will fail because provisions were not made for a smooth transition from the older generation to the younger.

Failing to make plans can also lead to disagreements between family members. In most of the cases, whatever Mom and Dad want is fine with their children, but if no plans are made, the plan for dividing assets will be determined by default. Then nobody's happy.

Retired farmers should also check on using losses from renting their land to offset other income. There should be no problem in using losses from a share rent agreement to offset other income, because a farmer "materially participates" in such an agreement. However, if a farmer is not materially participating (with a cash rent agreement, for example), any "passive" losses may only be used to offset passive gains. There may be an exception to this provision for farmers who cash rent if they materially participated before they retired. To find out how the regulations apply to a particular situation, farmers will need to consult their financial planners.

Some of the provisions of the new tax law will help retired farmers. The tax rates have been decreased, and personal and standard deductions have increased. Overall, the net effect should be lower taxes.

Retired farmers and those planning for retirement have to deal with a new set of circumstances. But careful tax planning, estate planning, and retirement planning can help them make the most of their nest eggs.

While many farmers know how to deal with the financial challenges of farming today, some are ignoring other equally important problems. For example, family farms can also be destroyed by stresses on farm marriages, stormy family relationships, poor management training of farmers' successors, conflicting needs of on- and off-farm heirs, and complications of retirement.

Farmers today find themselves facing many problems. A financial planner who understands the problems that farmers face and who can communicate with the farmer will secure the engagement.

"The advantages of working with military retired officers are that they tend to be decision makers. They appreciate a job well done and they will offer you strong referrals to their associates in the armed forces and associates in their new careers."

—JOCELYN R. KAPLAN, CFP

Jocelyn Kaplan, CFP, is president of the Northern Virginia firm Advisors Financial Inc., a Registered Investment Advisory firm. Previously, Kaplan worked as a financial planner, case writer, and insurance agent for a varied group of firms, acquiring the expertise needed to develop her company. She is registered with the NASD and has been admitted to the Registry of Financial Planning Practitioners.

A former radio talk show host, Kaplan is an articulate, knowledgeable, and personal speaker who regularly speaks at meetings and seminars. She is an alumna of Northwestern University and is included in *Who's Who in American Women*.

Working With Retired Military Clients

A career in the United States military often involves sacrifices. A pay scale that is lower than the private sector's, possible separation from spouses and children, and the requirement to move one's home on a fairly regular basis are examples of such sacrifices. However, an attractive incentive associated with a military career is an excellent noncontributory retirement plan. After twenty years of service an individual can retire with an income that equals 50 percent of his or her final pay. In addition, many of those who retire from a career in the military are young enough to start a second career. The combination of the military retirement pay and the income from a new profession creates a different financial dynamic that can benefit from the services of a personal financial planner.

Income received while on active duty consists of nontaxable dollars in the form of housing and subsistence allowances, with the balance being taxable income. Also, some individuals maintain residency in states that do not tax military service income. These factors allow many of those on active duty to pay less income taxes than those in the civilian community. This is in sharp contrast to the situation after retirement. Retired officers often obtain high-paying positions in the private sector. This income, plus the retirement pay, all of which is now taxable on a federal and state level, results in a much higher income tax liability than that experienced while on active duty. In addition, if expenses do not increase to match this new income level, there can be substantial discretionary, investable income. Both of these changes present excellent financial planning opportunities.

A key decision that *must* be made before an individual retires from a military career is whether to elect to participate in the Survivor Benefit Plan (SBP). This plan pays a monthly income for life to a surviving spouse or dependent children after the death of the retired military individual. If one maintains his or her active-duty status after twenty years of service, survivors are automatically covered under this plan at no cost. Upon retirement, however, an election must be made whether or not to participate, and the choice is irrevocable. The cost of the SBP is approximately 10 percent of retirement pay for the maximum benefit. This benefit is paid for by an allotment with *before*-tax dollars. Various levels of benefit can be elected up to 55 percent of the retired military pay at death.

One advantage of participating in the SBP is the ease of administration. The payment is allotted from one's retirement paycheck, and the benefit comes to the survivor without fail on a monthly basis with an annual cost-of-living increase. For those families who have shown no savings pattern or experience in managing money, electing the SBP may be the proper decision.

The disadvantages of the SBP are numerous. Flexibility is limited. One cannot opt out of the plan once it is chosen. Therefore, if one's financial situation changes, due to an inheritance, for example, one must continue to pay for the benefit. If the potential recipient of the SBP dies before the military retired individual, the benefit that has been paid for is never received. Also, if the survivor dies soon after the retired member of the armed forces (as actuarial tables often indicate), then the cost will have far exceeded the benefit. Finally, when the survivor becomes eligible for social security, the SBP is reduced by the social security benefit provided by the deceased retiree's active military service. The amount of the reduction cannot exceed 40 percent of the amount of the SBP payment.

The SBP should be viewed as one element of a family's risk management program. It pays a benefit in the event that the family has insufficient time to attain the level of wealth that would provide a comfortable unearned income.

Life insurance is typically used to mitigate this risk. Therefore, where a need exists, the costs and benefits of the SBP should be compared to a life insurance program. Since the SBP is paid for on a before-tax basis and life insurance premiums with after-tax dollars, additional calculations are necessary to make a fair comparison. Next, the planner must determine the amount of life insurance that equals the SBP benefit stream, bearing in mind that the benefit increases annually with Consumer Price Index increases. Therefore, the use of a low capitalization rate in a capital needs analysis is necessary to take inflation into account.

It is often possible to illustrate a life insurance program that compares favorably in the areas of cost and benefits to the SBP by using a universal life insurance policy. In addition, you gain flexibility. As the family's wealth increases, the face amount of the policy can be reduced. If the surviving spouse dies first, then the retired military individual can change the beneficiary if a need still exists, or the cash value of the policy can be used for other purposes.

Numerical comparisons between the SBP and a life insurance program can be endless. Naturally, as assumptions change, so can conclusions. The SBP is paid for by allotment and life insurance premiums are typically paid voluntarily. However, the life insurance premium can be paid by allotment if established prior to retirement. If the financial planner doubts whether the family will continue premium payments or has concerns whether survivors can handle a sizable life insurance death benefit, then perhaps the SBP is the best choice. These concerns aside, a life insurance program usually provides the flexibility that is not inherent in the SBP program.

The following are highlights of a few of the many benefits available to a retired member of the armed forces. Veterans Group Life Insurance (VGLI) is an optional, five-year, nonrenewable term insurance policy for $50,000 that may be converted to a permanent individual policy at its expiration. The cost is $4.08 per thousand for those over the age of 35. This may be a cost-effective benefit, depending upon the age at retirement. Retired members of the uniformed services and their qualifying dependents are eligible to use military medical facilities or the Civilian Health and Medical Program of the Uniformed Services (CHAMPUS). This program is offered at no cost, but the benefits are subject to deductibles and coinsurance provisions. There are health insurance programs that are offered in the private sector that pay the difference between the total medical charges and CHAMPUS payments. Other benefits available to retired members include educational assistance programs and VA mortgages.

Members of the armed forces have a complete physical examination before they retire. If there is evidence of a service-related disability, the retiree may receive payments from the Veterans Administration. These payments will be tax-exempt if a waiver of equivalent retired pay is executed. Retirees are eager to point out health problems in order to receive this tax-free benefit. However, this may later create insurability problems when they apply for commercial life or disability insurance. Military retirees usually are in possession of their medical records if they are needed for insurance application purposes.

Military homeowners on active duty have up to four years to purchase, build, or occupy a new residence in order to defer capital gains tax on the sale. The standard rule is two years. The four-year time frame may be extended under certain circumstances, including being stationed overseas or being required to live in base housing.

Many individuals in the armed forces will convert their personal residence into a rental property when they are stationed in a new location. The benefits of this strategy need to be reexamined in light of the Tax Reform Act of 1986 and new passive income rules, lengthened depreciation schedules, and the elimination of capital gains.

Military retirees enter second careers because they prefer to work and/or because their retired pay will not allow them to maintain their standard of living. Often they are motivated by the ability to save for a more comfortable second retirement. The combination of the retired pay and income from the second career typically allows for surplus, investable cash. Since many expenses were paid for by allotment during active-duty years, retirees are accustomed to regular, automatic savings programs, and this is highly recommended. Also, the financial planner should carefully examine the retirement plan and vesting schedule of the new employer. With careful planning, the military retiree could look forward to a comfortable second retirement with benefit streams from retired pay, pension benefits from a second career, social security, and income from personal investment assets.

The advantages of working with retired military officers are that they tend to be decision makers. They appreciate a job well done and they will offer you strong referrals to their associates in the armed forces and associates in their new careers.

An excellent reference text in this area is the *Uniformed Services Almanac,* which can be ordered by writing to P.O. Box 76, Washington, D.C. 20044.

Chapter VII

Working With
Other Professionals

Mark Bass, CFP, CAP
Bruce E. Winter, J.D. LLM, CFP
Michael J. Bobal, Jr.
Neil Ross, CFP

"The depth of relationship you desire with the CPA community is truly a function of your integrity and willingness to share information, reciprocate business, and, more importantly, keep the client's financial goal accomplishment as everyone's number one objective."

—MARK BASS, CFP, CPA

Performance, Praise, and Profits: Working With Your Client's CPA

Mark I. Bass, CFP, CPA, is President of Pennington/Bass Companies, Inc. Mark holds a BBA degree with a major in economics from Baylor University and a B.B.A with a major in accounting from Texas Tech University. In 1975, he was the youngest person to become a Certified Financial Planner, and he has been admitted to the Registry of Financial Planning Practitioners. Mr. Bass currently serves on the Board of the International Association for Financial Planning and has served on the Board of the Institute of Certified Financial Planners. He was the chapter President for the West Texas IAFP chapter.

Mr. Bass has lectured for several colleges, universities, and professional and civic groups and has written articles for professional financial planning periodicals. He has been quoted in several magazines and newspapers and has appeared as a financial commentator on radio and television.

For a long time financial planners have recognized the importance of the CPA in providing financial advice to clients. As a result, many financial planners seek a method of working with a client's CPA that benefits the financial planner, the CPA, but, most importantly, the client. For after all, are we not working for the benefit of the client?

The CPA too often has been referred to as "the deal-killer." There is no question that as a group they are seen as ultraconservative. It is understandable that this perception has grown from the fact that most CPAs provide advice on a reactive (versus proactive) basis and deal with matters of compliance as opposed to taking the initiative to accomplish the client's financial objectives. I submit to you that many of us are negative (or outright afraid) of things or people we don't know and understand. Therefore, financial planners on behalf of their clients must educate CPAs regarding the financial planning process, financial products, and the benefits that accrue to the client. Financial planners must also illustrate the benefits of this process that accrue to the CPA. The financial planner may in fact need to overcome the concern of a CPA regarding "financial planners" who may have not really provided quality service or even an appearance of the financial planning process.

How, then, should a financial planner work in conjunction with a CPA? I've been in the financial planning profession since 1971 and feel fortunate over that period of time to have worked in harmony with my clients' CPAs. We haven't always agreed, but by and large, I have had pleasant relationships. I became a CFP in 1975 and a CPA in 1978. Both of these designations have been helpful. My CPA was an unplanned evolution of the study of accounting which I initiated so that I might better communicate with CPAs and understand the CPA's perspective. Consequently, the first recommendation I would have to a financial planner who wants to work with CPAs is to study accounting enough to gain the CPA's perspective. As an alternative, associate with someone (a financial planning associate or staff person) who is a CPA. In either case, I encourage the financial planner or his or her associate to be active in the local chapter of CPAs as well as the local IAFP chapter and/or ICFP Society.

Second, communicate clearly and often regarding those things that affect your clients' tax positions. One of the best CPA relationships I have is with a CPA with whom I reviewed a mutual client's financial plan *before* it was implemented. The CPA was shocked that I would do such a thing! We didn't agree on every single proposal, but we did agree conceptually on the problems and solutions to help the client. How far a financial planner must go in actually walking through the client's financial plan is dependent on what the client/CPA relationship is, and how willing the client is for you to share the financial plan with the CPA. This needs to be determined by the financial planner in the data-gathering interview.

Third, it is advisable for the financial planner to send the CPA tax projections and cash flow projections to get his or her input and to provide current information on the tax ramifications of various financial products and strategies being utilized. This is particularly beneficial to the financial planner/CPA relationship when the client has been referred to the financial planner by the CPA. This helps alleviate the feeling of the CPA that the financial planner is "stealing" his or her client.

This leads to point number four. If a CPA refers a client to me and if the CPA is doing good work for the client, I always tell the client his CPA is providing quality service. I've done this both in the CPA's presence and in his or her absence. Genuine praise and affirmation has always helped the various intertwined relationships of financial planner-client-CPA. I also will call or write a CPA to express appreciation for referring a client to me.

A fifth helpful tool in relating to CPAs has been the maintenance of a mailing list of CPAs to whom I send a variety of information. This includes reading material of interest (in areas of tax, economics, finance, and even nonbusiness material), current offering lists, generic news regarding financial products, Christmas cards, news about our firm, and newsletters. Many times updates regarding a specific financial product will be sent to the client and his or her CPA. I also provide the CPA with information as I receive it regarding any particular product's tax ramifications or change in projections.

Of particular note is this level of communication placed in practice in the case of financial programs that do not perform according to projections or even have significant financial troubles. I have received a great deal of positive feedback from CPAs who simply appreciate being informed in this circumstance. Frankly, I want the client and the CPA to know what I am doing to help rectify the situation.

Finally, I ask CPAs for their input on what characteristics and services they seek in a financial planner. I also ask if they plan to make financial planning a part of their accounting practice. If so, I offer assistance to them in the transition process. You may wonder why. The reason for this is to maintain a good relationship, the end result of which is the CPA/financial planner's utilizing my services in the implementation process.

These six things may sound like so much common sense, yet in my experience, they are rarely done completely and consistently by most financial planners. It cannot be overstated; these things I've mentioned have *contributed significantly to my practice*. The depth of relationship you desire with the CPA community is truly a function of your integrity and willingness to share information, reciprocate business, and, more importantly, keep the client's financial goal accomplishment as everyone's number one objective. With this in mind, everyone wins.

"The difficulty in meeting your clients' wishes with respect to estate planning is that you, as a financial planner, are not licensed to practice law. You must therefore depend on an estate-planning professional who is a lawyer to assist you."

—BRUCE E. WINTER, JD, LLM, CFP

The Role of an Estate-Planning Attorney in Financial Planning

Bruce E. Winter, Esq. is an attorney specializing in taxation in Boca Raton, Florida. He has an extensive knowledge of financial planning. He completed his J.D. degree in 1973 from the University of Pittsburg School of Law. In 1974, he completed his L.L.M. in taxation from New York University. He is also a Certified Public Accountant and a Certified Financial Planner. Mr. Winter holds a B.B.A. degree from Ohio University.

Mr. Winter is a member of many professional associations, including the American Bar Association, the Florida Bar Association, the International Association for Financial Planning, the Palm Beach Tax Institute, and the Boca Raton Income, Estate and Business Planning Council.

Estate planning is the process for an individual to control the disposition of his assets to his loved ones with the least amount of delays, expenses, legal fees, and taxes. Estate planning is critical for each and every one of us but obviously becomes more critical as age increases. Since I am an attorney and financial planner living in South Florida, estate planning has become an important aspect of my practice. My particular practice is somewhat unique because of my background as an attorney, certified public accountant, and certified financial planner.

In our organization, we have twelve professionals, including five estate planning attorneys, three of whom are also certified public accountants. Two of our attorneys have master's degrees in taxation, one from Boston University and the other New York University. One other attorney has a master's degree in business administration. Also in our organization we have seven other financial planners, all enrolled in the College for Financial Planning, with aspirations of becoming certified financial planners. We also have one individual, a Chartered Life Underwriter and Chartered Financial Consultant, who is the insurance professional of our organization.

My firm, unlike most other firms, has expanded under the concept of providing total financial planning services to individuals on a highly specialized basis because of the depth, experience, and professional degrees of our associates. Nevertheless, I am writing this chapter on financial planning and estate planning from the standpoint of assisting you in selecting that proper estate planning attorney who can complement your financial planning practice.

As all good financial planners should recognize, estate planning is merely one aspect of a comprehensive financial plan. Estate planning for many clients is a major concern and a major part of their financial plan. Obviously, the benefits from optimal estate planning are not realized until one's death. However, the dollars that can be saved upon one's death in both probate and federal estate taxes can be significant. In order to properly help your client in the estate-planning area, you need to work with an attorney who has expertise in the estate-planning field. Law, unlike many other professions, in most states does not require degrees of specialization. Consequently, all lawyers, whether they are estate-planning experts or not, are licensed to prepare wills and trusts. Not all lawyers, however, are competent to recognize and handle advanced estate-planning matters. Therefore, in order to meet a particular client's wishes as they relate to his or her estate planning, it is necessary for you to find a lawyer who is a specialist in the estate-planning field.

From my personal experience, most clients, when it relates to estate planning, have certain basic objectives in mind. First, they want to be certain that their assets pass to their loved ones and others in accordance with their wishes. Second, most of my clients would like this process to occur as rapidly as possible after their death without delays. Third, my clients prefer to minimize legal fees charged for estate administration as it relates to the size of their probate estate. Consequently, the ability to avoid probate has strong appeal to my clients. Without going into greater detail on probate avoidance techniques, an obvious approach is to prepare living trusts for the benefit of your respective clients and place their assets in the living trusts in order to minimize their probate exposure.

Last, most of my clients do not want to pay unnecessary additional taxes on account of their death. They generally do not understand the federal estate tax structure. To the extent that a married couple can take advantage of their respective $600,000 unified credit exemptions and pass a combined total of $1,200,000 to their children without federal estate tax consequences, they want to take advantage of this opportunity. The obvious approach is to establish a marital deduction trust and a unified credit trust, either of which can be part of a living trust, which is highly preferable, or, alternatively, part of a testamentary trust included within a will.

The difficulty in meeting your clients' wishes with respect to estate planning is that you, as a financial planner, are not licensed to practice law. You must therefore depend on an estate-planning professional who is a lawyer to assist you. Unfortunately, many lawyers do not understand estate planning. Even if they do not understand estate planning, many lawyers would not be inclined to acknowledge that estate planning is beyond their expertise. Preparation of a will, without the attorney's understanding all aspects of the will, may not address all of a client's wishes as it relates to estate planning, such as the minimization of federal estate taxes and the reduction of probate expenses. Consequently, it becomes necessary for you, as a financial planner, to seek out those attorneys who are specialists in estate planning in order to have proper wills and trusts prepared on a timely basis to help you with your financial plan as it relates to estate planning. The attorney selected should have the communication skills that are necessary to make your client feel comfortable with his services. In fact, the appropriate attorney will make you appear to be a better financial planner because of your knowledge and awareness in selecting a competent professional to assist you in this specialized area.

It is my recommendation, in the selection of an attorney to assist you with the estate-planning aspect of a financial plan, that the attorney have an advanced law degree in taxation and/or estate planning. There are attorneys who go to law school an extra year (fourth year) in order to specialize in either tax or estate planning and receive a master of law degree. These professionals often are part of a large firm or may have their own practice limited to their legal expertise. In Florida, for example, it is possible for an attorney to be board-certified in estate planning by the Florida Bar or, alternatively, to be designated by the Florida Bar in the areas of wills, trusts, and estate planning. I strongly recommend that the attorney you select have these special degrees, credentials, and/or background.

In addition, and possibly even more important than the extra schooling, is an attorney's experience in the estate-planning field. Does the attorney understand what your client's wishes are? Is the attorney willing to prepare living trusts which, in the future, will result in reduced legal fees when it comes to estate administration for that particular client's estate? What are the communication skills an attorney has with your clients? Is he or she personable? Does the attorney have a rapport with your clients, or is he or she merely a technician to whom your client cannot relate? In addition, does the estate-planning attorney have knowledge of financial planning and the financial-planning process? Does he or she understand what your role is with your clients and what his or her role will be? Furthermore, is there an opportunity that you can network with this attorney and receive referrals from him or her to expand your financial planning practice?

Lastly, I would like to mention the matter of your prospecting for new clients. We have found in Florida that the opportunity to speak to many people through seminars is an excellent technique. In Florida, particularly Broward County and Palm Beach County in South Florida, you can read the newspaper on a Sunday and see as many as two dozen seminars being offered for the upcoming week in the areas of financial planning, investments, estate planning, and particular insurance products. What makes the seminars sponsored by our office rather unique is that we offer a seminar on both financial planning and estate planning.

When a prospective client sees that an attorney is speaking along with a financial planner, there will be greater credibility to the substance of a financial- and estate-planning seminar. Obviously, as a financial planner, it is critical that you receive the credibility and respect of your prospective clients. Doing a seminar with an estate-planning attorney may be an opportunity for you to get greater exposure and awareness in your community with respect to your particular financial-planning skills. Should you follow this technique, it becomes absolutely critical that the attorney you select to assist you with the seminars have extremely strong communication skills and be able to convey his or her expertise to your potential clients at their level. Merely confusing your prospective client by having an attorney speak in Latin phrases and in other legalese will alienate your potential clients, as opposed to making them want to utilize your services.

If you integrate estate planning into a financial-planning seminar, I suggest that you talk about such issues as legal domicile, how to avoid probate, the advantages of living trusts, and how to avoid federal estate taxes through properly planned trusts and use of the unified credit exemption. Other topics that are of interest are the disadvantages of jointly held property and the use of generation-skipping transfers.

Because it is a critical aspect of comprehensive financial planning, estate planning must be a major concern for financial planners. Although it is necessary for planners to understand what estate planning actually entails, no one is more qualified to consult with than an attorney who specializes in such matters. Financial planners must remember that the practice of law without a license in most states is a serious offense. Planners must realize that working with an estate-planning professional is essential.

"The most frustrating thing for a financial planner or client is the delay that is usually involved in the loan approval process."

—MICHAEL J. BOBAL, JR.

Understanding Banks and Selecting the Right Banker

Michael J. Bobal, Jr. is Vice President and Treasurer of Central Bank, Hollidaysburg, Pennsylvania. In addition, he is an instructor at Saint Francis College, Loretto, Pennsylvania. Mike holds a B.S. degree in business management from Indiana University of Pennsylvania. He is also a graduate from the Bank Administrations School of Banking at the University of Wisconsin. Mike is presently enrolled in the Certified Financial Planners Program and is a member of the International Association for Financial Planning.

The process of selecting a bank and banker should be given the same considerations as when one is selecting another professional to perform joint planning. The attributes of both the bank and banker should mesh with your firm. A relationship with a financial institution should be based not only on services, but also on client base and personality traits. The ideal institution should complement your firm and strengthen the relationships between you and your clients, not destroy them. In the following paragraphs I will outline some of the attributes and services that should be reviewed when one is selecting the appropriate person and institution for this relationship. However, before anyone can endeavor to establish such a relationship, you must first understand what makes a bank and banker tick.

To understand a financial institution, you must first realize that it is quite common for banks to view financial planners, stockbrokers, and other financial service companies as adversaries. This view stems from the perception that these companies are encroaching on our deposit and loan business. Deregulation of the banking industry is slowly eliminating this barrier by enabling banks to increase their services, financial planning, etc. Now that financial institutions are able to offer financial planning services, we are viewed as potential competition for established planning practices. While banks may lack the experienced personnel, they do, however, have two important aspects. Those aspects are an established client base and the public's perception of a bank as being trustworthy.

While this situation is considered by most to generate an adversary relationship, I feel that the time could not be better for a financial planning firm to establish a working relationship with an institution. In order to break this barrier, you, the planner, will have to make the institution comfortable knowing that your services will complement those of the banks and not detract from their services and their client base. The easiest way to make a banker comfortable is to take the time to learn the bank's products and policies. Make it known to him that the reason for learning their products and services is to enable you to discuss them intelligently with your clients. Make it apparent that you will be recommending their institution to your clients. Relationships that I have experienced in the past have broken down in this area and have turned out to be one-sided.

A bank's most valuable product is its lending programs. Loans are important to an institution because of their yields. These yields are higher than those available from alternative investments. Loans, therefore, have the greatest impact on the bank's net income. Because of this situation, banks place a high priority on developing loan relationships. Quite often a commercial loan officer's bonus or compensation is based on new loans generated. The easiest way, then, to break this barrier is to refer your clients to this institution for loan services.

In looking for general attributes of a financial institution or banker, the most important aspect is the management style. Are the real power and decisions made by a centralized group, or are the respective departments or officers able to operate with some authority? This decentralized authority is very important when one is dealing with the lending function.

The most frustrating thing for a financial planner or client is the delay that is usually involved in the loan approval process. The easiest way to ascertain what type of management style is being utilized in this area is to ask the bank officer exactly what his lending limits are. Most institutions and officers are reluctant to make this information known, so you may have to obtain it in a roundabout way. This should, however, be one of your main concerns. The last thing you want is to establish a relationship with a banker who has a lending limit that can not meet the needs of your clients.

Ultimately, you will be dealing with client loan requests that exceed the individual's lending limit. This brings up the second aspect to be ascertained in the lending area, which is actual turnaround time. This is the actual time that it would take for a loan to be processed from start to approval by committee and for the documents to be prepared and signed.

The size of an institution doesn't seem to have an effect on turnaround time for a loan request. I have been involved with large institutions whose size would encourage you to assume that getting through the red tape would be longer, but this has not been the case.

Another area within the institution's and officer's management style are their actual personalities. Are the institution and its officers aggressive and creative, and are they willing to go the extra mile to solve your client's problems and requests? Aggressiveness and creativity will spill over into their products and services. The more aggressive and creative institutions tend to be market leaders when it comes to developing new products and services.

The actual size of an institution should have little to do with the selection process. I have been involved with several institutions, both large and small, and a general summary is not possible. The only time that size would be involved is in the event you are dealing with clients' loan requests that would exceed the institution's legal lending limit. The legal lending limit is a percentage of the bank's capital accounts.

SERVICES

The following paragraphs contain a brief discussion on the more recent services offered by banks. The main topic of the discussion centers on services other than the typical loan and deposit accounts.

There is a rule of thumb in the banking industry that states, ''Twenty percent of a bank's customers account for 80 percent of its deposit dollars.'' The first service that I would like to outline has been developed to maintain control of this 20 percent customer base.

''Select or private banking,'' as it is called, has been gaining notoriety in the banking industry. Select banking is exactly as its name states—it is a group of services offered to a select few. These individuals are in the ''20 percent base'' and are often considered super-earners. The main goal of this area is to coordinate the needs of the client throughout the institution.

The client is assigned a person who acts as his private banker. This person is the customer's designated contact officer at the institution. The private banker gets involved in every aspect of the client's relationship, ranging from loan requests to the various deposit activities. The banker is involved in both the client's personal and business relationships.

The services offered by this department have been increasing to include other nontraditional services, such as investment management. The real benefit of this department, from a financial planner's perspective, is not necessarily the services being offered, but that the individuals within the department are able to eliminate much of the time involved in processing a client's request. You will see an increase in these types of services being offered in order to maintain the ''20 percent client base'' as pressure from competition is continually being placed on the institution's customer base.

The following services are a few offered by a typical trust department.

Trust departments can be very valuable to a financial planning practice. They are willing to get involved with the client as little or as much as requested. The real benefit of these departments is that they are willing to perform the required administrative and record-keeping responsibilities without being involved in the actual planning or in acting in the investment advisory capacity.

The services outlined below are a few offered by trust departments.

Living Trusts

The living trust area, specifically the revocable trust, is being utilized more extensively as an investment management vehicle during a client's lifetime and not just after death. The institution is involved in the administrative details of the trust and in the investment advisory capacity as requested. The client or planner can exercise control over the investment decisions as well as disbursements of the income and principal of the trust, while avoiding the administrative details.

Custodial Services

Placement of requested investment transactions can be accomplished through the trading department. Statements are provided detailing transactions, and a consolidated statement is prepared with the information needed to complete the client's tax return. Actual custody of the securities and other documents is provided. The client or planner is also notified of any events affecting his holdings, such as stock splits.

Investment Advisory Services

In addition to the custodial services offered, a client can receive investment recommendations as well as investment and portfolio analysis. The institution is also willing to take full investment responsibility on either an extended or temporary basis. An agency agreement is utilized in establishing this relationship.

The following two services are important to a financial planning practice that frequently deals with business in the cash management area. The first service is what is typically called "zero balance checking."

Zero Balance Checking

The business client maintains one parent deposit account that is utilized as a sweep account. In addition to the parent account, several affiliate accounts are established whose purpose may range from payroll to accounts payable. Throughout the business day, entries are made to the affiliate accounts for both deposits and withdrawals. At the close of business, all accounts are automatically reviewed, and funds are either withdrawn from or deposited to the parent account in order to maintain a zero balance at the affiliate account level. A report is generated daily detailing the activity in both the parent and affiliate accounts.

The real benefit from this type of account, in addition to automatic transfer of funds and daily reporting of the company's cash picture, is that it increases the funds available for investment on a daily basis.

The second service dealing with business relationships is what is referred to as an "account analysis."

Account Analysis

This is a statement provided to the client that identifies the average collected balance of the client's deposit account in addition to services utilized and the fees associated with the services. The client is given an earnings credit based on his average deposit balance, which is used to offset charges incurred on the various services used. This statement contains a caption termed "balances available for additional services." The amount on this line can be either positive or negative. In the event that it is positive, it is a signal that a weakness may exist in the client's cash management process and that funds are available for other investments. On the other hand, if the number is negative, it is a clear sign to the institution that compensating balances aren't sufficient to offset the charges and that a monetary fee may be appropriate.

I have attempted to give a brief outline as to what to look for in a bank or banker and their services. There are considerable intangibles involved in selecting a bank that can't be described in a few paragraphs. However, there is one main question to ask yourself when attempting to establish this relationship, "Do the bank, banker, and their services complement my planning practice?" The last thing to remember when you are maintaining this relationship is to learn the bank's services and make it known that your clients will be referred to his or her institution. The banker in turn will refer clients to you, and the relationship will be a long-lasting one.

"You look for the professional who provides three things: service, service, and service! Service is comprehensive risk management, insightful questions, and good advice on products."

—*NEIL ROSS, CFP*

How to Secure the Right Property and Liability Coverage (and Broker or Agent)

Neil Ross has been involved as a fiduciary in the financial services profession since 1966 as a registered representative and as a licensed real estate salesperson. Currently, Mr. Ross is a licensed insurance broker and owner of the Neil Ross Insurance Agency, a general insurance agency offering all forms of insurance. He is a licensed real estate salesperson in Colorado, holds an NASD license, and is a Registered Investment Advisor with the Securities and Exchange Commission.

Mr. Ross received a bachelor of arts degree from Franklin and Marshall College in Lancaster, Pennsylvania, in 1966 and holds a Certified Financial Planner designation, which he received in 1981. He is a member of the Institute of Certified Financial Planners and the International Association for Financial Planning.

When we try to search out the mysteries of life, do we seek the chicken or egg first? When we want to find the appropriate insurance coverages for our property and liability exposures, do we research the kinds of coverage we think we should have, or do we seek out the broker or agent first?

If you are a neophyte in the insurance marketplace or even if you have some experience, the insurance professional with whom you deal can save you valuable premium dollars and, more importantly, provide the correct advice and/or products for your property and liability risk management needs. Please note that I refer to the areas as risk management; from the largest company to the individual household, the need to address this subject is only a matter of degree. Insurance purchased from a risk pool or insurance carrier is one way to approach the management of risk. We must assume that all insurance is by the nature of the relationship a waste of money (save for cash value life insurance, which should only be purchased with the anticipation of being used in one of two productive ways—estate liquidity during your lifetime or estate liquidity at your death), a darned if you do, darned if you don't proposition, a Catch 22 if you like. I can't afford to walk around without insurance but, well, I really don't want to use it. Some unpleasant, distasteful event in my life will have precipitated the need to use the insurance—my car was stolen, the house caught on fire, my kid bit the neighbor's dog, and so on.

What other actions can we take to address risk? First and most common is risk retention or self-insurance. We can do this by assuming the whole risk as we would if we did not purchase comprehensive or collision insurance on our automobile policy. With finite, limited (this being relative to each person's financial capabilities) loss, this form of retention is sometimes prudent; always judge this action in the context of your historical experience. Ask yourself questions like: How many automobile accidents have I been in during my life? What kind of target is my car statistically for theft? What kind of crime area do I live in?

A second form of risk retention revolves around the use of deductibles. The higher the deductible, the lower the insurance cost. You must ask what are the savings attributed to each of these various options you could choose relative to the dollar loss at risk.

The next way to address risk is through safety precautions and/or security measures. By way of example, let's take three different sets of circumstances for your home or office. You live in a small community with little crime, so you begrudgingly put a door on your residence or place of work. Friends from your younger days live and work in Suburbia, U.S.A.; they not only have the doors but, as prudent people, have the proper locks. The third set of circumstances brings us to a high-crime urban area, where they need not only the doors, but locks, bars, and alarms as well. Each of us has a home and a place of work. Each of us, however, manages that risk differently.

To avoid a malpractice suit a surgeon scrubs down before an operation to avoid the risk of infection. You, the general contractor, require your employees to take the safety precautions of wearing hard hats and steel-toed shoes, and so on.

Be very careful in analyzing this finite versus infinite (the size of the loss cannot be fixed with any reasonable certainty) exposure. The infinite exposure poses the most difficult question to answer and manage and is by far the most important aspect of the risk management process.

Now that we have reviewed different ways to manage risk, let's direct our attention to the commercial insurance carrier/risk pool representative, the insurance broker, and the agent. What is the difference—in theory, that is—

between the broker and the agent? The former will usually work with and represent a number of different companies, while the latter will usually work with and represent only one or a limited number of companies. Who is the best for you? If you believe Raymond Burr in the ads you have seen over the past several years, not only is the broker the most impartial professional for the task, but the members of the Independent Insurance Agents of America® fill the bill the best. Maybe yes and maybe no? With any label or any profession, as long as you know the kind of individual you are dealing with in terms of professional expertise, integrity, and honesty, you can find sound advice on either side of the fence. There is an inherent conflict of interest with *any* licensed insurance representative (broker or agent). They generate their living from commissions received in selling a product, not giving advice. You should understand that the agent who probably deals with one company, such as a direct writer like American Family Mutual or State Farm, will be limited to one or a few resources for those insurance needs. You, the financial planner, should note how agents initiate and direct the interviews. Do they say, in effect, "This is the coverage and this is the cost." or "What exactly do you need and how can I assist?" Does the agent ever recommend a product or company he or she does not represent because it's the best for your set of circumstances? If you find the second scenario, you have probably found a very trustworthy agent to whom you should always turn for your clients.

Similarly, with brokers do you have a broker who always has the right product at the right price, or a broker who has the right questions about your client's needs? Establish an easily manageable network of two to four property and liability resources and always, *always* compare products and cost. It is simple; with the proper coaching (from those two to four advisors), you can refine this process for you or your staff to a very short, cost-efficient and effective task. I caution you to compare products; although insurance regulation in each state creates a certain amount of standardization and more similarities than dissimilarities in comparable products from one company to another, it is those dissimilarities which become important to your clients. Ferret out those dissimilarities which may make a big difference.

Not only have we, the counseling public, been under the misconception of the benefits of the broker-agent advantage, but also we have been misled to believe that once we establish a relationship we must be loyal and have all our insurance with one licensed individual. Wrong! It is most assuredly not necessarily in your clients' best interests to put all their insurance coverages with one firm. Surely, there are sometimes discounts for multiple policies, but do you ask what is the premium basis from which you are discounting and what type of product are you getting? You must understand that the insurance industry has been fostering this misconception, because vertical selling is very profitable to those insurance companies. The one exception to this rule of thumb is where convenience, marginal cost differences, and superior professional expertise and integrity are exhibited. This does happen from time to time; however, more common is the ability to find different companies for specific needs or groups of needs.

What do you look for in the chicken/egg debate? You look for the professional who provides three things: Service, service, and service! First, service is comprehensive risk management, insightful questions, and good advice on products (generic) and appropriate and inappropriate insurance. We've all heard of being insurance-poor. Do I have an advisor or a salesperson in this relationship? Pick the former. Second, service is the friendly, efficient way in which the professional and his or her staff attend to your questions and changing insurance needs. Do they review periodically to make sure those needs are in tune with potentially changing circumstances? Last, service is the way in which your professional's organization gets down to the nitty gritty, mundane, boring job of accurately doing the paper work and administration of your account. If you can find this service triad, you're one step closer to achieving the best risk management for your clients.

Since property and liability insurance encompasses a broad spectrum in the marketplace, I will give you some guidelines and buzz words that will initially simplify the process for you. For purposes of this discussion, property insurance is that area of insurance covering risk and potential loss to your personal (portable) or real (appurtenant to the land) property. Liability insurance, sometimes referred to as third-party insurance, indemnifies you against claims arising out of possible loss due to bodily injury or property damage of a third party (a party not incidental to the insurance contract between the insurer and the insured).

How do you investigate the proper property and liability insurance to cover the wide range of risks listed on the exhibit pages (pp. 355–56)? A word for patience. When you first start this comparison process, it will take a lot more time than after you have several clients and added experience. It gets much easier. Although property and liability coverages are separate forms of insurance, you can find most forms of insurance on automobiles, real and personal property, and businesses in comprehensive packages (a combination of property and liability insurance). The likelihood is that if the exposures can be covered in one policy, the coverages will be broader and the cost less.

Let's take a look at the most common forms of insurance packages. Again, a word of caution. In our litigious society people have become paranoid about potential, albeit remote, catastrophic loss. I do not advise people to buy insurance simply because of this environment. What are the exposures, and what is the potential loss that cannot be handled without insurance? You can advise a client to become insurance-poor. Do you advise clients to buy a $10,000,000 personal umbrella policy when a $1,000,000 to $3,000,000 policy is sufficient for their set of circumstances?

The automobile policy you and your client should look for is the personal or family auto policy (PAP or FAP). This contract can include liability, medical and/or no-fault insurance (personal injury protection), uninsured and underinsured motorists, physical loss to your vehicle (comprehensive and collision), and other miscellaneous optional coverages like emergency road service, rental reimbursement, communication devices, and death and dismemberment. Liability limits should provide enough coverage to protect your client's assets in case of a loss. You need insure only up to a sufficient underlying limit if you carry an umbrella policy for catastrophic loss; you need not overlap liability coverages. Medical coverages are customarily purchased in non-no-fault states and sometimes as supplements in no-fault states. No-fault insurance or personal injury protection coverage varies from state to state but usually covers medical costs, lost wages, and a death benefit for you and your passengers, no matter whose fault the accident is. Liability and no-fault are mandatory in most states. The uninsured motorist and underinsured motorist are often overlooked coverages which should be carried in limits compatible to your client's liability needs. The costs for the UM and UIM are usually nominal relative to the potential recovery.

The commercial auto/vehicle policy is written on the basic form or newer basic auto policy (BAP), both of which are usually more limited than the PAP or FAP. Care should be given to hired and borrowed auto coverage and nonowned coverages on business policies.

For simplification of this discussion, we will divide property insurance into real and personal. When you need insurance in both areas, the package concept will almost always apply.

A key buzz word when one is looking at real property coverage is a "named exclusion" policy. This coverage rather than a "named peril" policy is always more desirable. In the first case your property is covered for risks of accidental direct physical loss unless specifically excluded, whereas the latter covers risks of accidental physical loss caused by specific perils. Try to secure named exclusion coverage on real property. In most cases you will be able to secure named perils only on personal property. Scheduling and inland marine contracts sometimes afford named exclusion coverage. Have your insurance representative supply you with a list of the exclusions and perils in both contracts and spend some time explaining each contract to you. In conjunction with so many property policies you will find the liability coverage packaged with the property coverage. Labels used by several insurance companies that you will find in the more complete packages, both personal and business, are "special form," "all risk," "deluxe form," "extra," "special deluxe," and "comprehensive." Even with the use of these labels, it is still most important that the broader contract be offered for your client (ask the insurance representative).

Here are a few more helpful hints with property insurance that are often abused in this country. First and foremost is the practice of insuring property for its full appraised or market value. The market value takes into account both the value of the improvements and the value of the land. As a consumer and for insurance purposes you are concerned only with the replacement cost of those improvements. Let me give you an example. You purchase a home or a small office building for $300,000. In each case the replacement cost of the improvement is $150,000 and the value of the land is also $150,000. Your liberal lender in today's market decides to give you an 80 percent loan to value (LTV) mortgage, or $240,000, and proceeds to tell you to purchase $240,000 of hazard insurance. Why? In almost every state in this country the insurer would be obligated to pay for only the replacement cost of the improvement, or $150,000. You would have been paying insurance premiums for which you will never be able to collect. Let your lender know that they have lent you $90,000 of the $240,000 secured by the land. I recently insured a home for a new owner in my area for $500,000. The previous owner's broker was insuring the same structure for over $800,000 (the appraised value). This brings us to two more points. On both real and personal property, you should try to secure guaranteed replacement cost or replacement cost as opposed to actual cash value (ACV). The more desirable coverage takes into account your original cost plus appreciation to replace the property. The second, ACV, pays only for the original cost minus depreciation. If you live in an area where older properties were built with labor-intensive costs, you should be aware that the market value could be below the reproduction cost of the improvement. The major point here is to make sure that your property insurance insures the current reproduction value of your property, neither more nor less.

What are the implications to you, the financial planner, of allying yourself with an insurance representative who is less than thorough? I can only recommend that you inquire of legal counsel in your area the precedents in your jurisdiction of such association where poor or incomplete services occur. More importantly, as a professional, how would you feel if a client you referred to an insurance representative were to experience a large loss not covered or only partially covered because of a poor risk management relationship? Your own professional standards will make it easy for you to search out compatible insurance support to your practice.

In summation, how do you as a financial planning professional want to relate with an insurance professional? The person who solicits you with a desire to identify, analyze, and review your client's risk management needs without mention of specific products is the true professional you need. The insurance product is only the by-product of a thoughtful, comprehensive risk management planning process.

Look for the chickens first and make sure that they don't lay any eggs.

EXHIBITS

The listings below are not intended to be all-encompassing but rather to give the reader an idea of the scope of risks we are faced with.

Personal Property for Individuals

Automobiles
Clothes
Household goods
Artwork
Jewelry
Coins, precious metals
Sporting equipment
Boats and related property
Aviation
Recreation vehicles
Collectibles
Cameras
Personal tools
Insurable interest in a residential tenancy

Personal Property for Businesses

Automobiles
Furniture
Fixtures
Equipment
Inventory
Materials
Supplies
Tools

Real Property for Individuals

Detached single-family primary residence or second home
Condominium or cooperative unit as primary residence or second home
Single-family rental property (detached, condominium, cooperative)
Multifamily rental property
Apartment building
Office building
Mercantile building
Industrial or manufacturing building
Farm or ranch property
Unimproved land

Real Property for Businesses

Single-family rental
Multifamily rental
Apartment building
Office building
Mercantile building
Industrial or manufacturing building
Farm or ranch
Cooperative complex
Condominium complex
Undeveloped land

Liability Exposures for the Individual

Assault or battery
Automobile
Breach of contract
Comprehensive personal liability
False arrest
Fraud
Libel
Slander
Trespass
Voluntary medical payments

Liability Exposures for the Business

Automobile
Business contracts
Comprehensive general liability
Contractual hazard
Directors and officers
Employers
Errors and omissions
Libel
Slander
Malpractice
Manufacturers and contractors
Nonownership
Products and completed operations
Voluntary medical payments

Chapter VIII

Professional Organizations

Alexandra Armstrong, CFP
Larry D. Hayden, CFP
Dianna Rampy
Ronald P. Meier, CPA
Paul Richard

"I can say unequivocally that it had been a worth-while experience and one that contributed greatly to the development of my career and practice."

—ALEXANDRA ARMSTRONG, CFP

The Value of Giving Your Time to Financial Planning and Other Related Organizations

Alexandra Armstrong, CFP, is President of Alexandra Armstrong Advisors, Inc. and Chairman of Alexandra Armstrong Associates, Inc. She received her B.A. in 1960 from the Newton College of the Sacred Heart. In 1977, she was the first financial planner to achieve certification in Washington, D.C., and in 1984, Ms. Armstrong became the first to be admitted to the Registry of Financial Planning in Washington, D.C.

Ms. Armstrong has appeared in many industry publications, has been quoted in numerous magazines and newspapers, and has appeared on national television including "Good Morning America" and "Wall Street Week." She was selected by *Money Magazine* as one of the seven outstanding financial planners in the United States and was featured on the cover of *Changing Times*. In 1986, the *Executive Financial Woman* designated her one of the 25 most successful women in the financial services industry.

In addition to her professional achievements, Ms. Armstrong has received many awards including Washington D.C.'s "Business Woman of the Year" award. She has served as national President and Chairman of the IAFP.

Since 1987, I have served as President of the International Association for Financial Planning, a 24,000-member organization, so I may not be exactly objective about the value of giving your time to financial planning organizations. On the other hand, who would be better suited to state objectively whether, in fact, giving this much time is valuable? I can say unequivocally that it has been a worthwhile experience and one that contributed greatly to the development of my career and practice.

I first enrolled in the Certified Financial Planning course in 1976 and attended my first IAFP convention in the same year. At that time, there were about 800 people who attended in Atlanta, Georgia, and it made me realize how important the whole field of financial planning was, which was a new concept to someone who had been a stockbroker for most of her working career.

At the convention, I met some people in my local chapter and immediately became active. At that time, financial planning was in a beginning stage, and we had about 100 people in our local Washington, D.C. chapter. However, it was invaluable to me to attend these meetings to develop my knowledge of financial planning and to meet other people who were doing financial planning—at the time, they were hard to find. As in any other organization, new members are quickly brought into the main stream, and the IAFP was no exception. I became program chairman and the year following was elected president. The friends I made within the organization at that time and since then have been a real support to me when I needed answers.

The real benefit of being a member of the IAFP is that it is a cross section of people involved in financial planning, not just individual financial planners. So I was able to find accountants, attorneys, and insurance specialists to work with when developing my financial planning practice. Some people would say, "Would you not be spending time more productively if you were joining other civic organizations, where you could meet potential clients?" That is important, too; however, I have found that developing relationships with my peers in the field helped me when a client asked whether someone knew me or not. If I had not been active in the IAFP, he or she would not have known of me. Presumably, if I had done a good job on the chapter officer level, then it would appear that I might also do well as a financial planner.

To derive full benefit from your membership, I think it is important that you not only become a member of an organization but that you work for the organization. Certainly, one of the ways you can do that is by being an officer. It does take time, but if you find other people who are like-minded, you can spread the responsibility and get the job done. In addition, practical continuing education is the cornerstone of our profession, and the IAFP meetings provide an opportunity to become better educated on an ongoing basis, which is essential to us.

I have noted that past presidents of our chapter have remained active and continue to contribute to the growth of financial planning. They would not do that if they did not feel it was beneficial and helpful to themselves as well as to the industry.

You can also get this knowledge by attending the IAFP national conventions, whether it be the annual convention, the practice management, advanced planners, or the international trip. At these meetings, not only do you attend seminars where you learn, but even more valuable is meeting and talking with peers throughout the country and exchanging information with them.

I am also a member of the ICFP and have regularly attended their retreats, which offer another opportunity for exchanging information and ideas. I will no longer be a National Board member in October 1987. To answer the question of whether I will still remain active, I certainly will. It will allow me to be more active in the local chapter once again.

I think participation in your local chapter is essential to making and keeping you ahead of your competitors in the financial planning industry. The field we are in changes too rapidly. It is important to keep your information current by attending chapter educational sessions as well as by reading *Financial Planning* magazine, available to IAFP members.

The IAFP has developed a new section which I think will be particularly valuable to me as a member, and that is the broker-dealer division, which is open to all owners of broker-dealers. It is too easy to recreate the wheel. Why not gather together and become stronger broker-dealers, exchanging information about our broker-dealer relationships, as well as our financial planning practices? It is for this reason, as well as a desire to have more of a say with the NASD, that we have developed the broker-dealer section. This is an additional benefit of being a member of the IAFP.

In summary, I can say unequivocally that my experience as an IAFP member has been invaluable to me; in fact, it is responsible for a great deal of what I have been able to achieve professionally.

"It is the IBCFP's desire to bring about public trust and respect for our profession by maintaining high standards of ethical, professional conduct among certified financial planners."

—LARRY D. HAYDEN, CFP

The International Board of Standards and Practices For Certified Financial Planners (IBCFP)

Larry D. Hayden, CFP, is the Executive Director of the International Board of Standards and Practices for Certified Financial Planners (IBCFP). Mr. Hayden has extensive experience within the financial services industry in practice management, administration, and regulation.

Prior to assuming his position with the IBCFP, Mr. Hayden served as President of Hayden Financial Management, Inc., a fee-only financial planning and advisory firm. Previously, he was Executive Vice President and Director of Hanifen, Imhoff Inc.; President, Treasurer, and Director of Westamerica Financial Corp.; and President of REHL Associates. In addition, Mr. Hayden has served as a member of the Board of Governors of the National Association of Securities Dealers (NASD); Assistant District Director of the NASD; member of the Boards of Directors of the Rocky Mountain Better Business Bureau, Pittock Financial Services, E.J. Pittock and Co., Inc., and the Institute of Certified Financial Planners (ICFP). Mr. Hayden is on the Board of Trustees of Continental Heritage Mutual Funds.

Mr. Hayden received his CFP designation in 1982.

According to some estimates, nearly a quarter of a million Americans now call themselves financial planners. They range from brokers who work for large, multimillion-dollar corporations to independent, one-person enterprises. These planners might make their money from commissions, fees, or a combination of the two. For many of them, financial planning is only a small part of their activities and is done in conjunction with specialties in investments, insurance, accounting, or law. Some consider themselves consultants and do not market any specific products.

While the vast majority of these planners are legitimate, their wide variations in education, credentials, and approach have left the public understandably confused over what, exactly, they can expect from a financial planner. This confusion, along with the rapid growth of the industry and the unscrupulous behavior of a few, have led states and the federal government to consider regulating the industry more closely.

In the face of this situation, the International Board of Standards and Practices for Certified Financial Planners, Inc. (IBCFP) advocates a certification program that, I believe, will lead to greater public trust and acceptance of financial planners as professionals.

The IBCFP was formed in 1985 as an independent, nonmembership, certifying organization. Its charge is to maintain and enforce high standards of professional conduct among Certified Financial Planners. A primary objective of the IBCFP is to establish the Certified Financial Planner and CFP marks as industry hallmarks.* By vigorously pursuing this goal, the IBCFP foresees a day in the not-too-distant future when the public will come to expect a professional financial planner to be a Certified Financial Planner also because of the assurances this designation represents in terms of the planner's education, competence, and ethics.

Let me emphasize here that I am *not* saying that a financial planner cannot be competent unless certified by the IBCFP, nor am I saying that other financial planning organizations will no longer have an important role to play. What I am saying, however, is that if financial planners wish to be publicly recognized as professionals, it will be important for them to obtain IBCFP certification.

The certification process will be described later in this article, but essentially, IBCFP certification is public acknowledgment that the planner has fulfilled IBCFP education, experience, and competency requirements and adheres to its Code of Ethics. When certification is granted by the IBCFP, the planner may identify himself or herself as a Certified Financial Planner and may use the marks in accordance with IBCFP guidelines.

With this introduction, let's look at how and why the IBCFP was formed, its current organization and activities, and some of the issues facing the financial planning profession that have particular relevance to the IBCFP.

HISTORY

To better understand the IBCFP's position in the financial planning industry, a historical perspective is helpful.

In the early 1970s, the International Association for Financial Planning (IAFP) helped found the College for Financial Planning in Denver, Colorado.

---

*CFP and Certified Financial Planner are certification marks of the International Board of Standards and Practices for Certified Financial Planners (IBCFP).

Early graduates of the College were required to be members of the IAFP and adhere to the IAFP Code of Ethics. Then, in 1975, graduates became subject to the College's own Code.

In the late 1970s, an upswing in interest in financial planning led to the need for more training and education of planners, and many colleges and universities began to add financial planning courses to their curricula. A number of institutions offered the CFP program to students through formal agreements with the College for Financial Planning.

In 1985, the IBCFP was formed as a nonprofit corporation, and staff came on board in February 1986. The organization's headquarters are in Englewood, Colorado. The College for Financial Planning agreed to provide funding to the IBCFP for a period of five years. During this time period, the IBCFP is expected to become self-supporting, primarily from CFP examination fees.

In June 1986, the IBCFP acquired ownership of the marks CFP and Certified Financial Planner and was authorized to administer the CFP examination that leads to certification. During that year a Code of Ethics and Standards of Practice and Disciplinary Rules and Procedures were adopted. All current CFPs were asked to sign IBCFP declarations, indicating that they met the IBCFP's requirements for certification and subscribed to its Code of Ethics.

ORGANIZATIONAL STRUCTURE

The IBCFP is composed of a board of directors and three subsidiary boards—the Board of Examiners, the Board of Ethics and Standards, and the Appeals Board. The Board of Directors establishes policy and oversees the actions of the subsidiary boards. It is the board's intent to maintain a positive relationship with all industry groups and government agencies.

The Board of Examiners is responsible for developing educational standards for CFPs, establishing testing criteria, and reviewing IBCFP CFP examination procedures. This board is also charged with developing a model financial planning curriculum and reviewing college and university financial planning programs that are submitted to the IBCFP for registration.

The principal function of the Board of Ethics and Standards is to enforce the IBCFP's Code of Ethics by investigating, reviewing, and taking appropriate action for alleged violations of the Code. Complaint action can be initiated by consumers or other financial planners.

Four types of disciplinary action may be taken by the Board of Ethics and Standards: (1) private letter of admonition; (2) private censure; (3) suspension of the right to use the certification marks, not to exceed three years; and (4) permanent revocation of the CFP's right to use the marks.

The Board of Ethics must follow prescribed disciplinary procedures when reviewing complaints to ensure due process, and all decisions are subject to review by the Appeals Board.

IBCFP ACTIVITIES

Essentially, the IBCFP's activities fall into seven categories:

1. to register
2. to test
3. to certify
4. to enforce code of ethics

5. to promote public awareness
6. to cooperate with government agencies
7. to protect the public.

Let's look at what is involved in each of these areas.

Register • All candidates for CFP certification must enroll in a college or university whose financial planning program has been registered with the IBCFP. To be registered, the institution's financial planning curriculum must be submitted to the IBCFP's Board of Examiners for review. In addition, CFP candidates must file a registration form with the IBCFP indicating their intent to become a Certified Financial Planner. (The education requirement is waived for Certified Public Accountants, Chartered Life Underwriters, Chartered Financial Consultants, and attorneys who specialize in tax and/or estate and trust work, provided they fulfill the examination and experience requirements described below.)

Test • Three times a year, the IBCFP administers a six-part CFP examination at more than 200 exam centers around the country. As presently structured the examination covers: introduction to financial planning, risk management, investments, tax planning and management, retirement planning and employee benefits, and estate planning.

Past graduates of educational programs who have since been registered with the IBCFP may "challenge" the CFP examination as a step toward becoming certified. In these situations, the six-part examination is given at one sitting, over a three-day period. This CPF challenge examination is also open to CLUs, ChFCs, CPAs and JDs, as described above.

Certify • When a candidate for certification has passed all six parts of the CFP examination, has signed a declaration form to adhere to the Code of Ethics, and has met the experience requirement set by the Board of Directors (currently three years), the individual is eligible for certification as a Certified Financial Planner. Upon certification, the individual may use the marks CFP and Certified Financial Planner in accordance with IBCFP guidelines. As the owner of the marks, the IBCFP reserves the right both to grant and to revoke the right to use the certification marks.

To keep their certification, CFPs must register annually with the IBCFP and meet continuing education requirements as prescribed by the Board of Directors. Of course, continued adherence to the IBCFP Code of Ethics is likewise required.

Enforce code of ethics • A major objective of the IBCFP is to enforce its Code of Ethics. To do this, the Board of Ethics and Standards is authorized to initiate investigations, file complaints, conduct hearings, and render judgments. Through this process, the credibility of CFPs is enhanced and a higher level of professionalism is achieved.

Promote public awareness • The IBCFP intends to use the media to promote public awareness of the competency and expertise, as well as the limitations, of Certified Financial Planners. By doing this, it is hoped that CFPs will gain widespread public trust and respect.

Cooperate with government agencies • The IBCFP wishes to cooperate with and/or assist state and federal agencies in achieving appropriate, uniform regulation of financial planners. Through aggressive enforcement of the IBCFP code of ethics and the establishment of stringent educational and testing standards, the financial planning profession can develop without cumbersome or duplicative federal and state regulatory constraints.

Protect the public • The IBCFP's overall objective is to protect the public by setting high minimum standards of ethical conduct for the financial planning community. To achieve this goal, the IBCFP will conduct investigations of CFPs as necessary, following prescribed disciplinary procedures. It is the IBCFP's responsibility to maintain the integrity of the marks by preventing their unauthorized use and by monitoring the business practices of CFPs.

Although these activities seem fairly straightforward in scope, they mandate high professional standards and the cooperation of all CFPs. Such cooperative efforts will protect each CFP's investment of time, energy, and money spent in achieving CFP status.

ISSUES IN FINANCIAL PLANNING

Many difficult issues face financial planners today, and several of them have particular significance to the IBCFP. I would like to address three of these issues, namely: (1) defining what a financial planner is (and is not); (2) unifying the profession; and (3) regulating financial planners. Let me explain what I mean by each of these issues.

Defining "financial planner" • The public is justifiably suspicious of the term "financial planner," because as it stands today, anyone can hang out a shingle and call himself or herself a financial planner. In addition, the public knows that professionals in the real estate, insurance, securities, or accounting worlds frequently call themselves financial planners as a way to get their foot in the door. While the majority of these men and women are very competent in their fields, they leave the public with the perception that anyone and everyone can be a financial planner. This perception seriously hinders both our effort to be recognized as professionals in our own right and our effort to help the public realize that the term "financial planner" is more than mere words.

How can this problem be remedied? As a first step, let's take a lesson from other professions. In other words, what have they done to gain recognition by the public as a "profession?" Look, for example, at accountants. The professional designation for an accountant is Certified Public Accountant (CPA). When consumers see this designation behind the accountant's name, they know that this individual has met certain educational requirements, follows prescribed accounting procedures, and has proved competence in the field of accounting. In a sense, the designation defines what an accountant is.

The confidence people feel when they turn to these individuals for advice is what makes them true "professionals." Financial planners need to foster this same feeling of confidence on the part of the public. It seems only logical, then, that one way to engender this confidence is to promote one financial planning designation.

A goal of the IBCFP is to make the public aware that they can, in fact, trust the designations CFP and Certified Financial Planner as indicators that the individuals using these marks meet certain standards. Specifically, a financial planner who is also a Certified Financial Planner has: (1) met certain educational requirements; (2) met certain experience requirements; (3) agreed to participate in continuing education programs; and (4) agreed to abide by a Code of Ethics.

Indeed, the Code of Ethics provides a definition of Certified Financial Planners. According to the code, they are professionals who:

1. Perform services in an honest and forthright manner. This means, for example, that CFPs have agreed to disclose to clients how they are paid, what their areas of expertise are, what their limitations are, and what actual or potential conflicts of interest may exist.

2. Exercise reasonable and prudent professional judgment in the best interests of the client. This means that CFPs are required, to the best of their abilities, to provide objective advice to clients.

3. Keep abreast of developments in the financial planning field and offer advice only in those areas in which they are competent.

4. Perform financial planning services in a lawful, ethical manner in the client's best interests.

5. Maintain the confidentiality of the client's financial affairs, unless required to disclose information as the result of legal action.

6. Conduct themselves in all matters as a "professional."

Unification of the profession • This issue, in a sense, flows out of the one discussed above. How can the public be expected to recognize us as a profession unless we recognize ourselves as members of one profession with one professional designation? I feel that the IBCFP can be a catalyst for unifying financial planners.

Currently, our industry has several organizations, degrees, and designations, and each of them has made an important contribution to the industry. But I would suggest that we are now at a point where we are ready to take a further step toward professionalism by supporting one professional designation.

This does not mean that other groups will cease to exist. The Institute for Certified Financial Planners (ICFP) continues to function as a membership organization that provides continuing education and other services to CFPs. The International Association of Financial Planners (IAFP) has an important role to play as a trade association. The College for Financial Planning, the American College, and other colleges and universities will contribute through their educational programs and degrees in financial planning. But let us recognize Certified Financial Planner as the one designation of financial planning professionals, in the same way that accountants have "CPA" as a publicly recognized designation.

In the future, I would also suggest developing generally accepted financial planning practices so that when a CFP performs an audit of a client's financial affairs, the client is assured that the CFP will follow certain prescribed standards of practice as a bare minimum.

Naturally, this process of unification will require some sacrifices, effort and trade-offs by us all, but if we are to rise to the level of a profession, it is a price we must be willing to pay.

An alternative to government regulation • It is the IBCFP's desire to bring about public trust and respect for our profession by maintaining high standards of ethical, professional conduct among Certified Financial Planners. By doing this, the IBCFP hopes to relieve government of the burden of developing possibly unnecessary or duplicative regulation.

Educating the public as to the proper role of financial planners is another aspect of this issue. Many of those who advocate regulation do not fully understand what is involved in the financial planning process. There are misconceptions about the fiduciary responsibility of a financial planner, how planners are compensated, and what a financial plan should look like. The public needs help in understanding that CFPs may be generalists rather than specialists, and that their education as financial planners has been in learning how to take clients through the process of putting their financial affairs in order. Some financial planners may already have a specialty, of course, but it arises out of other training, or a specific area of interest (such as in securities, insurance, accounting, or law), and not from the Certified Financial Planner curriculum itself.

A definite need exists for financial planning services provided by professionals who are trustworthy and competent. However, government regulation in and of itself will not make a financial planner a better financial planner. The IBCFP certification procedures offer an alternative to strict government oversight. The road ahead is an uncharted one, but with all of our efforts and a sense of understanding, it is sure to lead to the emergence of a valued profession. We will find, too, that a vital, respected financial planning profession serves the financial well-being of all consumers.

"The ICFP works to promote the Certified Financial Planner as the most recognized professional in the financial planning industry. It does this by providing quality educational programming, promotion of the CFP designation, development of public awareness programs, enforcement of rigorous professional standards of integrity, sponsoring the development of financial product standards, and the monitoring and assistance in the preparation of regulatory rules and legislation."

—DIANNA RAMPY

The ICFP: A Mission of Challenge

Dianna Rampy is the former executive director of the Institute of Certified Financial Planners, a national nonprofit professional association based in Denver, Colorado. Rampy joined the Institute in January 1981 after serving seven years as executive director of the Association of Trial Lawyers of Iowa.

During her tenure at the Institute, membership growth increased dramatically from 1200 members in 1981 to the present 11,000. She is credited with the application of many innovative management techniques that assisted in the orderly expansion of services to members during the growth of the Institute.

Rampy attended Iowa State University and has participated in advanced management courses conducted by the American Society of Association Executives and the United States Chamber of Commerce.

As we head towards the last decade of the twentieth century, the need for the services of highly qualified financial planners has never been greater—nor have the challenges to those financial planners.

Consumers, the media, and regulators are confused about what sound financial planning incorporates and what the best vehicles for dispensing financial planning services are. Planners face dramatic competitive growth and an avalanche of new financial products. Virtually everything from the local weather to international terrorism affects the financial well-being of one's clients. And recently we witnessed the most dramatic change in the tax structure in 30 years.

Helping financial planners meet these myriad challenges is the principal mission of the Institute of Certified Financial Planners, a national professional membership association of approximately 11,000 members headquartered in Denver, Colorado.

The Institute was established in 1973 by the conferees of the first graduating class of the College for Financial Planning in Denver. Today, through the efforts of a volunteer board of directors and a full-time staff, the ICFP works to promote the Certified Financial Planner® as *the* most recognized professional in the financial planning industry. It does this by providing quality educational programming, promotion of the CFP designation, development of public awareness programs, enforcement of rigorous professional standards of integrity, sponsoring the development of financial product standards, and monitoring and assistance in the preparation of regulatory rules and legislation.

The Institute and its members share the conviction that a better-educated and more professional financial planner and a better-informed consumer best serve the interests of both parties.

One reason consumers have been confused or wary about financial planning is that while many people claim they are financial planners, many are in fact merely product pushers. They emphasize only insurance or equities or real estate, while ignoring the overall needs of their clients. To become a Certified Financial Planner, however, an individual must study and demonstrate competency in a broad range of disciplines vital to *comprehensive* personal and business financial planning, including insurance, taxes, investments, retirement planning, and estate planning. The curriculum emphasizes the interrelatedness of the financial areas and an objective analysis of a client's circumstances and goals. It emphasizes alternative solutions and periodic review of the plan to ensure that it continues to meet the client's needs.

The ICFP has also coupled with this broad-based background a tough code of ethics which provides comprehensive professional guidelines for its members. It contains a number of safeguards and disclosures designed to protect the public, including review and investigation of complaints from consumers and fellow ICFP members.

EDUCATION

Acutely aware of the complexities and the dynamic landscape of financial services and products, the ICFP considers the continuing education of its members as the ''heartbeat'' of the organization. This is what distinguishes a *certified* financial planner from all other financial planners. If one does not study to stay current with new industry and product developments, how can one provide quality service to one's clients?

To meet ICFP requirements, each member can obtain credits by attending the Institute's national and regional meetings, including the annual retreat and annual conference. The Institute recently launched an annual residency program for planners seeking to expand their educational horizons. And one can earn credits through continuing education events at societies, which, in essence, are local networks of Institute members. Beyond the immediate value of educational information, these conferences and local groups are excellent opportunities to share ideas and experiences with fellow planners, and to brainstorm the issues and challenges that affect one's practice. The societies are especially designed for this and to provide a local voice for financial planners.

In addition, the ICFP keeps its members informed and educated through a monthly newsletter, *Newsworthy,* and its much praised quarterly *Journal,* a technical publication unique in the industry for its emphasis on innovative, timely, and constructive concepts, theories, and professional management tools. In addition, case studies drawn from Institute meetings and seminars can be ordered to provide the planner with in-depth examples of how to advise a widow or a high-profile athlete, planning for one-time inheritances, and many other topics.

As do consumers, many financial planners find that sorting out the proliferation and diversity of new financial products is a complex and time-consuming task. Which ones are wise investments, and which are merely gimmicks? In response to the growth of products, the ICFP established, in 1983, the Financial Products Standards Board (FPSB). The Board, through task forces composed of financial planners, attorneys, accountants, and independent industry experts, develops and publishes standards in such broad areas as real estate, oil and gas, and mutual funds. The Board does not judge the merits of specific investments, but provides standards by which financial planners and the public can judge investment products as to their quality, risk, and appropriateness in meeting individual goals and objectives. These benchmarks are not intended as another form of industry regulation, but as a public service that will serve as an educational tool for financial managers, other related professionals, and the investing public, as well as assist in upgrading the quality of future investment products.

MEMBERSHIP SERVICES

The Institute of Certified Financial Planners provides a wide variety of services for its members. Its national referral service links consumers seeking financial advice to CFPs in their specific locales. In 1986 alone, the Institute handled 35,000 referral requests. Qualified members may participate in a cost-effective national cooperative advertising program which advertises members in national publications such as *Money* and *Changing Times.* Another cooperative effort to promote individual members and the CFP designation is the Yellow Pages program. The Institute can also provide camera-ready advertising slicks for individual CFP advertising.

Of critical concern to all financial planners, CFPs and non-CFPs alike, is the future direction of regulation of the financial planning profession. The Institute is working actively with state and federal agencies to ensure that such regulations will not only protect the public's interests, but will enhance the public's perception of this still young profession. The ICFP believes that the core of any financial planning regulatory initiative should be the enforcement and preservation of a "delicate fiduciary relationship between planner and client" that prevents the planner from taking unfair advantage of a client's trust. Consequently, the ICFP believes that anyone holding himself or herself out as a "financial planner" should register under the federal and state investment advisers laws. Mandatory registration should be coupled with full disclosure of a planner's background and conflicts of interest, strong penalties for noncompliance, and rigorous enforcement through federal, state, and interstate cooperation.

INFORMING THE CONSUMER

Misconceptions, lack of information, and lack of consumer motivation have hampered the financial planning industry since its inception. To foster a better understanding of financial planning and of who the qualified professionals are, the Institute is conducting an ambitious public awareness program through the grassroots and national media. CFP members have been quoted in or have written for such publications as *The Wall Street Journal, The New York Times, Christian Science Monitor, Sylvia Porter's Personal Finance, Money,* and the *American Bar Association Journal.* ICFP members and staff have also appeared frequently on local and national television and radio programs.

A VOICE

The benefits derived from personal financial planning—tangible and intangible—are many: determining and setting priorities, developing and setting in motion specific strategies for those priorities, planning for the unplanned. But those benefits can easily be lost in today's complex and fast-changing world if there is not careful structuring and consistent tending of a financial plan. For that, more and more people are turning to the financial professionals for answers and guidance. That those professionals are the best qualified, the most informed, and the most objective is the ultimate mission of the Institute of Certified Financial Planners.

"It was necessary to create a separate organization consisting solely of financial advisors compensated by fees, so that the consumer of financial planning services could more easily identify and contact financial advisors who did not have the conflicts of interest inherent in the other methods of compensation."

—RONALD P. MEIER, CPA

The National Association of Personal Financial Advisors

Ronald P. Meier, CPA, is president of the National Association of Personal Financial Advisors (NAPFA) for the 1987–1988 year. With over seventeen years' experience in the financial services industry, he has been a stockbroker with Dean Witter & Company, a CPA with Peat, Marwick, Mitchell & Company, and a banker with Republic Bank-Houston. Currently he is a personal financial advisor.

Mr. Meier is the author and instructor of personal financial planning courses for the Texas Society of Certified Public Accountants. He is the founder and editor in chief of a monthly newsletter entitled "The CPA Financial Planner" and coauthor of the two-volume *Guide to Personal Financial Planning,* published by Practitioners Publishing Company. He is a member of the International Association for Financial Planning, the Texas Society of CPAs, and the Colorado Society of CPAs.

The National Association of Personal Financial Advisors (NAPFA) was formed in 1983. In early 1987, the association had approximately 175 members.

NAPFA is an association of personal financial advisors. In that respect, it is similar to the International Association for Financial Planning (IAFP) and the Institute of Certified Financial Planners (ICFP). Many members of NAPFA are also members of the IAFP and/or the ICFP. What distinguishes NAPFA from these other two financial planning organizations is its members' method of compensation.

NAPFA members are compensated for their personal financial planning services solely by fees paid to them by their clients. NAPFA members are prohibited from receiving compensation in the form of commissions or as a consequence of the purchase of financial or investment products by their clients.

Most financial planners are compensated by commissions or by a combination of fees and commissions. The founders of NAPFA felt that financial advisors who are compensated, partially or wholly, by commissions cannot maintain their independence and objectivity with respect to financial and investment planning recommendations made to their clients. They felt that it was necessary to create a separate organization consisting solely of financial advisors compensated by fees, so that the consumer of financial-planning services could more easily identify and contact financial advisors who did not have the conflicts of interest inherent in the other methods of compensation.

NAPFA has two categories of membership—members and associates.

Associates are fee-only financial advisors who offer comprehensive personal financial planning services to their clients. They must certify on their applications that, in conjunction with these services offered to clients, they do not receive, directly or indirectly, any economic benefit from the purchase of financial or investment products by their clients.

Members must meet the same requirements, stated above, as associates. Additionally, members must have practiced, for at least two years, as fee-only personal financial advisors; must have a CFP, ChFC, or CPA professional designation or a baccalaureate or graduate degree from an accredited institution with a major in personal financial planning, accounting, law, taxation, or a business-related field. They must agree to complete 30 hours per year of continuing professional education in areas related to personal financial planning. And, they must submit to the NAPFA membership committee an actual, blind copy of a written comprehensive financial plan prepared for a client.

NAPFA members offer clients the following benefits:

1. Independence, objectivity, and lack of conflicts of interest in the providing of financial- and investment-planning advice.
2. No-load and low-load investment products to implement financial-planning decisions.
3. Loyalty to the client as fiduciaries, rather than loyalty to product suppliers, as agents, in the delivery of investment products to the client.

NAPFA strives to help its members become more effective as fee-only personal financial advisors:

1. By informing the public about the existence of fee-only personal financial advisors.

2. By providing networking opportunities for its members, so that members can help each other grow.

3. By providing information to members about available no-load and low-load investment products.

4. By helping its members represent, collectively, a substantial amount of buying power to attract the interest of suppliers of no-load and low-load investment products.

NAPFA also helps its members improve upon their abilities to serve their clients by providing educational opportunities throughout the year.

An annual national conference is held in May or June of each year for three to four days. Formal regional conferences are held at least once in each of NAPFA's five regions between September and March of each year. Informal conferences, retreats, and meetings are held on a local or regional basis periodically throughout the year.

Formal national and regional NAPFA conferences feature nationally prominent speakers on financial and investment planning topics, "how-to" workshops by successful fee-only financial advisors, and product presentations by providers of no-load and low-load investment and insurance products. Resource-sharing by members is also an important aspect of the formal conferences. All members attending these conferences are encouraged to bring practice management, marketing, and other resource tools that they use in their practices to the conferences. Round-table meetings are then used as a format for members to share these resources with each other.

Members and associates also receive a monthly networking newsletter that is 10 to 20 pages in length. The monthly newsletter is specifically designed to help NAPFA members share resources and ideas with each other on a frequent basis. Individual members share their successful practice management and marketing ideas through the newsletter; they inform other members of computer templates that they use and offer to share these templates with other members; and they offer to share specific investment product ideas with other members.

NAPFA has an active publicity committee that maintains contacts with members of the media to promote the ideals of fee-only planning. Each year since its formation NAPFA has received an increasing amount of local and national publicity from the media. NAPFA members have been increasingly called upon by members of the media as experts for the development of articles on financial-planning topics.

This publicity has resulted in an increase each year in the number of requests from consumers for information about fee-only planning and about fee-only planners. Consumers requesting information from NAPFA are provided with literature about fee-only planning and are given the names of fee-only planners within their states whom they can contact for further information. The NAPFA referral system provides members opportunities for obtaining new clients as a consequence of their affiliation with NAPFA.

NAPFA has also developed a "financial planner disclosure form" to help prospective consumers of financial planning services understand the conflicts of interest that may exist in the person or firm they are considering to help them with their personal financial planning needs. NAPFA asks consumers to send $1.00 with their request for a copy of the financial planner disclosure form. A copy of this form is reproduced at the end of this article.

NAPFA is also building a resource library for its membership. The resource library will include information on investment newsletters, on no-load and low-load investment and insurance products, on computer templates developed by

FINANCIAL PLANNER DISCLOSURE FORM

1. Does your financial planning service include:
   - ☐ A review of my goals.
   - ☐ Advice on:
     - ☐ Cash management and budgeting
     - ☐ Tax planning
     - ☐ Investment review and planning
     - ☐ Retirement planning
     - ☐ Estate planning
     - ☐ Insurance needs:
       - ☐ Life insurance
       - ☐ Disability insurance
       - ☐ Property/Casualty insurance
       - ☐ Other: _____
     - ☐ Other areas: _____

2. Do you provide a written analysis of my financial situation and your recommendations?
   ☐ YES   ☐ NO

3. How is your firm compensated for the financial planning services you provide:
   - ☐ Fees only (flat fee or hourly rate)
   - ☐ Commissions only (from securities, insurance, etc. that I might buy from your firm.)
   - ☐ Fees and commissions

4. If you charge a fee, what is it based on?
   - ☐ An hourly rate of $ _____
   - ☐ A percentage based on _____
   - ☐ A flat fee based on _____

5. Is your firm registered with the Securities and Exchange Commission?
   ☐ YES   ☐ NO

6. If "fee only", is your firm affiliated with a broker/dealer?
   ☐ YES   ☐ NO

7. If "fee and commission" (or if affiliated with a broker/dealer), approximately what percentage of your firm's annual income comes from:
   - ☐ _____ % Fees charged to clients
   - ☐ _____ % Commissions earned from clients' purchase of investment products.
   - ☐ _____ % Other (explain) _____

8. If "fee and commission" or "commission only" (or if affiliated with a broker/dealer), what percentage of your commission income comes from:
   - ☐ _____ % Insurance products
   - ☐ _____ % Annuities
   - ☐ _____ % Mutual funds
   - ☐ _____ % Limited partnerships
   - ☐ _____ % Coins
   - ☐ _____ % Stocks and bonds
   - ☐ _____ % Other (explain) _____

9. Will you furnish me with no-load (no sales charge) product alternatives, if available?
   ☐ YES   ☐ NO

10. Do you or any member of your firm act as a general partner, or receive compensation from the general partner, of investments which may be recommended to me?
    ☐ YES   ☐ NO

11. What is the average income in fees from a typical client?
    $ _____ (annual fee income divided by number of clients served)

    What is the average income in commissions from a typical client?
    $ _____ (annual commission income divided by number of clients served)

To the best of my knowledge, the above statements are true and correct.

Name _____

Firm _____

Signature _____

Date _____

Prepared by:

The National Association of Personal Financial Advisors
Post Office Box 2026
Arlington Heights, Illinois 60006

375

members for specific applications to special client needs, and on practice management and marketing tools and resources used by members. Information in the resource library will be available to any member or associate.

Further information can be obtained about NAPFA by writing:

National Association of Personal Financial Advisors
P.O. Box 2026
Arlington Heights, Illinois 60006

The National Center for Financial Education: A Golden Resource

Paul Richard is the author of the NCFE's course, the Dollarplan-Financial Education 101 and leads the instructor training program. He also edits the NCFE monthly newsletter and heads their speakers bureau. Prior to joining the NCFE, he was a principal in a direct marketing and public relations firm, specializing in direct mail and broadcasting.

In addition, he has spent the last four years promoting consumer financial education in a variety of entrepreneurial enterprises. He has been named an Entrepreneur of the Month by the American Entrepreneur Association magazine, *Entrepreneur.*

Mr. Richard is an accomplished public speaker and trainer of trainers and has written a training guide and manuals for instructors. He addresses both service clubs and financial planners on the need for financial education. He has authored articles for *Retail Banking Report, Public Relations Quarterly,* and *Financial Service Times,* as well as several business journals and newsletters. He is regularly quoted in a variety of media including *USA Today, Sylvia Porter's Personal Finance Magazine, Financial Planning Magazine,* and WCBS-TV, among others. He is listed in several *Who's Who* and has earned the highest award for achievement from the Dale Carnegie Organization.

"Because money doesn't come with instructions, education about money is one of the keys to having it." This statement is found on the mailings of *The NCFE Motivator*, the monthly newsletter of the National Center for Financial Education, a/k/a the NCFE.

The NCFE's founder was visionary Loren Dunton, who is known around the world as "the father of the financial planning profession." He earned the title after founding the College for Financial Planning, (Denver) the CFP designation leading to the Institute for Certified Financial Planners, the International Association for Financial Planning, and the *Financial Planning* magazine.

The NCFE is a nonprofit educational organization, consumer-oriented, which Dunton dedicated to helping people do a better job of spending, saving, investing, insuring, and planning for their financial futures. Another important and overlooked goal of the NCFE is helping the banking, securities, and insurance industries work together to get more discretionary dollars put aside for the future. Everyone in the financial planning profession, the financial services industry, and those considering entering the field should be aware of this valuable golden resource.

It is Dunton's contention that a one-percent increase in savings could mean $3\frac{1}{2}$ trillion dollars going to the financial services industry. Founded in 1982, the NCFE also cites an overburdened Social Security system and excessive consumer spending as national problems it is working to resolve. Part of the NCFE's efforts are directed towards educating and motivating consumers and then persuading them to choose and use a financial planning professional. Thus this valuable resource also has become an important advocate of the financial planning process. Planners and other professionals who are playing a part in helping the NCFE are reaping multiple rewards and find they have an advantage over others who aren't.

NEUTRAL POSITIONING

With more and more individuals entering the financial planning profession and new firms opening their doors everywhere, positioning in the marketplace is critical to success.

Because of its solid educational posture, playing a part in the NCFE makes good sense for planners and firms in the financial services industry. Many wrongly conclude that individual and corporate efforts towards educating the consumer about the financial planning process are the way to go. These efforts are largely unsuccessful, however, as consumers are very suspicious, especially now with so many calling themselves financial planners. So-called financial planning seminars put on by stockbrokers and others are often nothing more than product pitches. Consumer weariness is so widespread that *The Wall Street Journal* ran an article on consumer displeasure in November 1985. One result has been increased consumer interest and acceptance of noncommercial financial education. That's where the NCFE comes in, and they are allowing these financial planners representing the NCFE an opportunity to participate in this educational approach. Here's how.

NCFE CORPORATE SPONSORSHIPS

Corporations can now channel their "consumer relations and education" dollars through one umbrella-type organization that will not be influenced by one particular group. This assures objectivity which may not be possible otherwise. NCFE corporate sponsors underwrite specific projects such as student manuals, booklets explaining the financial planning process, and public education programs. Others provide funding on an annual basis to help the NCFE with office and operating expenses. Franklin Group of Funds made a $3500 grant available to the NCFE to pilot a high-school course in personal finance. VMS Realty made a similar grant for the initial publishing of the NCFE's Dollarplan Financial Education course manual. The NCFE works closely with sponsors to assure proper credit and media exposure for their support. In order to bring objective financial education to students and consumers nationwide, which is the NCFE's ambitious goal, corporate sponsors will be needed in every state and from every industry. Additionally, professional and trade associations, especially those from the financial services industry, can do a lot to further and enhance the programs from this consumer group, which so openly provides a third-party endorsement of the financial planning process.

PROFESSIONAL SPONSORSHIPS

Individual planners can also play an important part in the NCFE by becoming professional sponsors. Like corporate sponsors, they can tell their clients and prospects that they support consumer education. Any professional prefers to work with an educated client. Only the con artists prefer the ignorant. Professional sponsors often make NCFE consumer memberships available to their clients at a discount. In addition, they can purchase NCFE books and publications, often months before others, at substantial savings. Sponsors are also the first ones to have an opportunity to participate in NCFE Dollarplan Instructor programs, or to become members of the national speakers bureau, or to become educational consultants, all very worthwhile and credible in the consuming public's eye.

DOLLARPLAN FINANCIAL EDUCATION COURSES

It is both time-consuming and costly for a financial planner to educate a client on a one-to-one basis. That's why the NCFE's Dollarplan Financial Education Course makes sense. It allows planners, who are trained by the NCFE as instructors, to leverage their time and reach even more prospects through education. The neutral positioning of the NCFE is of special importance here, because the planner doing financial education for the NCFE finds prospecting much easier. As instructors for the NCFE, planners and others, including many CPAs, take the commercial edge off their sales and prospecting calls when they represent the NCFE. It's modeled after the old United States Chamber of Commerce approach. They chose for their membership committee local business people who needed prospects and gave them a legitimate neutral platform for approaching logical executives, that is, membership in the local chamber of commerce. Many of them employed what is commonly referred to as the doorknob close, also used effectively by Dollarplan Instructors. It's used at the end of the presentation about the NCFE and often goes something like this: "By the way, here is my other card. We do financial planning here in the community, and should you or any of your management staff be looking for financial planning services, our firm would like to be considered."

In addition to a handsome instructor's certificate engraved and suitable for display in an office, the NCFE provides Consulting Dollarplan Instructors (CDIs) with 100 business cards which include the planner's name and local telephone number. A CDI can also purchase NCFE stationery imprinted with his or her name and telephone number. The course materials are packaged in a three-ring binder. The program has received wide acceptance from employers, who use it as an employee benefit, credit unions, organized labor, and community colleges. The NCFE also has a course designed for first-year college students and high school seniors known as The Student Dollarplan (Financial Education 101).

NCFE NATIONAL SPEAKERS BUREAU

As most financial planners will tell you, it is difficult to obtain a speaking engagement before a local chamber of commerce or other civic and service club to speak about financial planning or some element of the process, such as investment strategies or tax moves. The message from the NCFE, however, is quite different, and the reception has been outstanding. In fact, organizations such as the Lions, Rotary International, National Exchange Clubs, and the chamber of commerce are eager to have their local clubs learn about the NCFE National Speakers Bureau. The NCFE message is noncommercial and of national importance.

Those invited to serve on the bureau are Dollarplan Instructors and NCFE Educational Consultants. An educational consultant must be either a CFP or a ChFC. The speakers bureau member's kit includes two scripted talks. Each are about twenty minutes in length, which provides ample time for questions and answers after the presentation. The titles are: *Social Insecurity and the Need for Financial Education* and *Financial Illiteracy and What You Should Do About It.*

Also included in the speakers' kit are publicity aids, news releases, suggested introductions of the speakers, suggested letters to local clubs to arrange talks, and samples of handout materials available from the NCFE. The speaker gets valuable exposure in front of these thought-leader groups and often receives valuable media coverage. Both talks conclude with a message about the NCFE financial education courses, which is especially helpful if the speaker is also a Dollarplan Instructor. Interested listeners are asked to hand a business card to the speaker if they would like more information. This facilitates a contact, and the speaker later calls on the prospect to drop off the requested material and perhaps cultivate a new financial-planning client in the process.

THE NCFE MOTIVATOR

Corporate sponsors, Dollarplan Instructors, and Educational Consultants are invited to submit articles for the *NCFE Motivator,* a monthly newsletter. Consumer-oriented, it is distributed to NCFE sponsors (who have the exclusive right to reprint it for clients, employees, and affiliates), instructors, consultants, members, and individuals who attend the Dollarplan classes. Several instructors take advantage of the space provided at the top of the newsletter for an imprint and send it on to clients and prospects. The main focus is on spending, saving, investing, insuring, and planning for one's financial future. Having an article printed in the newsletter, which is distributed nationally, adds credibility to any planner's resumé. Along with the newsletter, articles can be submitted for the Financial Wisdom bulletins and subjects suggested for ''consumer alerts.''

BOOKS, BOOKLETS AND CONSUMER AFFAIRS

All of Loren Dunton's recent books were done on behalf of the NCFE, and he has donated the royalties to the NCFE. They include *Your Book of Financial Planning,* which included chapters from financial planning professionals around the nation (Reston/Prentice Hall). Next was a book on the history of the financial planning profession, a must for everyone in the field or thinking about entering it. It's called *The Financial Planner . . . A New Professional* (Longman). In January 1987 Prentice-Hall released what will be the most influential book Dunton has put together. Titled *Financial Planning Can Make You Rich . . . And Thirty-Three Case Histories to Prove It,* it brings together 33 of the nation's top certified financial planners, who have written specific chapters and included actual case histories or financial plans. It represents a third-person endorsement, and a powerful one, too, for the financial planning process. It should be a must book for every financial planner and a bible for consumers interested in learning more about doing financial planning for themselves—using a planner.

''My Financial Planner Won't Let Me'' and ''Do Financial Planners Just Want to Sell Us Something?'' are the titles of some of the newer booklets and consumer-oriented pamphlets that the NCFE produces and makes available to financial planners to distribute to clients and prospects. Dunton is effective in the combination of education and motivation, which he includes in each book and publication from the NCFE.

Future titles include: *Twelve IRA Myths, Rate of Return . . . Illusion or Reality?,* and *How to Choose and Use a Financial Planner.* All NCFE books, booklets, and other publications or programs are made available to sponsors (professional and corporate), members, instructors, and educational consultants before others. This is another good reason that so many financial planners see more and more value in NCFE participation.

DEVELOPING EFFECTIVE PROGRAMS IN WHICH THE FINANCIAL PLANNER CAN ACTIVELY PARTICIPATE IS AN NCFE STRENGTH

For the financial-planning professional, telling clients, prospects, and other people of their involvement with the NCFE is added strength to a professional resumé or other marketing tool. Having an instructor's certificate and making speeches in the community about the need for financial education gives the professional planner something to talk to clients and prospects about that is noncommercial in nature and projects a deserved image of community service. Both are important aspects in building and developing a financial planning practice.

HOW TO GET INVOLVED WITH THE NCFE

If you are a financial-planning professional and interested in more clients, more prospects, a marketing advantage, community service, public speaking, community exposure, media and public relations opportunities and the like, you should be actively involved in the efforts of the National Center for Financial Education. Your company should be a corporate sponsor; you should be a professional sponsor, a Dollarplan Instructor, and a member of the national speakers bureau.

Chapter IX

Beyond Planning

Robert F. Bohn, M.B.A., Ph.D.,
CFP

Andrew M. Rich, CFP

Ben G. Baldwin, CLU, M.S.F.S.,
CFP, ChFC, M.S.M.

Nelson J. Kjos, CFP

Amy J. Howe

"As competition gets greater and the expectation of the public gets higher, having a masters degree in financial planning/services will be a distinguishing achievement which will set apart the professional."

—ROBERT F. BOHN, M.B.A., Ph.D., CFP

The Value of Higher Education in Financial Planning Services

Robert F. Bohn, M.B.A., Ph.D., CFP, is the Dean of the School of Financial Services and a Professor at Golden Gate University in San Francisco. He has been considered the "Father" of University Financial Planning/Services education.

Dr. Bohn is nationally known in the financial planning/services industry as an educational pioneer, founding the first School of Financial Services at Golden Gate University. He is also founder and 1987 President of the Academy of Financial Services, founder of the first IAFP student chapter, and founder of the nation's first financial and estate planning degree program at Brigham Young University.

Dr. Bohn is listed in *Who's Who in Financial Planning, Who's Who in California,* and *Who's Who in the West.* He is on the Editorial Board for *The Journal of the Institute of Certified Financial Planners,* was the guest editor of the first "Financial Services Marketing" issue of the *Journal of Professional Services Marketing,* was a columnist for the *Salt Lake Tribune,* and wrote *A Budget Book & Much More* as well as many others. His professional affiliations include membership in the Financial Management Association, the IAFP, and the ICFP.

INTRODUCTION

The emergence of the "financial services" industry has significantly impacted traditional financial institutions and created new career opportunities, requiring innovation in educational curriculum. The membership growth of the International Association for Financial Planning (IAFP) from 6150 in 1980 to 24,000 in May 1987 is reflective of the great number of new professionals entering the field. Also, during the same period, the number of Certified Financial Planners (CFPs) increased from 1990 to 14,000. Chartered Financial Consultants (ChFCs) were nonexistent until 1982; in May 1987 there were 14,557. The purpose of this article is to define the role of financial planning within the greater "financial services" industry and to identify the academic organizations impacting the development of this new profession, emphasizing the relatively recent role of higher education in raising the professional level of the financial planning professional.

FINANCIAL PLANNING—A COMPREHENSIVE PROCESS

Functioning as a forerunner to the popularization of "financial services" in the 1980s, the "financial planning" profession emerged out of the "mutual fund era" of the 1960s and the inflationary "consumer decade" of the 1970s. Financial planning is the *process* of coordinating a broad range of financial services products and strategies consistent with the client's goals and values in order to optimize a client's lifestyle—including transfer of wealth at death. Financial planning is to a client's financial well-being as holistic medicine is to a patient's personal health. The emergence of this new generalist created an innovative professional known as the "personal financial planner/advisor." The "financial services" industry includes not only financial planning, but also investments, real estate, insurance, banking, and employee benefits/tax/estate planning. The purpose of this new entrepreneurial professional generalist called the "financial planner" is to fit all of the client's disjointed financial and tax pieces into one client-oriented mosaic.

The ideal role of the new professional financial planner is to be the "financial coordinator" of a client's many financial and tax needs, calling upon specialists (e.g., CPAs and attorneys) when appropriate. Instead of being viewed as a "seller" of financial products/services, theoretically the financial planner is the "buyer" on behalf of the client in such a way as to optimize the client's total resources. While the theoretical model of personal financial planning gained prominence in the early 1980s, the implementation of the concept does not always meet its lofty goals. Instead, some institutions view comprehensive financial planning as only another marketing tool to sell financial products and services such as insurance, tax services, tax-advantaged investments, stocks, bonds, mutual funds, bank/S&L/credit union services, wills, trusts, money market funds, insurance, real estate investments, pension/retirement plans, and the like. Fortunately, enough true financial planners are emerging to fulfill the expectations of this new profession.

HIGHER EDUCATION'S ROLE

Though university business schools have a long history of educating professional corporate-wealth managers/strategists, they were slow in creating curric-

ulum to prepare professional personal-wealth managers/strategists because of:
(1) increased demands for their traditional business/accounting curriculum due
to large enrollment shifts from other academic disciplines in the 1970s and 1980s,
(2) bias against personal financial management as an academic pursuit, (3) lack
of awareness of the complex nature of the comprehensive financial planning
process, (4) lack of academically prepared professors to teach in the area, and
(5) disregard for the new market dynamics of the financial planning and services
industry.

When I was a professor at Brigham Young University, developing its undergraduate degree in financial and estate planning in 1977, I was surprised to
learn that it was the first undergraduate degree of its kind in the nation. Three
historical "firsts" were announced to almost 2000 attending the Dallas IAFP
Annual Conference (Sept. 20–23, 1978) by Robert Strader, then the IAFP Executive Director:

> You financial planners in this room and all of us for ten hard years have
> been seeking a national identity and a national definition of the financial
> planner. . . . We have been told that we will have arrived in the country
> when the financial planner grows, in fact, from the campuses of the col-
> leges and universities. . . . I don't know if you know it or not, but it is
> now a reality. The first university in this nation has a full four-year under-
> graduate program, which results in granting the bachelor's degree in fi-
> nancial planning. It is the first of many colleges and universities. You can
> imagine the pioneering work that had to be done by one great crusader
> and believer. That man is at the head table today, and I want you to know
> the man that established the program at Brigham Young University in
> Provo, Utah, Dr. Robert F. Bohn. I want you further to know that we have
> at this convention another first. Ten of Dr. Bohn's students (were) pro-
> vided a much lower registration fee. . . . I want you to see the first live
> human beings to walk off the campus as financial planners in the world.
> Will you ten students stand. . . . I want to announce another first. That
> group will establish the first . . . college/university chapter of the IAFP,
> and it is only fitting and proper that it be chartered on the campus of
> Brigham Young University.

After establishing the first IAFP student chapter in 1978 at Brigham Young University, the IAFP decided in 1983 to eliminate separate student chapters in favor
of having students affiliate with local professional IAFP chapters at a student
discount.

Business schools' initial lack of interest in the 1970s left room for other
educational alternatives to fill the void. For example, some family science/home
economics educators began shifting part of their curriculum in the direction of
family financial planning/counseling in the 1970s by expanding their family fi-
nance- and consumer-oriented courses to embrace this new career track in response to: (1) the increased emphasis upon university curriculum coordination
with career opportunities in the 1970s, (2) the changing role of women in the
work force, (3) the declining enrollments among the family science/home economics schools, and (4) the realization that most business schools initially were
ignoring this need. Consequently, two college approaches to educating financial
planning/services professionals developed in the late 1970s—one from the business schools and the other from the family and consumer science/home economics schools.

Illustrative of the differences of opinion between business professors and
family resource management professors with regard to financial planning/ser-

vices education were Brigham Young University's two undergraduate majors in two different academic colleges from 1979 to 1988. For about nine years, BYU students could major either in business management-finance, emphasizing financial planning in the College of Business, or major in "family financial planning and counseling" within the Family Sciences Department of the College of Family, Home, and Social Sciences. Because of the curriculum overlap, Brigham Young University's administration made the decision in 1987 to phase out its "family financial planning and counseling" major in favor of putting all of the curriculum in financial planning/services within BYU's Business Management Department.

In the 1970s and 1980s several family science and consumer-oriented departments extended beyond their traditional academic roles in order to prepare students for business careers in addition to consumer/home economics-related jobs. Examples of universities that went beyond stereotypical "home economics" curriculum to offer undergraduate family financial planning and counseling degree programs include: Brigham Young University (Utah; discontinued in 1988), Purdue University (Indiana), Iowa State University, Texas Tech University (also has an M.S. program), Ball State University (Indiana), and the University of Wisconsin.

Examples of business schools offering undergraduate and/or graduate(*) financial planning/services programs include: *Golden Gate University (California), *San Diego State University (California), *Georgia State University, *University of South Carolina, *University of Dallas (Texas), Brigham Young University (Utah), Baylor University (Texas), Wright State University (Ohio), California State University–Fresno, Western Kentucky University, Santa Clara University (California), Mary Hurst College (Pennsylvania), Metropolitan State University (Colorado), Old Dominion University (Virginia), University of Alabama, University of Dallas (Texas), and Drake University (Iowa).

Some university professors, such as Fred Tillman, feel that the primary focus for preparing financial planning/services professionals should be at the master's degree level. In 1982, he initiated Georgia State's financial planning concentration within the master's of insurance degree and in 1985 created a separate master's degree in personal financial planning.

In 1980, Golden Gate University (San Francisco) introduced its MBA in financial planning and San Diego State University instituted its M.S. degree in financial services. In 1982, I left Brigham Young University's Business School in order to restructure and direct Golden Gate University's financial services curriculum. Consequently, in 1983 I developed the nation's most comprehensive graduate financial services curriculum and in 1986 organized the first university School of Financial Services at Golden Gate University with the following graduate degrees: MBA or MS in financial services; MBA in financial planning; MS in financial planning–tax concentration; MBA or MS in financial services–investments concentration; MBA or MS in real estate; and MBA in risk management and insurance. In 1984, GGU introduced the United States's first MS degree in financial planning–tax concentration, which provides the professional with additional strength in taxation. Other financial services-related master's degrees offered by Golden Gate University include taxation, banking, and accounting.

While there is no formal Ph.D. program in financial planning or financial services, graduate students can tailor their Ph.D./DBA dissertation in the field at universities such as Golden Gate University, or declare a concentration in financial planning, such as Georgia State University's Ph.D. program in insurance.

EMERGENCE OF ACADEMIC RESEARCH
IN FINANCIAL PLANNING/SERVICES

As a result of the philosophical differences between the business school professors and the family resource management professors, two separate professional academic research associations have unfolded. Interested business professors established the Academy of Financial Services in 1984 (Thomas Warschauer, first president, and Robert Bohn, first president-elect) with a membership of 272, representing 160 business schools as of May 1987. Interested family science/home economics professors and extension specialists founded the International Association for Financial Counseling in 1983 and changed its name to the Association for Financial Counseling and Planning Education in 1984; its membership as of May 1987 was 122.

As higher education is becoming involved with the financial planning/services curriculum, greatly needed research in the area is being generated. Before the creation of the two aforementioned professional academic organizations (which publish proceedings of their academic meetings), the only refereed academic publication dedicated to financial planning was the *Journal of the Institute of Certified Financial Planners.* The Institute of Certified Financial Planners (Denver, Colorado) began its journal in 1979 and was founded in 1973 to enhance the professionalism of Certified Financial Planners. Tax Management Inc. (subsidiary of The Bureau of National Affairs, Washington, D.C.) published its first monthly *Financial Planning Journal* in January 1985. Haworth Press's new *Journal of Professional Services Marketing* (Binghamton, New York) is edited by William Winston, a Dean at Golden Gate University, with periodic special issues such as "Marketing for Financial Services" (Spring 1986: Vol. 1, No. 3), for which I served as the guest editor. Not until November 1986 did the *Journal of the American Society of CLU* expand its name to include "*and ChFC*" to reflect the expanding scope of the insurance industry into the broader area of financial planning/services. Neil Cohen, a finance professor at George Washington University (District of Columbia), is chairing the Academy of Financial Service's "Bibliographic Research Committee" and has developed valuable research resources for interested academics.

In 1980 I worked with Charles Atwell, who was then on the IAFP national board of directors, in order to hold the IAFP's First Annual Academic Symposium concurrently with its national convention. The IAFP's Sixth Annual Academic Symposium (October 2, 1985; Anaheim, California) had special historical meaning, because it was the first truly academic symposium that professors organized and conducted (Robert Bohn and Thomas Warschauer, cochairs) and formal academic papers were presented and critiqued as well as a proceedings published. The 1985, 1986, and 1987 *IAFP Academic Symposium Proceedings* are available through the IAFP (Atlanta, Georgia). Because of the emergence of academic meetings sponsored separately by the Academy of Financial Services (AFS) and the Association for Financial Counseling and Planning Education (AFCPE), the IAFP sponsored its last academic symposium during its national convention on October 4, 1987, in Atlanta, Georgia.

ALTERNATIVE FINANCIAL PLANNING/SERVICES EDUCATION

While most of mainstream academia initially ignored the need for preparing a new generation of financial planning/services professionals, various industry professional designations, self-study, and university extension division programs were established. The two most prominent industry designations are

(1) the CFP (Certified Financial Planner), which was conceptualized in 1969 and requires passing six three-hour examinations, and (2) the ChFC (Chartered Financial Consultant), which was established in 1982 and requires passing ten two-hour examinations. The College for Financial Planning (Denver, Colorado) originally controlled the privately owned CFP designation until it transferred the designation to the newly formed IBCFP in 1986. The College for Financial Planning became independent of the Society for Financial Counselling (which no longer functions) and the IAFP in 1972 and held its first CFP conferment for 41 recipients in 1973. The ChFC is administered by the American College (Bryn Mawr, Pennsylvania) which also administers the insurance industry's CLU (Chartered Life Underwriter), and in 1977 developed a self-study (plus two-week residency) MS degree in financial services. A CLU can take three additional examinations and obtain the ChFC; likewise, a ChFC can take three additional examinations and receive the CLU designation. Accordingly, most of the first ChFC recipients (2035) in October 1982, as well as the 14,557 ChFCs as of May 1987, were already CLUs.

In 1979, the College for Financial Planning instituted its "affiliate college program"; the first licensee was Golden Gate University (San Francisco, California), whose Center for Professional Development administers preparatory CFP classes on a nonacademic basis to help candidates prepare for the CFP examinations. As of May 1987, there were approximately 70 College for Financial Planning "affiliates" wherein typically the affiliate's extension division offers the helpful (but not required) classes to assist candidates in preparing for the CFP exams.

The CFP (Certified Financial Planner) marks were transferred from the College for Financial Planning to the newly organized, independent IBCFP (International Board of Standards & Practices for Certified Financial Planners, Inc.) in June 1986. Accordingly the IBCFP (Englewood, Colorado; Tel. 303-850-0333) is now responsible for administering CFP examinations and all other matters relating to the use of the marks CFP and Certified Financial Planner. The IBCFP is governed by the Board of Directors, which supervises the following subboards: Board of Ethics & Standards, Board of Appeals, and the Board of Examiners. The IBCFP Board of Directors in November 1986 approved the adoption of a CFP continuing education requirement, which begins January 1, 1988.

The May 1987 IBCFP examination date had important historical significance because it was the first IBCFP exam at which students from authorized academic programs were able to test directly through the IBCFP by paying a $100 fee per CFP exam, instead of having to register through the College for Financial Planning. Also, persons having a CLU, ChFC, CPA, or JD are now able to test directly through the IBCFP. The CFP exams can be taken at authorized testing centers around the United States in May, September, and January. Recognizing the importance of the master's degree in financial planning/services, the IBCFP requires one instead of the normal three years CFP experience requirement for graduates of authorized master's degree programs such as Golden Gate University's.

Many other adult extension divisions have jumped onto the financial planning/services bandwagon in the 1980s because their own academic departments ignored the need. The Adelphi University's "University College" (Garden City, New York) began its own certificate program entitled "Certified Financial Planner (CFP)" in 1978. The UCLA Adult Extension Division, with input from an advisory committee, began its own "Professional Designation in Personal Financial Planning" in 1981. It was so popular that the program is now offered throughout most of the University of California's extension system. Examples of other adult university continuing education divisions providing their own "certificate programs" in personal financial planning include: Boston University–Metropolitan College (Massachusetts), Oakland University–Rochester (Michigan), Fairfield University (Connecticut), Iona College (New York), City University (Washington), Old Dominion University (Virginia), University of Houston (Texas), and San Francisco State University (California; began in 1983 and discontinued in 1986).

In June 1985, the California Society of CPAs (Education Division) introduced a new CPA continuing education "Advanced Personal Financial Planning Certificate Program," which has seven modules, but requires a total of only 88 teaching contact hours (Tel. 415-321-1900). The APFP certificate program was sold to the American Institute of CPAs (AICPA) in early 1987, and 19 states as of May 1987 have begun the program. These 19 states represent about 50 percent of all CPAs in the United States. As of May 1987, 433 CPAs completed the APFP certificate program. Also, as of May 1987, 1900 CPAs completed the first APFP module.

While the professional designation programs and adult extension certificates are a helpful introduction to financial planning, they are not usually transferable into a regular degree program because they do not meet the necessary rigorous academic standards.

Because of the proliferation of so many designations and "certificate programs," the IAFP created in 1983 the "Registry of Financial Planning Practitioners" (RFPP) as a means of identifying those who are actually practicing the total personal financial planning process. The requirements of becoming an RFPP include: specified educational requirements, a sample financial plan, three years' experience doing total financial planning, client references, and passing the RFPP's "Practice Knowledge Examination," which was first given in 1984. RFPPs have been awarded to 720 candidates as of May 1987.

IMPORTANCE OF THE MASTER'S DEGREE

The emergence of so many nonacademic shortcuts to prepare for a "career" in financial planning has caused a credibility gap with many other professionals, because they had to complete demanding academic degree programs before entering into their own professions. Since personal financial planners (functioning as the "financial quarterback") overlap the traditional roles of investment advisors, insurance professionals, bankers, CPAs, real estate professionals, and estate/tax attorneys, it is understandable why other professionals would expect similar academic rigor in order to become a true "financial planning/services professional." **Accordingly, those willing to complete a master's degree in financial planning/services are achieving the highest national standard of educational preparation.**

While students obtaining a bachelor's degree in financial planning/services receive a more complete educational preparation than the CFP/ChFC and "certificate programs," those willing to complete the master's degrees in financial planning/services are equipped to make the most significant impact upon the quality of service being provided to clients. As the public and other professionals are becoming aware of the quantum difference between a graduate from a rigorous master's degree program and one who has completed a professional designation or extension program, they are demanding master's degree graduates who have the sophistication to deal with a broad range of financial products, strategies, and tax variables. Because of the professionalism and rigor of specialized master's degree programs in financial planning/services, graduates are discovering more satisfying career opportunities because of the enthusiastic response of the industry and public. In fact, I receive letters and telephone calls from employers and potential clients, who have heard of Golden Gate University's nationally known financial services graduate programs, wanting to employ our graduates.

In order for financial planners/advisors to make the same professional breakthrough as did medicine, dentistry, law, and accounting, they will have to recognize the necessity of professional preparation through universities offering bachelor's and preferably master's degrees. Probably the two most significant milestones to help raise the professional stature of the financial planning profession in the first half of the 1980s were the development of graduate programs in our nation's business schools and the creation of the Academy of Financial Services, which will continue emphasizing quality curriculum and research in financial services at our universities.

Those willing to climb the higher road to professionalism through a master's degree in financial planning/services as an integral part of their career preparation will substantially increase their heights of employment satisfaction. Some will complete their master's in financial planning/services in preparation for a career, while others will obtain the master's degree while working. As the competition gets greater and the expectation of the public gets higher, having a master's degree in financial planning/services will be a distinguishing achievement which will set apart the professional who was willing to walk the extra mile to prepare for "financial surgery" on his client. Likening it to the medical model, would you prefer having a "financial doctor" perform "financial surgery" on you after an educational preparation of six to ten examinations, or would you want someone with a bachelor's degree plus 19 to 21 additional semester graduate courses? While graduate education does not guarantee success, it provides graduates with an early vision, many new networking contacts, and a sound educational foundation, which, if used well, will substantially increase the probability of their becoming more successful in this highly competitive world than those who choose to take the easier and more travelled road.

Because of higher education's initial reluctance to respond to educating a new generation of financial services professionals and the lack of rigorous industry or government regulation, there are far too many people coming into financial planning/services careers with inadequate education. Nevertheless, those willing to take the time and exert the effort to prepare themselves educationally have tremendous opportunities to impact this new career field, earn substantial incomes, and provide valuable service to their clients. An important indicator of the direction of this new profession will be the number of people who are willing to go through the professional rigor of a master's degree in financial planning/services.

"Tax preparation and financial planning go hand-in-hand. . . . Taxation is the heart and soul, the nucleus, of financial planning."

—ANDREW M. RICH, CFP

The Financial Planner's Role in Tax Preparation

Andrew M. Rich, CFP, is President of AMR Planning Services, Inc., a Registered Investment Advisory firm. He holds a B.A. degree in economics from Queens College of the City University of New York and an M.S. in taxation from Long Island University.

Mr. Rich is the author of *How to Survive and Succeed in a Small Financial Planning Practice,* published by Reston Publishing Company, a contributing author to *The Money Encyclopedia,* published by Harper and Row, and is profiled in *The Financial Planner: A New Professional,* published by Longman Publishing. He has been quoted in numerous financial publications.

Mr. Rich is an Adjunct Assistant Professor of financial management at New York University and a member of the Adjunct Faculty of the College for Financial Planning. He is a Registered Representative licensed through USLICO Securities Corporation and a general agent for the Bankers Security Life Insurance Society. Mr. Rich is currently the Ethics Vice President of the Long Island chapter of the IAFP and is a member of the ICFP.

There are two schools of thought regarding the financial planner's role in tax preparation. The first school, the old school, takes a passive view and places the financial planner in a subordinate role to the accountant. The new school, on the other hand, places the financial planner in an active role and directly involves both the planner and client in the tax preparation process. Since my first day in practice, I have been an advocate of the new school methodology. Tax preparation and financial planning go hand-in-hand. Financial planners who shy away from tax preparation are missing a golden opportunity to expand their client base and to service their clients better.

THE NUCLEUS OF FINANCIAL PLANNING

Today's financial planner faces a myriad of challenges and crises in the diverse field we call financial planning. Just to keep up with the fundamentals of our profession is a challenge in itself. The modern financial planner must be fluent in investments, taxation, risk management, estate planning, pensions and employee benefits, accounting, psychology, and motivation. Nevertheless, of all the factors, taxation, in my opinion, is the heart and soul, the nucleus, of financial planning. In order to fully understand investments, insurance, or pensions, one must understand taxation. Tax is the essential ingredient that interrelates all the financial planning disciplines (Fig. 1). A financial planner weak in the knowledge of tax is usually a weak financial planner.

The key to meeting today's financial planning challenges can be better accomplished through an in-depth understanding of taxation. How can financial planners guide their clients through this fast-moving, ever-changing world without understanding the mechanics of tax? Unfortunately, reading books, articles, and professional services will not allow a practitioner to master taxation. It usually must be learned through a combination of academic study and practical experience. In essence, it would be very difficult truly to understand such concepts as the alternative minimum tax, depreciation, exclusions, installment sales, basis, and S Corporations without ever participating in the nitty gritty of preparing a client's tax return—a boring, but necessary, experience. As a result, accountants, CPAs, and tax professionals making the transition to personal

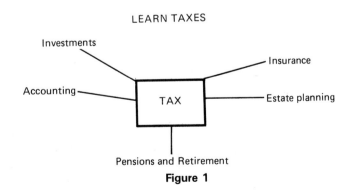

Figure 1

financial planning have a strong foundation which enhances their other financial planning skills.

WHY MOST FINANCIAL PLANNERS SHOULD PREPARE TAX RETURNS

I am firmly convinced that all financial planners, without exception, should have the knowledge in their firm to prepare taxes. Whether or not a firm chooses to prepare taxes, of course, depends on the markets in which they operate. Obviously, the majority of firms and individual practitioners who operate in the affluent marketplace and interrelate closely with CPAs, tax attorneys, and skilled tax practitioners most likely would not prepare their client's taxes. This would be especially true if the other professionals were giving the financial planner numerous quality referrals and the financial planner had a strong professional relationship with the tax professional or professionals. If, through networking, the tax preparation process can be accomplished, the financial planner has done the job. Nevertheless, the ability to prepare taxes should not be minimized, since it would enhance the working relationship with the tax professional and upgrade the planner's level of financial planning skills.

But not all financial planners practice in the affluent marketplace. Most financial planners, in fact, practice in the middle-income marketplace where clients have traditionally relied on outside accountants, tax preparation services and "do-it-yourself" skills. The chances of receiving significant referrals from other professionals would be minimal for most financial planners. Nevertheless, there is a great need in this marketplace to increase the skill level of tax services. Most middle-income clients not only would be receptive to financial planners who offered tax preparation services, they would be overjoyed. In essence, it just would be another link in fulfilling what most clients seek—one trusted adviser.

Since writing my first book, *How to Survive and Succeed in a Small Financial Planning Practice,* I have had the opportunity to speak in front of several thousand financial planners. My experience has shown that more and more planners are either involved with or beginning to understand tax preparation services. In effect, many of the planners who attended my seminars were accountants, CPAs and enrolled agents making the transition to financial planning. And as more and more accountants cross the threshold into financial planning, the industry can only benefit. This, of course, is the good news. The bad news is that the transition will increase competition among small planners and small planning firms and squeeze out many of the planners who are not providing full services. I predict that in the next five years, especially with increased regulation of planners, that many consumers will swing away from tax services in favor of full-service financial planners. In essence, accountants are no longer on the financial planning team, they are taking it over.

If you are already an accountant or in the tax preparation business, you are more than likely in full agreement with what I have said. Without doubt, tax preparation has been the secret of my success. It affords me the opportunity to understand my client better, to provide a higher level of total financial planning services because of that understanding, and to receive numerous referrals that I would not have ordinarily received. If you are not in the tax preparation business, then at least be fair with yourself. If my article makes the least bit of sense, then talk to as many financial planners that you know who are in the tax preparation business as you can. Has it helped them? Do they get referrals? Are they quality planners? And so forth.

THE REALITIES OF TAX PREPARATION

Assuming that you decide to take on the world of financial planning, what can you expect? First of all, forget financial planning during tax season. Your case load and all non-essentials must be put off until after April 15th. Then, give two weeks to a month to get your brain back into working order before you go back in the financial planning business. Most likely you will have a long list of clients to see and work to complete, which you were forced to put off during tax season. By September or October, you just may begin to think about looking for new business. If you are not in a marketing-free, referral-only business in three to five years you, in all probability, are doing something wrong. In a multi-planner firm, some of the tax preparation blues and down time can be overcome through networking.

Thinking about being able to prepare taxes and being qualified to prepare taxes are two different matters. Tax is a science that takes more than formal education, it takes experience. Fortunately, for the bulk of your clients, you can learn to prepare their taxes quite quickly; it is the complex returns that you think you can prepare, but botch, that will get you in trouble. Never try to prepare a tax return that is too difficult. Bring in a qualified professional and learn from that professional's expertise. It is not professional, or wise for that matter, to experiment on your clients.

Qualification to prepare taxes depends, of course, on the status of your financial planning clients. Planners in the more affluent and business market-places should have a good working knowledge not only of individual taxation, but also of partnerships, corporations, S corporations, estates, and trusts. I suggest the following courses:

Basic accounting
Individual taxation
Corporate taxation
Partnership taxation
Estates and trusts
IRS procedures and tax research

Whether you take graduate courses, undergraduate courses, continuing education courses, or correspondence courses is not that important. What is important is that you learn the material inside out and know how to apply it in a practical situation. However, if you are going to invest a great deal of your time learning about taxation, I would suggest you seriously consider an advanced degree, since it offers excellent credentials as well as knowledge.

SUMMARY

If you have a small- to moderate-size practice in the middle income markets, you may be missing the boat if you are not preparing your client's tax returns. Tax preparation enhances your overall level of financial planning, provides a needed client service, brings in significant extra income, allows you to better understand your clients, sets the stage for a faster build up of clients and referrals, and places you in a strong position to compete in the rapidly changing field of financial planning.

"In today's world, if the agent cannot communicate to you a solid understanding of life insurance, what you are buying and why, it may well be because the agent does not understand the products."

—BEN G. BALDWIN, CLU, M.S.F.S., CFP, ChFC, M.S.M.

Selecting Quality Life Insurance Products for Your Clients

Ben G. Baldwin, CLU, M.S.F.S., CFP, ChFC, M.S.M., is president and owner of Baldwin Financial Systems, Inc., a registered investment advisory firm involved in financial education, consulting, and planning for corporate and individual clients. He holds a B.A. from the University of Rochester and an M.S.F.S. and M.S.M. from the American College. Mr. Baldwin is the originator of the Baldwin System Financial Plan.

Mr. Baldwin serves as an adjunct faculty member with the College for Financial Planning. He is a contributing author to Prentice Hall's *Financial Planning Can Make You Rich* and was profiled in Longman's *The Financial Planner . . . A New Professional.*

Mr. Baldwin was a founding member of the Greater O'Hare chapter of the International Association for Financial Planning and served as president in 1982 and 1983. He also is a member of the Institute of Certified Financial Planners, the American Society of CLU & ChFC, the Chicago Estate Planning Council, and the Million Dollar Round Table.

Selecting quality life insurance products is a pleasure and a wonderful opportunity these days. The existence of a very volatile economy, an unpredictable regulatory environment, technology that allows us precise management of numbers, and the demand by the consumer for quality and full disclosure has forced the insurance industry to be creative and innovative. They now recognize that the goodwill of their customers is most important. If you don't recognize this glowing description of the life insurance industry, it is because the description probably applies to less than 10 percent of the industry at this time. The other 90 percent is still trying to figure out what is going on. The good news is that 10 percent of the industry is being responsive and servicing the consumer. It is our job as financial planners to assist our clients in doing business with that 10 percent. The object of this article is to help you do just that and to help you select quality life insurance products for your clients.

There are two initial steps that we should take on our way to selecting quality products for our clients. The first is to select a quality company, and the second is to select a quality agent. Let's deal with the company first. In selecting a quality company, I assume that one-half of the life insurance companies selling and servicing life insurance products today will no longer be in business ten years from now. The accuracy of this assumption may be debated; however, it forces me to conclude that I do not want my clients insured by any of the disappearing companies. We must evaluate the survival potential of the companies we recommend. The companies that I expect to survive are the consumer-oriented companies, offering quality products, whose primary business has been life insurance with a century or more of experience in that business. They are mutual companies and/or the stock company subsidiaries of mutual insurance companies, that is, the household-name companies such as Metropolitan, Prudential, Equitable, John Hancock, New England Mutual, New York Life, Mutual of New York, Connecticut Mutual, Northwestern Mutual, Massachusetts Mutual, and others with similar histories. I avoid companies that have the potential to become the cash cow subsidiaries of publicly traded companies whose primary business is other than insurance and financial services. In other words, avoid those companies owned by piano manufacturing companies, the Baldwin-Uniteds (no relationship to this author), and the like.

Those are my prejudices; I do not always trust my own prejudices, so I look for more qualified authority. I look for someone who spends more time evaluating life insurance companies than some of our state insurance commissioners, Joseph M. Belth, the editor of *The Insurance Forum* (published monthly by Insurance Forum, Inc., P. O. Box 245, Ellettsville, Indiana 47429). If you are looking for quality information regarding what is going on in the life insurance industry, I would recommend Professor Belth's publication. Let me quote from his December 1986 edition:

> When a buyer selects a life insurance company the financial strength of the company should be an important consideration. To be conservative on this point, I have suggested the consumer buy only from a company with an A+ rating from the A. M. Best Company. To be more conservative I have suggested the consumer buy only from a company that was recommended in the strongest language in 1975, and was rated A+ in 1976–1986. The 113 life insurance companies meeting this test are listed in the supplement to our October 1986 issue.

It is easy for me to go through Professor Belth's issue and highlight less than two dozen companies that fit both his description of quality and my own, and I believe it will be just as easy for you.

The next item in our selection process is the agent. Some of you may be thinking that we should be using no-load life insurance products and thus eliminating the sales commission normally paid to an agent. If it was possible to find a "quality" company with a broad spectrum of "quality" products from which you could choose, this might be a viable alternative. The only company that is on Professor Belth's list, and in certain cases on my own, that fits this description is USAA of San Antonio, Texas, which does business primarily with military service personnel. If such a company is a viable alternative for you and your client, the question becomes, which of the following is more cost efficient for your client? The client may pay the financial planner a fee or pay an agent commissions to assist in product selection.

There is no question that the agent should "earn" the commission paid. The commission will be earned by assisting you and your client in evaluating "quality" in a manner that fits your client's individual situation. Let me recommend that you "hire" an agent in the same way you would hire anyone else to assist you in a staff position; that is, by reputation, education, ability to communicate client alternatives and to recommend, with sound reasoning, individual products tailored to your clients' needs. In today's world, if the agent cannot communicate to you a solid understanding of life insurance, what you are buying and why, it may well be because the agent does not understand the products. In this case, you have not found the appropriate professional with whom you should be doing business. Keep in mind that only about one-third of the licensed sales force is adequately licensed to sell all of the life insurance products available today. The other two-thirds of those licensed to sell life insurance have not passed the National Association of Securities Dealers (NASD) test required to sell equity-based variable life insurance products. If an agent is limited by lack of licensing, or by lack of product availability from the company with which he has associated, you need to be aware of these limitations. Should such limitations eliminate that agent from consideration as your life insurance professional?

The first job of the agent is to make sure that your client understands the generic description of the life insurance products on the market. I use my Product Analyzer (Figure 1) to communicate the basics of life insurance to clients in an efficient and comprehensive manner. As you read over the matrix, you will find that it is self-explanatory and describes the key characteristics of the various products on the market. The client can make a "chocolate, vanilla, strawberry" type of selection, depending upon individual taste and the specific personal life insurance needs. In my search for quality life insurance products for my clients, the first criterion is what the client wants. It is irrelevant whether my tastes would be different from the client's. For example, if a client chooses mortality and expenses only (that is, term insurance), and elects not to allocate any plus dollars for investment, I will not stop to discuss whether this is appropriate for the long-term need at this point. The primary job of the life insurance professional is to get the protection in force as soon as possible. Take the client and the beneficiaries off the risk and put the life insurance company on the risk. The professional life insurance agent knows that once the required life insurance is in force, the secondary question of how to structure the policy can be determined at a more leisurely pace. In most cases, all premiums allocated to the term life insurance in the first year can be credited toward any policy into which the term insurance is converted. Also, the question of insurability and the cost of term insurance will have been determined.

A Baldwin System Financial Plan™

BALDWIN FINANCIAL SYSTEMS PRODUCT ANALYZER

	General Description	Investment Vehicle	Investment Flexibility	Premium Flexibility	Face Amount Flexibility	Appropriate For
TERM – Mortality & Expenses ONLY						
Non-Guaranteed Term	**Lowest Cost** *Poor Quality*	NONE	N/A	**NONE** *Increases Yearly*	NONE	*Very limited situations*
Yearly Renewable and Convertable Term	**Quality Term** *After Tax Life Insurance*	NONE	N/A	**NONE** *Increases Yearly*	NONE	*Limited Cash Flow Temporary Needs Protection NOW*
TERM "PLUS" - Mortality & Expenses "PLUS" ADDITIONAL DOLLARS FOR INVESTMENT						
Whole Life	**Tried and True** *Basic Coverage Dividends make it great.*	*Insurance Co. selected Long term bonds and mortgages*	**NONE** *To change investment of capital, borrowing from the policy and reinvesting is required.*	**NONE** *Billed premium remains level. Dividends can provide reduction or elimination. Loans Available*	**NONE** *If you want more, you buy new, IF you can pass a physical.*	*The Conservative Older Insureds* *Substandard Insureds*
Universal Life	*"How much would you like to pay . . . . . When ?"*	*Annual Interest Sensitive Investments*	**NONE** *To change Investment of capital requires WITHDRAWAL of capital.*	**MAXIMUM** *Just enough for Mortality and expenses, or AS MUCH AS YOU WANT.*	*Increase it or decrease it as it suits your life setting . . . Stay Healthy for major increases.*	*Younger Insureds Variable Needs Like Short Term interest rate investments.*
Variable Life	*We will put it where You want it.*	*Common Stock Bond Funds Guaranteed Interest Rates Zero Coupons Money Markets etc., etc. . . .*	*You Name It. You Split It. You Move It. You Borrow It. Both fixed and variable rates.*	**NONE** *Billed premium remains level. Loans Available*	**NONE** *If you want more, you buy new, IF you can pass a physical.*	*The Investor. An alternative to . .Buy Term, Invest Difference.*
Universal Variable Life	*"You Decide !" How much . . . Where . . . When?*	*Common Stock Bond Funds Guaranteed Interest Rates Zero Coupons Money Markets etc., etc. . . .*	*You Name It. You Split It. You Move It. You Withdraw It.*	**MAXIMUM** *Just enough for Mortality and expenses, or AS MUCH AS YOU WANT.*	*Increase it or decrease it as it suits your life setting . . . Stay Healthy for major increases.*	*The Investor. An alternative to . . Buy Term, Invest Difference. I want it MY WAY !*

Copyright 1985 by Ben G. Baldwin, CLU

Figure 1

If the client does not have any particular "taste" that determines the type of policy that should be placed, and if the client and the financial planner ask my counsel in selecting among the alternative products, I would proceed in the following manner.

The first question is to determine if the client has funds available over and above what is required for mortality and expense charges that could be allocated to life insurance. If such funds are not available, we don't need to go any further. If such funds are available, then we can go about evaluating the opportunities available to the client under the "term plus" categories of the Product Analyzer. The election to put additional dollars with the life insurance company is an investment decision and an "alternative use of funds" question. Once the client is aware that there are charges for expenses and mortality costs in every life insurance policy, no matter what it is called, charges that must be paid if the policy is to remain in force, then the client can understand the following simple mathematical concept. He or she must earn enough money to pay both the annual premium for the mortality costs and expenses and to pay the income taxes due on those earnings. We can determine the amount of money the individual must earn in order to pay the premiums into that life insurance product. For example, if your policyowner has a $1000 premium to pay and is in the 28 percent marginal federal income tax bracket, he or she would divide the $1000 by $(1 - 0.28)$, or 0.72, and find that (disregarding state income tax), the earnings required to pay the $1000 premium amount to $1388.89. The earnings of $1388.89 would be split—$388.89 to pay the taxes ($1388.89 × 28 percent) and the $1000 to the insurance company to pay premium.

The alternative to this method of paying the mortality and expenses charges of a life insurance policy would be to have an investment fund held by an insurance company that would earn a return not subject to current income taxation. This return could be used by the policyowner to buy coverage which alternatively could be purchased with after-tax earnings. Suppose, for example, that this client had $12,500 in a certificate of deposit, currently being renewed at 6 percent taxable interest, which would result in $750 of taxable income. Of that, $210 would go to income taxes, if we assume a 28 percent marginal tax bracket, and a net of $540 would be retained. The client could, on the other hand, put this $12,500 into a life insurance policy and, if we assume a return of 8 percent on those funds, earn $1000 of interest for the year. If, say, the insurance company requires $1000 from this policy to pay the mortality and expense costs within this policy, the client has a choice. Choice one: He or she could retain the CD, earn a net of $540, and continue to pay for mortality and expense charges with after-tax earnings. This would require a $1,388.89 of earnings to pay the $1000 premium, resulting in a net of $848.89 ($1,388.89 − $540.00) out of pocket. Alternatively, the client could put the $12,500 into the life insurance policy and let the untaxed earnings service the mortality and expense charges. This would eliminate any out-of-pocket expense. By combining the investment decision with the life insurance decision $848.89 has been saved, an 84.9 percent discount on the mortality and expense charges under consideration—and how often have you heard the admonition not to mix investment decisions with life insurance decisions? What poor advice!

This procedure will help your client to understand that if there is a choice between paying term premiums with after-tax dollars or with pretax dollars the latter is by far the least expensive way to pay them. The time and money required to shift from paying premiums with post-tax dollars to the pretaxed earnings on an investment will depend on each client's individual situation.

Once the client has decided upon "Term Plus," the next question should be which "flavor" of the "pluses" available should be chosen? If the client and the financial planner have definite investment tastes, they can choose the insurance company's general portfolio (whole life), or short-term interest rates (universal life), or equity investment alternatives with a fixed premium (variable life). However, if they ask my advice, you will find me suggesting the following.

I will take the Product Analyzer and go to the three columns labeled across the top, investment *flexibility*, premium *flexibility*, and face amount *flexibility*. I will then draw my client's attention into the body of the analyzer and, as illustrated in Figure 2, I will write the word "boo" in any boxes that say "none" to any of the flexibility questions, and I will put a "yea" in the boxes that indicate that my client retains the right to flexibility. I will suggest that in today's world I would choose flexibility over inflexibility. Give me a life insurance product with investment flexibility, premium flexibility, and face amount flexibility, and

A Baldwin System Financial Plan™

BALDWIN FINANCIAL SYSTEMS PRODUCT ANALYZER

	General Description	Investment Vehicle	Investment Flexibility	Premium Flexibility	Face Amount Flexibility	Appropriate For
TERM - Mortality & Expenses ONLY						
Non-Guaranteed Term	Lowest Cost *Poor Quality*	NONE	N/A	NONE *Increases Yearly*	NONE	*Very limited situations*
Yearly Renewable and Convertable Term	Quality Term *After Tax Life Insurance*	NONE	N/A	NONE *Increases Yearly*	NONE	*Limited Cash Flow Temporary Needs Protection NOW*
TERM "PLUS" - Mortality & Expenses "PLUS" ADDITIONAL DOLLARS FOR INVESTMENT						
Whole Life	**Tried and True** *Basic Coverage Dividends make it great.*	Insurance Co. selected *Long term bonds and mortgages*	NONE *To change investment of capital borrowing from the policy and reinvesting is required.*	NONE *Billed premium remains level. Dividends can provide reduction or elimination. Loans Available*	NONE *If you want more, you buy new, IF you can pass a physical.*	*The Conservative Older Insureds* *Substandard Insureds*
Universal Life	*"How much would you like to pay . . . . . When ?"*	*Annual Interest Sensitive Investments*	NONE *To change Investment of capital requires WITHDRAWAL of capital.*	MAXIMUM *Just enough for Mortality and expenses, or AS MUCH AS YOU WANT.*	*Increase it or decrease it as it suits your life setting . . . Stay Healthy for major increases.*	*Younger Insureds Variable Needs Like Short Term interest rate investments.*
Variable Life	*We will put it where You want it.*	*Common Stock Bond Funds Guaranteed Interest Rates Zero Coupons Money Markets etc., etc. . . .*	*You Name It. You Split It. You Move It. You Borrow It. Both fixed and variable rates.*	NONE *Billed premium remains level. Loans Available*	NONE *If you want more, you buy new, IF you can pass a physical.*	*The Investor. An alternative to . .Buy Term, Invest Difference.*
Universal Variable Life	*"You Decide !" How much . . . Where . . . When?*	*Common Stock Bond Funds Guaranteed Interest Rates Zero Coupons Money Markets etc., etc. . . .*	*You Name It. You Split It. You Move It. You Withdraw It.*	MAXIMUM *Just enough for Mortality and expenses, or AS MUCH AS YOU WANT.*	*Increase it or decrease it as it suits your life setting . . . Stay Healthy for major increases.*	*The Investor. An alternative to . . Buy Term, Invest Difference. I want it MY WAY !*

Copyright 1985 by Ben G. Baldwin, CLU

Figure 2

we can design it to serve client needs today, and redesign it to serve client needs tomorrow. Indeed, in many cases the policy can emulate the results the client would have under any of the other ''Term Plus'' products by the way the client directs the insurance company to invest the ''plus'' dollars.

Once this process is complete, the client and the financial planner can specify to me what they define as a ''quality life insurance product.'' First, it must be a product that will survive and be serviced during the client's lifetime. Second, it must provide competitively low expenses and mortality charges with acceptable contractually guaranteed maximum charges. Third, it must have access to acceptable investment alternatives managed by outstanding investment managers. The job of proving that the life insurance product being scrutinized is ''quality'' can then be delegated to the life insurance professional, with the financial planner assisting the client in demanding the complete disclosure necessary for them to make a fully informed selection.

The wonderful new world of life insurance exists today because all the required information is available. The opportunities available to improve your client's economic well-being through life insurance have never been greater. Your clients are beginning to pay off life insurance policy loans because alternative investments are not paying the high interest rates they used to pay and because the deductibility of the loan interest is being phased out. This results in substantial amounts of investment capital being invested in older, sometimes underperforming, life insurance policies. There is a wonderful opportunity today, depending upon the circumstances, to make 1035 tax-free exchanges of underperforming life insurance policies into contracts that respond more flexibly to changing economic conditions. It is incumbent upon all of us to determine if our clients have a choice, and if they do, to present them with the alternatives available in the new world of quality life insurance products.

"Stock market participants fail by underestimating defense and by overestimating offense (the possibility of how much a stock can go up)."

—NELSON J. KJOS, CFP

The Stock Market Triangle of Developing the Art of Conservative Money Management

Nelson Kjos is President of Nelson Kjos & Co., Inc. and Chairman of the Board of Barrington, Ltd., both registered investment advisors based in Southfield, Michigan. Mr. Kjos founded his firm in 1967 with $370,000 under management which has grown to over $65 million. He developed the Technical Tick Index in 1969, which is the major marketing timing tool of the firm.

Mr. Kjos is affiliated with many professional organizations. He is a member of the Institute of Certified Financial Planners, the International Association for Financial Planning, where he served as former Director and former Vice President of education for the Southeastern Michigan chapter, the Metropolitan Society of Detroit Certified Financial Planners, and the National Corporate Cash Management Association.

At the College for Financial Planning, Mr. Kjos was an adjunct faculty member. In addition, he is an author and frequent speaker at investment seminars and has been interviewed on television.

The most important factor in our triangle of conservative money management (Figure 1) is risk (uncertainty). Risk is the nemesis of all money managers. Most professional and nonprofessional stock market participants are their own victims in misestimating risk. Why? Because stock market participants do not understand the most significant risk to an equity or mutual fund portfolio: market risk. As an example, three important changing factors of market risk are

1. The inflation rate (the cost of money).
2. The rate of economic growth (the business cycle).
3. Program (arbitrage) trading (which causes violent swings in the major market indices).

The opposite of offense, of course, is defense. Defense is also called adjusting for market risk. Stock market participants fail by underestimating defense and by overestimating offense (the possibility of how much a stock can go up). In general, Wall Street is overly enthusiastic when buying and reluctant to recommend selling.

Entrepreneurship is the second side of our triangle. All money managers should be motivated to think of their client's money as their very own. Most successful money managers who manage their own portfolios are active on both the buy and sell sides. Protecting portfolio assets is a constant that never changes. Therefore, observing other successful entrepreneurs in stock market finance is a study in not being a victim of change.

The third side in the triangle is the educating of your clientele. Communicate to your clients what are reasonable expectations of portfolio performance. In other words, what is old-fashioned financial conservatism? My answer— peace of mind and reasonable economics. Clients should realistically keep their money manager for a minimum of one three-year performance cycle. The performance cycle consists of one central-achiever (CA) year of twelve to fourteen percent return; one overachiever (OA) year of twenty percent return or more; and one underachiever (UA) year of six to nine percent return (but not necessarily in this order). Mathematically, the mean of the three minimum percentages comes out to 12.7 percent. My argument? What is wrong with averaging 12.7 percent for three, six, nine, etc. years?

It is the money manager's responsibility to educate his or her clientele. Doing so is only being fair to your clientele and to yourself. The money manager is not supposed to be a superman or -woman. Just be prudent in sharing with your clientele the importance of reasonable and consistent asset perpetuation. After all, isn't this what investors, not speculators, would call portfolio success?

Figure 1

For those stock market participants who disagree, maybe their expectations are unrealistic and they are closet speculators, not investors. If so, remember that you, the money manager, are in charge of formulating an investment policy that you believe in and of recruiting like-minded prospects to become your clients.

Ask yourself, would you like a conservative or an aggressive clientele? Only you, the money manager, can decide.

"The paraplanner significantly lightens the work load of the planner, allowing him or her to handle more of the tasks requiring the planner's particular expertise."

—AMY J. HOWE

Financial Paraplanners: The Missing Link in the Modern Financial Planning Practice

Amy J. Howe is the coordinator of the Financial Paraplanner Program at the College for Financial Planning in Denver, Colorado. A graduate of the University of Kentucky, Howe has directed the development of the Financial Paraplanner Program since its inception in September 1983.

Ms. Howe has published articles on using a paraplanner effectively in *Best's Review* and the ICFP *Journal,* and has addressed ICFP and IAFP groups on related subjects. She completed the Certified Financial Planner professional education program in September 1986 and is currently an M.B.A. candidate.

Use of paraprofessionals in the service professions is not a recent phenomenon. Professionals in fields such as medicine and law have long employed paraprofessionals as a means of maximizing productivity and quality of service to clients. The emergence of paraprofessionals in these established professions occurred, for the most part, as the profession matured. Unlike its more established counterparts, which have matured and developed over centuries, the financial planning profession is maturing virtually overnight. The number of consumers seeking financial planning services has increased rapidly over the past decade, and these consumers are sophisticated, demanding a corresponding sophistication of service. The struggle to meet the needs of consumers has involved the emergence of new products, improved technology, and, perhaps most importantly, the emergence and development of a new breed of paraprofessional—the financial paraplanner.

Many financial planners have found the financial paraplanner to be an indispensable member of the financial planning team. A financial paraplanner may be defined as an individual with general training and education in the financial planning field who assists a financial planner with technical and technically oriented tasks that do not require the planner's level of expertise.

The typical financial planning practice or department within a larger organization employs two classes of individuals: professional staff members (usually one or more financial planners) and clerical staff members. The clerical assistant performs such tasks as answering the phone, typing, filing, and computer data entry, while the financial planner does everything else. Typically, there is little or no overlap between the responsibilities handled by the planner and those handled by the clerical assistant. Each has a distinct role in the practice. Because the clerical assistant usually is trained in general office skills, it would rarely make sense for the financial planner to delegate any of his or her responsibilities to a clerical assistant lacking an understanding of the technical aspects of financial planning.

While this arrangement may make sense in the very early phases of a practice's development, most successful financial planning practices grow to a point at which the work load finally exceeds the staff's capacity to handle it efficiently. If the work is bottlenecking because of the number of responsibilities that the professional staff must handle, many practices attempt to resolve the problem by adding financial planners. A more practical solution, however, may be the addition of a financial paraplanner. A true "missing link" in the practice, the financial paraplanner possesses a basic understanding of financial planning and is able to assume a number of technically oriented responsibilities that may not be delegated to traditional clerical staff. By assuming such responsibilities, the paraplanner significantly lightens the workload of the planner, allowing him or her to handle more of the tasks requiring the planner's particular expertise.

Adding a paraplanner to the financial planning team allows the practice to handle more business. Of course, this same result may be achieved by adding another planner; however, it cannot be achieved as economically. Because the paraplanner handles the lower-echelon planning responsibilities, he or she does not command the salary of an individual who assumes the full gamut of financial planning responsibilities. Paraprofessional staff provide an intermediate link in the structure of the financial planning practice, thus allowing more appropriate allocation of responsibilities.

Because financial planning practices differ in terms of administrative procedures, services provided, personnel, classes of clients served, and so on, the specific role of the paraplanner differs from practice to practice. Deciding which tasks are appropriate for the paraplanner to perform in the financial planning practice is perhaps the most difficult, but most important, decision facing the financial planner who employs a paraplanner.

Determining the paraplanner's responsibilities within the practice should begin with a thorough analysis of the responsibilities being performed by the financial planner. In a small practice, the financial planner frequently has a hand in every aspect of the business. He or she is involved with the technical aspects of generating financial plans, client services, public relations and marketing, and practice management. Each task performed by the financial planner in these areas should be evaluated to determine if it can be handled more appropriately by the financial paraplanner. In general, tasks that can be handled adequately by the financial paraplanner should be assigned to him or her.

Several more specific criteria may be used, however, in allocating work. First, responsibilities unique to the financial planner's job should always be retained by the planner. For example, the planner's function is to provide financial advice to clients; this is a responsibility that cannot be delegated to a subordinate. Second, repetitive tasks generally should be handled by someone other than the planner. If the task is a repetitive matter that requires technical knowledge, such as completing the data survey using form documents provided by the client, the task may be handled efficiently by the paraplanner. Additionally, technically oriented details that require a substantial amount of time, such as research, should be delegated to the financial paraplanner. Finally, the paraplanner may be assigned tasks that require, in addition to technical knowledge, a "layperson's perspective," or the ability to perceive events as clients do, such as the production of a newsletter for clients.

While the paraplanner's role varies, technical support comprises the bulk of the paraplanner's job in most practices. A primary responsibility performed by paraplanners in this area is data gathering. The paraplanner facilitates the data-gathering process by transferring information from the forms, policies, and documents provided by the client into a format that is readily useful to the planner as he or she begins developing the financial plan. In many practices, the paraplanner also is involved in the fact-finding interview with the client and planner, providing the planner additional insight and a fresh perspective on the client's attitudes, objectives, and concerns.

Since the paraplanner assists in the data-gathering process and therefore is familiar with the client's financial information, he or she is in a good position to perform a preliminary analysis of the client's financial situation by identifying certain financial strengths and weaknesses. By commenting on the adequacy of the client's emergency fund, appropriateness and adequacy of existing insurance coverage, size of consumer debt, existence of wills, and so on, the paraplanner allows the financial planner to focus on complex financial concerns and strategies for handling them.

Research is another time-consuming, yet essential, task frequently performed by paraplanners. Because the paraplanner is familiar with financial planning concepts, he or she is capable of researching new financial products, laws affecting the planner and client, and other matters.

Through working closely with the financial planner and the client, the paraplanner's knowledge and expertise builds rapidly. The more advanced paraplanner, while not fully qualified to develop a financial plan, is able to counsel clients on a number of specific financial concerns, such as budgeting, purchase of relevant financial products, basic tax strategies, asset accumulation methods, and so on. And, by handling clients who do not require a full-fledged financial plan, the paraplanner generates revenue that otherwise would not be available to the practice.

Although technical support comprises the bulk of the paraplanner's job in most practices, paraplanners frequently assist with other tasks. If the practice provides newsletters or seminars for clients, the paraplanner may be involved in producing these services. In the area of client services, the paraplanner monitors the client's progress in implementing the financial plan and is able to respond to client questions. In addition, many paraplanners assist the financial planner with public relations efforts by coordinating the planner's speaking engagements, ghostwriting speeches and articles, writing and distributing relevant press releases, and facilitating the planner's relations with the local media. Finally, the paraplanner may assist in practice management by supervising other staff members and establishing procedures.

Because the paraplanner's responsibilities are technically oriented, the financial paraplanner selected in the hiring process must possess, at minimum, a basic understanding of financial-planning concepts. This knowledge may be derived from education, experience, or a combination of the two. Education that may be helpful to a paraplanner in performing his or her job includes course work in finance, accounting, and other business-related subjects offered through traditional colleges and universities, or nontraditional educational programs, such as the Financial Paraplanner Program℠ offered by the College for Financial Planning in Denver, Colorado. The Financial Paraplanner Program, which is conducted on a self-study basis, provides basic education on the financial planning process, the time value of money, risk management, investments, tax planning, retirement planning, and estate planning. It is the only educational program currently available that is specifically designed to meet the needs of financial services support staff.

Because the paraprofessional role is relatively new in the financial planning field, it may be difficult for planners in many areas to locate an individual with experience as a paraplanner. However, an individual who has experience in a financial planning practice—in an increasingly responsible capacity—may be qualified, as may an individual with experience in another segment of the financial services industry, such as banking, insurance, or securities.

When selecting a paraplanner, the financial planner should consider the individual's personal skills and attributes, as well as education and experience. Because the paraplanner works closely with clients and staff members, it is essential that he or she have excellent communication skills. In addition, because the paraplanner handles a wide range of responsibilities, the individual selected for the position must have strong organizational skills, being able to focus both on detail and the big picture, while working largely unsupervised. He or she also must have a strong desire to learn and grow within the position to fulfill the needs of a growing practice. Finally, he or she must possess an understanding of his or her own limitations, being able to recognize where his or her expertise ends and where the planner's begins.

The importance of ongoing education for the paraplanner cannot be overemphasized. The paraplanner has heavy involvement in the financial planning process and substantial contact with clients; therefore, it is essential that the paraplanner be dedicated to keeping abreast of issues and developments relating to financial planning and the paraplanner's job. The paraplanner's ongoing education program should include taking relevant courses, whether through self-study, like the Financial Paraplanner Program, or through local colleges or universities. Course work should cover such topics as finance, accounting, law, taxes, insurance, investments, management, speech, writing, and so on. Other activities that should be included in the paraplanner's education program are memberships with applicable organizations, such as the International Association for Financial Planning (IAFP), regular reading of trade publications, and attendance at relevant seminars and workshops. Finally, the paraplanner should obtain licenses and registrations that add to his or her value in the financial planning practice.

Financial paraplanners are rapidly emerging as a necessary part of any growth-oriented financial planning practice. Like their counterparts in other service professions, paraplanners serve to leverage the professional's time in an efficient manner. However, the paraplanner's benefit to the practice is dependent on appropriate allocation of tasks to the position, the paraplanner's education, experience, skills, and personal attributes, and his or her commitment to ongoing education. The financial planner must take substantial care in determining the paraplanner's job responsibilities, in selecting a competent paraplanner, and in providing adequate and ongoing training. Properly trained and utilized, the financial paraplanner is an indispensable member of the financial planning team, contributing strongly to the ultimate success of the financial planning practice.

Appendix A

Directory

Armstrong, Alexandra, CFP

> Alexandra Armstrong Advisors
> 1140 Connecticut Avenue, N.W.
> Suite 505
> Washington, DC 20036
> (202) 887-8135

Arowesty, Jill

> AMR Planning Services, Inc.
> 146A Manetto Hill Road
> Suite 200
> Plainview, NY 11803
> (516) 433-0828

Jill Arowesty is Director of Financial Planning and Director of Research and Communications at AMR Planning Services, Inc. She is a Registered Representative licensed through USLICO Securities Corporation, an Agent of Bankers' Security Life Insurance Society, and provides full, comprehensive financial planning through AMR. A CFP candidate, Ms. Arowesty also coordinates the affiliated planner program designed to provide support services such as computerization, plan writing, an in-house training to planners.

Baldwin, Ben G., CLU, M.S.F.S., CFP, ChFC, M.S.M.

> Baldwin Financial Systems, Inc.
> Equitable Financial Companies
> 5 Revere Drive
> Suite 500
> Northbrook, IL 60062
> (312) 498-7111

This firm was founded by Ben and Maureen Baldwin in 1982. The mission is to use all available means to enable as many people as possible to be competently in control of their personal financial affairs. The firm uses the systems they have developed, speaking engagements, seminars, teaching, and the selling of financial products to accomplish this mission.

Barry, James A., Jr., CFP*

> The Barry Financial Group, Inc.
> The Barry Plaza
> 40 S.E. Fifth Street, 6th Floor
> Boca Raton, FL 33432
> (305) 368-9120
> (800) 432-3029 (Florida only)

Most people resist change, yet change is constant. Be the captain of your financial destiny. Take charge of your financial house, realizing that there are two basic kinds of monies: people at work and money at work, and there is no question in my mind, nor should there be in yours, which lasts longer. Surround yourself with "OPB—Other People's Brains." Stay with your game plan. I wish you clear sailing.

*Admitted to the Registry of Financial Planning Practitioners

Bass, Mark, CFP, CPA

Pennington/Bass Companies, Inc.
1001 Main, Suite 100
Lubbock, TX 79401
(806) 765-7471

Mark Bass, CFP, CPA, is president of Pennington/Bass Companies, Inc. Pennington/Bass Companies is a dynamic financial planning firm that continues to grow by associating with and developing comprehensive financial planners around the country. Pennington/Bass provides continuing education to planners as well as a full line of products, planning services, and creative marketing ideas.

If you are interested in joining one of the premier financial planning firms in the country, please contact Mark Bass, CFP, CPA, or Lee Pennington, CFP at (806) 765-7471.

One phone call can make you one of those rare financial planners who continues to be on the cutting edge.

Bobal, Michael J., Jr.

RR 2, Box 303
Hollidaysburg, PA 16648
(814) 695-4438 (office)
(814) 695-9025 (home)

Mr. Bobal specializes in establishing financial services and trust departments for community banks. As a community banker, he has realized that even though the demand is there, it is not cost-effective to form a new department. He offers services to institutions in various degrees of sophistication which enable them to maintain customer contact and to increase revenue without the typical costs involved in forming and/or expanding a trust department. Programs are also available for credit unions and CPA firms. Additionally, he offers financial planning to businesses and individuals.

Bohn, Robert F., M.B.A., Ph.D., CFP

Dean, School of Financial Services
Golden Gate University
536 Mission Street (Main Campus)
San Francisco, CA 94105
(Satellite facilities: Walnut Creek, Los Altos, Novato, Monterey, Sacramento, Orange County, Los Angeles, and Seattle)
(415) 442-7221 (office)
(415) 820-4479 (home)

Golden Gate University offers the nation's most comprehensive financial services-related master's degrees: M.B.A. or M.S. in financial services, financial services—investments concentration, or real estate; MBA in financial planning, risk management, and insurance or banking; MS in financial planning—tax concentration, or taxation. Founded in 1901, GGU is one of the major centers in the western United States for professional education in business, public administration, and law. Sixty percent of the students are graduate students and 40 percent are undergraduates. GGU is one of California's four largest private, independent universities with full-time/part-time day and evening undergraduate/graduate degree programs. Students can also take classes on a nondegree-seeking basis to enhance professional competency. Three trimesters per year (beginning September, January, and May).

Burke, James J., CFP
> Burke & Company Asset Planning, Inc.
> P.O. Box 502
> 356 South Oyster Bay Road
> Syosset, NY 11791
> (516) 932-1100

Several years ago, a friend advised me to read Andrew Rich's book, *How to Survive and Succeed in a Small Financial Planning Practice,* and told me that it would be helpful in getting my fledgling practice off the ground.

The book was extremely useful to me, and, in fact, probably saved me several years of learning by trial and error. I subsequently met Andy, and he became my friend and financial planning mentor.

It is, therefore, an honor to have been asked to contribute to this book. I am certain that it will be a valuable guide to as many people as Andy's first book has been.

Burns, Leo R., CFP
> IDS Financial Services, Inc.
> 42 Main Street
> Leominster, MA 01453
> (617) 537-4588

Leo is a member of the IDS Gold Team Financial Planners. Gold Team Planners are an elite group of experienced and professional planners selected from among more than 5700 IDS Personal Financial Planners. At this writing, there are 24 Gold Team Planners in the country. Gold Team Planners provide two customized financial planning services on behalf of IDS: IDS Gold Team Consulting Service and IDS Gold Team Financial Planning Service. The main objectives of both services is to assist clients in identifying financial-planning objectives and to implement appropriate planning techniques. The services provide written recommendations to assist in achieving planning objectives.

Chapman, Lisbeth
> Financial Services Times
> 437 Newtonville Avenue
> Newton, MA 02160

Financial Services Times is the nation's independent news, product, and feature newspaper for financial planners and the financial services industry. It reaches 76,000 professionals every month. It is edited for financial planners from a variety of backgrounds: insurance, securities, accounting, real estate, banking, and consulting. An annual subscription is only $29.95—a small amount to invest in your future as a planner. For financial services and product suppliers, *FST* offers the largest circulation and lowest rates—an efficient and economical way to reach the entire financial planning and services community.

Clinard, Joseph H. Jr., CFP
> DESCAP Planning, Inc.
> 200 Vanderbuilt Motor Parkway
> Hauppauge, NY 11788
> (516) 273-9100

DESCAP Planning, Inc. established its corporate headquarters in Hauppauge in January 1980 and has since become one of the major financial service groups to enter the area. In the early 1970s, the founders of DESCAP set out to create an organization that would be able to provide the necessary financial services and products to fulfill the complex and wide-ranging needs of Long Island's industrial and professional community, as well as those of the individual consumer.

Cohen, Martin J., CFP

P.O. Box 9005
Rockwall, TX 75087
(214) 475-8662 (metro)
(214) 722-6783

Martin J. Cohen, CFP, is a Dallas-based financial planner who provides financial and investment services to individuals to assist them in the accumulation and preservation of wealth. His mission is to define the lifestyle goals and objectives of individuals and to help, through the blending of services and products, to enable those clients to achieve those goals. Mr. Cohen has a national and international client base.

Coombs, Ben, CFP

Petra Financial Group, Inc.
6351 Owensmouth Avenue, Suite 207
Woodland Hills, CA 91367
(818) 346-8601

Petra offers full financial planning services to individuals and small business owners as well as asset management services. We service Los Angeles and Ventura County areas in Los Angeles, California. We work on a fee basis with a credit for securities commissions.

Danielson, Deborah L., CFP

D.L. Danielson & Associates
101 Convention Center Drive
Suite 1203—Penthouse
Las Vegas, NV 89109
(702) 734-7000

Creating "your" image is very important! It sells you long before you have the opportunity to sell yourself. Time spent in careful consideration of your options will pay off handsomely. Your office should always provide a win-win environment. You feel good, your staff feels good, and your clients feel good. If all this is true, you should have no problem building a successful and rewarding practice.

Darany, Michael Anthony, CFP

The Consortium Group
11430 North Kendall Drive, Suite 106
Miami, FL 33176
(305) 596-3650

The business philosophy of The Consortium Group has always been to provide a place that individuals can rely on to handle their financial affairs. As a result of our structure, we are able to coordinate every aspect of their financial needs. This includes services like a total financial analysis of their insurances and investments, a review of the estates, trusts, and wills, and preparation of tax returns. All of these elements need to be examined in order to manage a client's affairs properly. We are able to act as financial and business consultants for various types of ventures, including structuring limited partnerships, mergers and acquisitions, and obtaining financing for new and established businesses.

Dohan, Michael R., Ph.D.

Family Financial Consultants, Inc.
1 St. Marks Place
Huntington, NY 11743
(516) 549-1805

Family Financial Consultants, Inc. provides a full range of financial consulting and management services to families and individuals on a fee-for-service basis only. Our services range from consultation on personal financial problems, family budget development, and tax preparation to comprehensive financial planning, portfolio management, household expense and income accounting, and direct management of day-to-day finances for individuals and families. We welcome working with financial professionals specializing in the other areas of financial planning.

Dunton, Loren

National Center for Financial Education
P.O. Box 34070
San Diego, CA 92103

Founded in 1982, the NCFE is a nonprofit organization dedicated to helping consumers do a better job of spending, saving, investing, insuring, and planning for the financial future. The NCFE has programs for both individual financial planners and corporate sponsors, including Dollar Plan, a basic level educational program. For more information, contact Paul Richard, Director of Education.

Fain, P. Kemp, Jr., Ph.D., CFP

Asset Planning Corporation
238 Peters Road, Building A
Knoxville, TN 37923
(615) 690-1231

Dr. Fain founded Asset Planning Corporation in April of 1975. Asset Planning Corporation offers financial planning and asset management services to the public. Dr. Fain has helped develop very innovative and cost-efficient methods for providing financial planning to individuals and families. His methods depend upon the high level of planner training and experience available through management services, such as portfolio management for cash and securities. Prospective clients may wish to review the 10-year track record of portfolios managed by Asset Planning Corporation.

Frechette, Jerry L.

Financial Planning Consultants, Inc.
The Financial Planning Building
2507 N. Verity Parkway
Middletown, OH 45042-0430
(513) 424-1656

Financial Planning Consultants, Inc. has developed and marketed computer software for financial planners since 1971. The early programs have been considerably refined and are now available for PC-compatible equipment. The ProPlan comprehensive planning software has 1300 users, including several major accounting firms, life insurance companies, and many independent planners. The Text Library System has three unique elements: 284 generic documents for financial service customers ranging from 1 to 14 pages, a master implementation checklist of 642 items, and a communications and disclosure record system consisting of agendas and letters.

Freeman, Richard B., MBA

DESCAP Planning
88 Post Road West
Westport, CT 06880
(203) 454-3377

Thanks to the following for my professional development:

- Andrew Rich—he taught me CFPI. I have owed him dinner for three years but do not remember why.
- Barry Cliff—the first to tell me the joys and sorrows of this business. The best at helping me make money for my clients.
- Vern Hayden—the best at teaching how to survive and prosper in this business.
- My wife Chris—for putting up with this madness.

Hallihan, Jacqueline H.

National Regulatory Services, Inc.
Main Street
Lakeville, CT 06039
(203) 435-2541

National Regulatory Services, Inc. (NRS) provides registration and compliance services for broker-dealers. For new broker-dealers, this includes counseling, application preparation, compliance manual preparation, and coordination of all aspects of the application.

To begin the process we offer a preliminary Advisory Committee report, encompassing a review of state, securities, examination and net capital requirements, and other issues.

NRS also provides compliance services for existing broker-dealers, as well as a microbased back office computer software system, "BOSS," for back-office support.

Similar services are also available for investment advisers.

Interested persons should contact National Regulatory Services, Inc.

Hayden, Larry D., CFP

International Board of Standards and Practices for
    Certified Financial Planners, Inc. (IBCFP)
5445 D.T.C. Parkway, Suite P-1
Englewood, CO 80111
(303) 850-0333

The IBCFP is an independent, certifying body for all CFPs. It is charged with maintaining and enforcing high professional standards of conduct among Certified Financial Planners and is a nonmembership, not-for-profit organization. The IBCFP owns the marks CFP and Certified Financial Planner and is dedicated to gaining widespread public recognition for the marks and for the profession as a whole. For more information about the IBCFP and how you can become a CFP, write the IBCFP at the above address.

Hayden, Vern C., CFP
Financial Services Advisory Co.
88 Post Road West
Westport, CT 06880
(203) 454-3377

In addition to managing a private practice, Vern has a very active consulting practice. He consults in all areas of building and managing successful financial planning operations. He also consults on issues related to marketing, especially seminars. He has a very practical, simplified, cost-effective seminar package. It is currently being repackaged and will be available for about $1000.

Vern is also a professional speaker and is available to speak and/or give workshops at conventions and other functions.

His clients have included major insurance companies, broker/dealers, and financial planning companies, both large and small.

Heath, William C., CFP
Center for Financial Planning
4800 Sugar Grove Blvd.
Suite 200
Stafford, TX 77477
(713) 240-7177

In 1972, William C. Heath began providing services for tax returns and accounting. He founded the Center for Financial Planning (CFFP), a Texas corporation, in August 1983 to provide comprehensive financial planning for the general public and for financial planners needing an affiliation to allow them access to high-quality financial planning and plan implementation through various related products. In April 1986, the first branch affiliate was established in California and combined the management and marketing skills of the California staff with the quality professional services offered by the Texas staff. In developing the first national financial planning/services firm, CFFP will capture a substantial share of the market. For further information on the Center for Financial Planning, contact Mr. Heath at the above address.

Heifetz, Wendy J.
Wendy Heifetz, Inc.
550 W. Merrick Road
Valley Stream, NY 11580
(516) 825-2277

Wendy Heifetz, Inc. meets the training challenge for the brokerage firm, financial institution, and insurance company administrator who must look ahead. An innovative training plan and a unique class-scheduling arrangement has already created a demonstrable 96 percent success rate, a performance standard that leaves the training industry's traditional leaders far behind.

A representative of this dynamic program is prepared to meet with you to review a scheduling plan that assures an enthusiastic learning experience to your personnel—and licensed brokers for your firm.

Herman, Stephen P., M.D.
109 West 70th Street
New York, NY 10023
(212) 595-0457

Dr. Herman is an assistant professor of psychiatry at Cornell University Medical College. He is in private practice and specializes in adult and child psychiatry.

Hogarth, Ronald P., CLU, CFP
Bretschneider & Associates, Inc.
600 Oxford Valley Road, Suite 213
Langhorne, PA 19046
(215) 946-1900

Taking good care of your clients is taking good care of your business. They and you will be generously rewarded.

Howe, Amy J.
College for Financial Planning
9725 E. Hampden Avenue
Denver, CO 80231-4993
(303) 755-7101

The College for Financial Planning is an independent, nonprofit educational institution established in 1972 to provide career-enhancing instructional programs for financial services professionals. More than 30,000 individuals currently are enrolled in the College's programs, chief among them being the Certified Financial Planner (CFP) Professional Educational Program, Financial Paraplanner Program, and advanced studies courses in the areas of investments, taxes, retirement planning, and estate planning. Through its highly respected programs, the College continues to be an important influence in the financial planning industry.

Huxford, David C., CLU, CFP
Financial Computer Support, Inc. (FCS)
Route 4, Box 527
Deer Park, MD 21550
(301) 387-4445

APUG provides planners with client asset and portfolio management software, computer consulting, and significant discounts on hardware and planning software such as IFS, Planman, Proplan, and Softbridge.

APUG's CAMS system provides data management to track clients, their family members, assets, and underlying transactions. Financial, cash flow, and managed asset client statements show client values and portfolio activity. A TODO module that tracks tasks to be done by each staff member is included.

Additional modules automatically reprice portfolios via Dow Jones, bill clients for services rendered, and track staff time.

Iseman, Murray, CLU, M.S.F.S., ChFC, M.S.M.
U.S. Equities, Inc.
950 Glebe Road
Arlington, VA 22203
(703) 276-3547

U.S. Equities is a wholly owned subsidiary of the USLICO Corporation. It provides a full array of financial planning services to its affiliated insurance companies: United Services Life, United Services General, Bankers Security Life, United Olympic Life and Provident Life. The existence and support of this separate corporation illustrates USLICO's commitment to the financial planning movement.

Johnson, Dale S., Ph.D., CFP
Financial Planning Consultant and Writer
105 Radnor Avenue
Villanova, PA 19085
(215) 527-2620

Dale Johnson provides consulting services as an independent contractor in market development, communications design and marketing, practice management, and distribution systems for financial planning. He specializes in the following activities:

- Designing communications packages for financial planning practices, including library text, client communications materials, and software support.
- Developing and presenting seminars and workshops on topics related to implementing the financial-planning process and installing it in a professional practice.
- Publishing books and monographs on the practice, procedures, strategies, and techniques of financial planning.
- Providing presentations and talks for professional membership societies.

Kaplan, Jocelyn R., CFP
Advisors Financial, Inc.
8321 Old Courthouse Road
Suite 250
Vienna, VA 22180
(703) 883-0300

As a financial planner, I get the most satisfaction from working with those clients who are task-oriented and who are willing to make the effort to implement a financial plan. For the most part, I have found that my retired military officer clients fit into this category.

If other financial planners wish to enter this marketplace, I can provide reference information and ideas for marketing. Feel free to write or call.

Kemple, Glenda D., CPA, CFP
Carter Financial Management
5956 Sherry Lane, Suite 1100
Dallas, TX 75225
(214) 363-4200

Financial planning is so much more than mere number crunching, the "science" of financial planning assisted magnificently by the computer. The key, however, to financial success is the application of the "art" of financial planning. This includes designing the correct portfolio mix and motivating the client to implement the financial plan. Good communication skills and the ability to understand the client's needs are necessary.

My practice specializes in working with high-net-worth individuals and professionals, such as attorneys and doctors. I especially enjoy the situation where a client needs planning and asset placement after a divorce settlement, at the sale of a business, or after an inheritance is received.

Kessler, Judd, CFP
Abacus Data Systems, Inc.
2775 Via De La Valle, Suite 101
Del Mar, CA 92014
(619) 755-0505

Fast Plan III incorporates the latest technology in financial planning software from the company who developed the first database management system for financial planners in 1982. At $6995, FastPlan III is simply the best integrated database and financial planning system around today. Call Abacus to find out why FastPlan is the first choice of successful Certified Financial Planners.

Kjos, Nelson J., CFP
Barrington, Ltd.
26711 Northwestern Highway, Suite 309
Southfield, MI 48034
(313) 358-4750

Barrington, Ltd. specializes in equity portfolio management and covered option writing. The firm presently has $65 million under management. It uses the Technical Tick Index, developed by Mr. Kjos in 1969, as the major market timing tool of the firm. Barrington caters to individual investors or to financial planners who wish to place their client's money under private management. His definition of the stock market: ''The stock market is a business of crisis, of sudden ups and downs, that constantly occur.''

Krause, Lawrence A., CFP
Lawrence A. Krause & Associates, Inc.
500 Washington Street, Suite 750
San Francisco, CA 94111
(415) 362-1200

Lawrence A. Krause & Associates, Inc. is a San Francisco-based personal financial planning and advisory firm with offices throughout the Bay area. Mr. Krause's firm has a national reputation both for integrity and quality and for dealing with high-net-worth clients. *Forbes* once stated, ''Larry Krause is at the pricey end of the financial planning spectrum.''

Mr. Krause's marketing expertise is also well-known. In that regard he has shared with his peers his knowledge of how to attract wealthy (and not so wealthy) clients in a book he coauthored entitled *Marketing Your Financial Planning Practice: How to Turn Your Image into Profit*. This book is currently available through Longman Financial Services Publishing Inc., Chicago, Illinois.

In addition, he is the author of the *Money-Go-Round* and the currently released book published by Simon & Schuster entitled *Sleep-Tight Money*, a book used extensively by financial planners as a gift to clients or for seminar and/or classroom use.

LeClair, Robert T., Ph.D.
Financial Data Corporation
P.O. Box 1332
Bryn Mawr, PA 19010
(215) 525-6957

Dr. LeClair is a coauthor, with Stephen Leimberg, of ''The Financial & Estate Planner's Number Cruncher'' and ''Financial Planning TOOLKIT,'' software packages for use with Lotus 1-2-3. For additional information on these programs, contact Financial Data Corp. at the address indicated.

Lieberman, Anne M., CFP

Lieberman Associates Financial Planning
700 Larkspur Landing Circle
Larkspur, CA 94939
(415) 925-1124

Lieberman Associates Financial Planning operates in association with Lawrence A. Krause & Associates. Lieberman and Krause coauthored *Marketing Your Financial Planning Practice: How to Turn Your Image into Profit*. Lieberman also coauthored (with J. Edson Clinton) *Mastering Money: How to Create Your Own Financial Plan*. Both books can be obtained from Longman Financial Services Publications, (800) 428-3846—Customer Service. Lieberman Associates works primarily with high-net-worth clients.

Lindquist, Gale, CFP

Planning Consultants Unlimited, Inc.
1 Suffolk Square, Suite 220
Islandia, NY
(516) 467-5247

First and foremost, PCU would like to thank Andy Rich for his successful completion of this guide. I hope you enjoyed reading this book as much as we enjoyed contributing to it. Through guides such as this one, both our knowledge and insight increases. The following is an insight into my company:

PCU is an independent financial planning firm specializing in privately owned small to mid-sized businesses. We are a full-service firm in that in addition to comprehensive financial planning, we offer accounting and tax preparation services. We are also well equipped to implement our plans, as we represent over 40 insurance companies and have a full line of brokerage services. My thanks again to Andy, and may each of you reach your personal goals.

Lochray, Paul J., J.D.

College for Financial Planning
9725 E. Hampden Avenue
Denver, CO 80231
(303) 755-7101, ext. 222

By familiarizing himself or herself with conduct that approaches the unauthorized practice of law, the financial planner can avoid such actions and the liability that can result.

Lochray is the author of *The Financial Planner's Guide to Estate Planning*, published by Prentice Hall, Inc.

Longden, Claire S., CFP

Butcher & Singer, Inc.
65 Broadway
New York, NY 10006
(212) 422-1111

Total-concept financial planning for high-net-worth individuals and small businesses has been Claire Longden's forte since she received her CFP designation in 1979. She is an independent planner with investment banker Butcher & Singer. Compensation is fee only. Implementation is available through her firm if required. Plans are individually written with direct and specific advice to the client, including tax, estate, insurance, and investment planning with expert emphasis on redeployment of assets.

McGee, Judith Headington

Associated Investment Advisers
North 222 Wall Street, Suite 314
Spokane, WA 99201
(509) 458-2600

In difficult economic times, the need for professionalism and peer support is greater than ever. Support the professional organization of your choice—the ICFP and IAFP need you.

Meier, Ronald P., CPA

Professional Investment Planning, Inc.
P.O. Box 5638
Kingwood, TX 77325-5638
(713) 359-6666

Professional Investment Planning, Inc. is a fee-only personal financial planning and registered investment advisory firm. Comprehensive personal financial planning, including tax, estate, retirement, and risk management planning, is offered to clients. Objective investment planning advice is available to clients, since the firm does not accept, directly or indirectly, commissions as a consequence of the purchase of investment products by clients. The firm offers a sophisticated investment monitoring and management service on a continuing basis after completion of the initial investment plan. Those interested can contact Professional Investment Planning, Inc. at the above address.

Miller, James, Ph.D.

Financial Information Group
P.O. Box 7108
1603 Solano Avenue
Berkeley, CA 94708
(415) 549-1730

Launching a new product or service? Expanding your firm? We specialize in developing successful marketing plans, lead generation strategies, and marketing materials for financial services firms.

Proven strategies tailored to your target market and special services will reduce risk and increase your profits. Call upon our direct response experts for the brochures, direct mail, advertising, seminar plans, telemarketing campaigns, audio- or videocassettes, newsletters, press releases, newspaper articles, or other marketing materials to attract the kind of prospects you want and convert them into profitable clients.

Montgomery, Henry I., CFP

Planners Financial Services, Inc.
3500 W. 80th Street #670
Minneapolis, MN 55431
(612) 835-9000

I would not want you to think my comments on due diligence were divinely inspired. Every word is a drop of my blood, a former client, a year of my life. They may be tough words, but I learned them the hard way. I had to, or I would not still be around. How long will you last? What will you do for your next career? Think about it a bit before you hand over your life to some well-meaning but ignorant product purveyor or sponsor.

Morrow, Edwin P., CLU, ChFC, CFP

Confidential Planning Services, Inc.
Financial Planning Building
Middletown, Ohio 45042-0430
(513) 424-1656

CPS provides practice management services to financial planners, including public relations, marketing, administrative manuals, training, audiovisuals, and computer hardware and software. We place special emphasis on compliance and minimizing professional liability through disclosure and record systems. Software includes Pro-plan comprehensive package for affluent clients with simplified input for moderate customers. Text Library System includes 680 pages of documents and a planner's master implementation checklist of 642 items. We have been serving planners since 1976.

Ober, Stuart A.

Securities Investigations, Inc.
P.O. Box 888
Woodstock, NY 12498
(914) 679-2300/2301

Securities Investigations, Inc. is one of the nation's foremost due diligence and research organizations. Through its innovative approach to financial investigative research and reporting, SII has added a new dimension to the concept of due diligence and has been cited as maintaining "standards beyond the ordinary requirements for full disclosure." SII publishes "The Ober Income Letter," the only newsletter devoted solely to real estate and oil and gas income, and *Investment and Tax Shelter Blue Book,* the professional directory for the investment shelter and financial planning industries.

Oberst, Robert J., Sr., Ph.D., CFP

Robert J. Oberst Sr. & Associates
218 Broad Street
Red Bank, NJ 07701
(210) 842-2300

Dr. Oberst is president of Robert J. Oberst Sr. & Associates, a firm specializing in financial planning. He hosts a television program on financial planning and is a frequent and popular professional speaker. Dr. Oberst is available for lectures and seminars.

Parkins, Raymond A., Jr., Ph.D., CFP, ChFC, CLU

The Parkins Investment Companies, Inc.
1600 E. Robinson Street
Orlando, Florida 32803
(305) 896-9384

Dr. Parkins is President of The Parkins Investment Companies, Inc., an asset management firm. The firm, established in 1974, has four operating subsidiaries: The Parkins Investment Advisory Corporation, a registered investment adviser; The Parkins Investment Securities Corporation, a registered investment securities broker/dealer and member of NASD; The Parkins Investment Properties

Corporation, a licensed real estate and mortgage broker; and The Parkins Investment Partnership Corporation, a real estate investment banking and management firm.

The firm's objective is to provide a complete range of asset management services for successful individuals, corporations, and individual trustees of retirement plans. Services include portfolio management, plan administration, tax return and financial statement preparation, investment securities brokerage, investment property brokerage leasing and management, and capital formation through real estate investment banking.

Professionally, Dr. Parkins is a member of the Board of Regents of the College for Financial Planning and also is a member of the Board of Directors of the International Board of Standards and Practices for Certified Financial Planners, Inc. (IBCFP).

Price, Felice, CFP

Felice Price Financial Services, Inc.
5976 W. Las Positas Blvd.
Pleasanton, CA 94566
(415) 462-6910

Felice Price has had an active planning practice since 1977. She provides comprehensive financial planning for individuals and businesses with emphasis on high-net-worth and/or high-income clientele. Services also include diversified investments in securities and insurance.

Ms. Price wishes to thank Tom Shipley of CIGNA and Les Grubin of Anglo-American Agents, her career mentors.

Rampy, Dianna

Former Executive Director
Institute of Certified Financial Planners
Two Denver Highlands
10065 E. Harvard Avenue, Suite 320
Denver, CO 80231

The Institute of Certified Financial Planners is a national professional membership association based in Denver, Colorado. Its membership is comprised of Certified Financial Planners (CFP) and those persons currently seeking the CFP designation. Benefits and services include "Newsworthy," a monthly current events newsletter; *Journal of the ICFP*, a quarterly technical publication on financial services strategies, trends, and theories; the annual membership directory; conferences and meetings, which include the annual retreat (college campus setting), the annual conference, the residency program, and regional conferences; regulatory and legislative liaison; professional code of ethics; and professional development products such as brochures, case studies, and audio cassette tapes.

Rich, Andrew

AMR Planning Services, Inc.
146A Manetto Hill Road
Suite 200
Plainview, NY 11803
(516) 433-0828

• General financial planning specializing in taxation, mutual fund investing, retirement planning, and hourly consultations. • Registered with the Securities and Exchange Commission as a Registered Investment Advisory corporation.

Mr. Rich acts as a consultant to both individual practitioners and firms needing advice and/or training in financial planning, including the development of in-house training manuals and other written materials. He is available for seminars and lectures to practitioners and the public.

Richard, Paul

National Center for Financial Education (NCFE)
P.O. Box 34070
San Diego, CA 92103

The NCFE is a nonprofit public education organization which offers courses in personal finance to consumers through employers, credit unions, community colleges, and adult education programs. NCFE Consulting Dollarplan Instructors are comprised of financial planning professionals, CPAs, and others who represent the NCFE in their local communities. They enjoy the neutral educational posture of the NCFE and the many opportunities it creates for them that they might not have otherwise. The educational programs are supplemented with a national speakers bureau, which, through a neutral position, also opens many doors for members.

Riva, Ron

National Regulatory Services, Inc.
Main Street
Lakeville, CT 06039
(203) 435-2541

National Regulatory Services (NRS) provides registration and compliance services for registered investment advisors. For new investment advisors, this includes counseling, application preparation, compliance manuals, and coordination of all aspects of compliance planning. Interested persons should contact NRS.

Rosenberg, Lee Evan, CFP

ARS Financial Services, Inc.
125 Franklin Avenue
Valley Stream, NY 11581
(516) 872-0077

ARS Financial Services is a professional planning organization designed to objectively coordinate a client's financial affairs into a total financial plan. ARS uses the team approach to meet client objectives best. The staff includes Certified Financial Planners, Certified Public Accountants, and other financial advisors. For more information regarding a rewarding affiliation with ARS Financial Services, Inc., contact Lee Rosenberg, CFP, or Anthony Spatafore, CFP, at the above address.

Ross, Neil, CFP

100 South Spring Street
Aspen, CO 81611
(303) 925-2800

All too often our profession, which deals with dollars and bottom lines, loses sight of an ultimate goal. We so often hear first, foremost, and only how much money this or that person expects to make from his or her work. There is absolutely nothing to apologize for in that goal, but is that the only goal of the financial planning professional? If you are professionally uncompromising and hold only the highest standards for yourself, for what you expect to give to your clients, and for what you expect to share with the industry, you will not have to worry about how much money will be forthcoming. The rewards materially and otherwise will be abundant.

Sackler, Lori Reisman, CPA, M.S.
25 East Clinton Avenue
Tenafly, NJ 07670
(201) 569-4258

Lori R. Sackler provides financial planning, investment and insurance counseling primarily to professional career couples and single women, including divorcees and widows. Ms. Sackler is committed to providing innovative and uncompromising quality in planning and implementation and has over ten years of experience as a tax advisor, investment consultant and financial counselor. She is available to speak before professional associations, colleges and financial planning groups.

Sandstrom, Carol A., CFP
Fast Start, Inc.
P.O. Box 5148
Largo, Florida 34294-5248
(813) 584-0099

Fast Start, Inc. is a consulting and referral firm specializing in independent financial planners and their broker/dealers. Fast Start functions as a national clearinghouse for broker/dealers interested in competing for planners' business and also offers a complete spectrum of consulting services including broker/dealer selection, transfer, operations interface, compliance, and practice management.

Fast Start offers the registered representative objective advice on the pros and cons of choosing between major wire-house affiliation or the initiation of an independent practice.

Schaeffer, Karen P., CFP
Schaeffer Financial
7855 Walker Drive
Suite 620
Greenbelt, MD 20770
(301) 220-0111

Schaeffer Financial shares office space with Hibbard Brown & Company, a full-service broker/dealer committed to meeting the dynamic needs of the independent financial planner. In addition to maintaining a diverse financial planning practice, Karen conducts workshops for planners on topics including marketing, compliance training, and practice management. She is available for individual consultation, negotiating fees based on services rendered and expenses.

Seglin, Jeffrey L.
Seglin Associates
186-A Savin Hill Avenue
Boston, MA 02125
(617) 265-9620

Seglin Associates is a consulting firm that provides marketing, editorial, and writing services. Among the books Seglin has written are

America's New Breed of Entrepreneurs. Acropolis Books, 2400 17th Street N.W., Washington, D.C. 20009. $14.95.

Personal Financial Planning in Banks. Bankers Publishing Co., 210 South Street, Boston, Mass. 02111, (617) 426-4495.

Serving the Small Business Market. Bank Administration Institute, 60 Gold Center, Rolling Meadows, Ill. 60008, (800) 323-8552.

Financial Services Marketing. Forthcoming from Prentice Hall, Englewood Cliffs, N.J. 07632.

Sestina, John E., CFP, ChFC

SMB Financial Planning, Inc.
3726-J Olentangy River Road
Columbus, OH 43214
(614) 457-8200

Mr. Sestina is a vice president of SMB Financial Planning, Inc., a professional financial planning firm which counsels individual clients on an objective, fee-only basis. The firm's guidance includes cash-flow management, investment management, tax planning, disability planning, education planning, retirement planning, and estate planning.

Sharkey, Eileen M., CFP

E. M. Sharkey & Associates, Inc.
2755 South Locust Street #206
Denver, CO 80222
(303) 759-4262

Eileen Sharkey provides general financial planning services for a fee to individuals, small businesses, and corporations. Her areas of expertise include tax, investment, and retirement strategies. Asset management services are also offered. She is a regular contributor to professional and consumer publications and is a popular speaker for professional organizations throughout the United States.

Stitt, David M.

Gem Financial Corporation
Post Office Drawer M
Middletown, OH 45042-0912
(513) 422-4045

Nothing is more important in selecting a computer than dealing with someone who is honestly interested in what your needs are. Advances in technology are not nearly as important as knowing that the system will work and do the job you need done. Find a local dealer you trust and can count on for service, especially if you are buying your first system.

Suver, Jerry L., CLU, CFP

Confidential Planning Services, Inc.
The Financial Planning Building
Middletown, OH 45042-0430
(513) 424-1656

CPS furnishes practice management support to a network of over 120 independent financial planning firms in the areas of training, marketing, audiovisuals, manuals, public relations, and software. It offers two financial planning software programs:

1. ProPlan, a comprehensive, integrated software program which gives users the maximum flexibility and accuracy in creating financial plans.
2. Text Library System, a financial-planning software program offering documents on over 250 financial topics, objectives, assumptions, and Master Implementation Checklist.

Sweet, John C.

John C. Sweet & Associates
1580 Blanchard Court
Wheaton, IL 60187
(312) 653-8545

John C. Sweet & Associates is a management, marketing, and business planning consulting firm that specializes in helping financial professionals develop and focus the people, time, and financial resources necessary to meet long- and short-term personal and business goals. Consulting services are offered through John and his nationally recognized, uniquely qualified professional associates. For information regarding available services and client references, write or call John personally at his office.

Waller, Laura, CFP

Laura Waller Advisors, Inc.
Suite 1109
201 E. Kennedy Blvd.
Tampa, FL 33602
(813) 221-1956

Laura Waller has a general financial planning practice dealing with individuals, couples, and small businesses. Her experiences include serving as the Southern Regional Director on the National Board of the ICFP and as Director of the Board of a Tampa bank.

Walker, Lewis J., CFP

Walker Capital Management Corporation
4340 Georgetown Square, Suite 608
Atlanta, GA 30338
(404) 452-7222

Subscriptions to Lewis Walker's client newsletter are available at $30 per year; send check to Walker Capital Management Corporation at the above address.

Winter, Bruce E.

Winter Financial Advisors, Inc.
2300 Corporate Blvd., N.W.
Suite 139
Boca Raton, FL 33431
(305) 994-0100

Winter Financial Advisors, Inc., is an investment advisory firm registered with the Securities and Exchange Commission and the Florida Department of Securities. The firm is committed to providing comprehensive financial planning services to individuals and corporations throughout South Florida. They provide competent financial planning advice and information consistent with the client's goals and objectives. The company consults on asset management, risk management, income tax planning, investment portfolio analysis, retirement planning, and estate planning.

Bruce E. Winter, P.A. is a law firm with five attorneys specializing in wills, trusts, estate planning, taxation, and corporate law. Bruce E. Winter is the sole owner of both companies.

Woodwell, Donald R.

D & D Royalties, Inc.
20 DeHart Drive
Belle Mead, NJ 08502
(201) 874-0952

D & D Royalties provides:

1. Preparation of manuscripts for specialty and general books on investing, financial planning, and computing.
2. Consultation services for financial-planning practices on automation.
3. Lectures on uses of computers in practice management, client record keeping, and computation.

Wyatt, Lindsay K., AFP

Wyatt Investment Advisory, Inc.
2625 Cumberland Parkway, Suite 280
Atlanta, GA 30339
(404) 438-1976

Ms. Wyatt has created a broad range of communications materials and services for independent financial planners, including brochures, client newsletters, seminar programs, and advertising campaigns. Her *Financial Planner's Guide to Publicity and Promotion* can be obtained from Longman Financial Services Publishing, 500 North Dearborn Street, Chicago, IL 60610, telephone 1-800-428-3846. Ms. Wyatt's services as a communications consultant and speaker are also available to financial planners and professional organizations.

Ziedins, Aivars, M.S.F.S., CFP, CLU, GRI, ChFC

Ziedins & Company, Ltd., Financial Consultants
300 S. Jackson Street, Suite 500
Denver, CO 80209
(303) 355-7391

Ziedins & Company, Ltd., Financial Consultants is a full-service financial planning firm based in Denver with ten professional and support staff members. Ziedins's clientele includes doctors, dentists, and other professionals, business executives and small to medium-sized businesses, among other personal accounts. A fee schedule is available.

The president and owner, Aivars Ziedins, is a nationally known speaker and has written *Personal Financial Management* (Farnsworth, 1985) available from Ziedins for $5.00 each.

Ziedins can provide implementation of the financial plan, with securities offered through FSC Securities Corporation, a registered Broker/Dealer, member NASD/member SIPC.

Index